You're the Director… You figure it out.

The Life and Films of Richard Donner

James Christie

Published in the USA by:
BearManor Media
PO Box 1129
Duncan, Oklahoma 73534-1129
www.bearmanormedia.com

978-1-59393-527-6

Printed in the United States of America.
Book design by Brian Pearce | Red Jacket Press.

Table of Contents

Foreword 5

Acknowledgements 7

Taking a Shot 11

Early Years 29

New York City 41

King of the Pilots 53

Death, Destruction, and a Kick in the Balls 77

Brando, Bagels, and the Man Of Steel 93

American Dreamer 143

True Romance 167

A Goonie Life (Hip, Hop! March, March! Everybody Let's Go!) 189

Lethal Combination 207

Bah, humbug… Bill Murray 225

The Wishing Spot 243

Lights, Camera… Action! 285

Fun with Dick and Mel 311

Out of Time 331

Post-Credit Sequence 351

Notes 361

Filmography 371

Select Bibliography 391

About the Author 395

Index 397

Foreword

Leave Your Ego At The Door.

The words leap from a sign on the wall of Richard Donner's office. The sentiment is typical of Dick, a perennial straight-shooter who abhors the politics of vanity, a man who remains one of the most balanced, levelheaded people I know. He is widely recognized for his intelligence, passion, and wicked sense of humor, but perhaps his most brilliant quality is the passion he brings to an industry so often sustained by extremes of personality. For as long as I have known him he has never been anything other than steadfastly humble and modest — at times positively embarrassed to receive personal credit or praise. "I'm just a traffic cop, Kid," he once pleaded to me. "Here directing traffic." Yet Dick's record speaks for itself: from seminal television work to big-budget movie blockbusters, his half century in show business is defined by a remarkable creative flair, supreme technical proficiency, and intuitive sense of the public zeitgeist. I have been privileged to work with him on six motion pictures, and know from experience that he deserves to be judged in the rank of filmmaking greats.

One of his many attributes as a director is his ability to sign actors whose essential ingredients fit that of a character. It's hard to imagine anyone other than Christopher Reeve as *Superman*, or a different pre-teen ensemble forming *The Goonies*. When I first met Dick, and he offered me the role of Martin Riggs in *Lethal Weapon*, I think it was because he thought I was nuts. He was probably right!

On set, he is a giant of infectious enthusiasm. His boundless energy inspires all around him, and ensures that the creative process remains fresh, fun and exciting. Most important is the invigorating atmosphere of artistic freedom and collective participation that Dick creates. His productions become a liberating space where ideas and suggestions are encouraged from every member of cast and crew, regardless of rank or experience. Such selflessness is a wonderful directorial skill, and cast and crew feel a great loyalty and urgency to give him everything they've got.

Of course, allowing a say differs from having a vote, and Dick's filmmaking success is ultimately dependent upon his own artistic instincts. A true strength is his ability to temper narrative and spectacle. By utilizing improvisation and rehearsal to further character development, Dick ensures that his protagonists are "larger than life," but not parodies. His characters always exist within a framework of reality, which makes audiences care to believe in them, and care to believe in the wonderful escapist fictions that they are a part of.

Dick Donner is a tough, physically imposing guy with a personality as wide as the Grand Canyon. But underneath the somewhat gruff exterior is a quietly sensitive man who loves people and loves life. He is a dear and loyal friend whom I have known for more than twenty years.

Dick mostly chooses to shun the limelight. The minute someone points at him and says, "You're great!" you'll find him hiding in a closet somewhere. But the truth is that he is a unique talent from whom I have gleaned so much over the years. I am thrilled that his life and career are finally to be documented with such a comprehensive biography, and hope that his immense contribution to Hollywood history is remembered with the dignity and high regard it so richly deserves.

Mel Gibson
Santa Monica, California
April 6, 2009

Mel Gibson is an actor, writer, producer and Academy Award–winning director. His films include Braveheart, What Women Want, Ransom, Signs, *and* The Passion of the Christ. *He starred for Richard Donner in the* Lethal Weapon series, Maverick, *and* Conspiracy Theory.

Acknowledgements

The best thing about writing a book like this is the chance to spend time with so many people you're really excited to know. One could certainly do worse than to meet with Richard Donner, and listen to him recall the pivotal moments of his life and career.

In addition, I would like to offer my thanks, alphabetically, for their help in sharing memories of specific conversations and events: Sean Astin, Stuart Baird, Harvey Bernhard, John Calley, Jeff Cohen, Joan Cohen, Danny Farr, Corey Feldman, Gene Freedman, Mel Gibson, Bob Gilbert, Danny Glover, John Glover, Stephen Goldblatt, Kerri Green, Bob Harman, Derek Hoffman, Geoff Howard, Ke Huy Quan, Brian Jamieson, Steve Kahan, Margot Kidder, the late László Kovács, Alan Ladd, Jr., Lisa Lange, Jennie Lew Tugend, Kathy Liska, Peter MacDonald, the late Tom Mankiewicz, the late Guy McElwaine, David Morse, Jerry Moss, David Petrou, Roy Pickard, John Richardson, Ilya Salkind, Diana Scarwid, Lauren Shuler Donner, Michael Thau, Liv Ullman, Jim Van Wyck, David Warner, Amy Wright, and Vilmos Zsigmond.

I am particularly thankful to my agent, Winifred Golden, of the Castiglia Literary Agency. Winifred is talented, dedicated, and loyal. She has been there for me whenever I needed her. I am also, of course, grateful to my publisher, Ben Ohmart, for his continued patience and support.

What to say of the incomparable Cece Neber Labao? If my incessant nattering of "thank you" each time we speak hasn't already tipped her off, then she should know that this book would simply not have been possible without her. Cece (and Derek Hoffman) put me in touch with many people who have worked with and for Richard Donner. She is as wonderful a person as you are ever likely to meet, not to mention the maker of the finest Iced Tea in Beverly Hills!

Clark Kent might say that Jim Bowers and Dharmesh Chauhan are swell. They are. Both encouraged this book from the point of when it was little more than an idea (Jim also supplied me with some rare images from his vast collection of Superman memorabilia to serve as illustrations).

I owe much to my parents, Jack and Susan, my brother Stuart, to Bill and Judy Scavuzzo, and to the Gutheim and Spellos families. Most importantly, I am thankful for the support of my wife, Danielle, whose faith provided me with the strength to tackle the task, and my son, Liam, who gave me the energy to see it through. I could not have done it without them.

James Christie
Orlando, Florida, 2009

"Neverland had been
make-believe in those days,
but it was real now."

J. M. BARRIE, *PETER PAN*

Taking a Shot

He had pulled some audacious stunts in his time, but this was crazy. Here he stood, never more insignificant, more insecure, a young man literally shaking with fear. Where exactly was the exit in this place? In an epic bluff the aspiring filmmaker Richard Donner had charmed his way into the office of Otto Preminger — OTTO PREMINGER! — esteemed director of *Bonjour Tristesse*, *Anatomy of a Murder*, *Exodus*, *Advice and Consent* and *The Cardinal*. Eminent and influential throughout American theatre and film, he was a veritable living legend.

Preminger appeared in person as he did in the trades. His head was bald, his brow furrowed, his right hand impressed firmly upon his cheek. He stared unmercifully at him from behind his desk. He had recently purchased the movie rights to a new novel from New York writer Lois Gould entitled *Such Good Friends*, a wry comedy of sexual infidelity and retribution that he intended to helm.

Donner, too, had read an advance copy of the book and had immediately fallen in love with it. With but a few television credits to his name, he just knew that he could turn it into a great movie. "Mr. Preminger," Donner began. "You have a book called *Suck*... err... *Such Good Friends*."

"Yes, yes," he replied.

"Well, I think you're one of the great producer-directors of all time. Here's a great opportunity for you to produce a picture and let me direct it."

"What are you talking about?" Preminger demanded, his sharp Austrian accent rising with his blood pressure.

"I want to direct *Such Good Friends*, and I would love you to produce it so that I could learn from you."

"Get out of here!" the triple Academy Award nominee roared, following a suitably dramatic pause. "GET OUT OF HERE!"

Donner, suffering the suggestion of a bowel movement, dutifully obliged.

Once he made it home, his telephone began to ring. Call after call after call. Everyone was eager to find out if the shocking rumors were true. Had the upstart really tricked his way into Otto Preminger's office? Had he the *cajones* to demand Preminger produce a movie for him? Surely nobody was that suicidal.

Of course, it was true. Several years prior, shortly after he had arrived in Los Angeles from New York, Donner had impressed actress Joan Crawford while directing her in a commercial. "Do you direct movies or television?" she had asked him.

"No, I'm doing this," he had informed her, referring to advertisements.

"You should be," she replied. "Who's your agent?"

At the time he had no representation, so Crawford referred Donner to her own management team, the Preminger/Stewart Agency on Sunset Boulevard. It was here that he had once briefly met Ingo Preminger, Otto's brother, and although no professional arrangement came of the meeting, it was Ingo's name that Donner would use to gain access to Otto in the future. No doubt there would be ramifications.

Friends and acquaintances consoled him and offered advice. Some flat out told him that he'd likely never work again. Maybe they were right, maybe they were wrong. Donner tended not to see things the way other people saw them. He'd always been different that way. Win, lose, or draw, he had taken a shot, which was all one could ever really hope to do in life.

Invariably, the first thing that people mention about Donner is "The Voice." In line with the biggest of his blockbuster movies, it is often a thunderous timbre that commands instant attention. Steven Spielberg once likened its scope to that of "the public-address system at Candlestick Park." The voice, however, is just one characteristic. The sweeping smile, the puppy dog eyes, regularly fired by a cheeky, mischievous glint, and the dancing fingers that frequently animate hand gestures, all betray the ageless energy of Richard Donner. The immediacy of *The Omen*, the vibrancy and color of *Superman*, and the thrills and spills of the *Lethal Weapon* series can all be attributed to his power generator personality propelling the action forward from a hidden, off-camera space. "Dick has this hugely youthful attitude," says Stuart Baird, who edited eight of his films. "He just comes on the set and there's no question who's the director because he's all over the place shouting. He's a personality director, and it's great working with someone that big and theatrical."

Donner is a tall man, handsome and tanned, with a crop of silver hair. At eighty, his youthful glow lends him the appearance of a man fifteen years younger. He is known as an inveterate practical joker. *The Omen* producer, Harvey Bernhard, remembered, "One day we were coming back from the editing and I was carrying a tote bag, and we were walking from SoHo to where we were living, about four miles. I said, 'Jesus, Dick, I am so tired, I can't carry anything. I'm just worn out!' And he just casually walked along.

I got home and opened the bag, and he had put about 15 pounds of lead in the damn thing!"

Recalling a moment in New York scouting locations for *Superman*, screenwriter Tom Mankiewicz disclosed to *Variety*, "I found myself in front of Florsheim's in Times Square. And we were ready to go to lunch. I said to Dick, 'Go on ahead, I need to get a pair of shoes.' And he said, 'You're not going to buy Florsheims, are you?' I said, 'Dick, my feet hurt. I need some shoes.' And he put up this fuss. I finally said, 'I'll see you at lunch.' I get to the restaurant and the waiter comes up and says, 'By the way, are those Florsheims?' And I said, 'Why, yes.' Then later at the hotel, the elevator operator says, 'Oh, are those Florsheims?'... Months later, we're on a soundstage with Marlon Brando, getting ready to shoot. And Brando's looking at the script and he's mumbling and grumbling. And this goes on for a bit. I'm getting embarrassed. Here's Brando, displeased with my script and he's grumbling around. And suddenly, Brando looks down and says, 'Are those Florsheims?'"

Actors certainly connect to Donner's presence. Says David Morse, who played Jerry Maxwell in the 1980 film, *Inside Moves,* "The force of his personality was completely contagious, and you really felt a great sense of ease with him. You never had the sense that this was the beginning and the end of the world, that life was somehow more important than the film you were making, but at the same time that made the film the most important place you needed to be."

Concurs Diana Scarwid, an actress nominated for an Academy Award for her role as Louise in the same film, "[He was] a great coach, a great leader, the type of person that if you were a brigade of men you would want him out there in front guiding you, making you be strong and taking the best care of you that he can. He's a true artisan with great personality, great presence, who knows how to use that power for good."

Yet, while there is no denying that he is larger than life — forever playful, of good humor, seemingly carefree — the hyper-excitable, hyper-confident persona projected to the world is not the complete Richard Donner. Few might peg him as a closet contemplative, but behind the fun and jokes is an intensely private man. "He seems so tough," says his former girlfriend, actress Liv Ullmann, "and he's so big in the way he talks, but that's not who he is inside."

Donner is undoubtedly strong, fiercely independent, still sizzles with the chutzpah that drove him into Preminger's office all those years ago, but to peel away layers is to discover a man more complex than we know, more complex than he would like us to know. He is deeply sensitive, can be, at times, an introspective soul, a figure not immune to moments of insecurity and self-doubt — particularly over the release of his films. He is not a little shy. "If he goes out to do an interview I'm surprised by how nervous he seems," describes his cousin, the well-recognized actor, Steve Kahan. "He gets the fumbles. When he's not in control, you can see that he's not totally at ease like he is in real life."

Richard Donner is one of the most successful film directors in history. His career spans more than five decades, a passage of time witness to explosive collaborations with Gregory Peck, Marlon Brando, Gene Hackman, Michelle Pfeiffer, Mel Gibson, Jodie Foster, Sylvester Stallone, Julia Roberts, and Bruce Willis — to name but a few. His pictures, which have grossed billions of dollars in theatrical box-office revenue alone, resonate with generations of moviegoers. Donner himself has never received his critical due, and he is far from well known (genre fans aside). His film titles roll easily off the tongue, but his name does not.

Donner began his career as an actor in New York during the fifties, studying under David Alexander and Dort Clark at the Greenwich Village Theater. It was after he was cast in *Of Human Bondage,* a live television production for director Martin Ritt, that his focus changed. "Your problem is you can't take direction," Ritt advised him. "You ought to be a director." The advice was taken to heart. When Ritt immediately offered him a job as his assistant, Donner gleefully accepted. Then, after a period of time, he met George Blake, a man who would become a determining influence in his life.

The dynamic Blake was an Academy Award-nominated director who specialized in documentaries and commercials. He took Donner under his wing, schooled him not only in the art of direction, but also the art of humanity. Blake believed that it was the emotional connections he made, the friendships he formed, that mattered most in life, and he approached everything he did with love and with humor. The two men traveled across the country and formed a close bond, before Blake's untimely death from a heart attack at the age of thirty-eight.

It was in 1958 that Donner moved to California and earned an opportunity to helm an episode of the Western serial *Wanted: Dead or Alive,* starring Steve McQueen. The irascible McQueen bullied him throughout his debut. When a worn-down Donner finally submitted to the pressure, and asked the star how *he* would set up a particular shot, the actor lambasted him: "You're the director. You figure it out."

It was a bumpy start in network television, but on the west coast Donner's career took off. He enjoyed prolific success on such popular series as *The Twilight Zone, The Man from U.N.C.L.E., The Wild Wild West* and *Kojak,* until he stole headlines with his first theatrical success: *The Omen* in 1976. The creepy tale of a child Antichrist was a major international smash, helped in part by a sensational marketing campaign that promised "The Film the Devil Did Not Want You to See." During filming, rumors abounded of a hex on the production. The closest that Donner came to being cursed was during the casting process, which brought forth, quite literally, his most painful moment. Looking for a suitable child actor to play young Damien the Antichrist, the director stumbled upon four-year-old Harvey Stephens. The cherubic blond-haired little boy didn't offer the presumed appearance of the devil incarnate, but he nonetheless proved to possess an entirely satanic rage. "Now, when I yell, 'Action!' I want you to come at me and try to beat me up, and when I yell cut, you stop. Right?" explained the director, who had arranged a screen test for the boisterous infant.

Stephens nodded, beaming with excitement. Like a flash of lightning, he streaked across the room and kicked Donner straight between the legs. Hard. As the pained filmmaker collapsed onto the floor, writhing in agony, Stephens jumped on top of him — punching, kicking and scratching his now almost motionless victim in a wild frenzy.

"Cut... cut...," Donner wheezed, his eyes full of water.

Stephens instead stepped up his assault, only to be dragged off by the producer Harvey Bernhard and a group of frightened crewmembers.

"Dye his hair black. That's the kid," the director groaned through a cut lip.

Originally conceived as an *Exorcist*-style schlock-fest, Donner molded *The Omen* screenplay into a powerful mystery-suspense-thriller by eliminating its many clichés and placing emphasis on compelling, well-rounded characters.

Made for a little over $2 million, *The Omen* grossed $61 million in the U.S. alone. It was a phenomenon that inspired three sequels, a television movie, and a 2006 theatrical remake. Crucially, the blockbuster success propelled Donner to in-demand, A-list filmmaker.

Next came *Superman* with Christopher Reeve. As a child Donner had reveled in the comic strip adventures of the popular American icon, and he was determined that his movie version should deliver the same passion and energy. The original screenplay, however, had failed to meet his standard. Hindered by parody and camp, Donner deemed it more in tune with the *Batman* television series than the reverential epic he had in mind. The director flew to France to meet with the European producers who were funding the picture, and conveyed the need for a complete overhaul. He contacted his friend, Tom Mankiewicz, for the task. "Get up! Get up! Get up!" he bellowed at hyperspeed. "This is Dick Donner — I'm calling from Paris."

"What are you doing in Paris?" replied the writer, whose credits included the James Bond hits *Diamonds Are Forever*, *Live and Let Die* and *The Man with the Golden Gun*.

"I'm going to direct *Superman*. It needs a massive rewrite, and you're going to do it!"

"Dick... it's five in the morning!"

"Look, there's a woman coming to your house right now with the script, and I told her that you were too nice a guy to go back to sleep. She'll be there any second — call you later."

Mankiewicz received the enormous five-hundred-and-fifty-page screenplay — enough for at least two movies in one — and went back to bed. The phone rang again.

"Are you reading?" Donner demanded.

"It's too heavy to get upstairs," quipped the acerbic scribe.

Mankiewicz concurred that Siegel and Shuster's comic creation deserved better treatment, but he did not feel it was the right project for him. He called Donner when the director returned to Los Angeles and informed him of his decision.

"Look, I really want to work with you," Mankiewicz told his friend, "but I don't think I'm going to do this."

"You've got to come over right now," Donner insisted. "Just come on over."

The reluctant screenwriter made the short journey to the director's house, figuring he would at least listen to what he had to say.

When Mankiewicz rang the front door bell, his friend answered, clad top-to-toe in an ill-fitting Superman costume provided to him by his producers. From ear to ear Donner grinned, stood proud in full regalia, his enthusiasm so infectious it was out of bounds. "Just try the suit on," he insisted. "If you try the suit on you'll do it."

Mankiewicz laughed hysterically as his friend surged past him, bounded across the front lawn, his one arm pointing up to the sky, attempting to fly.

In that one moment it was clear that Richard Donner had to direct *Superman*. Not because of the $1 million salary, or the array of big name talent attached to the project, but because he yearned to turn what was once make-believe into something real. The late Mankiewicz observed, "If you give Dick a myth like *Superman* he immerses himself in it and he believes in it, he will do it as if he is a member of that cast. If you asked Dick to direct a restoration theater or a comedy of manners he wouldn't know what the hell to do. He would turn and say to me, 'These people aren't saying anything real! Where's the heart in here?' It's the difference between standing back from a myth and commenting on it while you're doing it, and immersing yourself in it and becoming the myth. There's integrity to it."

The incredible struggle Donner faced in bringing *Superman* to the screen would ultimately pass into movie lore. He knew he was in trouble from the moment Marlon Brando suggested that he play his character, Jor-El, "as a green suitcase." Fortunately, the superstar actor owned an alternate suggestion in the event that this idea proved too far-fetched: a bagel that speaks electronic sounds.

After an eighteen-month shoot beset by bitter political infighting and an extraordinary battle to develop revolutionary special effects, *Superman* was released to wild, record-breaking box-office success. Donner wowed audiences across the globe with a visually spectacular blockbuster like nothing before; the amazing technical advancements developed at his behest allowing audiences around the world to buy into its tagline, "You'll Believe a Man Can Fly!"

In tune with audience demand for unabashed escapism, Donner had also instinctually understood the need to "play it straight." He worked tirelessly to create a tangible romance between Superman and Lois Lane to which moments of action and humor would complement. "The love story has to work," he had instructed Mankiewicz at the time of rewriting the screenplay. "If the love story doesn't work, the picture doesn't work."

In the end, Donner's warm affection for his fictional all-American hero permeates the entire film. He handled its grandiose moments and its more lighthearted and witty scenes with equal straight-faced aplomb. "Dick really was the guardian of the Superman myth," says David Petrou, author of the bestselling *The Making of Superman: The Movie.* "From the beginning he said, 'This legend created by Siegel and Shuster, I grew up with it, lots of kids grew up with it, and if you laugh *at* it, then our film will be a failure. If you laugh *with* the characters, that's something else."

The legacy of Donner's direction was a phenomenon that has swept the box-office. *Superman* led to record-crushing franchises such as the *Batman*, *Spiderman* and *X-Men* series, and more than thirty years later his seminal picture remains the creative benchmark by which these and all comic book movies are judged. (Filmmakers Christopher Nolan, Sam Raimi, and Bryan Singer have each publically cited Donner's contribution as being of influence to them.)

Donner's next project was startlingly smaller in physical scope, but no less powerful in emotion. The independently financed and distributed *Inside Moves* was an uplifting drama of hope in the face of adversity; an intricate, textured exploration of the psychological barriers people place in front of themselves, and which must be overcome in order to be the best that we can be. Donner's emotionally-charged effort garnered rave reviews, and an Academy Award nomination for supporting actress Diana Scarwid. A deeply personal film noted for remarkable performances and a Capraesque tone, it remains Donner's most complex and affecting picture. The film earned the director the best reviews of his career, but in lacking the support of a major distributor it failed to score at the box-office.

Donner himself could, perhaps should, have been nominated for an Oscar for *Inside Moves*. It is possible that a scathing interview he allowed just weeks after the release of *Superman* may have hindered his chances. Angry and disappointed that his cinematographer, Geoffrey Unsworth, and production designer, John Barry, were not to be nominated for their contribution to the comic book hit, he claimed the Academy of Motion Picture Arts and Sciences to be "a disgrace... the most political, ridiculous thing I've ever seen." Such a statement was typical of Donner, who despite being ferociously intelligent has never played the complicated political game of Hollywood. He knows but one way to shoot — from the hip (preferably with both barrels).

The Toy, starring Richard Pryor and Jackie Gleason, and *Ladyhawke*, starring Matthew Broderick, Rutger Hauer and Michelle Pfeiffer, followed. Donner was then hired by Steven Spielberg to direct *The Goonies*, a buccaneering quest of adolescent friends searching for the buried treasure of a mysterious pirate named One-Eyed Willy. Spielberg had conceived of the idea, and had written the story upon which the screenplay would be based, but although the project was one that was close to his heart he was adamant that Donner should be the man to bring his creation to life. When Donner asked him why, the auteur mogul responded firmly, "I need an even bigger kid than me."

Pre-teen fun at its very best, the legacy of *The Goonies* continues to grow. You may overhear children of that era, now grown adults, comically reciting such glorious dialogue as "That's what I said, Booty Traps!" or "I smell ice cream" with their friends. You may witness children of the nineties, now students on college campuses, proudly wearing their *Goonies* T-shirts or eBay-sourced merchandise. And as the film airs on cable networks across the globe, and with a DVD release readily available, an entirely new generation of children falls in love with it. Says actor Sean Astin, who, as hero Mikey Walsh, made asthma inhalers an unlikely fashion accessory of the eighties, "Everywhere I go all over this planet, there are *Goonies* fans that are desperate for a sequel."

The key to such resonance lies in Donner's unique brand of energy and enthusiasm, and the authentic performances he elicited from his cast of children. Desiring his charges to behave before the camera as they might in real life, the filmmaker invited his young cast to improvise. "He wanted kids to talk how kids talk," says Jeff Cohen, who played Chunk in the movie. "I remember early on in *The Goonies* he'd ask us, 'When you're talking with your friends what kind of slang do you use?' Dick's big thing is verisimilitude and that's what he got with *Goonies*."

The Goonies was lensed at breakneck speed. So much so that after filming had wrapped Donner planned an immediate vacation to recuperate. His executive producer, Steven Spielberg, had other ideas. He booked the child cast onto a private plane — complete with parents and guardians in tow — and broke into Donner's holiday home in Maui. "Hi, Dick! We've come to visit you!" the kids screamed as the exhausted director walked through the door.

Full of crackling dialogue (the kids cuss, swear and insult each other's mothers in a fashion only kids can make endearing), slapstick humor and goodies and baddies so clearly defined that you literally want to boo and cheer along with youthful exuberance, *The Goonies* bristles with the same careful blend of naivety and knowingness that Donner brought to *The Omen* and *Superman*. So invested was he that during shooting he claimed, "I never saw it as a fantasy or a fairytale. It's a true story [that] we just happen to be documenting the lives of a group of kids in a little town known as Astoria, and the kids call themselves the Goonies."

For the iconic *Lethal Weapon*, Donner brought a previously marginalized genre into the mainstream, created a billion-dollar series, and set the template for a generation of supersized action movies that defined nineties cinema (its impact was such that the picture became the progenitor of an entirely new sub-genre: the action-buddy film). Donner's ability to extrapolate the "real" from "unreal" was crucial to this. Says he, "All the car chases and explosions are quite honestly child's play, because you surround yourself with so many people who do it better than you. The challenge is to make the characters work, so that the audience really cares if they come through... If the characters [in a movie] don't come to life, and you don't either love them or hate them, then you don't have a movie. [If] after a few moments you're not committed to the people that are within that element you're lost. You don't care."

In addition to elevating the action genre, *Lethal Weapon* dramatically reinvented the way black people are portrayed on screen — a contribution noted by the NAACP (National Association for the Advancement of Colored People) when they awarded Donner an Image Award for Best Picture of 1987. Although *The Defiant Ones*, *In the Heat of the Night* and *48HRS* pre-date it as bi-racial buddy flicks, black actors had struggled for years to escape roles as downtrodden (often unemployed) men surviving on wisecracks alone. As Roger Murtaugh, African-American actor Danny Glover played a successful professional who lives with his family in a modern suburban home — a stark contrast to Mel Gibson's rootless loner. "There wasn't any racial casting in the screenplay," Glover recalls, "the role could have been played by any actor. It didn't have to be a black actor. What really appealed to me was that Murtaugh had a family. In films at that time the black protagonist didn't have a family."

Donner remembers *Lethal Weapon* fondly as a groundbreaking picture of quality, but his recollections always start and end with Mel Gibson, the superstar actor and director with whom he formed a tremendous friendship. *Lethal Weapon* was the first of six screen partnerships, and the forging of a tight familial bond, despite their differences in opinion. "He's a very special person in my life," Donner admits. "I find him a fascinating man. Although we have different political philosophies [Donner is a staunch Democrat, Gibson a proud conservative], I respect him for his because in his own way he can validate them — and a lot of people can't. It's a hard thing to say you love somebody, but I love this kid. He's an amazing boy."

"His views are very strongly held by him," says Gibson, "and I'm not going to try and get into a spat about it. I think his [political ideology] is real interesting in some areas, but I'll express [my opinion] and he's respectful of that, but it's not like we're coming from the same space at all."

Like many friendships, there have been ups and downs, bumps in the road, but a relationship based upon love and mutual respect continues to this day. On February 15, 2009, the pair were photographed at the Beverly Hilton Hotel in Beverly Hills, where Donner was present to receive the Golden Eddie Filmmaker of the Year Award from the American Cinema Editors group. Recently, Joel Silver, whom Donner had brought on board the *Lethal Weapon* franchise as a co-producer, approached Gibson to appear in a fifth installment. In doing so, he was careful to exclude Donner from his role as producer/director of the series. The veteran director believes that Gibson declined out of loyalty to him.

In recent years Donner has directed *Scrooged*, *Radio Flyer*, *Maverick*, *Assassins*, *Conspiracy Theory*, *Timeline* and *16 Blocks*. His film achievements are undoubtedly formidable, yet to date they have been afforded only the most cursory of critical glances. In *The New Biographical Dictionary of Film*, film critic David Thomson cuttingly dictates that, "Mr. Donner has made several of the most successful and least interesting films of his age. And no one doubts it's over yet."

It is difficult to recall a filmmaker of comparable stature so summarily dismissed, especially interesting when given that, from within the industry, a different perspective emerges. "I had the best time of my career working with Richard," testified the late cinematographer, László Kovács, of *Easy Rider* fame. "He was very much an influence on me. It's just a joy working with him. He's a very visual director, and also wonderful working with actors, so it's the ideal combination. He's a truly great filmmaker."

The smash hits *The Omen* and *Superman* belong to a select group of films released during the late seventies that forever changed Hollywood, but Donner's input to this seismic ideological shift in American filmmaking has been overlooked. It is not completely clear as to why.

Perhaps it is because Donner's signature hit did not arrive until he was forty-six, when he was already a veteran of more than a hundred television shows, that he somehow failed to ignite journalistic imagination. (In contrast, George Lucas was thirty-three when *Star Wars* was released, Steven Spielberg a sprightly twenty-eight at the point that *Jaws* swam into theaters).

Or maybe it is because after *Superman*, a picture that established him as the putative author of the comic book movie, the vast reach of his *Lethal Weapon* series saw Donner's career forever entwined with the action-adventure genre.

Thus, certain critics may believe that they have the filmmaker summed up — firmly bracketed in traditionally non-prestigious categories. "A lot of people he worked with, including myself, got a lot of accolades from working on his pictures," says Stuart Baird, "but he seems to have been sidestepped. It's like [film critics] have never taken him seriously, and because they've never taken him seriously they can never take him seriously [in the future]."

But Donner has tackled challenging, mature subject matter to contrast against his mainstream, popcorn entertainment. *Inside Moves*, arguably his best film, is a powerful artistic vision into which he poured his heart and soul, a picture lacking recognition only due to a shortfall in financing and a poor distribution strategy that spelled doom at the box-office. "Some of Dick's most beautiful movies just aren't well known," says *The Goonies* actress Kerri Green. "*Inside Moves* is just one of the most heartbreaking films ever, [but] most people have never heard of it."

Yet it would seem that the biggest single factor behind Donner's comparative lack of acknowledgement might be Donner himself. His happy-go-lucky manner can certainly blind people to the genuine artist that resides within. "That personality marches out in front of him like a flag," says actress Margot Kidder, "and people find it very distracting. In a way, the personality is what people take and they don't look any further."

"If he were some brooding, miserable artist in the corner weeping," agrees Jeff Cohen, "it would be different. He's a very gregarious person. People like him. He's just a very fun, strong, bold personality."

Although a solid promoter of his movies, Donner desires to avoid the show business limelight. He habitually deflects attention away during interviews, answers personal questions in a limited, generic fashion. "He does try to shun the attention and he throws it on other people," says Mel Gibson. "Or he sends it up. Makes light of it. But there is a real talent and a real genius there."

As a filmmaker, he is unwilling to peddle myth and falsehood in order to envelope himself within a fabricated aura of mystique. "He wants to have a good life and a real life," says actress and former flame, Liv Ullman, "and a warm life with love and a life with family. He would rather have that than be a mythical director, even if he makes movies as good as so-called mythical directors."

Donner's films are driven by that great American quality, the capacity to wonder, that he seems to so naturally embody. As Mel Gibson confirms, "I think when you make a film as a director your personality's all over it, and he's no exception. At the end of the day he's kind of putting himself out there and leaving his mark on it."

And yet Donner has never entirely revealed himself in his work. Certainly his energy and passion, his sense of mischief and prank, and — most importantly — his unerring belief in the power and importance of love and friendship, are universal themes that connect each of his films. But what of the pivotal moments in his life, the critical chain of events that drive his optimism?

Donner's childhood would appear to have been idyllic, but it was not entirely without heartache; one major loss in particular would haunt his family for many years. His cousin, Bobby Brauer, was just two years younger than him. In a way he was the brother he didn't have, a loving, affectionate lad whom Donner palled around with whenever he would visit from his home in Forest Hills, Long Island. On one occasion, when Donner was seven, he returned from school for lunch and found that Bobby and his mother, Aunt Tess, were there (so, too, was his Aunt Francis and her daughter, Judy). While he and Bobby played, Donner's sister, Joan, listened in on the adults as she so often did. "Bobby couldn't catch his breath the other day," she overheard Tess report to Hattie and Francis. "We were so scared and worried about him."

Some time afterward, Donner's mother informed Joan that, "Your cousin Bobby is very sick and is in the hospital. Your aunt and uncle are staying in your bedroom for a while, and you're going to have to sleep in Dick's bedroom." That night Donner and his sister huddled, listening to the grownups crying. Desperate for news in the days that followed, Joan periodically plucked up the courage to inquire. "He's still very sick," was the most she could seize from her mother. After a while Bobby's parents, Herman and Tess Brauer, left the family home. Their son was still sick, likely for a very long time, Donner was told. An unknown while later, Joan again asked her mother, "When is Bobby going to come home?"

With great tenderness, it was explained that Bobby was never coming home.

Devastated, Joan went to her brother. "Did you know Bobby died?"

"Yes," he answered solemnly. "What else could it have been?"

Five-year-old Bobby had lost his battle against the undisclosed illness, dying at the house at 475 North Columbus Avenue in Mount Vernon, New York, while Donner and his sister slept at the home of a school friend. The

Brauer family would never recover from the tragedy. Although Tess later gave birth to a second boy, William ("Billy"), who has become a renowned artist, her husband Herman slipped into alcoholism.

In 1972, Donner's father, Fred Schwartzberg, experienced sudden chest pains and a shortness of breath. When hospital doctors in New York discovered that he had suffered a series of minor heart attacks, they informed him that he would require several days of observation and treatment. Donner's sister, Joan, a divorcee and single mother who was pursuing a career as a psychologist, called her brother in California to inform him of the news. "Should I come right out?" he asked her.

"No," she replied. "The doctors don't think there is any immediate danger."

The next day, Joan visited her father while en route to a consulting lecture. "Dad, are you really sure it's okay for me to go?" she checked. "Do you feel okay?"

"Yeah, I'm okay, I'm okay," he assured. "You just go on with your plans, everything is okay."

When she left, her father smiled to her. "Goodbye, Monkey," he said.

During the drive to her class, Donner's sister was anxious. "Monkey" was the pet name her father had given her as a child. Something was wrong. She could feel it. With her mother at home suffering from a cold, and her brother in Los Angeles, somebody needed be with her father. She contemplated turning around but talked herself out of it. She was being paranoid. When Joan arrived on campus there was a message waiting for her. Fred Schwartzberg had suffered a severe heart attack and had died, just moments after she had left the hospital.

Donner was shattered by the death of his father, especially anguished by his decision not to travel immediately to New York, of being denied the opportunity to say goodbye. He was also angry. What had gone so terribly wrong? Donner suspected medical error, and in part he was correct. In order to control Fred's diabetes his doctors had injected him with insulin (he normally treated his condition orally). Some years later, the medical profession would learn that the intravenous treatment of diabetes in patients with heart disease could induce heart failure.

Donner has known these and other instances of unabridged pain, tragedies within his family of which he will not speak. And while he truly is a perennial optimist, the battle to remain positive can be, at times, a heavy burden. Indeed, Donner sometimes struggles to reconcile the "positive thinking" belief by which he lives with the hardships and tragedies he encounters. When one lives life to the mantra that the glass is always half full, how does one cope when it is discovered to be empty?

Donner once joined Mel Gibson at a children's hospital in Sydney, Australia. Gibson remembers that halfway through the afternoon the director simply disappeared. He found him sobbing behind the door of an adjacent room, unable to cope with the plight of the many sick children.

"There's a very private side of him that he gives you a small glimpse of from time to time," Gibson observes. "I don't think he's necessarily trying to cover stuff up, it's just not everybody's business to be out there on display. It's the same sort of thing with all of us, it's just a natural, human tendency to try and obscure our vulnerabilities. It's hard to stick your heart out there on a plate just in case somebody comes along and decides to tap dance on it."

Donner and Gibson were deeply affected by the time they spent on the children's ward. Appalled by an apparent lack of funding for much-needed equipment, the two men publicized the shortfall in finance (with the help of various news outlets) until the Australian government agreed to provide the required medical instruments.

To some, Donner's reluctance to outwardly express his inner pain is more reflective of a life led in the glare of show business. Explains Stuart Baird, "He doesn't reveal a lot about himself, perhaps because he doesn't want to show any vulnerability. Hollywood is a town [that] if you show any vulnerability it's looked upon as a weakness, or a means of controlling you. It's like the adage [that] if you show that you care too much, they've got you."

Donner is quick to avoid aspects of life that cause him pain and discomfort, and rejects movie projects upon the principle. He has abandoned numerous quality scripts simply because he does not wish to become absorbed by the deep, dark spaces on offer. One such movie he turned down was *Silence of the Lambs,* the screenplay for which he found "really disturbing."

For much of his adult life, Donner's fear of commitment and vice-like grip on bachelordom were legendary. No one, least of all him, anticipated marriage. Then, in 1986, he stunned friends and family by announcing his engagement to Lauren Shuler, the producer who had hired him to direct *Ladyhawke* and who had become his best friend and truest confidante. The spur of the moment ceremony, to which numerous friends and family were invited, was to be held in the backyard of his home in Hollywood on Thanksgiving Day. On the day of the wedding, however, there was a last-minute hiccup. Donner was in the shower when, nervous over the occasion, he inadvertently put soap in his eye. Not a little soap, but an entire bar. Tears ran down his face. Then the swelling began. Shortly afterward, he could no longer see. "I can't get married," he explained to Lauren in a state of panic.

But of course he did.

More than twenty years later, their marriage continues to thrive. They are partners in the highly successful production unit, The Donners Company, based in Beverly Hills, a business that associate Kathy Liska — an eighteen-year veteran of the company — describes as "a mom-and-pop" venture. Says she, "Nobody ever wants to leave this company. They know that no matter what would happen to any of us, the Donners would be there to take care of it."

The Donners support various charitable organizations (including Lupus Research, the Natural Resources Defense Council, The Environmental Association, Guide Dogs of America and Canine Companions for Independence), but are most well known for their support of the prevention of cruelty to animals. During the nineties their campaign to return captive killer whale "Keiko" into the wild made international headlines. Their activism saw the star of the hit film *Free Willy* flown from the U.S. to Iceland, where the whale eventually swam into open water off the coast of Norway. The story aroused attention to the poor living conditions numerous marine mammals are subjected to, and captured the public imagination. Keiko was featured on the cover of *Life* magazine and in a popular documentary, *The Free Willy Story*, for the Discovery Channel. (Donner would later threaten to front a boycott of the Olympic Games because of controversial whaling practices.)

Be it for a press interview or a movie premiere, or for any recent public engagement, Donner can be seen proudly wearing a prominent anti-fur emblem — a socio-political sympathy he has snuck into many of his more recent films. For *Lethal Weapon 3* he applied the slogans "Fur is Dead" and "Only Animals Should Wear Fur… Except For Tasteless Pigs" to vehicles that appeared in the picture. In *Assassins*, Electra (played by actress Julianne Moore) vandalized a ladies fur coat with spray paint during an elevator ride. "It was a very bold and wonderful statement," says Lisa Lange, an executive with PETA (People for the Ethical Treatment of Animals). "We cheered."

The animal rights group honored the Donners with a special Twenty-Fifth Anniversary Humanitarian Award in 2005, but the vast majority of the couple's philanthropic efforts are conducted without fanfare — strictly no press releases or media blitzes. They rarely, if ever, court publicity, as it is the semblance of a normal life that they treasure the most. They escape Hollywood whenever they can, typically to their favorite spots in Maui or Orcas Island— the latter a place where Donner seems as happy in command of a tractor, maneuvering heavy boulders, as he is directing any of his films.

"Dick was never looking for Hollywood glamour," describes his childhood friend, Danny Farr. "Dick was always laid back. He'd rather be in the garden than get involved with a 'flashy' lifestyle. I always respected that in him — he never went for the scene, he did his own thing."

"To have lived in Hollywood all those years," says Liv Ullmann, "and to still be a real person, I think that is just magnificent. He's a real person. There's nothing phony about him… He hasn't allowed the world to wonder who he is because he's lived an ordinary life. I think the most important thing for him is life, and then comes the movies."

That Donner's films have achieved stratospheric fame is axiomatic. Equally as clear is the fact that, from the point of his very earliest success, Donner recognized personal celebrity as a trap and worked hard to find his way around it. He succeeded beyond measure.

"He was full of Hell."

JOAN COHEN (DONNER'S SISTER)

2

Early Years

He was an unruly boy. Inattentive, hyperactive and impulsive, the young Richard Donner was a tiger of a lad who rejected authority and whose enormous energy, boundless as it was, seemed to concentrate only on that which pleased him. From his earliest days he decreed that life was going to be lived his way, on his terms — even if he dug himself into trouble along the way. His mother, likewise a powerful personality, was forced to improvise some creative, nontraditional tacks in an attempt to keep him in check.

"I'm running away! I'm leaving!" her ten-year-old son once obstinately stormed.

"Here you are," she replied, passing him a pre-packed suitcase hidden in a closet by the front door. "Go."

Muted by shock, Donner paused to contemplate an unexpected play.

"I know now that I'm not really loved," he conjured indignantly. "I was adopted."

"Oh, Dick, who on Earth would ever adopt you?" quipped his mother.

The youthful Donner was a rascal and a hell-raiser, a boy whose hair-trigger temper and keen awareness of his physicality led to many a wrestle and fist-fight. At school his grades were crippled by apathy, more a symptom of a barely existent attention span than a lack of intelligence. Surprisingly, his teacher at William Wilson Elementary School, Miss Burton, was less than concerned. "Don't worry about him," she once declared to his parents, matter of fact. "He'll be supporting you someday. We'll read about him in the newspapers."

Donner fully earned his reputation as a mischievous wild child. "He was terrible," says childhood friend, Gene Freedman, "and a lot of people didn't like Dick because of all the crazy and stupid things that he did." Yet it was difficult to remain angry with him, a fine-looking lad blessed with thick locks of sandy-brown hair and piercing brown eyes. "He was always quick to try and make things right," Freedman continues, "Dick would literally give you the shirt off his back. He is one of the sweetest, most considerate people that I've ever known."

Richard Donner, nicknamed Dick, was born Richard Donald Schwartz-berg, on April 24, 1930, in the Bronx, New York City. He was raised in the northern half of the neighboring Mount Vernon, a typical suburban com-munity traversed by few public highways and just two railroads. Children played in front of close-knit homes, rode bicycles along tree-lined streets, traveled to friendly neighborhood stores — taking breath of the palpable sense of safety that hung in the air. Remembers another childhood friend, Danny Farr, "It really was a fabulous place to grow up. If you took me there today, I could tell you the name of everyone who lived there, and in what house. We had good lives. We came from a good town, had good friends and we had a lot of fun."

Donner was the only son of Harriet ("Hattie") Harowitz, a tall, attractive brunette known not only as a long-legged beauty but as a woman of intel-ligence and sharp wit, and Fred Schwartzberg, a furniture maker for Bronx Parlor Frames and Sons, who'd inherited an honest, determined work ethic from his father, Aaron Schwartzberg. Both Hattie and Fred were Jewish, of eastern European extraction. Their courtship had begun while Hattie was still in her teens. Believing that Fred — who at twenty was two years her senior — was "simply adorable," she had befriended his sister, Nellie, as a means to engage him in conversation. After Fred had passed a stern inter-view with Hattie's younger brother, George, who was barely a teenager at the time, they began their courtship, and were subsequently married on Sep-tember 13, 1925.

Donner lived with his parents and his older sister, Joan, in a comfort-able house at 475 North Columbus Avenue. It was a liberal household full of fun and laughter, one visited often by friends and relatives. It was a place of respect but of few rules. Good-natured teasing became a family staple. Although at times he secretly felt very shy, Donner was colorful and funny, highly skilled in understanding when and how best to provoke a smile or a giggle, able to keep pace with his parents and their many visiting family and friends. The dynamic, outgoing atmosphere honed the advanced inter-personal skills that would serve him so well in life. "He learned very quickly that he could get by on his personality," says his sister, Joan Cohen, "and he knew how to charm people."

No matter his havoc-wreaking ways, or his many volcanic moments, it was possible even then to believe that somehow, some way, he was going to *make it.*

Hattie Schwartzberg was everything a mother should be — loving, nur-turing and extremely proud of her children. "She was a special person," says Donner's cousin, Steve Kahan. "I never saw her upset. My only memories of her are those when she had a smile on her face. And she was always great to the kids." Hattie was also very smart, quizzing her young son, who would be so full of energy and spirit when he came bouncing in the door from school. "How was school today?" she pressed.

"Fine," he replied, awkwardly.

"Did you do anything wrong?"

"No."

"I know you're lying because you've got that red spot on your forehead again." Donner would run to the closest mirror. Sure enough, there was a big red spot on his forehead. "I don't know how that happens!" he protested, before confessing his crimes. The tell-all mark in question was always there, for it was lipstick from his mother's kiss that greeted him at the door, but the only time he ever noticed was when he was caught in a lie.

Hattie was extremely close to her own parents, Joe and Ida Harowitz, and to her four sisters and one brother, whom she would see regularly. Her mother and father were "old world" people who spoke only heavily-accented English. Joe was an especially fascinating character, an intensely quiet man normally to be found in the corner of a room playing pinochle with a cigarette dangling precariously from his mouth, or sitting in his favorite chair in the living room, reading the *Forverts*, a Yiddish newspaper. Despite his quiet nature, his family remembers him as a man with a determined spirit, a man who made money, lost it, and won it back again — at least that had seemed the pattern when Hattie and her siblings were growing up. The Harowitzs would routinely live in a nice house and drive a nice car, but it was only ever for a couple of years at a time, as they would inevitably be forced to sell both. Just as inevitable was the fact that, after having moved to a lesser house and having driven a lesser car, Joe would always find a way for his family to clamber back to the top.

He was a tailor by trade who survived much of the Depression as he owned an enormous pair of sheers, giant cloth-cutting scissors the size of a forearm that, when used correctly, could be utilized as effectively as a precision instrument like a lathe, or another purpose-built machine tool. Joe was also a modest entrepreneur. During the early twenties, for instance, he had purchased a small, independent movie theater in Brooklyn. The move had shocked his entire family, but it proved so successful that he was soon able to own further picture houses across New York City. In the twilight of her teenage years, Hattie had been enlisted to play piano, offering musical accompaniment to the silent features, while her younger brother, George, was responsible for running reels to different projectionists in different locations. This task was an important one, and greatly time sensitive, as Joe would often show the same single movie in his various theaters, staggering the start times so that once a reel had finished in one theater, George could run it safely to the next. The thirteen-year-old made the job famous when he fell down a ladder exiting a projection booth and broke both his arms.

Joe continued with his movie theater experiment into the thirties, long enough for Donner, his grandson, to own vague memories of being sat transfixed in the middle of an auditorium. As Donner's mother and her sisters gossiped among themselves, he remembers being locked into the gaze of one Edward G. Robinson.

Joan Cohen remembers that, being such a quiet man, it was a surprise to see her Grandfather Joe rise to address guests at a party held in celebration of his golden wedding anniversary. He spoke assuredly and left a strong impression. "I have something to say that I don't think any of you know," he informed those in attendance. "Today is not only my wedding anniversary, it's also my birthday."

Family members looked on perplexed, for it was not his birthday.

"Grandpa, what are you talking about?" enquired a confused grandchild.

"Yes," he declared, "because I didn't start to live until I married my wife."

Such actions by Donner's family greatly impacted his childhood and his future mindset as an adult — ultimately driving the messages and values inherent in his work as a filmmaker, and the firm ideals he would apply in his personal life. Like his grandfather (and indeed his father, who doted upon his mother), Donner would become entirely committed to love and romance. He mentions Lauren Shuler, his wife of more than twenty years, in almost every interview, consistently emphasizing that she is "the best thing that ever happened to him."

Fred Schwartzberg was an infant when he arrived in the U.S. from Russia. With a brother and three sisters, he was one of five siblings who had grown up in the same apartment building in the Bronx as his future wife, Hattie Harowitz.

Fred loved to laugh and had a great sense of humor. Steve Kahan believes that, "Dick's like his old man [because] his father was a big joker." Fred may have been a prankster, but he was also a disciplined, steadfast man, the product of a strict Germanic upbringing. His passion was motorized vehicles and he had worked as a salesman for a series of car dealerships. He gave up his dream of operating his own agency following his wedding, when his father, Aaron, insisted he join the family furniture business.

Fred would begin his commute from Mount Vernon into the heart of New York City before daybreak, and would not return from the factory until after dark. The hours were long, and he was exhausted, but he would nevertheless make the time to return home with a small present for his children. With money for luxuries sparse, a favorite gift became a bag of Indian pine nuts, which he would lay on a table and split equally between Donner and his sister. Indicative of their personalities, his son would shell a nut and eat it as fast as he possibly could, while his daughter would first shell her entire portion, so that the nuts could be collectively savored. Once Donner had gobbled his share, the tantalizing sight of Joan's uneaten portion was too much for him to tolerate. Somehow, anyhow, he would distract her. "Mom's calling you," he pretended. "Don't you hear mom calling you?"

Her head could be turned but for a second and the pine nuts would be gone.

As much as he tried, Donner never could get the better of his older sister who, like her mother, was extremely intelligent. Despite his initial protestations of innocence, Joan knew that her younger brother found it impossible to conceal guilt. She cleverly devised a scheme to rein in her sibling and to ensure that, in the end, he always told the truth. Whenever the shadow of suspicion fell upon him, which was often, Joan pulled out a specific playing card named "Blue Boy" from a deck of cards. "Blue Boy says, 'YOU'RE LYING!'" she declared emphatically.

Scared, Donner immediately confessed his crimes, although afterward he sought to destroy the power of the card. Finding his sister's deck, he tore up the rogue "Blue Boy." It was not long until he gave cause for his sister to cross-examine him further. When she did, she once more reached for the mysterious pack of cards. Confident that "Blue Boy" had suffered a terrible death by his own hand, Donner grinned cheekily. To his horror, "Blue Boy" appeared resurrected.

"Blue Boy says, 'YOU'RE LYING!'"

The cycle continued. Donner didn't realize that although he destroyed the particular card, his sister had an entire deck — fifty-two of them ready to serve as replacement.

Innocence and naivety always kept Donner in check. He was an exceptionally trusting boy, a fact that left him susceptible to manipulation. (Some within the cutthroat world of Hollywood filmmaking would use this to their advantage, for the trait stayed with him into adulthood.) All that he really wanted was to have fun. He was an outdoor child, practically minded, as evidenced by his passion for conducting mechanical repair (or disrepair) on whatever form of machinery he could lay his hands on. Most fun were the games that could be played with a weathered tennis ball and a rusty pocketknife, not to mention a treasured bag of marbles. His favorite games were "Immies," a marble contest in which every kid in the neighborhood intended to be declared champion (the sharpest shooter won a penny a piece, and collected the marbles of all the other children), "Stoop Ball," played on the sidewalk by throwing a ball against the stairs leading up to a building, and "Mumblety-Peg" (pronounced "Mumbly-Peg"), a venture well-suited to Donner's personality, for it required much in the way of bravado. Played with two players and a pocketknife, the winner was the boy who could throw a knife into the ground as near to his own feet as possible.

Schoolwork and household chores were irritating distractions, rarely completed, if attempted at all. When indoors, Donner was likely to be listening to a radio serial or reading an adventure novel or a comic book, the latter of which proved much to the displeasure of his parents. He was not a prolific reader; in fact, it was only the fantasy genre that seemed to hold his interest. He did enjoy Mark Twain, whose Tom Sawyer he seemed to have a little in common with, but he simply reveled in the collective works of Herman Melville, H.G. Wells, and Jack London. Donner would draw upon his childhood love of fantasy to launch his movie career. He infused *The Omen*, *Superman*, and *Ladyhawke* with a passionate desire to believe — to invest wholeheartedly in impossible myths, just as he had done as a child.

As a youth he was transfixed on the headlining hero of the *Action Comics* line: Superman. The brainchild of Ohio teenagers Jerry Siegel and Joe Shuster, Superman could leap one eighth of a mile, raise tremendous weights, and run faster than a speeding locomotive. A social crusader who battled gangsters and corrupt politicians, the immigrant from another star fought to uphold truth and justice in a Depression-ravaged America, all the while falling in love with news reporter Lois Lane.

For Donner, comic books were candy for the brain, and Superman was the sweetest tasting one of all. (He was devastated when his mother threw out his collection during a cleaning spree.) Many a night when he turned out his bedside lamp and readied for sleep, he would focus on the star-filled night through the frame of his bedroom window and dream of the orphan from a doomed planet many millions of years more advanced than Earth. Many a following morning, he — like countless other children — would attach a makeshift cape to his shoulders and pretend to fly. Donner did not know it at the time, but one day, far into the future, his path would again cross with the superhero, and in the most spectacular way.

As of 1941 an old barn still stood on Rolling Acres farm, as did a dog kennel and a caretaker's abode that consisted of a tiny living room, a kitchen with a coal stove, two small bedrooms and a lone bathroom. There was no official residence, for the main building had been burnt to the ground by a fire, and the land — although a vast hundred-acre lot — was in no condition to be farmed. The realtor, Hess, did not believe it could be sold, despite the fact that the property in Clinton Corners was once owned by an heir of John A. Roebling, the pioneering chief engineer of the Brooklyn Bridge.

Fred Schwartzberg immediately fell in love with it. He had often whisked his family away for the weekend to Upstate New York — even as far as

Connecticut and Massachusetts — merely to survey available land and to dream that one day it could be his. Now his dream was to become a reality.

As Hattie refused to be away from her family and friends in Mount Vernon, Rolling Acres farm would need to be rebuilt to accommodate them, too. Fred and his best friend (and brother-in-law), Saul Kahan, started by renovating the empty barn, installing a kitchen and two bathrooms. In just three short years they would restore the dilapidated property to the extent that the multiple families could utilize it as both a weekend retreat and a summer home. Fred's children would affectionately recall that Rolling Acres was "always a family reunion."

For an eleven-year-old boy, life on the farm was a grand adventure. "He loved that life," says boyhood pal, Danny Farr. "He loved being in the country. He loved the animals. He loved everything about being up in Clinton Corners." Donner towed behind him his mud-splattered Radio Flyer wagon, collecting in it assorted finds from various expeditions of the seemingly infinite space. Hermit, an adopted Collie dog that traipsed by his side, was his loyal chum.

Donner tended to chickens, calves, lambs, cows and horses, naming each and every one of them. He and his sister begged their father not to sell them to the local butcher. Fred would eventually relent, discharging them instead to Charlie Trippolette, a neighboring farmer. Donner remembers, "We were so stupid because my father would always buy chickens and lambs from [Trippolette]. Eventually, when we grew up, we realized we'd eaten our best friends."

Charlie Trippolette taught Donner how to use a rifle, and paid him a quarter for every groundhog or woodchuck he killed. A hole dug by either animal could lead to a cow or a horse breaking a leg. He was also close with a man known only as Weiss, a farmer who owned a German Shepherd dog that Donner adored, and who paid him to clean the pasture out of the metal plough wheels of a tractor. Donner enjoyed the money that such tasks earned him, but if something did not hold his attention he had no patience for it. He was quickly distracted and grew bored easily, just as he would do as an adult. In the mid-eighties, Donner planned to direct the vampire flick *The Lost Boys*, pitched by him to Warner Bros. as "*The Omen* meets *The Goonies*" — a scenario that left studio executives drooling. A promising screenplay was already in hand, but when the development process failed to move at sufficient speed, Donner lost first his excitement, then all interest. On the recommendation of his wife, he passed the project onto Joel Schumacher, who would deliver a timeless cult classic.

Very late in his adult life Donner would be diagnosed with A.D.D. (Attention Deficit Disorder), but during his youth his inability to focus for any length of time likely frustrated his father, although Fred was impressed by his son's passion for machinery — one of the few things that did hold his attention. The young boy could often be found disassembling and reassembling farm equipment, although, like his father, it was motorcars that obsessed him the most. He knew the details of every make and model, loved to place his hands out of the window and pretend they were the wings of an airplane.

Fred Schwartzberg's pride and joy was his 1940 Oldsmobile with automatic transmission that he left for Hattie during the week while he worked in the city. Sometimes, Hattie would teach her excited son how to drive safely across the pasture. After these lessons, however, he grew tortured to see the vehicle parked, and he fantasized about putting the pedal to metal and tearing across the farm in his father's dream machine. As the summer grew to a close, he stole his chance. He grabbed the keys and tore off into the distance. Faster and faster he sped, grinning cheekily from ear to ear, until he lost control and became beached in the mud. When he spun the wheels in an attempt to free the car it caused it to bog down further into the ground. Panic set in. It was a Friday, and his father would soon need picking up from the train station. "Oh my God!" he screamed at his mother and sister as he ran into the house. "What am I going to do?"

A phone call was placed and Trippolette arrived with his tractor to rescue the stricken Oldsmobile. Donner frantically washed the car down before they departed to pick up his father from the train station. He pleaded to his mother along the way, "Don't ever tell him. Please don't ever tell him."

Hattie would indulge him, as she typically did, but would hence break into song whenever the dishes needed washing, "Oh, the mud is deep! Deep is the mud!" The passionately sung lyrics always brought her son to attention.

A few years later, once he had earned a learners permit, Donner was involved in a more serious car crash in Mount Vernon. The Oldsmobile belonging to his parents was stored in a garage directly opposite a local church. As Donner reversed, a car chauffeuring a bride and groom ran a yield sign and plowed straight into the back of him. Fred returned home to a damaged Oldsmobile and, amazingly, a pending lawsuit — the newlyweds suing him for "non-performance" during their honeymoon.

The U.S. entered World War II in 1942. The protective Schwartzbergs sheltered their children as best they could. The conflict was not discussed, although it was impossible for Donner, a boy approaching his teenage years, to avoid such a pervasive reality. He observed citizens of Mount Vernon departing their community dressed in armed service uniforms. Some, brothers of his friends even, would not return. Reading breaking events from the newspaper headlines, he learned distaste for war, although he wanted to play his part in the effort. He saved his chewing gum wrappers to make big balls of tin foil, and collected ration stamps — especially those for gasoline. At night he made sure that the blinds were drawn and that all of the lights were out. His father patrolled outside to inspect his work.

The war years caused the Schwartzbergs to suffer financially. Business at the factory declined, and it was not long before Fred was unable to maintain payments on the house in Mount Vernon and the farm in Clinton Corners. He could not bear to give up his beloved Rolling Acres, so he foreclosed on the house and rented his family a cramped apartment at 630 Gramatan Avenue. It was a bitter pill for the proud man to swallow, but yet again he and his wife, Hattie, shielded their teenage children from the hardship. (As an adult, Donner would choose to be the same way, refusing to reveal his darkest moments to those around him.) Says his sister, "All that I remember from that move is, 'Oh, what fun!' They made us believe that we were moving to an apartment because it was closer to things and we wouldn't have to drive as much."

At A. B. Davis High School in Mount Vernon, Donner appointed himself his sister's protector. "I remember Joan as being the most beautiful girl in that entire high school," says Gene Freedman. "She was just absolutely gorgeous."

When Joan, the football queen, hosted a house party at which a group of older boys arrived uninvited, Donner ran upstairs to his bedroom and grabbed his pellet gun. "I stood on a table behind a door," he recalls, "and when this one guy came through I hit him on the head with my shotgun as hard as I could. I remember he chased me, but some other people protected me."

His nobleness did occasionally slip, as it did when he chanced upon Joan's diary. Curiosity forced him to administer the smallest of peaks, which was promptly followed by another, and then another. Soon his sneak peeks amounted to the entire contents, writings that revealed his sister's strong feelings for Rick, a close friend of her boyfriend, Chuck.

"So, you going out with Rick tonight?" he teased her in Chuck's presence.

"No," she replied, her cheeks reddening. "I'm going out with Chuck."

Casually, Donner quoted an incriminating passage that he had memorized from the diary, before posing the question, "Sis, you got a dollar?"

At fifteen, Donner fell in love with Mimi Horowitz, one of the prettiest and most sought-after girls in Mount Vernon. She had straight brown hair, brown eyes, liked to dress funny, her clothes always buttoned up wrong, a style that reflected her quirky personality.

Determined to win her favor, Donner would rarely visit without a dozen red roses in tow. The end result was a six-month courtship that Horowitz ultimately ended. "I think it really broke his heart," Freedman believes, "and hurt him for a long time in his relationships with other women."

Before the demise of the romance, the young couple had attended their annual high-school dance, held at Glen Island Casino, as Mount Vernon lacked the facilities to cope with such an event. The duo traveled together by car with his sister, whom Donner turned to upon arrival.

"Don't bother me," he warned sternly, keen to express his freedom. "You don't bother me, I won't bother you. You don't even know me."

"I don't even know you," was her easy reply.

In an attempt to convince the bartenders at the dance that they were old enough to buy alcohol, Donner and his two great friends, Danny Far and Gene Freedman, had persuaded some former soldiers to lend them discharge pins that they then attached to their own shirts. He was confident the ploy would work, but, as he later discovered, the plan was missing one very important aspect. As such, just a short while later, Donner was forced to return and tap his sister on the shoulder.

"Hey, Sis!" he bopped. "How is everything? How are you doing? Are you having a good time?"

"Uh, huh."

"Say... do you have any money?"

"No, Dick. I didn't bring any money."

"But you must have brought money!" he pleaded. "I don't have any money, Sis. Please! I'll pay you back. I'll pay you back double!"

Joan resisted the temptation to remind her brother that they did not know each other, and decided instead to give him what little money she did in fact have in her purse. The exchange was typical of their relationship. Half the time they were poised to kill one another, but they were family, and for the Schwartzbergs, family was everything.

"He didn't take much very seriously. We had some experiences together that were hysterical. He was a lot of fun and he was game for anything."

DANNY FARR (CHILDHOOD FRIEND)

3

New York City

His head appeared a little oversized, his ears, too, perhaps, but during his transition to adulthood Richard Donner was undoubtedly handsome. At sixteen he had grown tall and he possessed a strikingly deep voice. His distinctive laugh boomed — driven forward by a refreshing, natural confidence every bit as powerful as his vocal chords. His ability to charm people, that great advantage during his boyhood, remained, and took on new and highly pleasurable outcomes as it related to women. "Scarsdale was our stomping ground and we did run around up there with all the women in town," chuckles Donner's pal, Danny Farr. "Dick was popular with the girls."

Donner, however, was a restless young man and never strived to settle down. Age had calmed him only a little - his unfiltered excitement still at times bordered on hyperactivity. He remained willful, stubborn, and uncompromisingly independent. He struggled to exert patience and possessed a blustery temper, even if it was only short-lived. More severely, he lacked a comprehensive sense of direction for his life. Unlike his friends, who left Mount Vernon to pursue their college ambitions before marrying their high-school sweethearts, extending his own academic résumé was sadly out of the question. "Dick was not a great student," says Farr. "[He] just didn't put the effort into it, at all."

To Donner, it was his way in life or the highway. He was expelled from A. B. Davis High School in Mount Vernon for "a practical joke that misfired." Even now Donner refuses to reveal the details, for fear of upsetting his family, a clear indicator of the seriousness of the event, even after so many years. He only says, "I was a kid. School and I didn't get along, and I was asked to leave."

The expulsion was the cause of great distress to his exasperated parents, who promptly enrolled him at Blair Academy, a boarding school in New Jersey. "It didn't do much for him as far as straightening him out was concerned," continues Gene Freedman, another friend. "I remember going over there with Danny [Farr] to visit him at boarding school, and he was confined to quarters, which meant that he was in his room and not supposed to go out. I remember Dick climbing out the window, over the roof, and dropping down to the ground so that we could all go out to have something to eat and have a few beers."

It was not long until Donner was also kicked out of Blair, when surprisingly he chose to join the Navy as part of a special one-year enlistment program being offered by the armed services.

While training, Donner was asked if he had a profession. He lied and said he was a photographer for a film company. Thus, after camp, he was assigned to a four-man photography division on the U.S.S. Sicily CVE-118, the smallest aircraft carrier in the fleet by five feet. Donner would fly off of the ship with young hotshot pilots, too young to be scared. The year he traveled the globe was defined by completing public relations tasks and "a lot of experiences that I can't talk about."

Upon his discharge, and when pressed by his father, he decided to at least take a shot at college. He signed onto a business curriculum at Packard Junior. In the evenings he cleaned furniture at a factory showroom belonging to the father of his friend, Danny Farr.

When Donner received a letter advising him that, as a navy reserve, he was expected to report to his unit every Wednesday and for two whole weeks of the summer for seven years, he went to his employer for assistance. A letter was written explaining that if Donner were held to his commitments, it would result in him being terminated from his job. The letter was enough to earn his release.

If his family hoped that his armed service experience might encourage greater focus and dedication, they would be disappointed. While he reluctantly attempted his obligations, Donner struggled. For the most part he remained a phenomenon of inattentiveness and impulsiveness, failing with anything beyond his immediate short-term satisfaction.

From the offset the young man skipped his day classes in order to hop on the subway and explore New York. From the bleakness of World War II had evolved a vast neon-lit prosperity; it was a vibrant, optimistic city brimming with purpose. As he puts it, "You could go anywhere in the world, or what you thought the world was, [by] going from one end of New York to another." Donner had lived for movies in Mount Vernon, where he and his friends would hide out in theater bathrooms so that they could sneak around and catch two movies, plus whatever shorts were running, for the price of one film. Likewise, as a young adult, his favorite destination was the theater district at 42nd Street and Broadway, a place to catch all of the latest movie releases.

He continues, "You'd go in and see one performance, but they would never empty the theater. So you could see double movies. You'd see two movies two times." There are many autobiographical moments in Donner's 1992 film *Radio Flyer*, including the one in which protagonists Mike and Bobby (Elijah Wood and Joseph Mazzello) employ the very same trick.

It is not clear at which point during his time at Packard that Donner first dreamed of a life as an actor. The idea ruminated, gathered some momentum as he struggled day to day in school and at the furniture factory, but the concept remained outlandish and far-fetched. He remembered well a "Black Sheep Uncle," George Auschmen, a producer of live musicals whose shows had once played at Madison Square Garden. Auschmen's career choice was frowned upon, deemed irresponsible, and he existed on the periphery of the family circle. "Nobody really respected him until they wanted to get tickets to his shows," Donner quips. (Nonetheless, on one of the few occasions he interacted with him, Donner had been thrilled to go backstage and get a glimpse of the inner workings of theater. Afterward, his uncle took him for a ride in his brand-new Lincoln Continental — a big car for a big personality.)

The fifties were a groundbreaking era. The "teenager" had been born and kids were beginning to find their own mold in life, rather than simply following in the family footsteps. Still, Donner fretted over his father, who was leading the family business: Bronx Parlor Frames and Sons. "[My father] never had the opportunity [to go to college], and he wanted me to do it. He always thought I would come into his business. He had a little furniture factory, really tiny. He and everybody [there] worked their butts off all day and all night and — God love him for it — he thought that he was going to give it to his son. It was difficult, but my mission was somewhere in entertainment."

When Donner finally mustered the courage to confide in his parents his ambition, he was cheered by their reaction. Fred Schwartzberg had suffered a similar conflict many years before, when he had so yearned to sell cars for a living. Donner continues, "He was really hurt that he hadn't followed his own dream of running a dealership selling cars. He hadn't been able to stand up to his father. When I made my decision, our family business wasn't good. It was a unionized, tiny little shop. [So] I think although he wanted me in, in his heart of hearts he wanted me to do something else."

If he really, truly wanted to leave school and pursue acting as his chosen career, Donner's parents insisted he be able to support himself. After a brief spell working as an assistant for Mecca Film Labs, he stopped by the offices of a non-union film company, Harvey Productions. With typical self-assuredness, he talked them into paying him $18 a week to paint sets and to shuttle film equipment, lying that he knew how to drive the trucks.

In the evenings he studied acting, and formed a loose friendship with a fellow actor, Steve McQueen. The future icon dubbed the "King of Cool" was a complex personality. An irascible, combative man always spoiling for a fight, he was the product of a traumatic childhood (as a baby he was abandoned first by his father, and then by his alcoholic mother). He could be unpredictable and was awkward to get along with, but Donner liked him nonetheless. Throughout his life Donner has been sensitive toward difficult, at times unpopular personalities, drawing reward from offering them the faith and encouragement that others would not.

Their Navy experiences, and their passion for motor racing, were common bonds. McQueen was a keen bike enthusiast and competitor who, in an act of radiant kindness, would later generously gift Donner a Triumph motorcycle.

At the Provincetown Players, a theatrical group based out of the Greenwich Village Theater that specialized in experimental, non-commercial work, it was his acting coach, David Alexander, who mentored Donner. Although a slight man in terms of physical stature, Alexander projected a large and powerful presence. "He was a wonderfully talented director," says student of teacher. "He believed that if you wanted to act, or do anything in life, that you diversified and took in as many theories as you could until you found your own. He didn't believe in any strict method. He didn't think people should study with him too long."

It was likely Alexander who first brought Donner's attention to the term "verisimilitude." Defined as "the appearance of being true or real," the word would become a governing force throughout Donner's life and career. Alexander encouraged his students to find "the truth in themselves," a philosophy that Donner would later draw from. "I have my own sense of verisimilitude when it comes to each and every project," he told *Variety* in 2008. "It's a reformation, to a degree, of Method acting principles transformed for directing: Find the reality. I look for the reality in the situation, rather than the farce." From the mysticism of *Ladyhawke* to the action of *Lethal Weapon*, in any great fictional myth, the director believes, audiences require a framework of reality so as to truly invest themselves in the material. Donner even had Marlon Brando boldly open in *Superman* with the promise: "This is no fantasy, no careless product of wild imagination." He has sought to impose such a tone upon all of his projects, primarily through narratives that tread a fine line between naivety and knowingness.

In many ways, his dedication to this principle, one that originated with the influence of Alexander, can be seen as a primary reason for his sustained success as a filmmaker.

Donner was good looking, and he had some talent as an actor. Like many other young Jewish performers of the time, he contemplated changing his name. Thus Richard Donald Schwartzberg morphed into Richard Donner. (His sister, Joan, had suggested Donner, for it was close to Donald, his middle name.) He worked off-Broadway and made some walk-on appearances in television advertisements that impressed his family. "I remember him doing a Lava [soap] commercial," Donner's cousin, Steve Kahan, recalls, "[where he was] walking into a bathroom and washing his hands. I thought he was the biggest thing in the world." The commercial was a split-screen episode featuring two people washing their hands in separate sinks, who then proceeded to dry their hands on different towels. The message was obvious: to use Lava soap was to leave your towel clean and white, to not was to leave it filthy. Donner happily provided filthy hands.

For the most part, however, the budding actor struggled to make his chosen career a success. He eventually won a small speaking role on the live television show, "Of Human Bondage," a part of the *Somerset Maugham TV Theatre* series (originally titled *The Teller of Tales*) directed by Martin Ritt. Ritt was a former actor-turned-director, and a respected tutor at the renowned Actors Studio. There, his star pupil was Paul Newman, whom he would later guide to an Academy Award nomination for his performance in *Hud*.

Ritt was a big deal, a fact that made Donner nervous. He recalls, "At the old NBC Studios, the director's booth was way up in the balcony. We used to call it the 'God Booth.' There was a long spiral staircase leading down to the stage, and I could hear Marty taking every one of those steps, clank-clank-clank."

During rehearsal the young actor repeatedly fluffed his lines. "Your problem is you can't take direction," an exasperated Ritt finally advised. "You ought to be a director."

"Easier said than done," Donner blurted, typically bold and forthright.

Impressed by the brazen response, Ritt offered Donner a role as his assistant on two subsequent live television shows, an opportunity he reveled in. Intermittent jobs working for other directors followed, but the promise of a behind-the-scenes part in the entertainment world was snatched away from him just as quickly as it had appeared. When NBC Studios ceased production for its summer-season hiatus, the only employment Donner could find was as a salesman for a cardboard company.

In the evenings he visited the parents of Gene Freedman, a lifelong friend who had moved away to college. He loved the Freedmans, one of the few families he knew that owned a television set. On one occasion over dinner the father, Chauncey, turned to him.

"Dick, are you enjoying the job you're doing?"

"Chauncey," he replied. "I absolutely hate it."

"Well, what would you really like to do?"

"I would really like to do something in showbiz," Donner confessed.

Chauncey Freedman paused. "Well, I have a very, very good friend by the name of George Blake, who is doing something in television. Television commercials. If you'd like, I'll introduce you to him. He's recovering from a heart attack and he's looking for an assistant."

At just thirty-four, George Blake was already an Oscar nominee, his documentary *A Voice Is Born* (the moving profile of a Hungarian tenor, Miklos Gafni, who learned to sing while imprisoned in a concentration camp) having been nominated for an Academy Award several years prior. The precocious New York filmmaker had since established George Blake Enterprises, his own production company based on Madison Avenue that specialized in commercial work.

Blake was a heavyset man who liked to drink and smoke (pleasures he was determined not to conduct by half). He was funny, charming, and full of humor, full of jokes. Inside him a giant engine roared, straining on the rev limit, never a pause for cruise control. In the words of Donner's sister, Joan Cohen, Blake was "bigger than life, a wonderful guy. He lived life to the fullest... and he thought nothing could ever stop him."

Since his heart attack, however, Blake had conceded the need for somebody to drive him around. Donner was hired to be his gofer, and quickly endeared himself to his new employer during the many hours they spent together on the road. A dynamic bond was formed. As Gene Freedman describes, "Dick was a very handsome guy and had a huge personality. He had a great big laugh... He was very easy to get to know very quickly."

Within a year Donner was a full-time assistant, an alacritous pupil who amassed countless hours on film sets and in editing suites, absorbing all that he could. At night he studied script materials, which he would report on the next morning. "Dick was George's protégé," Joan Cohen states. "He found him, and he was training him."

Thus, Donner was carefully nurtured into the world of film. Says he, "With live television, you had to make the actors concede to the equipment, because you weren't taping. It was one take, right through. The cameras were really the stars, because the actors had to move and choreograph themselves and their lines to the camera. When I saw film - where you could shoot a scene and then shoot it over from a completely different angle without seeing the camera — right then and there I fell in love with film."

The director welcomed Donner into the home he shared with his wife, Jean, and their children. The two men would spend hours playing with a vast electric train set in the basement, a lifelong hobby of Blake's.

Donner has rarely spoken publicly about his close relationship with Blake, a man who was, in all likelihood, the most important, most influential figure in his young adulthood. For him it is too highly emotional, too deeply personal a subject. When asked during interview in 1997 what he felt he had learned from Blake, he could only summarize: "Humanity. He was wonderful with people and he thought it was relationships that ultimately counted (even in the work). He believed a director should approach actors as if he too were an actor, and then work with them. Somehow, he always got inside a character. He felt film people were fortunate to be doing what we were doing and that sets should be happy places. He had a brilliant sense of humor. Also, he gave me an insight to where I wanted to go in life."

The statement was a positive tribute, but in no way did it give justice to the breadth of impact Blake had. Their crossing of paths certainly changed Donner's life forever. "George loved Dick like a son," Freedman believes, "and George was so smart, and so good at what he did, [that] I think Dick realized that if he was ever going to go anywhere in the film industry, that George had a lot to teach him. He paid attention, and he wanted to become a clone of George Blake, which I think he did; only he did it in spades."

One day Blake fell ill, and allowed Donner to stand in for him on a TV spot for the gun maker Remington. The young apprentice was nervous and worried, invited friends onto the set for moral support. He did not need them. From the offset it was clear that he had talent. He executed the contract with great aplomb, leaving no indication that it was in fact his debut assignment. Next was a commercial for Camel cigarettes that starred General Claire Chennault (a United States military aviator who had commanded the "Flying Tigers" during World War II), before he and Blake made a memorable trip to California to lens a promotion for Philip Morris. During another bleak winter on the east coast, the two New Yorkers cared not a bit, for they were sharing a poolside room at the Hollywood Roosevelt Hotel, basking in brilliant sunshine. In their rented Buick convertible the two men set off down the famous Sunset Strip. "Where are we going?" Donner inquired.

"To where your wheels get wet," Blake replied.

They drove until they reached the ocean. The sky was clear, the weather sunny, it was a perfect California dream. Palm trees swayed in the foreground; to view the distance was to witness beautiful, snow-covered mountains. Right then and there, Donner fell in love with the Golden State.

In the months that followed Donner continued to helm various commercials for GBE, and piloted episodes of the *Candid Microphone* series (the precursor to *Candid Camera*). He became such a valued asset that Blake offered him a share in the profits of the company, and allowed him input into its future vision.

Donner's parents, however, remained nervous of his mischievous nature. Once, when their son legitimately won a television set in a raffle, his parents refused it — entirely convinced that it was either a scam, or that somehow they were to be presented with a bill for the expensive merchandise. Nonetheless, as a director, the twenty-five-year-old finally saw a path for his professional life. He possessed the natural eye of an artist, and his empathy for actors and his infectious personality were simply made for managing cast and crew. As a person, Donner discovered through Blake the kind of man that he wished to become.

It was the fall of 1955, and each day was a new thrill, a fresh adventure. Together, as business associates and as friends, Donner and Blake were young, successful, had the world at their fingertips. And then it ended.

Donner was in Pennsylvania, filming a commercial, when he received the news. "I got a call one morning. 'Come home, George had a heart attack and died.' And I was destroyed. Destroyed. Destroyed."

At thirty-eight, George Blake was dead. The untimely loss shook Donner to his core. He struggled greatly in coming to terms with it, if in fact he ever did. Blake had been so young, at the height of his vitality and power. He had been so bright, so *alive*. Donner wondered: What was the cycle of life? Where did it all come from? How could such a tragedy happen?

The pain, the intense battle to remain positive of mind, brayed through him, forging a void that would never entirely go away, and would ultimately impact the majority of the most important decisions he would ever make.

George Blake had been more than a mentor. He had been his best friend, his truest confidante, a man whose humanity and belief that friendship was one of the great virtues of mankind was so affecting that, consciously or subconsciously, Donner would make it the message of his own life.

Following his death, Blake's distraught widow, Jean, assumed control of his production unit, George Blake Enterprises, which she intended to run in tandem with the company salesman, Phil Frank. Donner remained as loyal servant for a transitory period, but as he was not offered a full partnership, he formed Signal, an independent effort run in conjuncture with friends George Tompkins and Chick Green (who had also worked at GBE as a salesman). Both men were colorful characters, although especially Green, who at 6'4" stood out for being the shortest of five brothers. An inveterate smoker who could puff three packs a day, he was known for his energy and wit.

The trio set up base in an office across the street from St. Patrick's Cathedral, where Donner insisted to his partners that the new company was not to steal a single GBE contract. In spite of their lack of capital, the group achieved great overnight success, although they were, as Donner recalls, "pissing the money away as fast as we could make it." Danny Farr confirms, "Every Friday night there was a party at their place." Any time a vast amount of cash was earned, it was depleted on trips to Bermuda.

A perk of running his own production company was the plethora of would-be starlets who mailed in photographs in the hope that Donner might find a role for them in one of his commercials. Freedman remembers, "I would come home from college, and Dick would say, 'Well, let's go down to my office and we'll get some names out of my file and we'll get some dates.' He had pictures and résumés of some of the most beautiful women in New York City. He'd go through the file and I'd say, 'I like this one.' He'd say, 'I like this one.' Invariably, when he called them, they knew who he was, and [knew] that he could potentially do them a lot of good by getting them on the screen. So he'd call these girls and make a date."

He continues, "What he would do is he would introduce me as the quarterback for West Point, or the shortstop for the New York Yankees. And all night long I would have to live that part; because that's the way I was introduced to these people. Of course, he was Dick Donner, the big director and producer, so I had to be someone of quality."

As a young man, Donner was a fiendish and frequent practical joker. "He was a master," describes his friend, Bob Gilbert. "He could spend three minutes with you and he knew exactly what the most embarrassing thing he could say or do would be. We were at a dance one night, and one of the women had a backless dress. He asked her to dance and he put his hand on her back, and then turned to the assemblage and said, 'Jeez, isn't it wonderful the way all those pimples on Judy's back have cleared up?'"

Donner was more than funny. He was slick. He once celebrated his birthday with some friends at a New York restaurant. When the group departed in separate cars, he followed Gene and Claire Freedman, who were accompanied in their vehicle by Bob and Doris Gilbert, and who happened to be carrying a chocolate cake from the dinner. Ever playful, Donner kept blinking the lights on his MGA convertible, giving the friends in front of him a hard time. As they drove up Park Avenue, Gene turned to Bob.

"I'll tell you what," he said, "if I stop at this next light, Dick will pull up alongside. Roll down your window, and when Dick looks up shove the cake into his face."

Freedman stopped at the light. Donner pulled up alongside. Gilbert dutifully slid the window down and launched. Somehow, Donner volleyed the dessert back, the cake landing on the defenseless Claire Freedman, whose hands were caught in a fashion accessory of the time known as a "fur muff."

"You got chocolate cake all over my muff!" she screamed.

"You shouldn't have been sitting like that," Donner advised in deep voice, reveling in the double entendre.

As the light turned to green, he screeched away, leaving a thunderous roar of laughter trailing in the wind behind.

When debts for his company, Signal, built up, the business dissolved. Donner remembers, "We had a great time, but we soon ran out of money."

He freelanced for a while, until he was enticed by Filmways, a major television player, to relocate to California and become their main director of commercials. The unit was managed by Martin Ransahoff and John Calley, the latter a former producer for NBC who was ferociously intelligent and possessed a quirky, idiosyncratic, and energetic manner that made a firm impression. Donner found him particularly endearing, and the admiration was mutual. "He was very promising," Calley remembers. "Everybody was excited about him."

"You're the director.
You figure it out."

STEVE McQUEEN

King of the Pilots

In California, Donner became a major force in the television industry for the best part of two decades. He would direct more than a hundred episodes of shows as wide-ranging as *Letter to Loretta, Combat!, The Twilight Zone, The Man From U.N.C.L.E.* and *Gilligan's Island,* to name but a few. Nearly every time he helmed a pilot, it was commissioned as a series, a fact that earned him the industry nickname "King of the Pilots."

At first, Donner shot commercials for Bromo Seltzer, Volkswagen, and Ford, and oversaw (and acted in) a vast promotion for General Motors that aired throughout NFL season. After completing these and other assignments for Filmways, he began to work almost exclusively for Desilu Studios, where he petitioned for a shot at directing an episode of *Westinghouse Desilu Playhouse* starring Lucille Ball and Desi Arnaz. The closest he came to such an opportunity was helming a home appliance commercial that ran in between segments. It was a stressful shoot. "Desi and Lucy were into a bottle of vodka by noon," the director confesses. "It was terrible." As luck would have it, watching him cope was a producer, Ed Adamson, who was impressed with Donner's knack for managing difficult talent. "If you can work with these guys," he advised, "then you can work with McQueen!"

Adamson tapped Donner to helm an episode of the hit CBS show *Wanted: Dead or Alive,* starring Steve McQueen. As the show had grown in success, network powers had granted the temperamental star, performing in his third season as the hero, Josh Randall, an increasing level of power and influence. Adamson needed a resilient director at the helm, one who was able to go toe to toe with a star determined to flex his muscles. Donner loosely knew the actor from his time with the Provincetown Players in New York, but from the offset the challenge he faced was crystal clear. "He's an actor, and not, for Christ's sake, a director!" McQueen fumed when informed of Donner's hiring.

His character was billed as a gentleman bounty hunter, but, as Donner would find out, McQueen could be anything but gentleman like. While on the series, he earned a reputation as a perfectionist who wanted every shot to count for something, an actor who — since being awarded script approval and consultation rights over cast and crew — would hover close to his directors, dissecting camera angles and lighting setups.

From the very first moment he set foot on set to direct the episode "The Twain Shall Meet," Donner was undermined and attacked for "every conceivable hassle from the script to the quality of the canteen lunch." The barbs appeared mean-spirited; each putdown calculated and personal.

"Nope. That's not the way a gunfighter would do it," McQueen insisted over the way a scene had been set up on location.

"How, then?" Donner replied, conciliatory.

"You're the director. You figure it out."

As the young, nervy director struggled, the complex McQueen stormed off to his trailer in disgust. Donner was disconsolate. His dream chance had turned into a devastating nightmare. His bow in episodic television was a baptism of fire that left him wreaked with anxiety and self-doubt. Ed Adamson intercepted Donner on his way back to the crew bus. "Look, this is only your first day!" he assured him. "I bet by Monday you'll have him eating out of your hand!"

It was a Friday night, and Donner headed straight to the bar. He woke up the next morning with a hangover, his head ringing with memories of a torrid debut. Fortunately, he had some time to collect his thoughts. He had drawn a Friday as his first day on the show. Day two on *Wanted* would not arrive until after the weekend. On Sunday morning Donner called McQueen, who promptly summoned him to his home. The fledgling director paced the driveway for several minutes before a prop man opened the door. Once inside, McQueen refused to acknowledge his presence. "I gotta talk to you, man," Donner blurted, overcome with emotion. "Look, no hard feelings, but I quit."

The actor's mood suddenly changed. "Nobody quits my show," he rallied. "Come on. Let's you and me go for a ride in my new Jag." The pair set out in McQueen's production model XK-55, nicknamed the Green Rat, and went drinking, ironing out their differences over several bottles of Blue Nun. That night Donner crashed on the McQueen couch. In the morning the two newfound friends drove to the set together. With the air seemingly cleared, Donner breezed though his shot list for the day and regained all lost time on the show overall.

In "The Twain Shall Meet," his debut episode of network television, Donner opened with a medium shot of gunslinger Josh Randall readying in his room at the Allenville Hotel. Through the reflection in a dress mirror the viewer is introduced to a second protagonist, newspaper reporter Arthur Pierce Madison of the *Boston Evening Messenger*. Donner zoomed in on the reflection, framing both men in a close-up.

In the episode, Randall and Madison jointly pursue the fugitive, Jack Torrance. The director enjoyed the dramatic tension that his two lead characters presented him, one being a simple cowboy, the other a Harvard intellectual. He kept the tone serious but playful, the drama punctuated by some wonderful moments of subtle, incidental humor, particularly from his supporting cast, a lineup that included Mary Tyler Moore as the bar gal, Sophie Anderson.

Afterward, Donner met with the series star and their producer. "I'd like you to do more of the shows," McQueen informed him.

"Who's your agent?" Ed Adamson asked, keen to formalize.

"I don't have one," Donner replied.

"What do you mean, you don't have one?" McQueen responded.

"I don't have an agent."

McQueen recommended Donner to Stan Kamen, a leading agent for the William Morris Agency, who immediately secured him episodes on the Loretta Young vehicle *Letter to Loretta*. Kamen was an exceptional agent in more ways than one; he was an extremely tall man at a time when everyone else at the agency was short (it was rumored that the vertically-challenged William Morris refused to hire men taller than he). On "Quiet Desperation," Donner learned further differences between directing commercials and episodic television. He rehearsed a scene with Loretta Young in which she sat down at a table and ate breakfast. He readied to shoot. Once the camera started to roll, his star began her scene, picking up a coffee.

"Huh!" she snapped.

"Cut!" Donner yelled.

"What are you doing, Mr. Donner?" the actress asked, confused.

"I said, 'Cut.'"

"Why?"

"I thought you'd burnt yourself."

"That's... acting!" was the sage reply.

Donner flitted between *Wanted: Dead or Alive* and *Letter to Loretta* until, on "Barney's Bounty," his fifth and final chair on *Wanted*, he quarreled with McQueen again. This time the damage was permanent. The director had devised an elaborate camera shot that required the camera to travel up from the actor's feet to his legs, waist, and chest and finally to his face. It was an ambitious shot and the crew was hyped. McQueen, sipping coffee as he romanced an attractive girl on set, grew irritated by the effort. He was the star of the show, not some fancy camerawork. As Donner gave his signal to shoot, McQueen got up from his chair, walked in the opposite direction, and imposed a pause on proceedings by heading to the bathroom. Donner chose his words carefully, "Come on, Steve, please. This'll only take us a few minutes! We're all ready!"

"Well, man, I'm not. This dude's goin' to the can."

"Everybody take five while Mr. McQueen takes a pee!" Donner snapped back.

When McQueen returned, he headed straight to the director. "You will never work this show again," he enforced firmly.

Donner recalls the incident. "He came back and he just looked at me. McQueen could kill you with a look. This was not a dear close friend of mine, but I liked him and respected him... I wasn't surprised he fired me, because it was a face-to-face confrontation. Maybe I wasn't the smartest person in the world in the way I handled it... It was very hard on my career because I was just getting started. When you're fired from a series, it reflects on you. I was affected by it."

Nonetheless, with only a handful of television credits to his name, Donner was tapped to direct second-unit footage on his first feature film, the low-budget *X-15*. It would star David McLean, Charles Bronson, James Gregory and Mary Tyler Moore. James Stewart would lend voice-over narration. The picture was the brainchild of Tony Lazzarino, a brazen thirty-two-year-old entrepreneur who had been allowed unparalleled access by the U.S. Department of Defense and NASA to a hypersonic test flight over California. His camera operator, Jack Freeman, had lensed an extensive amount of footage of the multimillion-dollar rocket's journey forty-one miles above the Earth that Lazzarino intended to intercut with footage of actors performing in a fictional human drama.

Matt Powell, the chief test pilot for NASA, pilots a test mission of the world's first manned aerospace craft, the X-15. Lt. Col. Lee Brandon and Maj. Ernest Wilde offer support in their fighter jets, only for the X-15 to suffer a pressure failure. It is unable to launch from the B-52 bomber plane to which it is mated.

At Edwards Air Force base, Powell is shocked to see his former fiancée, Pamela Stewart. They quickly rekindle their romance, as Powell's commanding officers worry that the tension created by a series of aborted missions, setbacks, and delays will affect the pilots to an extent that they will not be able to perform during critical flights.

Maj. Wilde is onboard the X-15 for an engine test when a malfunction occurs, engulfing the craft in flames. He is briefly trapped inside the cockpit. His wife, Diane, pleads for news and learns that he is unharmed. Lt. Col. Lee Brandon assumes his turn to pilot the X-15, successfully establishing a world speed record of Mach 5.

The three couples, Matt Powell and Pamela Stewart, Lee and Margaret Bandon, and Ernest and Diane Wilde, enjoy a dinner and dance together, before a new test of the U.S Air Force rocket, piloted by Powell. Again, there is an explosion, and Brandon's fighter jet is hit by debris. Powell panics in the cockpit, and needs to be calmly guided through an emergency landing. Brandon is killed when his plane explodes on the ground.

Powell visits Margaret Brandon and her young son, Mike, to inform her of the news. Afterward, he and Wilde struggle to come to terms with events, before Powell again readies to fly the X-15. The maximum performance trial is a success. Powell makes it into space, achieving an altitude of one hundred miles above the Earth.

Lazzarino sold his idea to Frank Sinatra; whose company, Essex Productions, made an offer that United Artists couldn't refuse, securing $2 million in project funding.

Writer James Warner Bellah assisted in honing the screenplay, while cast and crew were assembled for a shoot lensed entirely on location at Edwards Air Force Base in Mojave, California. Just two weeks prior to the commencement of principal photography, the director suddenly left the picture. As Donner remembers, "I guess the director must have finally read the script. They came to me and said, 'Well, you're directing second unit — would you like to direct the picture?' So I said, 'Oh God, yeah!' I took it. I didn't know what to fucking do. I didn't know how to shoot a movie. I guessed that it was like a TV show, but it was bigger."

Incredibly, just weeks after making his professional bow in episodic television, Donner was to be a fully-fledged motion picture director. He was in awe — just as he later was when he visited Sinatra's office at the Warner Bros. studio lot to demonstrate some set designs. Building 102 was more than an office - it was an entire bungalow, detached from the main studio area, a space entirely reflective of Sinatra's iconic standing.

When Donner and crew arrived for their first day of shooting at Edwards Air Force base, their production trucks were ordered to a halt at the main gate. Representatives from the Teamsters labor union greeted Donner and Tony Lazzarino. "What's the problem?" Donner asked.

"You can't shoot up here," a Teamster responded angrily. "You've got to have man to man locally to [match] the crew you bring in."

"Well, that's not our decision. We can't say yes or no."

"Well, you're not coming in here."

The production dutifully obeyed and headed back to their hotel, where Donner received a call from Frank Sinatra.

"Turn around and go back."

"We can't," Donner offered meekly. "They won't let us shoot."

"Turn around... and go back."

The director returned to meet the same Teamster representative, who was suddenly alone. "Listen," he told Donner, "it's stupid to have an argument. We'd love to have you up in this area. Go ahead."

The gates opened to Edwards Air Force base. In one call, it appeared, God had spoken.

On *X-15* Donner did his best to grasp the incredible opportunity that had befallen him. Shooting was completed across seventeen days in April and May of 1961, but shortly into the editing process executive producer Howard W. Koch fired him. The director remembers only that, "I used to have lots and lots of arguments. I was very argumentative because it was my first picture and I was very opinionated. I saw it only one way, and I don't think that I had learned enough at that point to realize that others could really bring stuff to the table."

An interesting aspect of Donner's input to *X-15* was the father and son scene acted out by Charles Bronson and young Stanley Livingston. As Lt. Col. Lee Brandon shaves early in the morning, he bonds with his son, Mike, discussing "love stuff" and respect for women. The scene foreshadows a more emotional father and son moment in *Lethal Weapon 3*, played out by Danny Glover and Damon Hines, in which Roger Murtaugh attempts to instill in his son, Nick, what it means to be a man. Donner has always had an innate capacity for empathizing with people, and it may be that his own past experiences with his father are reflected in these scenes.

X-15 was an unremarkable start to a remarkable career. Unlike the explosive early efforts of Spielberg and Lucas, whose *Duel* and *American Graffiti* (Lucas' second film) would make them critical darlings and clear avatars of a new Hollywood movement, Donner's *X-15* was static, an anachronistic melodrama rooted in a fifties mode of filmmaking. Its visual style demonstrated little flair, and its narrative was ponderous. The bland, listless dialogue undercut both the competitive tension between the test pilot protagonists and the complexity of the romantic relationships with their wives. It offered little evidence to mark Donner as a future directorial talent to watch out for.

Unsurprisingly, the film crashed and burned on December 2, 1961. Yet, in the wake of free publicity generated by the real-life Major Bob White, who continued to break records in the NASA rocket plane, the picture was granted a second shot at success by exhibitors on April 4, 1962. Despite this publicity and a glittering (second) opening in New York sponsored by the National Aviation Club, the picture failed to register in the public consciousness.

While he steadfastly insists that he has no regrets in life, Donner has all but disowned his movie debut. "Stay up late one night and watch the worst television and you'll see it," he once informed a journalist.

"Careers are so curiously structured," observes John Calley, one half of the Filmways team who enticed Donner to the west coast. "Some people do the first film and it's an amazing success and they never look back, and others go along for a while and then suddenly explode into an enormous success."

Donner returned to television to helm two episodes of the serial *Have Gun — Will Travel* for the CBS network. The show starred Richard Boone as a hero noted for always dressing in black, a color that, for storytelling purposes, was normally associated with dark forces or villainy. (Donner would likewise flip this convention for his 1985 feature *Ladyhawke,* which featured the hero, Navarre, clad top-to-toe in black, pitted against the evil Bishop of Aquila, dressed only in white — a color typically suggesting virtue.)

He followed this series with yet another Western. *The Rifleman,* starring Chuck Connors as Lucas McCain, a rifle-toting rancher and single father battling criminal life on the New Mexican frontier, was airing for a fourth season on ABC.

Then Donner's new agent, Ben Conway, learned of an opportunity on the show *The Eleventh Hour.* Director Don Richards was due to helm the episode "Advice to the Lovelorn and Shopworn," but quit when NBC slashed his preparation time in half. Donner describes, "He was in a position to say, 'No.' I was in a position to say, 'I'll take anything I can get! I can prepare in an hour.'"

He was next hired by producer Gene Levitt to helm an episode of the ABC series *Combat!* The World War II action serial starred Rick Jason and Vic Morrow, the latter a former drinking pal of Donner's from his acting days in New York. The plot for "No Trumpets, No Drums" centered upon the accidental killing of a French civilian and the grief of the American soldier responsible, who resolves to take care of the man's orphaned daughter. Donner was thrilled by the script's emotional pull, and he was determined to extract the strongest possible performances from his actors. He visited the set during filming of the preceding episode, and cajoled the actors into remaining at MGM studios for improvisation exercises and script rehearsal.

During his tenure in television Donner immersed himself in the technology of production. He learned the intricacies of various cameras and their available lenses, of certain types of film stock, and was schooling himself in lighting techniques. He hated television's overuse of fill lighting, which allowed actors to walk around a set and always be perfectly lit. He preferred a more realistic use of light that allowed for more contrast, a setup that contributed to the mood and personality of the show, although this was invariably a more time-consuming process to arrange.

On *Combat!* the director discovered he would be able to express more artistic license. With his camera operator, Bob Hauser, Donner scouted the entire MGM back lot and handpicked a location for each scene, mapping in his mind a variety of elaborate camera angles and lighting setups that he wished to employ. Naturally, he refused to commit any of these to paper - much to the chagrin of the production manager. Producer Gene Levitt had failed to advise him of a house style of shooting, so Donner executed an exciting combination of tricky, handheld camera work, some traditional tracking shots, and low camera angles (designed to make the environment appear imposing and claustrophobic). It was instinctual, spur of the moment, and Donner loved every minute of it, grabbing the camera from his house cameramen and shooting much of the episode himself. He captured so much battle footage that his discarded film would be used in the future episode "The Little Carousel."

Donner was critical of his stuntmen on *Combat!* Many were used to "dying" three or four times a day, and their performances were lackluster. In his quest for verisimilitude, Donner was never afraid to tell them if he didn't believe them. Filming stunts and action set pieces was not an experience that Donner enjoyed. He was nervous for the safety of his cast and crew, for which he took personal responsibility, and would often quip to the wardrobe department of the need to keep a clean pair of pants on standby.

Despite his burgeoning career, the director watched little television. When it came time to lens his segment on *Combat!*, which was the season finale, he knew little of the back-story. For Donner, the show represented a training opportunity for his eventual career in movies, an ambition that was undimmed by the disappointment of *X-15*. Whenever a break was called for on set, he quickly downed tools and ran to grab a sneak peak of the latest MGM extravaganza being filmed on the lot, observing and learning, and dreaming of helming for the silver screen again.

The science-fiction series *The Twilight Zone* was born from the mind of the Emmy award-winning writer Rod Serling. The precursor to shows such as *The Outer Limits* and *The X-Files*, Serling's quirky mystery vignettes had proved a hit for CBS, the ultimate form of escapist television entertainment that transfixed a future generation of fantasy genre filmmakers. Steven Spielberg so admired the show that he twice attempted to replicate it, once with his controversial movie version (on which Vic Morrow and two young children tragically died), and again with his television series, *Amazing Stories*.

The ubiquitous Serling insisted upon quality, hiring only the very best television actors, writers and directors. Future stars Robert Redford, Robert Duvall, Dennis Hopper, Lee Marvin, Martin Landau and Jack Klugman made appearances early in their careers. Donner joined in 1963 for the fifth and final season of the series. His first episode, "Nightmare at 20,000 Feet," starred William Shatner (pre-*Star Trek*) as Bob Wilson, a man recovering from a mental breakdown who believes a "gremlin" is on the wing of the plane on which he is flying. It was an elaborate episode, perhaps the most complicated piece of television lensed at MGM studios, reliant upon operational airplane engines, simulated lightning, wind and rain, and multiple special-effect shots. Nick Cravat played the gremlin (an acrobat dressed in a furry costume, a slightly low-tech effect by comparison). Those on set felt his appearance was cheap and ridiculous, yet such is the resonance of the character, and the episode, that today two separate twelve-inch action figures are available for collectors to purchase.

The director enjoyed palling around with Bill Shatner, the pair dueling practical jokes between setups. With help from the visiting Edd Byrnes, star of *77 Sunset Strip*, it was Shatner's battle to win. As Donner described: "We were all exhausted — it was quite late — and when my back was turned, Shatner and Byrnes decided to stage a fight. I happened to look up at the wing of the airplane and saw this fight going on. I started running over, of course, and just when I got there I saw Byrnes hit Shatner, who went over the wing of the airplane, down 40 feet to the tank below!"

He continues, "I'm thinking Bill has to be injured, but what's running through my head is that now I have to shoot this whole thing over! What I didn't know was that they had dressed a dummy in Shatner's clothes."

Each installment of *The Twilight Zone* concluded with a twist, and "Nightmare at 20,000 Feet" was no exception. Bob Wilson breaks open an auxiliary door of the plane on which he is traveling, a desperate attempt to shoot the mythological creature. He is arrested and committed to an asylum. Yet, Donner closes with a shot of the airplane's damaged wing, perhaps tampered with, perhaps not.

He would pay homage to this finale in the conclusive, or perhaps non-conclusive, frames of *The Omen*, his 1976 mega-hit, a mystery-suspense-thriller that teased: Were events real? Or were they a put-on?

When a feature film production commandeered his set space, Donner was forced to film through the night in order to complete the episode (in the world of television there was simply no time to reschedule, and to not turn in your episode was career suicide). When the show aired, it became an instant classic, doing for the fear of flying what *Jaws* did for swimming in the open sea. Inspired by Nick Cravat's "gremlin," Steven Spielberg would borrow the name for his 1984 production *Gremlins* (directed by Joe Dante).

"Nightmare at 20,000 Feet" won Donner strong favor and he was retained to pilot five more *Zone* episodes. One of them, "From Agnes — with Love," starred Wally Cox, Marlon Brando's childhood friend and roommate in New York, whose TV show, *Mister Peepers*, had made him a household name. He would later provide the voice to the animated superhero *Underdog*, whose famous catchphrase was, "No need to fear. Underdog is here!" Donner found Cox to be more serious, less flexible than Shatner, but had fun working on an episode that was one of the series' lighter, more whimsical entries. On his final episode, "Come Wander with Me," Donner intended a misty, backwoods look, but flooded the set with so much smoke that the fire department was called to investigate.

In his early thirties, Donner directed as he lived - by the seat of his pants. He rarely planned anything, and objected strongly to his producer's demands for a shot list. His shooting scripts were immediately recognizable as his; they were the ones with the phone numbers and coffee stains scrawled across them.

Some in television's old guard may have viewed Donner's refusal to plan, or to analyze in detail, as haphazard and unprofessional. But Donner possessed a tremendous, natural instinct. When he read a script, Donner could film it in his head, knowing in his mind exactly how it should be done before arriving on set. And yet, staying true to the principles he learned from his acting tutor, David Alexander, who encouraged his students to find "the truth in themselves," Donner intended, as much as possible, for scenes to come alive as they happened, to be spontaneous. On *The Man from U.N.C.L.E.* he recalled that, "I used to do terrible things to Bobby Vaughn. Bobby used to take himself very seriously. His hair had to be perfectly straight. I used to run into the shot just before I yelled 'Action' and mess his hair up... Or I'd have a girl pop up in the middle of a shot holding a sign that says 'Smile.'"

If he wanted to simulate commotion in a scene, Donner would grab cameraman Til Gabani, and shake him to confuse the picture. In "The Giuoco Piano Affair," he jumped straight into the action, performing a cameo as a barroom inebriate.

Donner was not unchallenged on *The Man from U.N.C.L.E.* set. Word leaked that he had ordered, in the words of an insider, "The biggest director's chair I've ever seen." The gargantuan design became such a talking point that, once built, was too heavy to be carried from the prop department to the set. Donner was unsympathetic and ranted that, come hell or high water, he was going to have his beloved new chair. Arnold Goode, the production prop man, finally snapped. In front of the entire cast and crew he delivered Donner his new chair — a six-inch model replica.

The Man from U.N.C.L.E. was innovative television. The larger-than-life adventures of an international crime-fighting organization, a hearty mixture of action and humor; it perfectly suited Donner's tastes and sensibilities. He enjoyed the vision of writer and producer Sam Rolfe, who, according to associate producer, George Lehr, "fought very strongly for this concept where you had to walk the line between reality and make-believe, and you could step one direction one second, but you had to step on the other side of the line the next." It was Rolfe's sense of verisimilitude, the creative mantra that Donner had dedicated himself to which would provide the foundation to his film and television successes.

Donner's gig on *U.N.C.L.E.* was preceded by stints on shows as varied as *The Lieutenant*, *Mr. Novak*, *The Nurses*, *The Travels of Jaimie McPheeters* and *Perry Mason*, by which time he was firmly established as one of the industry's elite directors. His charisma and irrepressible energy generated a strong buzz; his ability to work within the strict confines of a formula and yet still draw something fresh and spontaneous duly noted. He was already known as an "actor's director," and had mastered the technological aspects of production, a fact that, when coupled with his unique natural instinct and flair, enabled him to shoot at great speed.

For his unrivaled ability to turn an episode into a series, Donner was dubbed "King of the Pilots." He was in on the ground floor on such shows as *The Wild Wild West*, *It's About Time* and *Bronk*. His television movie *Lucas Tanner* became the launch pad to a series by the same name, his *Senior Year* the precursor to *Sons and Daughters*. Yet, it is one pilot in particular for which Donner is most famous: *Gilligan's Island*.

CBS executives, and sponsors Philip Morris & Company and Procter & Gamble, had continually rejected the iconic American series until Donner brought his input to the first episode broadcast, "Two on a Raft."

Director Rod Amateau had lensed an unaired pilot, "Marooned," before being replaced at the helm by John Rich for "Two on a Raft." When Rich's episode also tested poorly, producers Sherwood Schwartz and Bill Froug (whom Donner had worked with on *The Twilight Zone*) brought Donner in for six additional days of shooting. His confidence and energy invigorated the cast and crew, and the show was sold.

The comedy sitcom featured the misadventures of an eclectic group of travelers, including a skipper, his dimwit first mate, a professor, an actress and a millionaire businessman, stranded on an unchartered desert island somewhere in the Pacific. Donner loved his time on the show - a kind of *Robinson Crusoe* meets *Laurel and Hardy*. He reveled in its slapstick humor and eccentric banter, but believed that, beneath the cartoonish veneer, the series produced an interesting microcosm of society (Sherwood Schwartz wanted the series to demonstrate how people work together when in trouble).

The move to California was a major step in Donner's life, a whole new challenge, and a whole new world. All the familiar things in life were nowhere to be found. In New York, his name — or at the very least his booming voice — were easily recognized. In Hollywood, he was just another face in the crowd. He knew relatively few people, but was constantly being introduced to new faces and new names, although at one of his very first social engagements he was warmed to see a man he knew from Mount Vernon across the room. They approached each other with great big smiles and shook hands.

"Ted Warchovski!" Donner roared.

"No, Ted Wallace," the man replied. "And you're Dick Schwartzberg?"

"No, Dick Donner."

One evening, Donner met Bruce Kessler and Lance Reventlow for dinner on Rodeo Drive. Kessler was a professional racing driver who had grown up in Beverly Hills, the son of a clothes designer. Reventlow, a wealthy playboy and entrepreneur, was the only child of American socialite Barbara Hutton and Danish nobleman Count Curt von Haugwitz-Hardenberg-Reventlow. For a period in his childhood he had been the stepson of iconic actor Cary Grant.

Donner had grown friendly with both men, due to the many hours he had spent at Lime Rock Park, Connecticut, where he raced against Reventlow's production model Jaguar X140 in his small MGA. If he ever moved to California, the pair had instructed, he was to make contact.

Surrounded by beautiful women, the trio ate Polynesian food and drank rum, when Ronnie Burns, the son of comedians George Burns and Gracie Allen, joined them at their table. He mentioned that he was looking for a roommate.

Filmways housed Donner in a small hotel on the Sunset Strip, before he rented himself a small apartment in La Jolla. The director was excited to view Burns' small cottage at 851 North Beverly Glen. It had a fireplace with a stone pit, a tiled bathroom, and two bedrooms that were so small that the bunks were built into a closet. Donner fell in love with it and agreed to rent a room.

One day Donner was alone at his new residence when there was a knock at his door. A shorter, red-haired man with big ears and freckled skin was squeezed in between two tall, beautiful girls. The man looked surprised and confused. "What are you doing here?" he demanded of Donner.

"What are *you* doing here?" the director volleyed.

"I live here."

"No," Donner replied. "I live here. Wait a minute. Who are you?"

"I'm Jimmy Boyd."

Boyd was a singer, a musician and an actor, a former child star forever famous for the song that became an international phenomenon: "I Saw Mommy Kissing Santa Claus." Boyd still lived with his parents, but had made an arrangement with Ronnie Burns to use the cottage as a love nest.

Donner was close friends with Burns, and spent a great deal of time with the sometime television actor at his parents' house, where he could find himself being entertained by comic icons such as Jack Benny and Groucho Marx. For a while, he was in a relationship with Burns' sister, Sandra, a divorcee and mother of two young daughters.

When his lease was up in Beverly Glen, Donner decided to move on. He settled on a new house that was being built on Mulholland Drive. From there he moved to a small house at 1207 Hilldale Avenue. But with the summer arriving and his family due to visit, Donner rented a small, luxury house in Malibu. When they arrived, his parents, sister, and her three daughters were wowed by the beach property that belonged to the Academy Award-winning actor Rod Steiger. The fact that Jane Fonda and her then-husband, Roger Vadim, were neighbors also thoroughly impressed his family.

Donner stocked up on beer and music, and hosted barbeques for his family and his Hollywood friends. Regular attendees were actress Tuesday Weld, whom Donner had briefly dated, and his good friend, writer, director and producer Jack Haley, Jr. Donner's greatest kick in Malibu came from seeing his father. "He had gone shopping in New York, and he had a pair of brown lace shoes, black socks, and a pair of strange shorts. That was his beach attire. That's what he thought he should wear. Within a week he was in a white T-shirt, khaki shorts, and wearing white tennis shoes with no socks." Fred Schwartzberg was a handsome man dubbed the "Silver Fox of Malibu" for his debonair manner and his silver hair and mustache. His pride for his son, and the successful life he had built, revitalized him. For his part, Donner reveled in the presence of his family, admitting, "I would have given anything to have had the money to have kept them there."

Summer of '42 served as a memoir for its author, Herman Raucher, detailing the events of his life during a summer spent on Nantucket Island in 1942, when he was fourteen years old. The screenplay was entertaining and affecting, charged with great humor and tenderness. Donner responded instantly to the material that took place during the era of his own adolescence. He optioned the motion picture rights and passionately set about to persuade a major studio to green light a screenplay. "When I had it, they [the studios] kept insisting it couldn't be done," he reminisced, "on the weird grounds that the public wasn't ready for a movie about masturbation. How do you deal with that sort of rejection?"

After toiling to no avail, his option lapsed, and Richard A. Roth, a producer, picked up the property. Roth convinced Warner Bros. to fund a picture with director Robert Mulligan at the helm.

Summer of '42 was released in 1971 to great success and was nominated for three Academy Awards (it won for Best Score). Donner was disappointed not to have filmed it. Might the picture have been as successful had he been given a chance? Where it could have taken his career, he would never know.

He continued to thrive in television, moving onto a new project, *The Wild Wild West*. In this cross-genre series, James West is a charming gunslinger teamed with Artemus Gordon, a man of gadgets and disguises, engaged in a mission to protect President Ulysses S. Grant and the United States of America from diabolical, half-crazed villains that plot to take over the nation and the world.

The show was the creation of flamboyant producer Michael Garrison, a colorful presence and unique personality whom Donner liked and respected. "I remember once we went to a big dinner party at his house," the director quipped, "and my date was very upset because he was dressed in a prettier dress than she."

Donner was friendly with the series star Robert Conrad, so it came as little surprise that when the actor failed to see eye to eye with Richard C. Sarafian, the original director of the pilot, "The Night of the Inferno," Donner was asked to re-film certain scenes.

CBS bestowed upon *The Wild Wild West* an impressive level of integrity, and Donner found that he was allowed the time and resources he needed to direct its many action-based sequences. The luxury of time, however, was not all it was cracked up to be. On "The Night of the Bars of Hell," he grew frustrated by Robert Conrad's insistence that he perform his own stunts. The director recalled, "There was a stunt planned where Conrad's [stunt] double would come through an upstairs wall and land on a card table, a table manned by other stunt men in order to aid the double in case he had trouble [with his landing]. But Conrad, without telling anyone, did the stunt himself. He flew through the wall and missed all but the corner of the card table, before landing on the floor. He got carried out. We had to shut down for almost a week."

In 1965, Donner helmed two episodes of *Get Smart*, a new NBC television series starring Don Adams as hapless secret agent Maxwell Smart and Barbara Feldon as his ever-faithful sidekick, "Agent 99." Full of ham-handed dimwittedness and self-deprecating humor, the spy spoof crackled and popped through its allotted runtime, making it an immediate hit for the network. Viewers were won over by Adams's enthusiasm and his clipped style of talking, and by the screen chemistry he enjoyed with his attractive co-star.

Of the two episodes he helmed, it was Donner's first, "Washington 4, Indians 3," in which Max attempts to infiltrate a rebel Indian tribe threatening the U.S. government with war, that proved his most intriguing.

In 1994, Donner would draw from the spirit of this episode for his movie adaptation of *Maverick*, a western adventure caper of fast-paced one-liners, and which, coincidentally, also includes a sequence in which its hero (played by Mel Gibson) dons a disguise as a Native-American Indian, for comic effect.

In their "Washington 4, Indians 3" script, the writers, Gerald Gardner and Dee Caruso, had injected subtle elements of moral statement with which Donner would have strongly empathized. In one scene, an admiral asks, "Exactly what do these Indians want?"

"They demand the return of all the territory we took from them," Smart's intelligence chief replies.

"Well, give it to them."

"But, Harry," interpolates an Army general, "it's *all* theirs. The whole country."

Of course, such prodding remained ever so gentle, and the tone was entirely appropriate to the lighthearted series format. Indeed, any message that existed could be considered diluted by the final scene of the episode, which appears to suggest that the only outcome for the American Indian is assimilation into the U.S. way of life — as depicted by "Red Cloud" joining the U.S. government dressed in business attire.

Although the episode, "Washington 4, Indians 3," offered viewers the first hint of Agent 99's feelings for Agent 86 (Feldon's character is visibly jealous when Max is being forced into marriage), for once Donner was not so interested in the potential for exploring romantic intimacy. He chose instead to focus on another aspect of their dynamic. Said he at the time, "86 is that little boy that everybody wants to mother. If I need a bit of business to fill a hole, I say, 'Hey, Barbie Doll, mother him up a little.' Barbie's perfect. Even standing around, she's working."

Donner realized that Feldon's Agent 99 was best played as the foil for Max's fragile wit. Playing it straight was paramount: there was no reason for a Feldon punch line to make Max look silly — he did that all by himself.

As he was on so many series of the day, Donner found himself under intense pressure to bring his episode home in less than three days. (This was necessary in order to meet the network goal of twenty-six to thirty-two episodes per season.) It was virtually impossible to meet such a deadline. Actors could fluff their lines, a camera shot or a boom shot might fail to deliver the desired result, or there could be glitches with the sound. And yet to not work within a specified time and budget remained career suicide. On every show, Donner found himself fighting the clock, with filming sometimes stretching until ten o'clock at night — even one or two in the morning.

Despite this, and marking the kind of attention to detail that would lead to his successful career in movies, Donner was described as shooting "endless footage" for "Washington 4, Indians 3." To move back and forth from studio to location was too complex, logistically speaking, so the director ensured that he had covered every conceivable angle before he wrapped.

Filming was held up on one occasion due to Adams's anxiety over riding a horse. Donner, a proficient horseback rider since his youth, did his best to coach his nervous star through the scene, but he would still need to take a great deal of care in the editing suite cutting around the actor's obvious look of dread.

There were other challenges, too. Because of her difference in height to Adams, and the social demand of the time for a leading man to be taller than his leading lady, Feldon would have to "shrink" for certain scenes. In a two-shot, she would be in bare feet, turning her ankles (causing her to quip that she was the only actress in Hollywood with calluses on her ankles), accentuating the disadvantage by slouching or leaning down. Adams, meanwhile, stood on an apple box, for added compensation. (Rather humorously, when the couple is filmed entering a room together, it is obvious that Feldon is at least two inches taller than Adams.)

After *Get Smart*, a comedic riff on James Bond, Donner soon found himself returning to helm further stints of *The Wild Wild West*. Despite the relative freedom he enjoyed on the series, he was growing increasingly frustrated with television, suffocated by an obligation to remain confined within the medium's strict formulas. He believed that stars held too much influence and power, and found that editors worked only for the producer and not for the director, much like in the days of the Hollywood studio system. He craved the broader canvas of film, where he believed he would find far greater artistic freedom.

Donner's guest stars for the installment "The Night of the Returning Dead" were comic pair Sammy Davis, Jr., and Peter Lawford. The Rat Pack royalty were sufficiently impressed by Donner to remember him for a movie they were planning. Thus, he would soon receive his wish to once more direct for the silver screen, an opportunity that would be complicated by the allure of a European capital, many beautiful women, and a plethora of alcohol and drugs.

Donner moved to London in the summer of 1967 to begin filming *Salt and Pepper*, a comedy from screenwriter Michael Pertwee. An Asian call girl, Mai Ling, who has frequented a nightclub in London, is found murdered. Colonel Balsom (a member of Britain's "Special Branch" police) informs proprietors, Charles Salt and Christopher Pepper, that Ling was actually a secret service operative - the sixth agent murdered in only two weeks. He declares that the British government is offering $150,000 to anyone who can crack the mystery.

Salt reveals to Pepper that he found a note on his couch belonging to the deceased — a seemingly important list of assorted names and dates. Their subsequent detective work earns the attention of a Colonel Woodstock, who orders his henchman to kill them both.

During a car chase, the heroes are pursued across the streets of London. Their bullet proof vehicle fires oil slicks to slow down the chasing villains, but eventually the machine breaks apart, and crashes into the River Thames. The pair flee to an apartment.

Pepper receives a phone call requiring he and his friend to report to a barbershop. When they oblige, they are launched through a secret doorway into a holding cell. They are drugged and held captive by Colonel Woodstock on board a mock navy submarine, from which they force an escape.

The sultry Marianne Renaud, who has secretly been contracted to kill Pepper, romances him at his apartment. Just as she attempts to shoot him, she is shot and killed by Salt, who has realized her murderous intention.

Salt and Pepper break into a military training college, where a "fake" Prime Minister (whom Woodstock is working for) broadcasts a television announcement warning the British government that he will launch a nuclear missile on a densely populated area of the British Isles unless they tender their public resignation.

Salt and Pepper battle their way to the fake Prime Minister, Woodstock, and assorted conspirators, whom they kill by firing a canon. The treasonous plot is foiled, and the duo receives a hero's reception on the streets of London.

Featuring a mad colonel, a grouchy police inspector, and wall-to-wall female eye candy, the farce was plentiful, perhaps distinctly British, even if the production clearly intended to capture the spirit of such early sixties Rat Pack capers as *Ocean's Eleven*.

Sammy Davis, Jr., and Peter Lawford would produce the film through their companies, Trace-Mark and Chrislaw, with assistance from Lawford's former agent, Milt Ebbins. United Artists supplied the funding and would distribute the picture.

Although several years past their Rat Pack heyday, Davis, Jr., and Lawford still made headlines. Donner had originally prepared to lens on location in London's Soho district, but the thoroughfares became so congested with fans hoping to garner a sneak peak of two movie stars that the production retreated to Shepperton Studios. Replicating the streets of London added an additional $144,000 to the budget.

Donner found London an exciting arena in which to test his romantic skills. His good friend, Alan Ladd, Jr., also based in the city at the time, remembers, "He'd come to my house and pick up my dog. I had a little Lhasa Apso that he'd take for a walk. The dog was a shill to pick up girls. He'd figured out what time the girls would get out of the [local] college and then he walked out with his cute little shaggy dog, and they all went, 'Oh, the sweet little dog!' and he'd pick up every day. If that dog could only talk."

Donner did not allow his pursuit of women to distract him from *Salt and Pepper*, unlike his stars, who were preoccupied throughout filming by the lustful nightlife on offer in London. In his biography of Davis, Jr., the author Gary Fishgall claims that Davis, Jr., and Lawford "liked to hop on their twin motorbikes and head over to Alvaro's, a disco on King's Road in Chelsea that catered primarily to youngsters half their age. When they weren't at Alvaro's, they could often be found in their suites at the Mayfair, hosting parties that overflowed with booze and drugs, notably marijuana, hash, and LSD."

During filming, Davis, Jr., became bedmates with an attractive London model. Shortly afterward, the young lady in question fell for Lawford's charms and promptly deposited herself in his company. Production closed for two days as the actors quarreled.

Dependent upon the quality of their nocturnal adventures, Davis, Jr., and Lawford arrived on set either late, or *very late*. Once in front of camera, they ruined take after take by cutting up during a scene. While Donner was typically open to improvisation, he tired of ramblings that had little to do with the movie plot, and usually ended with a racist joke as a punch line. "It was terrible for me," he recalled, "and I had no way of controlling them because they were the producers. What was I going to do, fire them?"

It was a torrid period. Donner rowed endlessly with his stars, who he felt were attempting to impose "black/white problems" on material the director believed to be "very superficial, a bigger than life comedy." In the end Donner extracted what he could from his actors and hoped for the best. Optimistic by nature, he believed the project could be salvaged in the editing suite. Two weeks after shooting wrapped, however, after he had attempted to omit some of the actors' more objectionable jokes in the cutting room, he was fired. Davis, Jr., and Lawford took the decision to personally edit *Salt and Pepper*. When United Artists criticized the quality of their version, they blamed the debacle entirely upon their inexperienced director.

A vapid, superfluous affair that failed to capture the essence of "Swinging Britain" or "American Cool," *Salt and Pepper* at least avoided being savaged by the critics. "The production is a lavish one," wrote *The Washington Post*, "though the movie never gets lost in its gaudy sets and mechanical gimmicks, and a thoroughly technical crew has kept the caper from diffusing into an elaborate home movie." *The New York Times* was moderately dismissive, calling the caper "merely nice spice on a familiar dish of comedy-melodrama." As he would do so often throughout Donner's career, Roger Ebert called it best. "At least nominally a comedy," he adjudged in his *Chicago Sun-Times* column. "... As you might guess, the movie is terribly short on running gags."

From a limited New York exhibition beginning on September 18, 1968, *Salt and Pepper* generated enough business to warrant a sequel, *One More Time*, released in 1970. It again starred Sammy Davis Jr., and Peter Lawford, but was directed by Jerry Lewis. It was an outright flop.

Donner returned to London in 1969 after an approach from Charles Bronson to direct him in the low-budget feature *Child Bride*, an edgy, *Lolita-*

inspired tale funded by the U.K.'s Rank Organisation and finance partners across Europe. Bronson was to play Scott Wardman, a middle-aged writer of pornographic novels who falls in love with a sixteen-year-old schoolgirl, Lola (Susan George). When the secret dalliance is exposed to Lola's family, the pair escapes to Glasgow, where they marry, before eloping to New York.

In the U.S. Scott is arrested and sentenced to thirty days in prison for striking a police officer at a street protest. Lola is left to fend for herself. When Scott is released, the relationship with his adolescent temptress begins to unravel, as both parties realize how little they actually know about one another. Lola returns home to England, the affair over.

The title *Child Bride* was changed to *Twinky* during production, which was lensed entirely on location and on a minimalist budget. Donner was happy to be back in London, the pop culture capital of the world, a home to some of the most exciting actors, musicians, artists and designers on the planet. He saw the difficult project as an opportunity to truly flex his directorial muscles.

In contrast to the anachronistic style of his cinematic debut, *X-15*, *Twinky* illustrates a high degree of experimental flair. It is an array of freeze frames, slow motion, stop motion, jump cuts, flashbacks and handheld photography, that owes more to an underground, guerrilla style of filmmaking than to the classical film form purveyed by Hollywood.

Despite the risqué subject matter, Donner infused the material with subtle humor. Whether it be a car full of horrified nuns staring aghast as Scott and Lola openly kiss, or a mother dropping breakfast on the floor before deciding to serve it to her family anyway, Donner ensured that *Twinky* was charged full of the incidental moments in life that so cheered him.

Released across the pond in 1970, *Twinky* did not secure a U.S. distributor until 1972. American International Pictures purchased it and rebadged it as *Lola*. It was screened in select theaters on June 11 of the same year.

Donner had been livid with Peter Lawford for coldly dropping him from *Salt and Pepper*, but the pair had since reconciled. "There was a bit of hero worship in my feelings for Peter," he remembered. "The women just flocked to him. It was unbelievable. I always wanted to be a pilot fish to Peter's shark — you know, the little fish that hangs on to the shark and eats up anything that falls out of its mouth? Peter had so many gorgeous girls around him I was content with his overflow. I did very well through him."

Donner was soon transformed into businessman, entrepreneur and full-time partygoer when he joined a group, including Paul Newman, Sammy Davis, Jr., Peter Lawford, Anthony Newley, Pierre Salinger (a former White House Press Secretary to U.S. Presidents John F. Kennedy and Lyndon B. Johnson) and his old friends Ronnie Buck and Peter Bren, in creating The

Factory, a major new nightclub in Hollywood. "[It was] huge," says John Calley, "[a] brilliant idea. The Factory was mobbed with people. It was sort of an early version of 'Studio 54.' It was celebrity owned and managed and therefore everybody was drawn to it."

"The Factory" was an exclusive loft venue with an elevator for an entrance. Donner could be found playing backgammon or pool, smoking a cigar while enjoying the music of Count Basie, or making the close acquaintance of a beautiful woman. He flirted with cocaine. "He was a player," describes producer Harvey Bernhard. "He was a big player. He was always laughing and he had a great sense of humor, a great laugh. He was just a pleasure to be around."

"The Factory" had begun life as "Mothas," a concept for an exclusive night-club inspired by a venue in Honolulu, Hawaii, that Donner and Sammy Davis, Jr., had frequented. "'Motha' was a word that Sammy brought to us and it was great," says the former. "We found a building on La Peer Drive in West Hollywood. It happened to be the old Mitchell motion picture camera fac-tory. Whenever we would have meetings, we'd say, 'Okay, we'll go down and meet at the factory.'"

After leasing a building and establishing a new name, the only serious point of disagreement between the multiple business partners came over the choice of restaurant menu. Paul Newman, with whom everyone was typically keen to agree, for the hope of making a film with him one day, had returned from the east side of New York with a very clear vision.

"I've got an idea," he proclaimed. "All we're going to serve at 'The Fac-tory' is omelets."

"Oh that's great, Paul," cheered the assemblage. "Wonderful."

Donner looked on rather shocked. "Hey, wait a minute, guys," he inter-polated. "If we're expecting people to come every night, then we've got to have a full menu. We can't just be serving omelets or they'll go other places for dinner."

The young director won out over the star, and for a while he was having the time of his life. He recalls, "As a single guy owning the top disco where everybody played, the most exclusive club with the most beautiful women, it was a great, great time in my life."

Exclusivity was the foundation of "The Factory," an underpinning that unraveled when one of the partners (whom Donner refuses to name) started to trade memberships for personal gifts. Soon a crowd came in that "started to push out the main crowd, and that killed it."

The demise of "The Factory" didn't place a halt on Donner. "I don't think Dick ever gave a thought to life," explained the late studio executive Guy McElwaine. "I really think he was just about working hard and having a good time. He didn't care [about his future]. He didn't have children. He worked hard. He made a lot of money. He was very popular with men and women, in terms of friends and girlfriends. People admired his life."

Women were drawn to Donner, taken by his good looks and his sense of humor, his incredible energy. They were turned on by both his confidence, and the hint of vulnerability he carried with him and allowed them to occasionally glimpse. "I don't know anyone less cheated in life than Dick Donner," says his cousin, Steve Kahan. "This guy had a good time. He was a magnet, no doubt about it. If I would drop by inadvertently without calling, he was never alone in his house. There were always one or two girls there." Donner had cared for his girlfriends, given them passion but not his heart. Nobody had come close to this, but that was about to change.

Donner's personal life was transformed in 1970 when he met and fell in love with Liv Ullmann. Eight years his junior, she was blue-eyed and fair-skinned, the archetypal Scandinavian beauty. Once married to a Norwegian psychiatrist, the actress was the muse of Academy Award-winning Swedish filmmaker Ingmar Bergman, the father of her young daughter, Linn.

Donner was vacationing in Nice, France, when he decided to visit the set of Terence Young's *Cold Sweat*. Ullmann was there, starring opposite Charles Bronson. During a break from filming, each star lunched separately, just the way Bronson liked it. As he sat with his wife, Jill Ireland, and their children, Ullmann ate alone with her three-year-old daughter. The actress remembers, "Linn, my daughter, was running over to his table, where his children [who were] the same age were sitting. He took my daughter in his hand and went over to my table where I was sitting and said, 'I would prefer that your child doesn't come over to us.' I would never forgive that because I was doing the lead in the picture [just] as he was doing the lead."

Donner consoled Ullmann, who was hurt and offended by the rudeness of her co-star. She found his openness irresistible. As she puts it, "He was a ladies' man… so tremendously handsome, charming, [and] interesting. And he immediately said, 'Here I am.'"

For Donner's part, he was strongly attracted to divorcees and single mothers like she. The brief romance was placed on hold when Donner returned to the U.S., only to resume two years later once Ullmann arrived in Hollywood. She had twice received the Best Actress Award from the New York Film Critics Circle, for *Utvandrarna* (*The Emigrants*) and *Viskningar och rop* (*Cries and Whispers*) respectively. Once on American soil she earned the cover of *Time* magazine accompanied by the caption, "Hollywood's New Nordic Star." And for *Utvandrarna*, Ullmann was nominated in the Best Actress category at the 1973 Academy Awards.

Although she would miss out on the ultimate prize to Liza Minnelli in *Cabaret*, her part in the ceremony made news headlines across the nation and around the world. It was Ullmann, standing next to James Bond star Roger Moore, who announced the name of the winner for Best Actor, Marlon Brando in *The Godfather*. Yet, in protest at perceived discrimination against Native-American people by the film industry, Brando had sent a proxy to the occasion. "Sacheen Littlefeather" (later discovered to be Maria Cruz, a Californian actress) famously refused the award on his behalf.

In Los Angeles, Ullmann was lonely and homesick. "You never see anyone," she complained at the time. "Nobody in the streets. Nobody at the windows of houses." Although tabloid rumors linked her to Warren Beatty and Glenn Ford, both of whom she was seen in the company of, it was to Donner that she ran. She continues, "If I hadn't had him [there] in Los Angeles, [my time] would not have been so good. He really took care of me, watched out for me. He was so, so wonderful, and I will never, ever forget it."

Ullmann knew nobody, so Donner introduced her to everybody, including his pals musician Quincy Jones and the recording executive Jerry Moss. He took her for long, romantic drives in his vintage Rolls-Royce, and when her sewing circle friends from Sweden came to visit, he played gracious host at his home in Hollywood. He even babysat her daughter, Linn, a dress rehearsal of sorts, a dry run for his entering into a stable family unit. He introduced Ullmann to his mother and to his sister, both of whom fell for her also.

Donner found Ullmann "talented, beautiful, a special lady with the biggest heart in the world," but suddenly he drew back. "I just fell hopelessly in love with him," the actress continues, '[but] he didn't fall hopelessly in love with me."

As had been the case in his previous relationship with Sandra Burns, a young and attractive single mother with two young daughters, Donner was strongly attracted to the notion of a ready-made family unit, but fled the commitment that it inevitably presented. Without warning, the most meaningful romance of his adult life ended abruptly.

"He was a good kid, [although] I wouldn't have wanted him as my own."

RICHARD DONNER ON HARVEY STEPHENS

Death, Destruction, and a Kick in the Balls

Terrorist bombs, plane crashes, and other grisly demises — the production of *The Omen* endured it all. Regardless of whether or not the series of frightful occurrences that occurred back in 1975 should be attributed to the demonic wishes of supernatural forces, or instead be considered hokum whipped up by an enthusiastic producer keen to sell his picture, the seemingly subcutaneous relationship between fictional and real-life horror remains a steadfast ingredient of its enduring legacy.

Before the producer Harvey Bernhard left the U.S. for filming in England, Bob Munger — the Los Angeles-based advertising executive who had pitched the original premise for the film — had warned him that "things were going to happen" on set. "He warned us that he thought the devil didn't want us to make the picture," Bernhard recalled, "and that we would have problems."

Gregory Peck, the star of Donner's eerie tale of a child Antichrist haunting the Earth, almost did not make it to the set at all. The actor arrived in the U.K., where the film was to be shot, after a turbulent flight across the Atlantic, during which the plane on which he was traveling had been struck by lightning. Bizarrely, the exact same fate befell David Seltzer, the film's screenwriter, when he traveled just a few days laters.

On November 18, 1975, barely a month into shooting, an IRA terrorist bomb exploded in a London restaurant, killing two and injuring twenty-three. The establishment in question was a favorite eatery of Peck's — although the actor had not dined there on the evening of the attack.

Donner did not think much of it when he was almost run down in the street while getting out of his parked car. A passing vehicle slammed by him, wedging him against the door. He was miraculously unhurt. Soon afterward, however, a lion trainer was killed at Windsor Safari Park, shortly after the director had filmed a scene at the compound. Rumors of a production curse soon began to spread.

It was one particularly tragic and gruesome event that sent those of a morbid disposition reaching for their crosses, and which stands out above the rest in horror production folklore. For a specific scene the producers had attempted to charter an airplane from a small airplane company, only to have their call returned with the news that there was a full charter on the day required, but if they liked they could have the airplane the next day for a quarter of the cost. On the day the original plane took off, it flew into a pack of birds and crashed into a busy motorway outside the airfield, killing a woman and three children in a car. The victims inside the car were the wife and family of the pilot.

Inexplicable tragedy would follow some of those involved with *The Omen* even after filming wrapped. Special effects supervisor John Richardson was injured and his girlfriend decapitated in a horrific car accident in Belgium. He had been on his way to the set of *A Bridge Too Far*, where filming was to commence just outside the municipality, Ommen.

Throughout the seventies, Donner continued to thrive in television. "I never regarded directing for TV as stiff dues," he was quoted as saying. "There were times when I wanted a bigger cut of the green, but I never disliked what I was doing."

He was commissioned to helm multiple shows at Universal, where he found a mentor in studio executive David Levinson. Donner was known as an "actors director" who elicited strong performances from his cast, appreciated as well for his innate technical skill and artistic eye, although it was Levinson who first encouraged him to become more involved in the concept of his shows, and to voice strong opinions to his scriptwriters. For the first time Donner started to read scripts the way *he* thought they should be shot, and not interpret them strictly the way they were written. With his enviable track record of success, he became pickier about the shows that he worked on, less prolific, dismissing opportunities to work on shows that were rigid in their approach, or would not allow him his input to the heart of what was going on. With Levinson's support, Donner demanded he be involved in all aspects of production, lending his own all-encompassing imprint to the shows that he chose.

He added *The Interns, Sarge, Cade's County, Bearcats!, Cannon, The Sixth Sense, Ghost Story, Banyon, Ironside, Kojak, The Streets of San Francisco* and *Petrocelli* to his résumé. When his NBC World Premiere Movie, *Sarah T. — Portrait of a Teenage Alcoholic*, was aired on February 11, 1975, it became the second highest rated show in the history of television. The touching movie of the week about a fifteen-year-old schoolgirl who descends into alcoholism after her parents' divorce starred a post-*Exorcist* Linda Blair, a pre-*Dallas*

Larry Hagman, and a pre-*Star Wars* Mark Hamill. In one scene during the movie Blair wears a T-shirt with the slogan "Pollution Is a Dirty Word" — a nod to Donner's environmental concerns, and a foreshadowing of his ability to sneak socio-political sympathies into his work.

"What if the Antichrist came back as a child?" Bob Munger teased to his friend, Harvey Bernhard. Inspired by the Book of Revelations, the Los Angeles-based advertising executive and born again Christian was pitching the premise for what would eventually become *The Omen*. The seasoned producer Bernhard immediately bought into the potential. Development capital was raised from a fifteen-page outline titled *The Antichrist* and screenwriter David Seltzer commissioned to write a fully-fledged screenplay — material that he dutifully completed in a rapid six weeks.

Although the success of *Rosemary's Baby* and *The Exorcist* had led to the revitalization of the horror genre, and the film industry was eager to satisfy audience demand for anything thrilling and chilling, Bernhard found the market to be flooded with too many similarly-themed scripts. Every major studio in Hollywood rejected him. He reached out to Mace Neufeld, the entrepreneurial manager of such diverse acts as Don Knotts, Gabe Kaplan, Jim Croce, and Neal Sedaka, a businessman keen to get involved in movie production. Operating on a guaranteed chunk of any future profit, Neufeld became an executive producer, and persuaded Warner Bros. that *The Antichrist* was *the* devil film worth investing in above the competition — extracting a seven-month development option on the property from the studio. A green light for a modest $1.5 million production was given, with director Charles Bail at the helm.

Harvey Bernhard's excitement at Warner Bros. was not to last. It turned out that the studio was firmly focused on its *Exorcist* sequel, *The Heretic*, to the detriment of his project. "They fucked us over," says Bernhard today. "They said it was 'too frightening.' Can you imagine?"

When his budget was slashed by more than a third as he scouted locations in Switzerland, Bernhard gave up hope of his picture ever getting made.

On a Friday afternoon Donner received a copy of *The Antichrist* from his friend, agent Eddie Rosen. He was told that Warner Bros. owned it, but were dropping it after the weekend. When he read it, he imagined not an *Exorcist*-style schlock-fest, rather an elegant mystery-suspense-thriller. If such hackneyed iconography as cloven hoofs, devil gods, gargoyles and witch covens could be eliminated, he reasoned, if the narrative had integrity, a sense of reality, then audiences might forgive the inherent, outlandish nature of the subject matter and embrace the film as a wonderful escapist entertainment. "All those rip-offs that came along after *The Exorcist* only did cult business because they gave you all the answers," he stated. "You saw devils on the screen, so of course you never had to wonder whether it was real. You knew it wasn't. For me, the holes in a picture of this type [horror] are when the answers are given."

Donner had first met Alan Ladd, Jr., during the early sixties, when "Laddy" was a talent agent working for Creative Management Associates. The director found the son of Alan Ladd (the star of the iconic George Stevens western *Shane*) to be intelligent, humorous, a man of integrity. Later in the decade Ladd, Jr., become an independent producer and moved to London, ending their professional ties, although he and Donner remained great friends. Laddy told the director that if he ever found a movie script he truly wanted to make, then he would do everything in his power to help him achieve it.

Ladd, Jr., had joined Twentieth Century-Fox in 1973, rising to head of production within a year (he would be studio president by 1977). He swiftly abandoned the cautious management style that had left the studio creatively moribund, marking his tenure with brave and dynamic leadership.

Donner sped to a dinner engagement with Laddy for which he was already half an hour late. When he arrived, he waved *The Antichrist* script in the air. This was the one, the one he had been waiting for. "You've got to read this!" he pleaded. "It's going to be in turnaround on Monday. I think it's very viable."

Donner had the perseverance, the eye for opportunity, now he needed the help of an old friend. Would Ladd, Jr., live up to the promise from all those years ago?

That Sunday, Donner placed a call to Harvey Bernhard. "Hi, do you remember me? I met you at a cocktail party once?"

"Yes."

"Well, you had a script called 'The Antichrist.'"

"Yes, yes."

"It was dropped by Warner."

"Yes."

"I sold it to Fox today. And I'm directing."

On Monday morning, Warner Bros. passed over their option on *The Antichrist*. Ladd, Jr., snapped it up for Twentieth Century-Fox and allocated a $2 million budget. Executive producer, Mace Neufeld, was ecstatic. "Listen, let's get rid of Donner," he enthused. "There's this other director we want to use."

"He brought it to me," Ladd, Jr., replied firmly, "and the only way I'm going to make it is if he directs it."

The audacious Neufeld had believed he could attract Robert Mulligan (*To Kill a Mockingbird* and *Summer of '42*) to helm, but Ladd, Jr., had demonstrated his loyalty to Donner. He remembers, "I wanted to give Dick the opportunity, obviously, because we had been friends for so long, and I thought that this was just the picture that could do it for him. I had a lot of faith in Dick that he would get the material right." It was Laddy who strongly encouraged his friend to "eliminate the obvious," and to "focus on mystery and suspense." As Donner affectionately reveals, "That's why he's such a great studio head."

Within four days *The Antichrist* had been dropped by one studio, purchased by another, issued a new director and a new vision. Shortly afterward it would have a new title. Because of a European picture entitled *Antichristo*, pre-production carried the working title *The Birthmark* (referring to the three sixes which appear on the body of the Antichrist). Donner and his producer would arrive at *The Omen* during filming.

David Seltzer commenced a new draft of the screenplay, one that eliminated the obvious and focused instead upon the mental deterioration of the script's central protagonists, Robert Thorn and his wife Katherine. With Donner he plotted the highs and lows of the script mathematically. Donner remembered, "We used a sheet of graph paper and traced each thrill on a scale of one to ten over the course of a projected running time of two hours. Of course, you want to start at the low end and climax with your Number Tens. There was a lot of shuffling and transposing of scenes, but the general idea was to start low, let the audience have some breathing room between the early shocks and then hit them repeatedly at the end. When they're begging for a breather, you keep the pressure building and leave them breathless."

Three days after Ladd, Jr., had green-lit the project, Donner and Bernhard departed for the U.K. for the start of an eleven-week shoot.

In Rome, the wife of the American ambassador gives birth to a stillborn baby. In a bid to protect her from the shattering truth, her husband, Robert Thorn, substitutes their dead child for an orphan born the very same night. Robert and Katherine move to London with their new son, Damien, where a series of inexplicable, horrific events occur.

During a lavish fifth birthday party held for Damien on a vast English estate, the boy's nanny commits suicide by jumping from a building with her head hung to a rope. Before he is impaled by a spire in a church cemetery, a priest warns Thorn of his adopted son's origins. His paranoia quickly mounts. Is he being punished for lying to his wife about their stillborn baby? Are these demonic acts?

Accompanied by a press photographer, Keith Jennings, Thorn travels to Rome and then to Jerusalem in search of clues. He meets archeologist Carl Bugenhagen, who informs him that his adopted son, Damien, is the Antichrist. Thorn does not believe Bugenhagen until his wife suffers a violent accident at home, and then falls to her death from the window of the hospital bedroom where she was recuperating. Thorn resolves to kill Damien and attempts to sacrifice his son at a church altar back in London.

Several actors of stature were approached for the role of Robert Thorn. Roy Scheider and William Holden gave a firm "thanks, but no thanks." Donner and Bernhard waited for a response from Charlton Heston, only for the studio to baulk at his salary demands.

Who could be Donner's legitimizing force, an actor whom audiences could believe in and who could help temper the outlandish elements of the script? Gregory Peck, possibly, but there was a stumbling block. Just a few months prior, the actor's son had been found dead in his home in California, the (apparent) result of a self-inflicted gunshot wound to the head, although no suicide note was found. Under the circumstances, Alan Ladd, Jr., felt it highly insensitive to send Peck a script in which his character would attempt to kill his son. Peck's agent, George Chasin, felt otherwise. The screen icon had not acted in more than three years, and Chasin anticipated that his client's emotional recovery would be assisted by a return to work. He passed the screenplay to Peck and conveyed Twentieth Century-Fox's generous offer of $250,000 plus a guaranteed 10% of the box-office gross. The base salary offer was more than twice the fee Donner would receive. The awarding of percentage points had the potential to earn the actor many millions of dollars, if the film was successful.

When he read the screenplay, the quiet, introspective star of such classic films as *The Guns of Navarone* and *To Kill a Mockingbird* was amused by what he considered a variety of obvious plot holes, and was not entirely impressed with some of the darker elements of the Thorn character (Peck was known to play characters underpinned by a basic decency and earnestness). What the star did acknowledge, however, was that the material had commercial potential. "The script held my interest as a Gothic thriller," he recalled during a promotional interview with *Cinefantastique* magazine, "and I thought if we could put this on screen it would be something exciting — shocking to be sure, with some quite ghastly killings in it... in spite of the contrivances of the script and the manipulative nature of the whole thing, it's sort of a roller coaster thrill ride for the audience."

Before he officially accepted the role, Peck wanted to learn more about the film's director, whose name he was not familiar with. "Who is he?" he demanded of his agent.

"Well, I've met him socially although I don't know him professionally," Chasin replied. "He's done one or two TV specials."

"Nothing for the theaters?"

"I'll have to look him up in the directory."

Donner flew out of London back to Los Angeles to meet with Peck in person. The director drove to the actor's house, and was greeted by his wife, Veronique. Donner's feet were trembling — Peck was one of the greats — but he pulled himself together. There was no idle conversation, no meaning-less chitchat. The two men got straight down to business, addressing each aspect of the production in detail. "What is it that I will bring to the prop-erty?" Peck asked.

"Validity," was Donner's immediate response. "You'll bring an honesty to this that will make it a mystery-suspense-thriller."

"That's the kind of movie I want to do," the actor replied.

In London, Lee Remick agreed to co-star as Kathy Thorn, the wife of the Ambassador to the Court of St. James. She had lived in the U.K. for sev-eral years and was enthusiastic to commit to a major motion picture being lensed in her adopted country. Prominent supporting roles went to British performers, including Billie Whitelaw, Patrick Troughton, Leo McKern and Martin Benson, largely due to tax incentives offered by the U.K. gov-ernment for basing the production in England. Donner was particularly excited to cast David Warner as the photographer Keith Jennings — the actor had starred in one of his favorite sixties movies, *Morgan: A Suitable Case for Treatment.*

Donner originally wanted the Antichrist to be a young girl, believing that he would receive a more sensitive performance, but after settling on a boy he and Bernhard toiled for a suitable child actor to play Damien the devil child. They spent days interviewing groups of four youngsters at ten-minute inter-vals, although many parents refused permission for their children to audition based on the film's controversial subject matter.

Four-year-old Harvey Stephens was submitted to casting agent Maude Spector by a local model agency. A screen test was arranged at Pyrford Court, an eighteenth-century, sixty-room mansion on a thousand-acre country estate. Upon meeting the lad, Donner asked him if he could convey menace, perhaps charge at him a little bit. Stephens caught Donner off guard when he implanted his right foot firmly in between the director's legs, enough to topple the director, who found himself under a deluge of blows to the head. An entirely satanic rage, coupled with the ability to inflict serious testicular injury on those who crossed him, won little Stephens the part.

Donner turned his attention to recruiting a cinematographer. Top of his list was Geoffrey Unsworth, who had photographed *2001: A Space Odyssey* for Stanley Kubrick and won an Oscar for Bob Fosse's *Cabaret.* Unsworth, how-ever, was committed to *A Matter of Time* directed by Vincente Minnelli.

Donner thus looked to Gil Taylor, a respected British cinematographer who had lensed *Frenzy* for Alfred Hitchcock and *Macbeth* for Roman Polan-ski. He had been Kubrick's cameraman on *Dr. Strangelove or: How I Learned to Stop Worrying and Love the Bomb.* Unfortunately, Taylor had suffered a sour experience at the hands of the intense Kubrick. He had been forced to submit to a written test on the art of cinematography, a slight that had embittered him against American directors.

Since his retirement from movies, Taylor ran a milk farm. When Donner called him and persuaded him to come in and talk over the film, Taylor arrived straight from the pasture, still wearing a giant pair of muddied rubber boots. He was dour, gruff, insisted he was tired of the film business. Donner bought him lunch at the studio canteen and shared some of his childhood memories of Rolling Acres in Clinton Corners, New York. The director pointed out that Taylor's harvest was all but in, and that his calving season wouldn't warm up until *The Omen*'s three-month shooting schedule drew to a close. Might he at least read the script? Charmed by Donner, Taylor called him the next day and agreed to come out of retirement (after *The Omen* he would photograph *Star Wars* for George Lucas).

The heavy burden of trying to deliver a $2 million movie in a mere eleven weeks, and a shoot that required location filming in three separate countries (the U.K., Italy and Israel), weighed heavily on Donner. The budget was tight and the logistics were complicated, but his perennially upbeat nature and clear sense of direction for the material won him many admirers amongst the cast and crew. "He was very charmingly enthusiastic and he would sometimes have difficulty expressing himself, because he was so bubbling over with ideas," David Warner enthuses. "You could tell this man loved films, and making them, and that was very infectious… he has a very forceful voice and a force-ful personality [and] you really felt that he knew what he was doing."

When veteran art director Carmen Dillon stood on a rolling dolly 60 feet off the ground, painting the stage ceiling at Shepperton Studios for the famed cemetery sequence, despite being well into her sixties, it was a testament to the levels of energy and enthusiasm that Donner inspired.

The filmmaker built a strong camaraderie on set. Special effects supervisor John Richardson, a veteran of more than fifty films who has collaborated with the likes of Steven Spielberg, Ron Howard, James Cameron, Renny Harlin and Chris Columbus, says that, "Dick is without doubt my favorite director of all the directors I've ever worked with. He has the ability to get more out of me than I knew I was capable of. He generates such infectious enthusiasm. I always felt, and I think most of the people that worked with him always felt, a tremendous loyalty to him."

At day's end, Donner would invite Harvey Bernhard, Gil Taylor, Carmen Dillon and Richardson back to his office at the studio for a glass of wine. The group would mull over ideas for the next day, kick them around, and get the creative juices flowing. There was never a rush to go home.

On Thanksgiving Day, Donner arranged for a specially cooked meal for the entire crew in order to celebrate the American holiday. He thanked his British friends for all of their hard work on the picture, and comically reminded them just how grateful he was that his country was no longer subject to their rule. The turkey made cast and crew so sleepy that the director ordered a wrap after a half day of filming.

Donner's original editor on *The Omen* was Ralph Kemplen, a respected professional who had cut *The Day of the Jackal* and *The Odessa File*. Donner and Kemplen failed to see eye to eye. Says Bernhard, "I was a very tough producer. I produced and Dick directed, and we got along like we were joined at the hip. I saw the dailies and I said, 'Dick, the editor isn't worth shit. It is no good and you have to fire him.' Well, Dick doesn't like to fire people. I said, 'I'll fire him.' And I did. And we got in Stuart Baird, who was a godsend."

The man chosen as replacement recalls, "I think I'd just finished *Tommy* for Ken Russell, and then I did *Welcome to My Nightmare* for Alice Cooper, who was doing a series of concerts in London. They [Donner and Bernhard] were obviously looking for a young editor who had done that sort of rock 'n' roll stuff, and I was the youngest cutter there was in features by a long chalk at that time. So we met and I said to Dick, 'But this is ridiculous. Why are you interviewing me when you've got an editor? You've got probably one of the top editors in the country. What do you think I can do that he can't?' He replied that it was 'a personality thing.'"

Donner and Baird formed an explosive film partnership. British camera operator Peter MacDonald, who knew the editor but did not work on *The Omen*, remembers, "At the time [Stuart] was hung really tight and very self-opinionated. Dick obviously got on with that. He wanted people who would challenge him and who would be inventive. Stuart was his own man, and Dick appreciated people who had this energy and courage." The talented Baird's confrontational style of working was exactly what Donner was looking for — a volatile youth hungry to drive the picture forward. Famed for their many heated exchanges, he and Baird would nonetheless become tremendous friends.

With Baird's wiry frame most often decked in a black corduroy suit topped by a fedora hat, replete with feather, Donner love to poke fun. "The legs were so tight you had to zipper them on," he quipped of Baird's choice of trouser.

The director quarreled with his chief camera operator, Gerry Anstiss, who imagined the film to be made up of the extreme low- and wide-angle shots that Donner wished to avoid. Donner preferred an "eye level" picture, one in which the audience gets to know the characters. He assumed physical control of the camera for several scenes, including one in which Damien suffers a panic attack in the car on his way to church, and another in which he speeds between the rooms of Pyrford Court mansion on his red tricycle.

Harvey Bernhard shielded Donner from the Hollywood moneymen as best he could. He was in constant contact with the executives from Twentieth Century-Fox, who were desperate to ensure the picture stayed on schedule and under budget. Although far from a high-cost picture, there were more than enough variables to cause a significant level of stress. Donner was filming with a major star, his special effects were all physical, and the weather was cold and dreary. At times, he allowed the stress of the shoot to show, occasionally losing his temper. Bernhard remembers Donner's temper. "He doesn't listen to anybody. He's off on a roll, so you'd better walk away or sit down, or say, 'Yes, Dick.' Until he calms down."

During other moments, when it all got too much, he would suffer from self-doubt. He would confide in his producer, a man who had become a great friend. Bernhard would stir two strong martinis and reassure his director of the fantastic job he was doing. Says he, "Dick Donner was a consummate director. There was not a position he could be put in that he couldn't figure out. His dedication was extraordinary. Morning, noon, and night he thought of this picture."

"I can remember Harvey [Bernhard] saying to me at one point that a lot of people in America were praying for us," recalled special effects supervisor John Richardson. "Because they didn't think the Devil would allow the movie to be made."

A series of strange occurrences had led the producer to believe that the Devil was against *The Omen* being made. For holy protection, he doubled up and wore both a Star of David and a Catholic cross throughout production. Donner found that, for the most part, shooting ran smoothly, even if some moments proved more difficult to film than others. For the scene in which Gregory Peck and David Warner are attacked by a pack of wild dogs in an Italian cemetery, so docile were the canines in question that — in a desperate bid to provoke a response — the actors (and stuntmen) resolved to stuff raw meat underneath their clothes. Likewise, when Lee Remick and little Harvey Stephens drive through Windsor Safari Park zoo and come under attack from frenzied apes, the sleepy primates were not keen to cooperate — even after Donner covered their car in bananas. (The apes *were* greatly interested in a hat that Harvey Bernhard was wearing — the crew fell about laughing after a baboon snuck up and stole it from him.)

Remick and Stephens sat in the front of the car. Donner was in the back, holding the camera. Next to him was a sedated leader monkey. When the baboons witnessed this abduction, they finally erupted into fury, launching a barrage of blows on the vehicle. The director excitedly captured the footage he required, but as he finished doing so, the leader monkey awoke from its sedation and started to tug on Remick's hair. Perhaps because of the fright the actress was more cautious when it came to Donner's future demands. Remick refused to perform a stunt for a scene in which her character, Katherine Thorn, falls from a second-floor balcony in her home, and Donner was forced into a famed moment of cinematic trickery. He built a "floor" onto a vertical wall at Shepperton Studios, and dollied an upright Remick toward it as though she were falling. The director avoided using a stunt double, and captured the close-up shot he desperately wanted.

In the screenplay, the violent fall called for a bowl of goldfish to come tumbling down with the actress, to smash violently next to her crumpled body. Donner purchased some dead sardines and painted them orange. He remembers, "Well, Harvey [Bernhard] came in and said: 'What are you doing with the dead fish? Put live fish in that.' And I said, 'I'm not going to drop live fish off here and have them hit the floor — it'll kill 'em.' And we had this *incredible* argument. And I said, 'Harvey, anybody says they're dead fish and you can have my profits on the picture.' I just couldn't drop live fish on the floor."

Donner was being paid a salary of $125,000 for his work on *The Omen*. His deal did not include a percentage of any profits; unlike Harvey Bernhard and Mace Neufeld, whose contracts assured them of vast fortunes, should the film become an unlikely blockbuster hit. As shooting progressed and Donner viewed his assembled footage, the commercial potential of what he was filming began to hit home. He started to realize: *The Omen* wasn't just viable — it was a potential smash. On set, he turned to Mace Neufeld. "Mace, c'mon, I'm the one that sold this picture that was dropped by every studio in town. I'd sure love to get a couple of points."

"Okay," the executive producer replied. "You deserve it."

"Oh great!"

Neufeld offered Donner two of his percentage points, should the film prove a success. The director called his attorney in California to make the deal official.

"If you keep having your lawyer call me then I'm not giving you anything," an irritable Neufeld declared, just days later.

"Jeez, I just wanted to put it on paper."

"Don't worry. You're covered."

In the main, Donner enjoyed a good relationship with Gregory Peck, who spoke glowingly of his director after filming was complete. He said, "It's an enormous help to have a man with good judgment, good taste, and who has a personal character you can trust. He's your audience… He drew me out and gave me every opportunity. The collaboration between the two of us — it was the best we could do."

The admiration is mutual. "He was really a man of great belief," Donner recalls. "He was incredible to work with. Incredible."

Despite such warm rhetoric, occasional moments of tension between Donner and Peck had ensued — with the lead actor prone to the odd moment of superstar tantrum. As a nod to his powerhouse status, the British cast and crew had been warned before filming began that they "shouldn't spend too much time talking with Gregory Peck." Donner vowed to remain tough. "Dick's willing to listen to everyone," says Bernhard, "but he runs the set. He's got the biggest voice in the business. I can remember once he yelled at Peck. Dick wanted to do it one way and Peck wanted to do it another. Dick prevailed. Dick yelled, I remember, and everybody sat down. He was dynamite."

In one scene, Donner instructed Peck to hold the gaze of another actor and not to blink, conveniently forgetting to inform him that the actor's eye he was holding was made of glass. Desperately attempting to hold the stare without blinking, Peck's eye dried up and began to tear. Donner got the reaction shot he wanted, although his star may not have been so amused by his prankish method for obtaining it.

A heated argument occurred as the pair prepared to lens a scene in which Robert Thorn learns of his wife's death. Peck insisted he should destroy the bedroom set in a violent rage. Donner was adamant that the actor should lie motionless on a bed, stunned and in shock. Peck stormed off set over the impasse. Donner knew that the actor would eventually calm down, but even still, he was only likely to receive one opportunity to film the scene the way he knew it should be done. He rallied his cameraman, his assistants and his operators, and rehearsed tirelessly.

"I'll do it your way, but it's wrong," Peck stated upon his return to the set the following morning. The scene was filmed in one take.

"Thank you Mr. Peck," Donner declared at the end of the shot. "Let's move on."

Taken by surprise, Peck requested another take, a chance to film the scene his way, but Donner insisted he had filmed exactly what was needed. The next morning, the star arrived to view the previous day's rushes with his director and the crew. As they got closer to revealing the disputed shot, the tension in the room rose exponentially. After seeing Thorn lie motionless on the bed, internalizing his wife's death, the lights in the room went up. Peck immediately stood up from his seat, and moved purposefully toward his director. "Mr. Donner, you were right," he graciously extended. "I couldn't have done it any better."

The actor shot his last scene as Ambassador Robert Thorn on December 24, 1975. He jumped straight onto a Pan American flight to Los Angeles to be with his wife, Veronique, for Christmas Eve dinner.

Principal photography officially wrapped on January 2, 1976. Donner would remain in London for several weeks to edit the picture alongside Stuart

Baird, during which time the director learned that Peck had met with Alan Ladd, Jr., in California to deliver his own widespread suggestions for the editing process. Soon afterward, he received a letter from the star. It read: "You may choose to think, that I am overstepping the bounds and being meddlesome; on the other hand, please remember that it takes some kind of courage to stick my neck out in this way [in making a low-budget horror thriller]. I could just keep quiet and hope for the best and not put my judgment on the line. In addition, I am quite sincere when I say that I will support the picture and do all I can to help it whether or not I agree with the way it is cut."

Donner conferred with Bernhard over an appropriate response, volleying a letter in return: "We appreciate the candor of your letter and certainly do not feel that you have over-stepped your bounds. You have contributed so much to this picture that it would be ridiculous for you not express yourself fully and clearly."

"Hey, Dick, what about instead of having Peck kill the little boy, the little boy kills Peck?" offered studio boss Alan Ladd, Jr., having viewed a rough cut of the film. Donner loved the twist. He asked for $5,000 to shoot an additional half a day, and he, Stephens, and a handful of extras descended onto the lawn at Shepperton Studios for the officially sanctioned pick-up shot. It began as a close-up of the boy with his back to camera, before Damien turns and stares right into the eyes of the shocked audience. "Just before he turned, I said, 'Look severe, look angry, and don't you laugh,'" Donner recalled. Of course, the rambunctious Stephens couldn't resist the temptation, and after a concerted effort he eventually broke into a wide (and appropriately demonic) grin.

"He kept fighting the laugh and we ended up with this wonderful smile. I said, 'That's it!' And everybody said, 'Don't do that, you'll ruin the movie. He's laughing at the movie.' Everybody fought me. [But] I felt what the smiling boy was saying was, 'Is this all true? Has this been a put-on? Am I the Devil?' At the first screening, when he turned, they all gasped, because he was alive, and they began screaming and cheering. It was perfect for me."

Donner wanted composer Jerry Goldsmith to score *The Omen*, but he had run out of money. Ladd, Jr., sanctioned the $25,000 fee. Goldsmith's mesmerizing soundtrack was suitably eerie and ominous, but also tender and poignant. Particularly striking and unsettling was his decision to incorporate Gregorian chanting from a black mass. When Fox executives caught a glimpse of the final cut, the excitement in the room was tangible. A decision was taken to push *The Omen* as Fox's major motion picture release for 1976, and a whopping $15 million war chest was allocated for its advertising budget.

The film nearly didn't make it to California at all, when *The Omen* "curse" presented another twist. Armed with the final answer print under their arms,

Donner and Bernhard's transatlantic flight from London ran into technical problems, and was forced into an emergency landing in Nova Scotia. "It really was a trip," says Bernhard. "I said, 'Oh shit. We're never going to get there.' It was frightening. We had the negative... [And] there wasn't any backup."

Despite the many moments of physical horror in *The Omen* — death by hanging, impalement or decapitation — Donner took the decision to make his experiment in terror a master class in suspense, succeeding largely because of what isn't shown. "It's classic narrative filmmaking," describes Stuart Baird, "Not relying on 'flash' but relying on character." The director's narrative emphasis was not on gore, but rather on something much harder to make successful: the convincing emotional descent of his central protagonists, who are driven into paranoid despair. "We treated the story as a coincidence," Donner recalled. "You can't tell Gregory Peck that somebody's wife was raped by a jackal and sired him a child. We treated it like he was surrounded by total insanity. I mean, coincidence after coincidence after coincidence until it drove him insane. And I think that was the success of the picture."

Donner's very strong personal take on the material at hand, his desire to "play it straight," to search for the reality in *The Omen* rather than the farce, was crucial to the film's eventual success. The approach would become his professional trademark, in many ways the key to the longevity of his career, and the reason as to why he would prove so often to be in tune with the public zeitgeist.

Donner had arrived.

"[Kids] don't want science. They want magic. They don't want hypothesis, they want immutable truth."

ROBERT PAUL SMITH
"WHERE DID YOU GO?" "OUT." "WHAT DID YOU DO?" "NOTHING."

Brando, Bagels, and the Man Of Steel

Superman was to be the biggest project of Donner's career. Two movies shot simultaneously but released a year apart — the epic production would eventually span more than eighteen months of filming across three continents, and utilize the skill of more than one thousand personnel. Yet with only a matter of weeks until the commencement of principal photography, the director remained without an actor for his lead role. Nick Nolte, Robert Redford, Jon Voight — even Sylvester Stallone — had all been linked as potential Men of Steel, but Donner rejected the idea of casting a named star, insistent that the role be given to an unknown performer.

Hundreds of young hopefuls were auditioned, none of whom seemed right for the part, and the situation became so desperate that Don Voyne, a Beverly Hills dentist to the wife of producer Ilya Salkind, a man with no previous acting experience, was screen tested, purely on the basis that he happened to look like Superman.

The start of shooting loomed ever closer, and the pressure mounted. To curb his anxiety Donner got high on grass, while screenwriter Tom Mankiewicz drank copious amounts of whisky. After a particularly hapless night spent discussing casting problems, the worried pair began to wonder what kind of mess they had gotten themselves into. They were being chauffeured to Donner's rented house in London when, some ways into the journey, a loaded Mankiewicz began to quiz the driver. "Eddie?"

"Yes, sir?"

"If you were making this picture, would you give the two people in the backseat $30 million to make two movies?"

The driver peered into his rearview mirror. "No, sir," he responded politely. "No, I wouldn't."

After a lengthy silence, Donner turned to his friend. "What are you thinking?"

"I'm thinking we're either going to have a huge hit," the pensive screen-writer replied, "or we're presiding over what will be one of the legendary flops in the history of film."

The release of *The Omen* became a national event. Elaborate trailers ran for months in advance, and sneak previews of the finished film were screened in more than five hundred theaters across America. Twentieth Century-Fox saturated the media with promotional material, including billboard and newspaper ads that read, "Good morning. You are one day closer to the end of the world." David Seltzer adapted his screenplay into a novel that was released six weeks before the movie. It became an instant bestseller. What had begun as an unfancied B movie made for $2 million, and which every studio in Hollywood had once rejected, was transformed into a bona fide summer blockbuster. *The Omen* premiered on June 25, 1976. It grossed $61 million on domestic soil (Donner was adamant it would have done five times the business, had it been released before *The Exorcist*). The Fox hierarchy, and in particular Ladd, Jr., were ecstatic over the success. The corporate euphoria was such that the studio felt encouraged to consider fully funding another piece of pulp cinema on their development slate, a little-known picture pro-visionally titled *The Star Wars*.

Critical reception was mixed. *Time* magazine heaped praise on *The Omen*, calling it a "brisk, highly professional thriller, in which an implausible tale is rendered believable by the total conviction with which it is told." The review also made positive comparisons with *Jaws* — Spielberg's history-rewrit-ing shark tale released the previous summer. "As did *Jaws*," continued critic Richard Schickel, "it offers, from start to finish, a lovely ominous mood, punc-tuated by increasingly horrific actions… everybody's in the soup for fair and the audience is suspensefully simmering along with them." Others disagreed. *The New York Times* described a "dreadfully silly film," while *The Washington Post* felt the picture lacked a "pervasive aura of malevolence, the sort of thing Polanski achieved in *Rosemary's Baby*."

Donner cared little of the critical reception, and chose instead to focus on the clear impact the picture was having upon the U.S. populate. In the shad-owy aftermath of the Watergate scandal and the Vietnam War, the idea of a demonic monster arising from the world of politics did not seem so fantas-tical. *The Omen*, it quickly became clear, had tweaked many a subconscious American fear, and its success left Donner feeling on top of the world. Out-side theaters where the movie was playing, he watched lines form around the block, and took photos of himself smiling under marquees, which he would mail to his mother. Inside, he sat with different audiences each night, always finding a seat in the front row, so that he could turn and revel in the fright-ened gasps of the assembled faces. When *The Omen* grossed more than $1 million a day for nineteen straight days, Donner dreamed that it would never stop. "He was successful as a TV guy," says his friend and editor, Stuart Baird, "but nobody thought he was going to make it. He was in his mid-forties, he thought the game was up — it was going to be TV for the rest of his life. [But with *The Omen*] he reinvented himself."

Such success commanded instant personal attention, and Donner was feted by Hollywood. "It's nice to be on top all of a sudden," he recalled to London's *Guardian* newspaper. "I've got offers and offers and offers. I'm spoiled rotten." Recognition outside of the industry was more difficult to come by. Twentieth Century-Fox worked hard to promote their new star director, and issued press releases that invited journalists to meet with him as part of a grueling series of publicity junkets. Having authored three previous movie failures, and with nearly two decades of television experience to his credit, Donner readied to become the newest overnight sensation. Although after *Jaws*, the rules of the game had changed. Future talents would forever be condemned to being judged in comparison to the youthful Spielberg, and Donner — a graying, middle-aged man bereft of sneakers and baseball cap — presented something of a conundrum. Here was no twenty-something film school graduate, no rebellious outsider with a view to challenging studio dominance. Here instead was something akin to a veteran, a man who counted the executive Alan Ladd, Jr., among his close friends. And as far as fashion accessories went, he was far more likely to be sporting a nice cardigan than the latest denim jacket. Was he "New Hollywood" or "Old Hollywood"? A "Movie Brat" or a "Movie Dad"? The answer was somewhere in between, but if the critics did not pose these questions, it was perhaps because they didn't care. Donner's purposeful and stylish handling of the material placed in front of him may well have been the most important factor behind the integrity of *The Omen*, but critical notices chose to focus upon the film's catchy premise and ingenious marketing campaign as the secret to its success. The director remained modestly indifferent. "The day *The Omen* came out," he told *Premiere* magazine, "I never had to prove myself again, ever, as far as I was concerned."

Harvey Bernhard lobbied hard for Donner to direct an *Omen* sequel. While he was reluctant to commit, he smartly refused to rule out his involvement and agreed to work on a story proposal. However, when an advance copy of the book *Inside Moves* landed on his desk, Donner determined that he would make Todd Walton's debut novel his next directorial venture.

The offbeat story focused on the bond formed between two men brought together by incredible hardship. A partially paralyzed youth, Roary, wanders into a bar and meets an extraordinary group of people, including bartender

Jerry Maxwell who is crippled by a leg injury endured since birth. Roary supports Jerry as a chance basketball game with a young rookie named Alvin Martin leads to a life-changing operation, and the dream of a pro-basketball career. Infused by their strong friendship, and the sunny outlook of fellow bar regulars, the two men face up to life away from the safe haven of their private world, and for the first time start to believe in aspirations beyond the confines of their physical conditions.

Such a low-concept premise would certainly have made for a nontraditional follow up to a breakthrough director's first hit, but the story had Donner hooked; its winning tale of love and friendship formed in the face of adversity played straight to his heart. There was just one problem. Despite his newfound status, Donner did not possess the necessary funds to option the book. His salary for directing *The Omen* had been $125,000, and the profit percentage points later promised to him by Mace Neufeld had not been forthcoming. "No way," Neufeld had angrily told him when asked. "Get them from Harvey [Bernhard]."

Donner was taken aback by the change of position. The incident was a very real, very stark introduction to what constituted honesty and integrity in Hollywood. The warning led him to establish the mantra: "Get it on paper, and get it signed." (He would not fully learn the lesson until after he had executed some poor judgment on both *Superman* and *The Toy*.)

Just as Donner prepared to take the idea of filming *Inside Moves* to Laddy, from whom he hoped to garner support, he received a phone call that changed his life forever.

"What's Superman?" had been the response of eccentric European producer Alexander Salkind to his son's business proposition. Ilya Salkind had first mooted the idea to his father for a feature-length picture based on the iconic comic book hero over coffee, on a Paris sidewalk, in 1973. Together with their business partner and family friend Pierre Spengler, they began to formulate a strategy for producing a viable commercial project that they hoped would spawn a franchise akin to the James Bond series. Although the trio had struck international success with their tongue-in-cheek film version of the classic novel *The Three Musketeers* (and a sequel, *The Four Musketeers*), their plans remained farfetched.

Their epic venture began by licensing the film rights for the Superman character from DC Comics, a task moderately complicated by the publisher being owned by Warner Bros. Once secured, a negative pick-up deal was struck with the studio to distribute the film across North America, leaving Alexander Salkind with the responsibility of financing and producing the project in full. Their main discourse for raising capital, and convincing a skeptical industry that their plans were credible, was to attach bankable names to the project. For two successive Cannes Film Festivals, the trio had unsuccessfully touted the Superman property. Few financiers, it seemed, believed that their staggeringly ambitious plans were achievable. Potential backers would remain unconvinced until author Mario Puzo, whose novel *The Godfather* had been so successfully adapted by Francis Ford Coppola for his Oscar-winning film, signed a $350,000 contract to pen a screenplay. Puzo's deal also included an entitlement to 5% of the gross receipts, should the project make it onto film.

What was to lend the project serious legitimacy was the shock signing of Marlon Brando to play Superman's father, Jor-El, for a reputed $4 million and a percentage of the gross — a record-breaking salary for only two weeks' work. The next casting coup was *The French Connection* star, Gene Hackman, hired to play Superman's arch nemesis Lex Luthor for a $2 million fee. Yet even with this majestic line-up in place, it was perhaps Alexander Salkind's next acquisition that proved the most satisfying: British director Guy Hamilton. With the *Goldfinger* helmer attached, the producers were confident that everything was in place for what was set to become the largest production in motion picture history.

The elation was not to last. Brando flatly refused to shoot in a country that had defined *Last Tango in Paris* as self-serving pornography and had arrested its director, Bernardo Bertolucci, on obscenity charges. The resulting switch from his preferred Italian production base to England would also save Salkind millions of dollars due to the strength of the Italian lira, but it cost Hamilton, who, as a British tax exile, faced stringent work restrictions in the U.K.

With Brando and Hackman locked in contractually to immutable start dates, and shooting to commence in just a matter of months, the task of contracting a name director usurped all others.

After leaving his role as executive vice president of Filmways, John Calley had joined Warner Bros. in 1968, where he held a variety of positions (including president) during a thirteen-year tenure at the studio. As of 1976 he operated as vice chairman, and was responsible for consulting directly with Alexander and Ilya Salkind over all aspects of the *Superman* production. As the primary distributor for the movie, Warner held a strong interest in crucial decision-making processes, and although hiring a new director remained the full responsibility of the independent producing team, Calley suggested Donner as a possible candidate.

It was early one Sunday morning when the director received the startling phone call, and in the most unlikely of position — while he sat on his toilet. "This is Alexander Salkind," uttered the heavily accented voice. "You know who I am?"

Donner answered in the negative. Continued Salkind: "I produced *The Three Musketeers*. We're doing *Superman* now, and we've just seen *The Omen* — would you like to do it?"

The offer was an astounding one. The producer guaranteed him $1 million to direct Puzo's whopping five-hundred-and-fifty-page screenplay as two movies lensed simultaneously but released a year apart. The director fumbled for pencil and paper and found the tattered business card of his hairdresser. On the back of it he frantically scribbled down the details of the production. "That's flattering," he responded, "but I'd like to read it first."

"You don't have to read it," the Polish producer replied. "Everybody likes it."

"Well, I'd feel better if I read it."

The full screenplay was couriered to Donner's house. He told genre publication *Cinefantastique* that, "It was a well-written script, quite honestly. But it was a *ridiculous* script... they [the producers] parodied a parody and kept compounding that felony all the way through until it became much like the *Batman* television series." In the book *Man of Two Worlds: My Life in Science Fiction and Comics*, the former head of DC Comics, Julius Schwartz, concurs: "Among the scenes that were dropped from the final screenplay, one dealt with his [Superman's] date with Lois, where he realized that he had neglected to bring a wine for their dinner, and he quickly scanned the world with his telescopic vision for a solution to his problem, saw that the Queen of England was just about to launch a ship with a bottle of champagne, and quickly zoomed across the ocean to England, snatching the bottle out of Her Highness's hands before it smashed against the ship's hull, and delivered it to Lois. The other scene dealt with Lex Luthor, who everyone knows was Supe's bald-headed foe. In the deleted scene, Superman is trying to track down Luthor and homes in on a bald guy in a trench coat, who he grabs and turns around... only to find a guy sucking on a lollipop who says to him, 'Who loves ya, baby?' — played by, of course, Telly Savalas, whose *Kojak* TV series was very popular at the time."

Another scene called for Lex Luthor to eat Kleenex tissue, a bizarre vignette inspired by the odd behavior of a literary agent representing David and Leslie Newman — the husband-and-wife scriptwriting team who had redrafted the Puzo screenplay. While this lighthearted tone may have been entirely in keeping with the conventions of the comic book genre, Donner instinctually understood that such a pandemic of parody and sardonic wit could quickly kill a motion picture. "You don't jack with the American Indian or Superman," he said after the film's release, "because that's our fable. In a funny sort of way, it's our history. My obligation, or my *challenge*, was to deliver Superman as honestly as possible."

As a youth, Donner had reveled in the comic adventures of the popular American icon, and now, as he had then, he still believed in the purity of the myth. As a self-styled symbol of clarity and hope, as a beacon for truth and justice, Superman's untainted values delivered the most romantic, most flattering answer to the question: *What does it mean to be an American?*

"These people were filmmakers from Europe and their approach, by my standards, was all wrong," he remembers. "Superman was something I remember as a kid, like white bread and butter, apple pie, and Mom's home cooking. This was Americana... and I was trying to defend it."

Producer Ilya Salkind disputes Donner's claim. He insists, "The camp element that everybody said we wanted to do was absolutely not intended. I know full well that the three or four camp scenes written by the Newmans would have been in the movie over my dead body."

Following a series of meetings, a reluctant Alexander Salkind acquiesced over the director's demand for an entire script rewrite, and Donner's long-time friend Tom Mankiewicz was brought onboard to attack the task. Known as "Mank," the screenwriter was charged by Donner to eliminate anything overtly camp or ironic, and to ensure that the focus of the two-movie script became the love story of Superman and Lois Lane. Episode one would begin on the doomed planet Krypton, the scientist Jor-El sending his infant son to Earth, where he is adopted by Jonathan and Martha Kent and raised as their own son, Clark. At eighteen years of age, Clark is summoned to his crashed spacecraft by a green crystal hidden within the wreckage, and heads north to the Arctic, where the crystal creates a giant home made from ice: the Fortress of Solitude. Here, the ghostly image of Jor-El appears. Tutored by his father on his alien heritage, and instructed in his super powers and earthly responsibilities, Clark emerges as Superman, flying to Metropolis and — as Clark Kent — embarking on a career as a newspaper reporter for the Daily Planet. Clark falls in love with Lois Lane. She, meanwhile, falls in love with Superman after he rescues her from a dramatic helicopter crash.

All the while, criminal mastermind Lex Luthor is plotting from his subterranean lair to hijack two nuclear missiles in an elaborate attempt to commit the crime of the century. When one of the missiles directly impacts the San Andreas Fault, Superman miraculously seals it, before dealing with the aftershocks of the resulting earthquake. After rescuing Daily Planet photographer Jimmy Olsen at the Hoover Dam, Superman is preoccupied by preventing California from being buried beneath the sea. Once it is saved, he remembers Lois, who is being sucked into the ground. Superman rushes vainly to her rescue. Unable to come to terms with her death, and struggling to cope with his own inability to save her (despite his extraordinary powers), he flies around the Earth's orbit at phenomenal speed, spinning the planet back on its axis, and turning back time so that he can save the woman he loves. Once accomplished, Superman returns to take Lex Luthor to prison.

In addition to eliminating the majority of its clichés, and fleshing out the characters in more vibrant detail, Mankiewicz accentuated the Christian metaphors inherent within the Superman story. Marlon Brando's Jor-El was written as God who expels General Zod (Satan) from Krypton (Heaven) during the film's opening sequence. Sending away baby Kal-El (Jesus) in his spaceship, the character says, "The son becomes the father, and the father the son." Later, when he speaks to his son in the Fortress of Solitude, Jor-El continues, "They can be a good people, Kal-El. They wish to be. They only lack the light to show the way. For this reason above all, their capacity for good, I have sent them you, my only son." It was as close a metaphor of God sending Christ to Earth as Donner and Mankiewicz could possibly get away with. The writer told *Time* magazine during production that, "Whatever Jimmy Carter is asking us to be, Superman is already. What we are really giving people is the Christian message: that we should all be honest, love each other and be for the underdog." The inclusion of biblical scripture in *The Omen* had served as a legitimizing force that — in the minds of audiences — had helped to counter some of the film's more unpalatable plot points. Donner was an avowed atheist, but understood how drawing upon religious inferences for *Superman* would assist in tempering the wildly fantastic subject matter, and would help lend a certain resonance to the story that might have otherwise been lacking. For his trouble, he would receive death threats that would be investigated by both the FBI and the U.K.'s Scotland Yard.

If *Superman* was Donner's opportunity to deliver an epic, then he wanted to surround himself with young and highly motivated personnel who would challenge him to push boundaries and stretch limits. Stuart Baird, his editor from *The Omen*, was immediately rehired. *Star Wars'* John Barry was contracted as *Superman's* new production designer. Cinematographer Geoffrey Unsworth was also signed, and brought with him his dynamic operator, Peter MacDonald, to lens the project. With Jerry Goldsmith unavailable, Donner would turn to another ex-television doyen, John Williams, to compose the film's musical soundtrack. Although the blockbuster phenomenon was still at an embryonic stage, Williams' record of delivering timeless anthems for event movies was already proven. With *Jaws* and *Star Wars* behind him, his iconic score for *Superman* would be his most expansive — bold, brassy action underwritten by tender, more traditionally romantic arrangements. The hero's motif that powered its stunning main theme would immediately ingrain itself into American popular culture.

Yet of all the factors crucial to Donner's official participation, and to the ultimate success of *Superman*, perhaps none was more pressing than achieving realistic screen flight for the very first time. To this end, the bullish director sought assurance from the Salkinds that, despite his own personal lack of development time, all necessary investment would be given to develop the required visual effects needed in order to convince an audience that a man could fly. A verbal agreement was struck, and Donner signed a contract with the producers, in Paris, in January 1977.

"*Superman* was a sort of maniac project," John Calley remembers. "It was this enormous [leap] toward the unknown… Everybody was optimistic, but terrified. It was one of those things that could have gone utterly wrong in so many different places at so many different points in production. It was a scary, scary project."

With eleven weeks until the commencement of filming, Mankiewicz raced against the clock to redraft the screenplay, as John Barry rushed to design and build sets that insiders were dubbing "Chez Brando." Donner worked closely with casting director Lynn Stalmaster in an effort to find suitable actors for the roles of Superman and Lois Lane. With time fast running out they seemed to have exhausted every possible option for the Man of Steel, until Stalmaster persuaded Donner to screen test the little-known but talented Christopher Reeve, a young actor who had impressed during an audition at the Sherry-Netherland Hotel on New York's Fifth Avenue, but who had been rejected on the grounds that he lacked the physical presence of a superhero. (Reeve stood at over 6'4" tall, but weighed a slender 190 pounds.)

Dressed in a makeshift costume with his hair blackened with shoe polish, his earnest sincerity and chiseled good looks impressed all assembled. Donner ordered Reeve to embark on an intensive bodybuilding regime, overseen by fitness instructor and actor David Prowse (Darth Vader in *Star Wars*), a schedule that included weight training, trampoline work and jogging, powered by a high-protein diet. By the end of production he would add more than thirty pounds of pure muscle to his physique.

Reeve was required to assist in the protracted search for a leading lady. He rehearsed scenes and screen tested alongside Stockard Channing, Anne Archer, Lesley Ann Warren, Holly Palance and Margot Kidder. It was during this process that Donner's vivacious enthusiasm proved a little overbearing for some of the more traditionally reserved British crewmembers. "He was obviously very loud," remembers Peter MacDonald. "In fact, I remember, when we did the tests, we had a different assistant director on it and he did say to him, 'Are you going to be this loud the whole time?' And Dick replied, 'Yes.' He said, 'Well, I don't think I'm interested in doing the film.'"

Due to the impending commencement of principal photography, screen testing for the part of Lois Lane would continue well into the start of shooting.

Before filming began Donner had telephoned Francis Ford Coppola for insight into Marlon Brando's personality, to which the director seconded the assessment of Jay Kanter (then head of production at Twentieth Century-Fox), who had previously advised that the heavyweight star "didn't like to work." Despite the warning Donner was shocked when, during his first in-person meeting with the famed actor, Brando laid out his interpretation of his character, Jor-El. "You know, I was thinking that maybe in space we don't look like people," the star proclaimed. "Maybe we look like a green suitcase or a bagel. Maybe we don't even speak at all; we just make electronic sounds..." Those surrounding the pair nodded approvingly. Fortunately, Donner was able to dissuade Brando of his ideas before cameras rolled for the first time on both *Superman* and *Superman II* on March 24, 1977.

Once on set, Brando made a strong impression. The acting legend had organized cue cards to be placed around the set with his dialogue written boldly in marker pen. "We had huge eight-by-four cards with his lines hanging up all over the place, and we had TelePrompTers on the cameras," MacDonald describes. "If we were doing something over the shoulder [of another actor], we would get a piece of sticky paper and put it on somebody's forehead." Brando also confided to MacDonald his uneasy relationship with film producers. "I learnt many years ago that if a producer gets a finger up your ass," he told the chief cameraman, "then it's a hand, and then the next time you look round it's a whole arm." The actor then handed producer Ilya Salkind a piece of paper to read. "You might think that's my telephone number," he enthused deadpan, "but that's my overage."

Brando baffled English actress Sarah Douglas. His obsessive efforts to feel up his co-star by forcing his hand through the leg vents of her shiny black jumpsuit earned him the nickname "Marvin Rando."

Luckily, Donner's own forceful personality quickly earned Brando's respect, although that did not prevent the star from occasionally testing his authority. The director once revealed during a seminar for the American Film Institute that: "We had this one very tricky thing to do, and I was ready to go... the night before, Brando had asked me if he could see *The Omen*. So I sent a 16mm print and projector to his house. He hadn't said anything about it all day, and I was wondering if he didn't like it. Anyway, I walked over and said, 'Marlon, come on.' He said, 'Oh, am I glad you're here. I was just telling them [his entourage] about *The Omen*. What a great film. Sit down, sit down.' I said, 'No, we're ready to shoot.' He said, 'Sit down, it's very important. What a wonderful film. How did you get the baboons do that with the car?' I said, 'Well, I just stood on the hood of the car. We released the baboons. And I yelled, 'Action.' And that goes for you, too.' He fell on the floor, got up, and came in. He was just wonderful, but he baits you all the time. He tests you every second."

Brando certainly enjoyed baiting the new Man of Steel. The disappointed Christopher Reeve only had one opportunity to deliver a line in the presence of the star (all other scenes between the pair would be shot independently of each other and edited together). The new Superman approached his one line of dialogue — "Who am I?" — with fierce dedication, rehearsing relentlessly in a quiet corner of the set until he felt he had perfected its delivery. Ever mischievous, Donner advised Brando of the young actor's anxiety, prompting Brando to respond to Reeve's line with his own unscripted dialogue: "Are you going to say it like *that?*" An embarrassed Reeve turned bright crimson as the entire crew fell about laughing.

Brando was greatly liked on the *Superman* set, and his screen performance was powerful. Although suffering from the debilitating combination of flu and jet lag, and irritated by wearing a wig and heavy costume in the one-hundred-and-five-degree heat of the studio floor, his turn lent the film a legitimacy it yearned for (and desperately required) if it was to achieve the unerring level of verisimilitude demanded by its director. His authoritatively delivered monologues not only bore responsibility for explaining the film's mythical context, but also invited the audience to suspend disbelief and embrace the fantasy as a temporary reality — in much the same wholehearted manner as Alec Guinness had achieved in *Star Wars* and Ian McKellen would later emulate in the *X-Men* series and *Lord of the Rings* trilogy. Biographer Peter Manso observed that he "delivered the Polonius-like adages much the way a Shakespearean actor might soliloquize."

Alexander Salkind suffered from a long list of morbid fears. His phobias dictated that he could never be around cats, ride on elevators, or travel by airplane. In order to raise the necessary finance for his movies he would instead travel across Europe by train. In an age before cell phones, the appropriate form for contacting him was to consult a train timetable, and estimate the exact moment he would be at a public pay phone on a platform at a Zurich station. To some, Salkind's phobias, coupled with his elfin appearance, may have connoted an endearing eccentricity. To others, the fifty-five year-old may have seemed paranoid and ruthless, an international businessman whose reputation was clouded by persistent whispers of financial impropriety. "Salkind was under indictment by Interpol," the late Mankiewicz asserted, "but had paid the nation of Costa Rica to receive a diplomatic passport. He was the Cultural Attaché to Switzerland, [and was therefore] immune to arrest."

Says John Calley of the father-and-son producing team, "From the very, very beginning they were the most difficult people [to work with]… Very mysterious, they'd reach in their pocket and take out five passports. It was like a Hungarian joke." (Widely believed to be Hungarian, Salkind was actually Polish.)

David Petrou, the author of the bestselling *The Making of Superman: The Movie*, and a close friend of Ilya's, remembers Alexander Salkind more affectionately. "I don't think [he] was five feet tall, but when he stood on his intellect and his ability to raise money, he was a towering figure."

Donner respected Salkind's virtually unrivaled ability to raise funds, extracting as he had millions of dollars in investment money from multinational sources (investors who Ilya Salkind humorously dubbed the "little gnomes in Geneva"). Yet his relationship with his new employer was one defined by a mutual, suspicious caution.

During production, an uneasy Donner would accept from Salkind a dinner invitation to an expensive London restaurant. The meal was a cordial experience, until the serving of dessert, when Salkind revealed his motive. "Mr. Donner, why do you have a lawyer?" he inquired. "You don't need one. Right now, you've got to trust me."

"Well," Donner replied. "I have to have a lawyer. Quite honestly, Mr. Salkind, I don't trust you guys."

The producer smiled, and politely excused himself from the table. The forthright Donner patiently waited for his return, until it dawned upon him that Salkind had left the building. He alone was left to settle the sizeable dinner check.

The Dorothy Chandler Pavilion in Los Angeles played host to the 1977 Oscar ceremony. Richard Pryor, Jane Fonda, Ellen Burstyn and Warren Beatty presented the event. Competition for the Academy Award for Best Picture was strong, with no clear favorite to choose from between *All the President's Men*, *Bound for Glory*, *Network*, *Rocky* and *Taxi Driver*. *The Omen* had grossed more than the combined total of three of the five nominees — not to mention having tweaked a not insignificant social nerve — but it was overlooked almost entirely. In 1973, *The Exorcist* had been nominated for both Best Picture and Best Director, but Donner's anomalous smash failed to make the shortlist for either statuette. Jerry Goldsmith, whose enchanting score was recognized for Best Music, received the film's sole Oscar. The composer had previously been nominated on an incredible sixteen occasions, although this was his first (and only) win.

The moment barely registered with the grossly preoccupied Donner, who was desperately trying to ensure that all of Marlon Brando's scenes were recorded in the limited time available. "Marlon, you've been just wonderful," offered a warm and appreciative Donner at the end of the actor's fortnight stint on the movie.

"Are you kidding?" Brando laughed. "At these prices I should be enchanting." The world's most famous film star then turned to Mankiewicz. "You know something?" he winked. "This film is a fucking valentine." Brando's good mood and enthusiasm was greatly appreciated. Mankiewicz had been warned before shooting began that the actor would be either "at your feet or at your balls." Mercifully, it had proved to be the former.

To celebrate Brando's time with them in London, a dinner was arranged at the Hungry Horse restaurant on Kings Road, a private meal intended to be devoid of unwanted fuss or attention. Yet Alexander Salkind, his spouse Berta Dominguez, and their son Ilya were in combative moods. To make matters worse, Berta — already deemed by Donner to be "nuttier than a fruit-cake" — was intoxicated. An intensely proud Mexican woman, and highly religious, the producer's wife had astounded crewmembers with her assertion that Ilya was "conceived of an immaculate birth," and she "could prove it." Berta slid into the booth between Brando and Mankiewicz. The uncomfortable scribe was still in the process of adapting Puzo's script, and each day Berta had returned his pages with her own suggested rewrites of his work. Fueled by alcohol, she quizzed the screenwriter over her suggested additions.

"Mr. Mankiewicz, I send you rewrites every day — what are you doing about it?"

"Mrs. Salkind, I really have to apologize," he replied. "I'm so snowed under at the moment, but I will certainly get to them."

Unimpressed with his response, Berta proceeded to announce the scriptwriter's salary to the table, compounding the degradation by ordering Mankiewicz to "get down on his hands and knees and thank her husband for hiring him." The embarrassed writer retorted venomously, "Mrs. Salkind, I'm always on my hands and knees when I'm talking to your husband as it's the only way I can look into his eyes." (Alexander Salkind stood, at best, at five feet in height.) Enraged, Berta grabbed for a steak knife, and attempted to bury it in Mankiewicz's chest. Fortunately, the quick-thinking Brando intercepted and forced her hand down on the table. "Will you behave?" he asked sternly before letting go. Berta nodded shamefacedly, only to lunge aggressively toward the heart of a shocked Mankiewicz for a second time. An uncompromising Brando was this time forced to wrestle the irate producer's wife out of the booth.

The hostility was too much for David Petrou, who was also an assistant producer for literary development for the Salkinds. "It got to be really ugly," he remembers. "… It got very nasty, with a lot of foul language." At past one in the morning he took to the street in search of a cab home, when he suddenly felt an arm on his shoulder. He turned around, and discovered a sympathetic Brando. "David, look, I'm sorry for all of that. You know people have a little too much to drink [and] they get out of hand. Please, why don't you come back in and join us?"

"Well, Mr. Brando, I've got a lot of work to catch up on, I have to be up early tomorrow."

"First up, cut the Mr. Brando shit. Just call me Marlon."

"I can't call you Marlon!" he protested. "Because to me you're Stanley Kowalski, you're Don Corleone, you're Julius Caesar…"

"C'mon," comforted the down-to-earth Brando. "Do me a favor. Take my car."

Petrou was driven home in the luxury of a chauffeur-driven Austin Princess. He never forgot the kindness.

With Brando's filming obligations fulfilled, the production went on a brief three-week hiatus, while Mankiewicz continued to rewrite the script, and Donner scouted locations in the U.S. and Canada. Upon return to the studio in England, a contrite Alexander Salkind approached the still-fuming screenwriter. "I am so sorry about my wife, Mr. Mankiewicz," he offered humbly. "Berta really shouldn't drink."

"Alex," was the reply, "if I ever see her again, if she's ever on the set, if she's ever in a room where I am, I'm going to leave the picture." The producer nodded solemnly in agreement.

When Donner and Mankiewicz were summoned to a meeting at the Salkind residence in London a fortnight later, Berta was notable by her absence. Or so the duo thought. During the course of the discussions, Donner excused himself to search for the nearest bathroom, which was located at the top of the stairs. Walking toward it, he heard a noise coming from one of the bedrooms. "Pssst," whispered Berta, peering nervously around the door. "Mr. Donner, please come over here. You know that I'm so sorry about Mr. Mankiewicz. He is such a wonderful writer, I'm so sorry I did that."

"That's okay, Berta."

"I'm just trying to help. Did you know that many people call me the 'Shakespeare of Mexico'?"

A stunned Donner returned downstairs to dryly inform his friend of the literary talent inhabiting the upstairs of the building. Mankiewicz shook his head, clearly unimpressed. "We're in a fucking nuthouse here," he proffered. "This is an insane asylum."

Mankiewicz enjoyed partying in London, a city he believed to be "the cultural center of the world." Donner was, by now, less enticed by the lustful nightlife. He occasionally frequented Tramps nightclub, but would rather spend the sparse amount of free time that he had relaxing at his house on Flood Street, where his next-door neighbor was Margaret Thatcher, the future Prime Minister of Great Britain. He installed venetian blinds on the ground floor of the building so that he could smoke grass undisturbed, away from the watchful eye of the local "Bobbies" who patrolled the street. Another pastime was restoring his vintage Rolls-Royce.

Almost a decade after they had first romanced in France, Donner was once more in a relationship with Liv Ullmann, who was preparing to tour North America in a theatre production of *Anna Christie*. For the after-show party in Toronto, she would have T-shirts that read "ANNA CHRISTIE" printed up as gifts for the entire cast and crew. She would invite Donner and give him a T-shirt, insisting that he had to wear it. She recalls, "After the premiere and [after] I'd taken off the makeup and everything... I came in and the whole restaurant had T-shirts that said 'THE OMEN.'"

Further tensions between Donner and his producers were quick to surface. Appalled at Guy Hamilton's original preparation work, Donner braced himself for the many months of innovation and experimentation required to achieve realistic screen flight. While the director readied for a tremendously exciting challenge, it did not appear that his financiers shared his daunting enthusiasm. Following Brando's departure, the main film unit had shot little more than tests and pick-up shots, progress that irked Alexander Salkind. Despite being promised that all necessary investment would be given to help develop heroic special effects, Donner found himself under intense pressure from his employers to deliver a final product as efficiently as possible — this in spite of the technical difficulties associated with creating a picture based around a man who flies. "Dick had this huge franchise picture on his hands, and he was going to go for broke on it," recalls editor Stuart Baird. "The Salkinds wanted to make it as cheaply as possible. Quality wasn't strictly their interest... When we started out, they were telling Dick, 'Do the best possible film' and all this stuff, then they start him before he's ready [filming with Brando] on the understanding [that] he's going to stop and start again. That [preparation time] was taken away from him. Then he's got a picture to shoot without knowing how the most difficult and the most significant parts are to be shot."

During production Donner recalled to *American Cinematographer* the technical difficulties: "*Star Wars* and *Close Encounters* enjoyed a tremendous advantage over our *Superman* project... When these spaceships came into the picture, they came in with a great deal of noise and light and, being inanimate, they could be computerized for multiple exposures on the film... In *Superman* we were dealing with a man who is flying. You could never repeat his movements precisely — even with the best computer in the world — because he's a human being. If a finger moved in the wrong direction or his cape fluttered slightly differently, you could never reproduce that exactly... [And] Superman does not make any noise or emit any light when he flies. This meant that there was a danger that his flying could seem uninteresting — especially if we simply had him going left-to-right, right-to-left, up or down."

Unkind whispers circulated among crewmembers intimating that instead of soaring the skies, Superman would in fact be patrolling the streets of

Metropolis on foot. Donner felt that he had been hired under false prospectus, and was aggrieved that the development time he felt he had been assured of, before he signed his contract, was not being honored. Determined to protect both the project and his fledgling movie career, he continually rejected the offerings of his special effects department that did not meet his standard for the Man of Steel. When pressured, Donner vented his frustration upon the producer, Pierre Spengler. The director told *Cinefantastique*: "Spengler was the liaison to Alexander Salkind, and he supposedly had this knowledge of production — but my God, I've been in this business long enough to know what a producer is, and it was ridiculous for him to have taken this job. As far as I was concerned, he didn't have any knowledge at all about producing a film like that. If he'd been smart, he'd have just laid back and let us do it; but instead he tried to impose himself. So, not only did we end up producing it, in a sense, but we also had to counter-produce what he was doing. It was *very* difficult."

Donner held Alexander Salkind culpable of parsimoniously stalling at the cost of developing believable flying effects, but he recognized that, as owner of the cinematic rights and instigator of the franchise, both he and his son Ilya were irremovable players from proceedings. He believed that Spengler — a man whose contribution he did not respect and who had committed the ultimate mistake of trying to tell him what to do — might be a different matter. Given the opportunity, he attacked and undermined the man whom he blamed most for his personal agony. Yet, in the eyes of Peter MacDonald, Donner may have been too confrontational. As he puts it, "I got the feeling it was more [that] Pierre was the front man sent out to do the dirty work. They [Alexander and Ilya Salkind] would plot in the back room what they wanted to do and Pierre would be sent out to do the dirty. And like anything, when you're the bringer of a message, you're the one that normally kops an earful. It was probably easier to blame Pierre for everything, which I think we all did at the time, when the actual culprits where the two Salkinds... The son didn't seem like a bad person, a bit of a playboy who got on quite well with Dick early on. I think it was more the father's influence. He just seemed to be one of those guys who had no humor or heart."

As flying tests continued, Donner and Mankiewicz were summoned to Zurich by Alexander Salkind to discuss a detailed agenda that included the impending U.K. arrival of Gene Hackman and the casting of Eve Teschmacher (Lex Luthor's glamorous sidekick). It was one of many occasions that Donner's presence had been requested, and it was becoming tiresome, especially with so much still to be achieved in London. The most likely reason for the director's compliance was his desire to persuade his producers to offer the role of Miss Teschmacher's to his preferred actress of choice. Donner had at first been keen on Goldie Hawn, but had realized that, at a cost of

$2 million, her services would prove too expensive. Now he intended that Ann-Margret be awarded the part. She would cost half the amount Hawn demanded — $1 million for two pictures.

After an unexpectedly cordial meeting at the hotel that doubled as the producer's European headquarters, Salkind confirmed his agreement over Donner's casting choice. Excited anticipation reigned as Spengler — operating from a phone booth in the hotel lobby — set to work negotiating a deal with Ann-Margret's representatives.

"We have just signed Ann-Margret for the role of Miss Teschmacher," he flatly delivered upon his return.

"Oh, God bless you, Alex!" Donner cheered. "This is so wonderful."

"You see, Mr. Donner and Mr. Mankiewicz," Salkind replied, "the money that you are costing me? But it's for the picture!"

"This is great, Alex," Mank offered, unable to control his delight.

Spengler left to conclude business, while Salkind, Donner, and Mankiewicz drank in the hotel bar. Spengler returned twenty minutes later.

"We have just signed Valerie Perrine for the role of Miss Teschmacher," the producer confirmed without shifting beat.

"What?" Donner replied.

"Valerie Perrine is cheaper, and she's very good."

"But, Alex, you just signed Ann-Margret twenty minutes ago," Mankiewicz interceded. "What are you going to do about that?"

"She can sue," was the peremptory response.

Soon after, Alexander Salkind again summoned Donner from London to Zurich. This time, Donner refused to attend, but asked Mankiewicz to go in his place. The screenwriter reluctantly obliged, if only to assist his exhausted friend. He remembered, "I had it in my contract — because I prefer not to write at the studio if I can help it — that I have a hotel suite wherever I go... So I check-in to Zurich and [I find] I have a single room. Now that didn't bother me, I was only spending the night, and it was a beautiful hotel, but I was warned [that] if you don't make the Salkinds live up to everything in your contract they'll start to take a mile and give you an inch. Now I'm thinking about that and the phone rings, and it's Alex Salkind. He says, 'Mr. Mankiewicz! Look at what your friend Mr. Donner has done to us! Here I am in my single room, calling you in your single room.' I go down the main staircase of the hotel, and I hear Alex Salkind yelling from down the hall. He was with his investors, and he had a huge suite. So later on in the bar I said, 'Alex, it's a little thing, and I really don't mind, but I have to ask you. When you called me and said, 'Here I am in my single room, calling you in your single room,' — you were in Suite 271 through Suite 278. It's such a little lie, a stupid lie, why do you do it?' 'I can't help it,' he replied."

Margot Kidder, a twenty-eight-year-old Canadian actress with a reputation for her earthy temperament and sexual aggressiveness, had beaten Lesley Ann Warren to the role of Lois Lane. Kidder had been an integral part of the Malibu scene during the early part of the decade, hosting free-spirited beach parties at the property she shared with Jennifer Salt, where she had introduced the likes of Martin Scorsese, Brian De Palma, and Steven Spielberg to one another — each a hungry young filmmaker with a point to prove and a reputation to make. She had since moved to Montana, where she had been married to writer Thomas McGuane, with whom she had a daughter, Maggie. Perhaps because of her recent divorce and her subsequent emotional state, when she arrived in London she exuded the exact delicate mixture of vitality and vulnerability that Donner was looking for in the part.

With his two leads in place, and in his own indomitable, uniquely playful style, Donner used humor in order to help the pair relax and to try and help them escape the burden of the multimillion-dollar franchise and forty-year legend resting on their young shoulders. Throughout filming Reeve would constantly be summoned by the command, "Hey, you in tights!" while Kidder would be brought to attention by the bellowing of "Divorce!" The actress recalls, "He took great delight in humoring me every day, and always made me laugh. I was really screwed up about going through my first divorce, a pretty life-shattering event, and he used that humor to tease me out of what could have been a disastrously morbid state… The key to good acting is being relaxed, and humor is possibly the most relaxing tool we've got as a species, and so I think there was a great deal of method to his madness."

Reeve was wholesomely clean-cut, and work-oriented — a former student of both Cornell University and the Julliard School of Performing Arts — the consummate professional. He was extremely bright, a concert-level pianist, flew his own plane. Yet, despite his good looks and vast array of talents, he could be a distant person, at times hard to engage. Kidder was more relaxed and seemingly self-assured. She was bold and irreverent, persistently unorganized, insisted on calling Donner "Harry" rather than "Dick."

Reeve and Kidder seemed the unlikeliest of matches. Both actors required vastly different types of personal direction. Says Kidder, "Chris at first decided to direct everyone, and Donner could have put him in his place, but he didn't. He saw that what was important was encouraging him. I was going through a divorce and was an emotional mess, and he saw that what was important with me was to get me through that and get out of me my humor unimpeded by my bouts of grief… I didn't often do the same thing twice, which Christopher found enormously frustrating. He'd whack his hand down on the table and go, 'I can't work with her!' And I'd go, 'Oh for fuck's sake don't you try and direct me, Chris Reeve!' Somehow Harry [Donner] accommodated to Chris' wishes and then to mine. Mine was a much more freewheeling [approach], [an] almost improvisational way of working, in the sense of going with what happened. And Chris' was very anal and he wanted to know where every pencil on the desk was before he did a scene. So we were at loggerheads a lot, Chris and I, we were like a bickering brother and sister... and he [Donner] would somehow make both of us feel like we were in the right."

According to camera operator Peter MacDonald, Donner couldn't always afford to play the understanding, encouraging surrogate parent. Says he, "Chris Reeve had to be — to start with at least — mothered along, because it was a huge responsibility to take on that part. He became stronger and stronger, but Chris was quite a quiet young man, and so Dick had [to employ] a mixture of coaching him, bullying him, [and] sometimes getting a little angry with him, as he did with Margot, if they weren't concentrating. With Margot, who is a lovely lady but sometimes a little off-the-wall, he got quite strong with her sometimes if she didn't concentrate."

The production moved from Shepperton Studios to Pinewood Studios, where construction work was underway on the interior set of the Daily Planet. The move allowed Donner to shoot many scenes that did not require complex special effect work, and gave the flying unit more time to hone various techniques. Nonetheless, the Daily Planet scenes from both *Superman* and *Superman II* would total an almost impossible number of shots for five weeks of scheduled filming. Most would feature the majority of the principal cast and dozens of extras each day, and one major sequence in particular would require the near-destruction of the newspaper office set.

Donner continued shooting in his normal style, insisting that plenty of time be devoted to improvisation with his cast, inviting suggestions and ideas from those around him — a non-mercenary approach that likely irked Alexander and Ilya Salkind. After many weeks of seemingly slow progress, the simmering tension between producers and director finally reached breaking point.

David Petrou observed in his bestselling book *The Making of Superman: The Movie*: "Ilya and Pierre claimed that Dick's slow, methodical pace — taking each shot from just about every possible angle — would bankrupt the production. Donner, on the other hand, accused the producers of trying to make major cutbacks that would threaten the success of the entire project... Loud shouting matches took place in Pierre's office between the producers and the director; Ilya and Pierre stopped visiting the sets; and finally Pierre refused to appear at all with Donner."

(More than thirty years later, Petrou remembers, "Dick didn't want each shot taken ten times. Not by any means. But he wanted them done right. If we looked at the dailies, at the rushes, and things were not to his liking, we'd do them over again. And I think the end product speaks for itself.")

"It wasn't a happy relationship between director and producers," MacDonald confirms. "Almost as a whole, you never felt that the production team really cared about the film, and were certainly, I felt, not supportive of Dick and how difficult the film was."

As Tom Mankiewicz put it, "Throughout the film they never gave [him] a budget. They never gave him a schedule... They kept screaming [to their investors], 'He's over budget! He's over budget!' And Dick kept saying, 'What is the fucking budget?' And then one day I remember Dick calling Alex Salkind... and [he] said, 'Alex, listen. Why don't you schedule the rest of the film for two days and I'll be seven months over?'"

Such was the level of acrimony and atmosphere of suspicion, Donner insisted to his crew that "they'd better be looking up. You never know when something heavy might fall."

Just days before the production mobilized to New York for all-important location filming, the deteriorating relations spiraled out of control. Alexander Salkind confronted his frustrated director during a conference with his multinational investors.

"Mr. Donner!" he demanded without preamble. "What is the basic problem with this picture?"

"The basic problem with this picture, Alex, is that you're an asshole!" the director retorted, apoplectically.

"No man has ever spoken to Alexander Salkind in that way," the shocked producer replied.

"I can't believe that, Alex," Donner countered provocatively. "Somebody must have called you an asshole before."

Some may have slinked away from such a decisive, seemingly finite confrontation, but political savvy was not in Donner's nature. He wore his heart on his sleeve, reasoning that if the immediate pleasure of letting loose with both barrels didn't always work to his advantage, it was at least to his credit, for he was staying true to the person he was — the willful, independent boy from New York who lived life his way and on his terms.

Infuriated by Donner's brazen affront, Ilya Salkind fired off a letter to the director's attorney, and began to explore the legal implications of replacing him with Richard Lester (undoubtedly in the hope that the fast working man behind *A Hard Day's Night* could shoot the remainder of the screenplay as efficiently as possible). When the news inevitably broke, disapproval spread quickly amongst cast and crew. "Dick called me into his office," MacDonald recalls. "It was the first time [that] I saw him looking really down and he said, 'I just want to warn you that I think I'm going to get the sack and Dick Lester's going to take over.' I said, 'I for one can assure you that if you were sacked the whole crew would go anyway. We came in with you and we'd leave with you.'" Special effects contributor John Richardson remembers, "I thought I had to go to Dick, which I did, and say, 'Listen, man, I'm with you. I'm your team. You go, I go.'"

Crucially, the embattled director also retained the support of Warner Bros., the primary distributor of the two movies for whom he had screened some early rushes. "We were thrilled," says John Calley of the footage. "What he was doing was amazing." Faced with a crew revolt and the potential for an expensive legal nightmare, Alexander Salkind acquiesced. Richard Lester was hired not as director, but brought onboard as an additional producer, whose primary responsibility would be to mediate between the feuding factions. Even so, the producers may likely have hoped that Lester's mere presence would be enough for Donner to storm off set in disgust. "[Dick] wasn't happy," says his cousin, Steve Kahan. "I know that he was really pissed off."

Ostracized from his employers, forced to suffer the humiliation of liaising with a peer (whom he ironically befriended for the remainder of the shoot), but still — for the time being at least — charged with delivering a picture that faced potentially insurmountable special effect difficulties, Donner's physical and mental health deteriorated. "I used to go into his office and he was so tired," says Margot Kidder. "He was worked to the bone and his back was in knots of tension. He was under a lot of pressure."

"I was really, really afraid for his health during the movie," Mankiewicz concurred. "He just worked non-stop… and that's why I thought out of sheer exhaustion one day it would get to him."

To make matters worse, Liv Ullmann had left Donner's house on Flood Street for New York, where she would perform on Broadway in *Anna Christie* from the beginning of April until the end of July. Her departure left him with nobody to confide in.

On numerous occasions, Donner did come dangerously close to the breaking point. *Superman* was by far the toughest fight of his professional life, one that ultimately required a combination of factors to rescue him from the brink.

Of all of them, perhaps none was more pressing than the commitment he had made to uphold the values and ideals of the Superman character, the primary reason for accepting the project in the first place. He had sworn an oath to himself to be the guardian of the Superman myth. He likely also drew strength from the memory of George Blake, his friend and mentor who had died so young, the man who had nurtured Donner's natural sense of optimism, and encouraged his belief that life was too precious and damningly short to dwell on its negatives. As such, even in the darkest moments of his production hell, Donner rallied to remind himself that he was living in one of the greatest cities in the world, overseeing a multimillion-dollar picture

featuring some of the most illustrious stars and creative talents in cinema —
an opportunity for which he had long yearned. For all the technical struggles,
political maneuvering, and the gross instability of his position, the moment
remained a gift. It had to.

In New York the temperature reached close to one hundred degrees. The
heat, coupled with a media circus and the general hustle and bustle of mill-
ing crowds and curious onlookers, made life uncomfortable and impeded
filming. Donner also had to make time for set visits by local dignitaries,
including Mario Puzo, New York Mayor Abe Beame, and the president of
DC Comics, Sol Harrison. Still, there were occasional moments of relief.
Donner had arrived via a brief stopover in California, and received something of a surprise in his hotel room. Lying in his bed was a fully inflated sex
doll dressed in a Superman costume. (John Richardson, in the city preparing
special effect shots, was the mischievous culprit.) Donner roared uncontrollably when he saw it, believing it so funny that he immediately snuck into
Geoffrey Unsworth's room to repeat the joke.

On the evening of July 13, filming was suspended due to a citywide power
blackout that plunged everyone and everything into total darkness. After an
uncomfortable night's sleep, the production awoke to news stories of riots
involving police and battling looters. In order to try and regain lost time,
Donner was forced to split his crew into two separate units so as to capture
all of the required footage.

In New York the production continued to accumulate a plethora of unpaid
bills. As his financial worries increased, Alexander Salkind stalled on money
owed to his creditors, delaying payments so that he could accrue some desperately needed bank interest. On more than one occasion, shooting suddenly
stopped. Then, on the very last day of filming, with rumors of a crisis envelop-
ing the production, Salkind — who would always wait until the last possible
moment to pay a bill — released a check to his creditors for $10 million. He
posed to David Petrou the question: "My dear boy, do you know what the
daily interest is on $10 million?"

"Frankly, Alex, I don't," was the reply.

"Well, better in my hands than theirs."

From the U.S. the production moved to Canada. Not required for this
leg of the shoot, Christopher Reeve traveled back to England to continue
working on the all-important flying tests. Just as in New York, the weather
in Calgary and Banff caused severe problems. Violent storms saw anticipated
filming stretch from days to weeks.

In an attempt to raise morale, a weekend party was arranged for cast and
crew on a hotel balcony in Banff. Television actor Larry Hagman, present
to film a minor role as an army colonel in charge of soldiers escorting an

atomic-tipped missile, provided the comic relief. Hagman filled plastic bags with powdered sugar, and taped them up so they appeared to be half-pound bags of cocaine. At the party, he waved them around in the air screaming, "Hey, everyone, look what I just got in the mail!" Donner was unaware of the prank, and more than a little uncomfortable when Hagman targeted him as the recipient of several bags of drugs. "Uh, no, no, no, thanks," he muttered, embarrassed, moving to escape. Hagman gave chase and dropped the bags, which flew over the parapet and exploded at the bottom, about 20 feet below. More than a hundred people looked on in shock at the ground blanketed by the mysterious white powder.

In preceding years, Hagman, an old friend of Donner's and a lead in *Sarah T. — Portrait of a Teenage Alcoholic*, had been desperate for roles. "Thank God for Dick," he confided to one production member, grateful for just two days' paid work. The person inquired as to what the actor planned to do next. "I'm going to do a pilot for some goddamn TV show," he responded, pessimistically. "It's called *Dallas*..."

As a member of the Commonwealth of Nations, Canada enabled the majority of the U.K. crew to travel across the Atlantic, unlike in the U.S., where for the most part local workers had to be utilized. Unfortunately, the mood of British crewmembers was not a good one. In Canada, it was flatly announced to the crew that they would only be paid half of their regular salary for location shooting (the remainder would be deferred until a later date).

Salkind was a brilliant financier and a shrewd businessman, but the sheer size of the production was crippling him. Upon return to the U.K. his son Ilya made the dramatic announcement that principal photography had wrapped. The production was placed on a financially-enforced hiatus, with the majority of main unit crew given their official notice. Not for the first time, *Superman: The Movie* and *Superman II* were in crisis, their successful completion hanging in the balance. Photo processing came to a standstill, and angry construction companies began repossessing essential equipment until outstanding bills were paid. Despondent, Donner and Mankiewicz returned to California. The Salkinds and Pierre Spengler conferred in Paris. During the chaos, the production's accounting department was held up at gunpoint. The robber left empty-handed. For all concerned, it seemed the money had simply run out.

Salvation appeared in the form of Charlie Greenlaw, a vice president of Warner Bros., who arrived in London for emergency talks and joined as yet another producer. In a short amount of time all parties agreed to cease shooting on *Superman II* — officially 75% complete — and to concentrate solely on the successful delivery of the original picture. Greenlaw promised the Salkinds a cash injection of $8 million — money primarily allocated for continuing effects tests and additional location shooting. In return, Donner's position was to be guaranteed. For their generosity, the studio would also require lucrative television and foreign distribution deals — a fact that did not sit well with the Zurich-based production team. Explains Petrou, "The Salkinds were independent producers, and they wanted to maintain control of the film."

Saddled with overwhelming debt, Alexander Salkind was effectively backed into a corner, and had little choice but to comply. As Warner's interest in the production grew, the producing team's share of any future profits diminished, and for that they blamed only one man. Deeply distrustful of their American director, they likely suspected him of being deliberately obstinate in his quest to perfect the film's flying effects, so as to purposely wrestle control of the picture away from them. Said Tom Mankiewicz, "When he [Donner] digs his heels in, he won't let go. With the Salkinds, for example, he made the film he wanted to make, goddamn it. Dick is very decisive that way, but the shoot took such a physical and mental toll on him that to even suggest that you wanted to string out the movie, you'd have to be a person with suicidal tendencies."

According to Stuart Baird, with the increased support of Warner Bros., Donner was able to weather the pressure applied by his producers, and to refocus his energy on the task at hand. Says he, "The Salkinds blamed Dick for spending too much money. They put him under horrendous pressure, but he has an amazing ability to let it roll across him. When you're the Guv'nor, you can't look as though you're being snowed by it. Dick Donner had this tiger by the tail, creating something for the Salkinds hugely better than they really ever thought they would get — and didn't really want."

As the production moved into 1978, nearly a full year since Brando had taken to the stage to officially launch the epic venture, a summer release looked impossible. Despite everyone's best efforts the production remained without a single effective flying shot. Indeed, the majority of special effects work remained untouched. After much industry and press speculation, the inevitable was confirmed, with Warner rebooking the picture for a Christmas release. In spite of the strained and uncertain nature of the shoot, Donner never lost his sense of humor.

One particularly rainy morning, Bob Harman, a crewmember tasked with developing flying effects, was walking down a country lane to Pinewood Studios. His car had broken down en route and he did not wish to be late for work. In the distance, he saw another vehicle approach. It was Donner in his Rolls-Royce. Harman stepped off the road onto a grass verge and hailed his boss for a ride. With a giant smile, the director sped up, deliberately driving his car into a puddle inches away from Harman, and doused him with muddy water. (After a hearty laugh, Donner did at least return to transport his rain-soaked colleague to the set.)

At the studio, the director taped an important notice to the door of the production office: "The management regrets it has come to their attention that employees dying on this production are failing to fall over. This practice must stop, as it becomes impossible to distinguish between death and natural movement of the unit. Any member found dead in an upright position will be dropped from the payroll immediately."

If ever there was a crewmember in danger of fulfilling Donner's prophecy, it was his editor, Stuart Baird, who was holed up in a cutting room, frantically attempting to keep pace with the relentless amount of footage that was still being shot. Although assisted by up to eighteen juniors, he was determined to cut everything himself, and to repay the faith Donner had shown in him since they had met on *The Omen*. Before the decision had been taken to cease shooting on *Superman II*, Baird had established two separate cutting rooms, between which he would run back and forth to edit the material. And as Donner became weighed down by the demands of filming, the editor's role became one of crucial importance. The cutting room was essentially transformed into the hub of the entire production.

The working relationship between the two men was a unique one, salted with mutual respect and close friendship, but peppered with occasional angry confrontation. Of the former, Baird remembers, "Dick doesn't like spending time in the cutting room. Some directors just love sitting in the cutting room from eight o'clock in the morning to eight o'clock at night, [but] Dick and I didn't work like that at all. He shot it and I cut it, [and then] we'd look at it in the theater. He gave me huge amounts of responsibility. The input I had very rapidly developed so that he was able to relax a bit because he trusted me."

Pouring through the infinite amount of footage often drove the passionate editor into frenzy. A pent-up ball of tension and stress, he was a heart attack waiting to happen. The brilliant but volatile editor worked himself into a stupor when Donner was late for their meetings. Instead of having something to eat or taking a nap, Baird would let his blood sugar level drop and his anger build. When Donner would eventually arrive, furious arguments would typically ensue, resulting in the director firing and rehiring his editor. To this day, industry fable dictates that, during one particularly fierce confrontation, Baird picked up a Moviola and threw it out of the cutting room window. (The editor denies the rumor, but admits that it makes a great story.)

Superman would require the best part of a year in order to complete the many special effects shots yet to be completed — the biggest single factor that was, quite literally, grounding the project. Donner drove his crew forward and kept energy and morale as high as possible. "He was everyone's buddy as such," describes Bob Harman. "He always had his arm round someone. He would say, 'This is what I want to see. How do you think we can achieve this?' He wouldn't take no for an answer, basically."

Birthdays were never forgotten, and in an attempt to keep the mood upbeat the filmmaker hosted numerous backyard barbeques — both at the studio and at his house on Flood Street — at which he provided fried chicken and homemade beer for his cast and crew.

The core unit of Donner, Mankiewicz, Reeve and Kidder grew particularly close, and during a brief production respite, vacationed in the south of France together. There was no real-life romance between Superman and Lois Lane. Reeve had met and fallen in love with the British model Gae Exton. Kidder remembers the crush she had on Donner. "He was vibrant, of course, and boisterous and open, and... appreciative of what I did and laughed like crazy. So, of course, I adored him, because he thought I was funny."

She continues, "I, like all actresses that work for him, fell a little bit in love with him, but he was very much attached to Liv Ullmann. What you had was this wonderful, visceral thrill going to the set every day because the divine Donner was there and you got to flirt at work. But you couldn't do more because you knew there was a girlfriend involved... As a man he's so charismatic that whether you call it falling in love, or getting a crush on, or whatever, even men are not impervious to that charm of his. So you just end up eating out of his hand... He's a very masculine character with a deeply soft side. He's just fucking irresistible."

Despite her mad crush on Donner, Kidder began dating Mankiewicz — a secret kept from the majority of those on set. One of the actress's fondest memories is of a surprise birthday party for her then-boyfriend. She had enlisted the staff at Pinewood to bake a giant birthday cake, arranged for it to be transported to Donner's house, and hired a stripper to burst out from inside it. Kidder remembers that the local Bobbies, whom Donner had befriended, "kept walking up and down outside, waiting for this babe to jump out of the cake." When she did, everyone cheered, especially the shocked Mankiewicz. All assembled spent the evening sipping margaritas and eating hot dogs — a little taste of home for the Americans abroad.

The long battle for visual authenticity on *Superman* was eventually won over the course of many months. The tenacity of Roy Field (head of the optical department), Denys Coop (creative director of process photography) and Wally Veevers (head of flying systems and process projection) paid dividends. Between them they mastered blue-screen technology, mobile front projection cameras and wirework to a level not previously achieved.

Credit is also due to Zoran Perisic, a former cameraman who had arrived in England from Yugoslavia in the sixties. Perisic had designed a revolutionary mobile front projection unit, but needed $25,000 to perfect the system. Donner, who felt it was imperative to making people believe that a man can fly, reflects today that, "the Salkinds refused to spend the money." Donner instead went to Charlie Greenlaw, who immediately approved the expenditure and ensured that the development moved forward.

Perisic had noted that with traditional optical work it was difficult to obtain an accurate depth of field, and he had been drawn to design a technique known as "Zoptic" to correct this. The elaborate system was a method of synchronizing zoom lenses in the projector and camera, a process that made Superman appear to fly toward or away from the camera without ever moving.

Although Donner's stubbornness and insistence on quality eventually paid off, he still faced a tense race to finish the film. With Warner Bros. sticking to a Christmas release, the director found himself frantically cutting negative, dubbing, and scoring, with only weeks to spare.

After more than three hundred and fifty official shooting days, an awesome 1,250,000 feet of film had been shot. As he sifted through the footage, Donner was hit by news of a tragedy. While shooting Roman Polanski's *Tess* on location in France, the immensely popular cinematographer, Geoffrey Unsworth, had collapsed and died from a heart attack. A widow, Maggie, and their three young children survived him.

The funeral was an emotional occasion. "Dick came to the funeral and was by the graveside, along with twenty or thirty close family and friends," remembers Peter MacDonald, who had worked in partnership with Unsworth for more than twenty years. "It was a bright but cloudy day, with a kind of soft light coming down. Dick put his arm around me and said, 'Look up. This is Geoffrey's type of day.' And I lost it totally."

Donner dedicated the first *Superman* movie to the memory of his trusted colleague and good friend.

Donner's completed vision of *Superman* is one of grandeur, a mythic ode to cinematic slight-of-hand that stands stoically as one of Hollywood's truest anthems for pure adventure, fun and romance. MacDonald recalls a crew screening in London: "There were two thousand people there: the crew and their families, and lots and lots of kids. When Superman flew, all the kids stood up and started screaming and shouting. And I knew then that Dick was right. I knew that he had his finger on the pulse of what the big audiences wanted. All the kids were screaming and shouting at Margot, 'Don't worry, he'll come soon!' Normally you go and see the crew showings and you all come out a bit depressed, but I came out feeling really good."

Donner had rightly anticipated America's appetite for a new tone and style of filmmaking, and offered its youth the magic and immutable truth that they so demanded. *Superman* was his tribute to a world of a bygone age, a time and place that ceased to exist, but a space that he instinctually knew audiences of the seventies yearned to revisit. From an archliberal came a film of some considerable conservatism, offering a product wholesomely uncomplicated and joyously fun. "He [Superman] is a lot of what America was a long time ago," explained Donner toward the end of shooting. "I'm a very liberal human being in my philosophies and my politics, and I find myself— in an odd sort of way — looking and respecting the conservative attitude of what Superman stands for now. And I see a lot of my philosophies now and I'm not very happy with them, and I almost wish I could go back to what once was and what America once was." *Superman* provided a vision of carefree optimism and hope, a temporary respite from troubles for both children and adults alike. With the affirmative philosophy so ingrained within his record-breaking space opera, George Lucas' *Star Wars* had convinced post-Watergate, post-Vietnam audiences that there was "a new hope." Perhaps more importantly than convincing people that a man can fly was Donner's ability to persuade skeptical audiences around the world to once again emotionally invest in truth, justice, and the American Way.

With the picture complete, Warner Bros. booked more than five hundred theaters in the U.S. for a nationwide release on December 15, 1978. They fueled the excitement with a $10 million advertising campaign. There was, however, to be high drama to the end. Having completed a cut of the picture, Donner and Baird traveled to the U.S. to hold preview screenings. Days passed, but the film never arrived. When contacted by Warner Bros. in regard to the final answer print, Alexander Salkind refused to release the negative to the studio. With exhibitors promising to sue if the film did not screen on schedule, it was the turn of Warner Bros. to be backed into a corner. Salkind demanded $15 million for the sale of marginal territories that would allow him to offset some of the colossal debt that he had acquired (ironically, the sale would in the end work out to the studio's fiscal advantage). It is alleged that for each day the studio refused to meet his new terms, he increased his demands by $1 million. That he could hold such a powerful conglomerate to ransom betrayed the bold confidence that had enabled him to finance the project in the first place and, in the end, Warner succumbed. After two rollercoaster years of epic highs and lows, *Superman: The Movie* was finally ready to fly.

New York filmmaker George Blake was a mentor and a best friend to Donner.
RICHARD DONNER

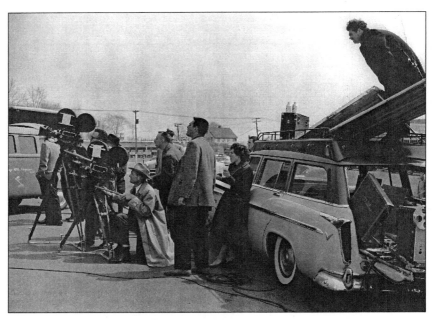

Donner directs commercials for George Blake Enterprises. RICHARD DONNER

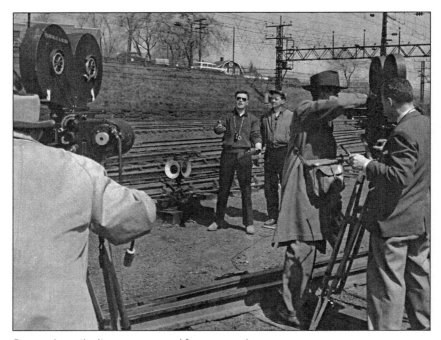

Donner happily discovers no need for a megaphone. RICHARD DONNER

For a commercial assignment, Donner chats with cartoonist and inventor Rube Goldberg (seated) and Broadway set designer William Riva (father of J. Michael Riva). RICHARD DONNER

Donner with Chick Green, a partner in his first production company, Signal Productions, Inc. RICHARD DONNER

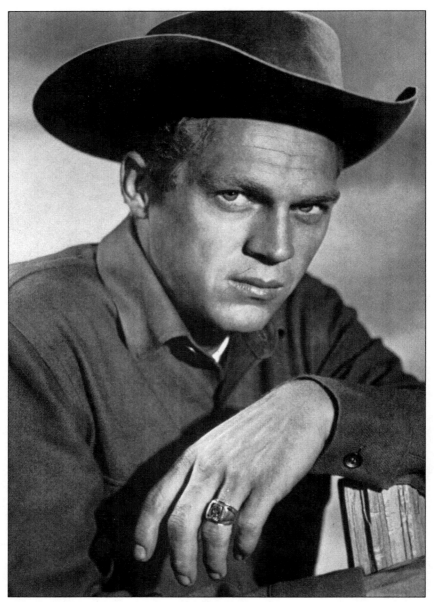

Steve McQueen as Josh Randall in Wanted: Dead or Alive. CBS/THE KOBAL
COLLECTION

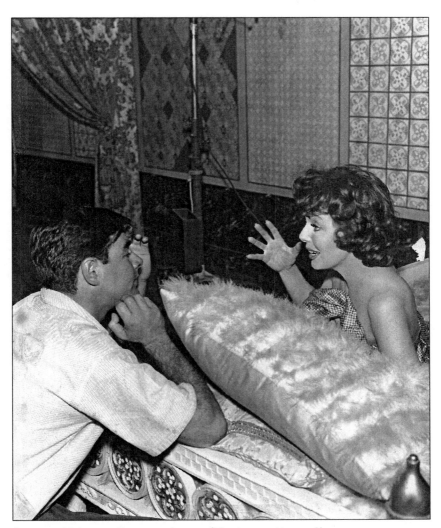

Donner with Loretta Young on the set of The Loretta Young Show. RICHARD DONNER

Donner credits his success to his parents, Hattie and Fred Schwartzberg. RICHARD
DONNER

David McLean as Matt Powell in X-15. UNITED ARTISTS/THE KOBAL COLLECTION

Donner duels Sammy Davis, Jr. on location with Salt and Pepper. RICHARD DONNER

Charles Bronson with Susan George in Twinky *(a.k.a.* Lola*).* WORLD FILMS/THE KOBAL
COLLECTION

Donner directs The Omen, *his breakthrough picture.* AUTHOR'S COLLECTION

Harvey Stephens as Damien, a child antichrist, in The Omen. 20TH CENTURY FOX/THE KOBAL COLLECTION

Christopher Reeve impressed Donner during a screen test for Superman. RICHARD DONNER

Donner dissuaded Marlon Brando from playing his character, Jor-El, as "a green suitcase." WWW.CAPEDWONDER.COM

Pierre Spengler vs. Dick Donner. Tom Mankiewicz observes. AUTHOR'S COLLECTION

Christopher Reeve strikes a pose for this promotional shot on Superman. DAVID PETROU

Donner reunites with his girlfriend, the Norwegian-born actress Liv Ullman, during the New York location shooting of Superman. DAVID PETROU

Donner relaxes with Gene Hackman on Superman. DAVID PETROU

Donner meets Queen Elizabeth II at the Royal Premiere of Superman *in London.*
RICHARD DONNER

John Savage, Diana Scarwid and Harold Sylvester like what they see on the basketball court in Inside Moves. AUTHOR'S COLLECTION

David Morse with John Savage in Inside Moves. AUTHOR'S COLLECTION

Richard Pryor as Jack Brown in The Toy. AUTHOR'S COLLECTION

Donner feels the strain during The Toy. RICHARD DONNER

Jackie Gleason as Ulysses Simpson Bates in **The Toy.** AUTHOR'S COLLECTION

Rutger Hauer with Michelle Pfeiffer in Ladyhawke. AUTHOR'S COLLECTION

Donner confers with Matthew Broderick during the filming of Ladyhawke.
AUTHOR'S COLLECTION

"It was an extraordinary gift for hope, a romantic readiness such as I have never found in any other person and which it is not likely I shall ever find again."

F. SCOTT FITZGERALD, *THE GREAT GATSBY*

7

American Dreamer

So tight was the race to finish that *Superman: The Movie* never enjoyed the luxury of advanced preview screenings. Fortunately, it did not need them. Cinematic history was rewritten as it amassed a record gross for a film premiering in the week before Christmas, and the highest attendance for a movie released during any holiday period. It flew high as the number one film at the U.S. box-office for thirteen weeks, and collected more than $300 million in worldwide ticket sales. It is possible that if it had achieved its original summer release date, traditionally the most profitable of seasons, *Superman* may have come close to challenging *Star Wars* for all-time box-office supremacy.

Such success did not yield a pot of gold for Donner or his producers. After paying both British and American taxes on his $1 million salary, the director would have earned substantially more had he simply remained in the U.S. helming movie-of-the-week TV specials. Donner was not alone in his fiscal misery. The Salkinds remained in perilous debt. "We owed money," Ilya recalls. "It was not a nice situation at all... We had creditors."

If the financial numbers at the box-office clicked, then so too did the review sheets, the vast majority of which were overwhelmingly positive. "Not since *Star Wars*, the all time champ, has there been such an entertaining movie for children of all ages," *Time* magazine decreed. "... [*Superman* is] pure fun, fancy and adventure." *Variety* concurred that *Superman* was "a wonderful, chuckling, preposterously exciting fantasy," while *Newsweek* raved that it "turns out to be surprisingly infectious entertainment, nicely balanced between warmth and wit, intimacy and impressive special effect, comic-strip fantasy and several elements that make the movie eminently eligible for Deep Thinking about rescue fantasies, cherubic messiahs and other pieces of popcorn metaphysics." It was superlative rhetoric for a superlative hit.

Any attempt to attribute singular artistic merit to such a multitudinous production as *Superman* is wracked with complexity. The film drew virtuoso efforts from luminaries such as John Barry, Stuart Baird, Geoffrey Unsworth and John Williams and, of course, Christopher Reeve. It was a triumph for the Salkinds, despite what Donner dubs "their interfering ways." But were it not for the idea of the son, or the financial determination of the father, there would have been no film for the director to make his own. Although make it his own he did.

"Dick and his whole concept of verisimilitude is largely responsible for the total success of the first film," says David Petrou, a member of the Salkinds' production team. "We had a story by Mario Puzo that was just ridiculous... it would have been about a four-hour movie. David and Leslie Newman were brought in, and they did a version that was like the *Batman* TV show. Dick brought in his friend, Tom Mankiewicz, the script doctor, and the script that you see on the screen is largely Dick and Tom's rewrites."

Indeed, it is Donner's personality, and his warm affection for his fictional all-American hero, which permeates the entire film. He had dearly loved Superman from his youth, when he frequently donned a makeshift cape and dreamt of taking flight. As chief creative force, Donner correctly handled *Superman*'s grandiose moments, and its more lighthearted and witty scenes, with equal straight-faced aplomb. From the very beginning he understood that his film would need to offer a pleasure to surpass those of the legendary Hollywood spectacles, and demanded that it would privilege audiences to witness that which had not come before. At the same time, his ideological approach necessitated that audiences not only be wowed by the complex, experimental and innovative visual effects, but that they should simultaneously *believe* that the fantastical events and situations could all be real. To achieve such verisimilitude, he skillfully teased a willingness to suspend disbelief by creating dynamic characters that explode into life, and by refusing to mock or parody his subject matter. "[He] was not afraid to wear his heart on his sleeve," waxes Margot Kidder, "and not embarrassed to believe in it."

If *The Omen* was his *Jaws*, a sleeper hit that hinted toward a strong thematic and stylistic integrity, then *Superman* was Donner's *E.T.*, an intensely personal film that resonated with millions. Stuart Baird concurs, "Dick was the perfect guy to make *Superman*. He respected it. He loved it. He wanted to convey all the feelings he had as a kid about it."

Superman was Donner's love letter to America, a celluloid ode to a young and brilliant nation's capacity to wonder. The picture's success left him feeling on top of the world, but his euphoria was tempered by developments in his personal life. He and Ullmann had separated — acrimoniously — after a heated row toward the end of shooting in London. Says she, "It was my fault. He showed me love and generosity in London as he always had done, and I kind of stood him up in a way [that] I shouldn't have. He became tremendously disappointed, and he lost his temper, and that was very frightening." Induced into a rage, Donner had violently torn down a poster image of Ullmann that decorated the wall of his U.K. home. He closed the door to his former lover, and it would be many years before the pair would eventually reconcile as friends.

Donner undoubtedly loved Ullmann more than he had any other woman, and theirs had certainly been the most serious of his many romantic relationships. After some previous false starts, their partnership had appeared to flourish — in spite of their struggle to reconcile two high-profile careers within the same household. In the words of close friend Alan Ladd, Jr., for much of his adult life Donner had been "very flighty. [With] one girl one day, one girl another night, that kind of thing." Ullmann had changed all of that, and there is evidence to suggest that the director may have finally been prepared to settle down and enter into a serious partnership. On this occasion, however, it was the actress who was perhaps less inclined to make a solid commitment. She continues, "What I do remember is that he was a very serious person once he felt that he was committed to something, and I felt that I was the one who wasn't."

Donner's memories of the relationship were warm. He remembered that he had once sent her a book with a pressed flower in it. On another occasion, while she was on a flight from Asia, he arranged for airline staff to celebrate her birthday each time they flew through a different time zone. But it was over now. The end of their romance confirmed his worst fears about long-term relationships. He would return to bachelordom with a vengeance, and, in his own mind at least, was unlikely to ever risk forming such an intimate connection again.

To recover from the physical and emotional strain that he had endured the previous two years, the director recuperated at his large, ranch-style house in Los Angeles. He was proudly renovating the property, adding to and expanding the already giant kitchen and living room areas, and building a guesthouse. Reflecting his personality, the house was one of impressive largesse and it offered an outdoor swimming pool with a stunning view of the city.

Dressed in beaten-up shorts and wearing a worn pair of flip flops, he spent most of his time either in his garden shed sipping from a six-pack of beer, or in his garage, tinkering with anything mechanical that he could lay his hands on. Copies of engineering magazines littered the floor of his house and all that remained of the milk in his refrigerator was penicillin. Given the choice, Donner would have preferred to sit down and watch a ballgame instead of the Oscars, although the 1979 Academy Awards provided him with plenty of food for thought. Christopher Reeve and Margot Kidder were present at the ceremony, which was once more held at the Dorothy Chandler Pavilion, but their involvement in the proceedings was limited to handing out awards instead of receiving them. As was appropriate for the Academy's treatment of special effect movies at the time, *Superman* won only one award — a Special Achievement Award for Visual Effects — which mirrored Kubrick's *2001: A Space Odyssey* and Lucas's *Star Wars* lone Oscar statuettes. It failed to convert its nominations for Best Editing, Best Original Score and Best Sound to Oscars.

George Lucas and Steven Spielberg had at least been nominated as Best Director, for *Star Wars* and *Close Encounters of the Third Kind* respectively, despite missing out on the final award, and given the rapturous reception for *Superman* Donner might have expected at least the same treatment as that bestowed upon Hollywood's wunderkinds. The back-to-back mega-hits *The Omen* and *Superman* should have ingrained Donner's name on the public consciousness. Yet while the director performed vigorously in his promotion of his new movie, he spent most of his interview time deflecting attention away from himself, and bestowing unfettered praise on his collaborators. Typical of his selfless approach, when the Academy Award nominations had been announced, he was most indignant of the treatment meted out to his British colleagues. In an outburst that may well have adversely affected his chances of ever receiving such an accolade, he told *Cinefantastique*: "I'm just totally disgusted, despondent, and have the greatest possible disrespect for the Academy of Motion Picture Arts and Sciences. Not for me. But how dare this select club of 3800 people look past Geoffrey Unsworth? If you look at the pictures that were nominated for best cinematography, it's a fucking sin that his name wasn't up there because his work far surpasses *anything* I've seen this year. How *dare* they treat him with such disdain and disrespect when that photography outclasses a hundred times over half the shit they have seen? What a genius of a motion picture cameraman he was; he was the master. And he didn't even get a goddamned nomination! I don't believe it. And art direction. They put up pictures like *California Suite* — duplications of the Beverly Hills Hotel. *Big deal!* Just *look* at what John Barry did for *Superman*! And he wasn't nominated either."

Relations had been cordial at the world premiere for President Carter in Washington, D.C., and at the Royal premiere for the Queen in London, but Donner found it difficult to dispose of his bitterness toward the producers of *Superman*. Haunted by nearly two years of violent clashes, and nervous to protect his newly established reputation, the aggrieved director aimed to disassociate himself from the chaos of *Superman*'s infamous budget and schedule by focusing firmly on Pierre Spengler. In one interview, Donner cited the Salkinds' "misplaced loyalty" to Spengler for "monies [that] were just flushed away — totally wasted," while in another he postured that, "If he's [Spengler] on it [*Superman II*] — I'm not." It was pure bravado, an emotional response toward the man whom he blamed more than any other for his personal agony.

Superman II was planned with Warner Bros. for a summer 1980 release. With no new financial incentive on offer, Donner's agent Steve Roth (operating at the freshly formed Creative Arts Agency under the auspices of Michael Ovitz) urged him not to return to England to complete the sequel. Yet *Superman* meant more to him than money. It was his passion. Says he, "I was determined to finish the job, for the reason that I wanted to protect what I had done."

If he was to achieve his cinematic vision as planned, Donner would need to recommence shooting by the end of February 1979, so as to avoid losing key personnel to other productions. Vindicated by the success of his first installment, he was aiming bigger and bolder for the sequel; a picture that he hoped would make the same kind of groundbreaking leaps forward in special effects technology. To do this, he intended two more months of principal photography followed by many months of second unit, flying unit and miniature unit work. In addition, he was also enthusiastic for further location shooting in the U.S., Canada and the U.K., and for Gene Hackman to return to film new scenes. The director was excited to revisit and reimagine what had been learnt during the course of the tumultuous first production, instead of relying purely on the existing footage shot during the difficult early months of 1977. Alexander Salkind was likely reluctant to meet such a commitment — even if he was prepared to tolerate the director once more. Wary that he might scare him away with his plans, Donner promised to walk away from the series once his opus was complete. Speaking to *Variety*, he bargained, "I'd love to see this thing go on and on, but I won't be a part of it past the second film. I can't think of a more appropriate story to spin future films off of, however." It was not enough. Via telegram, the Salkinds officially terminated his contract on March 15, 1979. Richard Lester was installed as his replacement.

Today, Ilya Salkind professes that Pierre Spengler attempted to reach Donner to resolve their personal disagreement. Says he, "Pierre did try and call him. He avoided the calls." Salkind contends that the director's refusal to talk, coupled with disparaging comments made through the press, is what ultimately necessitated the dismissal. Donner caustically rejects the assertion. "If Ilya Salkind says he wanted me to come back and do *Superman II*, it's bullshit. If anyone says they tried to get a hold of me, it's bullshit."

Donner's firing from *Superman II* is not likely due to the fact that he could not be reached by phone. The Salkinds had famously flown banners through the sky at the Cannes Film Festival to promote their message — if they really, truly, wanted to reach Donner, to make things work, they could have. Such was the resounding triumph that the filmmaker had presented to his producers that the built-in market for a sequel meant that it was already destined to be profitable — with or without his involvement — and, even if they had to reshoot certain scenes; Lester would likely be quicker and cheaper.

From the moment Donner had signed to direct *Superman* it had been more than a professional gig, rather a personal love affair, and his unceremonious divorcement from proceedings hurt deeply. "All I know is that Dick felt terribly, terribly let down," Stuart Baird recalls. "He thought that Warner Bros. were going to protect him, but they didn't." In point of fact, the studio was relatively powerless to prevent his firing, bound as it was by its original deal with the Salkinds. The late Tom Mankiewicz reflected that, "Warner was thrilled with the job Dick was doing and there was no question whose side they were on. The problem was that according to the deal they had made with the Salkinds, the producers had the right to make the picture [as they saw fit]. Their deal was with the Salkinds. Our deal was with the Salkinds. This wasn't a Warner Bros. picture, but a Warner Bros. release." Then-Warner vice chairman John Calley agrees, "Dick should have done the sequel. We would have been lucky to have him do it. It was heartbreaking, [but] the Salkinds were impossible… they got the rights and therefore had all the leverage, and they were very tough traders. They played hardball and essentially got what they wanted, when they wanted it."

In contrast, Ilya Salkind suggests the studio was content to relinquish the services of its director. Says he, "Warner knew that we [were the ones who hired] Brando and Hackman. We put the whole cake together… they felt very comfortable."

Donner initiated legal proceedings against his former employers, citing lost earnings from gross profits (Marlon Brando and Mario Puzo did the same), but he chose to conceal his innermost feelings over his firing, perhaps not wishing to draw too much industry attention to the debacle. He put on the best brave face he could muster, although those closest to him understood the pain he was going through. "It really broke his heart," Baird remembers. "You've never seen a man throw himself into his work like that, and [then] get screwed as badly as he did. Here's a man who worked around the clock, and that he didn't fall apart was nothing short of a miracle. And then they [the Salkinds] shafted him because of money."

As perhaps as unnaturally as an *E.T.* without a Spielberg, or a *Lord of the Rings* without a Peter Jackson, *Superman II* would be made — albeit completed by another.

Paramount's dynamic head of production, Bob Evans, had purchased the rights to Todd Walton's novel *Inside Moves* and commissioned the husband-and-wife writing team of Valerie Curtin and Barry Levinson to pen a screenplay. The physical disfigurement of the book's central protagonist, Roary, was softened, as were references to Vietnam, yet the adaptation remained largely faithful to the source material — despite added scenes not featured in the original novel, and the exorcising of others for reasons of narrative pace. One major departure from book to screen was the inclusion of a dramatic new opening sequence that detailed Roary's failed suicide attempt, the event that leaves him partially crippled.

Upon his release from hospital, Roary finds a new home in the form of Max's bar, a local hangout for a family of lovable misfits, the majority of whom are physically impaired. Chief among these is Jerry Maxwell, a charismatic bartender with a leg injury that prevents him from following his dream of becoming a professional basketball player. He is also involved in a damaging personal relationship with a drug-addicted hooker, Anne. Roary and Jerry quickly become close friends, forming a bond that helps each of them grow in self-esteem, and gives them the confidence to follow their dreams.

After a chance one-on-one game of basketball with local hero Alvin Martin, Jerry is offered the opportunity of an operation to cure his leg injury. Roary's dream is to feel like a "somebody," and with the help of his friends — Stinky, Wings, and Blue Lewis — he forms the resolve to buy a part ownership of Max's bar, and to woo the woman he loves, a waitress named Louise. With fears faced, personal demons exorcised, and collective spirits lifted, Max closes the bar for the first time in twenty-five years so that Roary, Louise and all of the friends can witness Jerry make his pro-basketball debut for the Golden State Warriors.

It was the agent Evarts Ziegler who sent the script to Donner. The filmmaker recalls: "I started to read and was hooked: This kid walks in and he goes out the window. And then he hits the Ford. Then he comes out of the hospital, and he goes into Max's bar — déjà vu. I realized it was *Inside Moves* but a whole different attack on it. And I couldn't put it down. I finished it, and I committed to Paramount that I would do the picture with them."

Donner was a natural born romantic, and to him *Inside Moves* was a positive, life-affirming piece. He recognized thematic qualities such as the triumph of the human spirit in the face of adversity, and the importance of love, friendship, tolerance and understanding. Roary was a metaphor for his own beloved post-Vietnam America: wounded and with low self-esteem, yet striving forward once more to love and to hope. Where *Rocky* had played to audiences' desperate desire to once more invest in the American Dream, *Inside Moves* could present itself as an extension of its Oscar-winning predecessor, offering the theater-going public the kind of heartwarming affirmation and celebration of human solidarity not seen since the Capra classic *It's A Wonderful Life* — itself an antidote to the horrors of war.

It quickly became clear, however, that Donner and Evans didn't see eye to eye over the material. The studio head deemed the subject matter too depressing, and wanted the screenplay extensively rewritten as a sports movie with basketball as its central theme. Forced into a creative impasse, Donner stalled until Evans eventually gave up on the project. When Paramount put the movie into turnaround, he purchased the rights to the novel himself.

Donner was courted by Bob Goodwin — who would later find success as an executive producer on *The X-Files* television series — and his Canadian business partner, Mark Tanz, both of whom were interested in producing a screenplay. The pair had no previous experience of filmmaking, although they were eager to learn. Crucially, they had money to invest, and were delighted to align themselves with one of the industry's most important directors. With their help, and by placing his own salary against the cost of the picture, Donner secured a $10 million budget. Goodmark Productions was formed and the three men took charge of a stylish two-story building off Sunset Boulevard to serve as their base. Donner's office was furnished with a giant wooden Howard pocket watch, a large bust of Abraham Lincoln, and a framed two-page handwritten letter from Todd Walton. There were posters for *X-15* and *Salt and Pepper*, some signed Ramon Santiago prints, and a giant Superman model hanging from above a window. On his desk sat his pride and joy: a Toshiba miniature component set he used for listening to *Supertramp* at high volume.

The director's immediate pre-production priority was to surround himself with an array of talented personnel — demonstrating once more his faith in filmmaking as a collaborative medium. The foremost of these bearers of prestige was László Kovács, the renowned cinematographer of *Easy Rider*. With Stuart Baird committed to cutting Ken Russell's *Altered States*, Donner turned to Frank Morriss to edit, while Charles Rosen was hired as production designer.

John Savage, a quiet but intense New Yorker who had shined opposite Robert De Niro and Christopher Walken in *The Deer Hunter*, was signed in the lead role of Roary. The actor was known to be a touch eccentric. "I don't know if [*Inside Moves*] was enjoyable for John Savage," quips actor Steve Kahan, who was cast as Burt, "because he's out there in the ozone.... He was very aloof, a weird guy."

The promising yet little-known character actor David Morse was cast as Jerry. "He was a very, very quiet guy," Kahn continues. "David didn't even talk on the sidelines, he just stood there. He was a very closed personality. He was like a deer in headlights; he really had a hard time communicating. If you were talking to him, you really became uncomfortable because he was uncomfortable. When he wasn't acting, he would stand away from everyone in the corner. After a while you realized it was too painful for both of you to interact. You just let him be." When offered, Margot Kidder declined the role of Louise, preferring instead to play the part of Anne. "I was in full manic depressive insanity," the actress confesses, "and I didn't want to play the leading lady, I wanted to play the screwed up drug addict. At that point [in my life] I saw acting as therapy to work out my demons, and I felt that if I could have played that destroyed character I probably would have done well." Sensing Kidder's emotional fragility, Donner refused her request and turned to the relative unknowns Diana Scarwid and Amy Wright for the roles of Louise and Anne. In both Todd Walton's novel and Curtin and Levinson's screenplay, bar regulars Stinky, Wings and Blue Lewis were written as young men. Searching for more of a contrast in his ensemble, Donner cast the much older Bill Henderson, Burt Remsen and Harold Russell. With casting complete, the production descended upon Silverlake, Los Angeles, in February 1980.

Filming *Inside Moves* was the realization of a dream for Donner, who had long desired to option and direct a novel of his choosing. His delight with his handpicked cast and crew, and his love for the material, was palpable, as he sensed the opportunity to direct an important movie that could have a profoundly positive effect on people's lives. He had never been happier, the power of his personality never more magnetic or contagious. As Diana Scarwid puts it, "The atmosphere there was so wonderful. There was this big, boyishly handsome man with a powerful nimbleness about him, and with whom you felt so secure. When you walked onto his set, you could hear him — he was 'The Commander' with wonderful stories and everybody loved him. His voice was like 'King Richard of Donnerville.' It was such a pleasure to be around that energy, and to be on set with this charismatic big daddy. I knew I liked him right away [because] he is what he puts out there. He *is* Superman."

Such mellifluous rhetoric is a clear reflection of the warm relationship Donner fostered with his actors, a bond crucial to the artistic success of the movie. In both Walton's novel and the eventual screenplay, the inhabitants of Max's bar depend upon each other's company as the essential purpose of their existence. Helping his actors to develop engaging, well-rounded characters became Donner's clear priority, with improvisation and creative spontaneity strongly encouraged. Scarwid continues, "Dick allowed us to feel the space… He was a great guider, a great actor himself, [and] he knew how to present things to actors to get them to feel more, and allowed you time to go to those places." In the end, Donner would choose to run the film's closing credits over a photograph of the entire production crew; a final, emphatic indication of the familial atmosphere.

Much of the responsibility for the visual look of *Inside Moves* was entrusted to László Kovács. Donner had admired his work for many years, as he had that of his Hungarian compatriot, Vilmos Zsigmond, and he happily allowed the cinematographer a generous level of autonomy. On the rare occasion the two men disagreed over a particular shot, Donner would diffuse the difference of opinion with humor. When Roary and Louise dance tenderly to the music of Frank Sinatra, Donner insisted that the camera zoom in tighter on the dancing couple. "No, you can't go any tighter," Kovács responded, firmly. "They [the audience] will see the [camera's] matte box in the mirror."

"László, with all that's going on in this party nobody's going to see a friggin' matte box that's 10 feet behind it," the director replied.

"Yes! Yes! Vilmos will see it!"

"Don't be ridiculous."

The scene was shot as Donner instructed. The next day Kovács received a telegram on set:

Dear Laszlo

Hope your picture's going well.

I happened to be at Technicolor looking at my dailies and I saw some of yours.

I saw a matte box in a mirror.

Vilmos

Kovács was beside himself until Donner casually revealed that he had sent the telegram — once again living up to his reputation as the ultimate practical joker.

Donner's legendary inability to recall names continued to haunt him as he often referred to László Kovács as "Vilmos." At first Kovács thought he was joking. Then he grew too embarrassed to correct him. Eventually, assistant director Mike Grillo was forced to bring Donner's lapses to his attention. When the real Vilmos Zsigmond dropped by to visit the set, the director had T-shirts printed up for both men. The visiting cinematographer was presented with one that read "MY NAME IS NOT LÁSZLÓ" and Kovács with one that read "MY NAME IS NOT VILMOS." Later they exchanged shirts and confused everybody.

Given his new reputation and the ownership of a source novel, Donner might have logically assumed that securing a distributor for *Inside Moves* would not prove too difficult. Yet his decision to fund and produce an independent feature without a deal already in place was a brave gamble. Nonetheless, it was one he was willing to take. Says he, "Steven Spielberg called me up and he said, 'You're doing what I really want to do.' I replied, 'What do you mean?' He said, 'You're coming off of two big ones and you're doing something little and personal.' And he had read my mind. It was a picture [that] meant so much to me... Where it fell into place in my career, I never even thought about it."

Most important to Donner was the empathy he felt with its inherent messages and values, and, perhaps, the potential for an intimate and small-scale production, devoid of special effects, that would serve as a form of recuperation following the stresses and strains suffered during *Superman*. Indeed, the only scene of *Inside Moves* that required detailed storyboards was Roary's suicide attempt — a free fall from the window of a local office building that would form the dramatic, attention-grabbing opening of the film. Since his earliest days in television, Donner had developed a morbid fear of filming dangerous stunts — a terror that grew increasingly ironic as his career later became entwined with the explosive, death-defying feats of the action-adventure genre.

For this particular stunt, six high-speed cameras were placed in position the day before, and tests completed featuring an articulated dummy. That night Donner struggled to sleep. In the rare moments that he could, he dreamt that *he* was falling from the window. The next morning he arrived on set ruffled and anxious, and immediately informed Mike Grillo that he would be staying in his trailer until stuntman Dennis Madalone was ready to fall. When he eventually left his trailer, he was confronted by a seventh camera that his mischievous crew had set up purely in order to archive his nervous reaction. Madalone's jump was successful, and was captured on film from six separate angles and at one hundred and twenty frames per second. One of Donner's worst fears — a serious injury or fatality on his watch — was allayed.

As the shoot progressed, Bob Goodwin and Mark Tanz grew increasingly anxious over their inability to secure a distributor. Pressure to secure a quick deal increased. Both men remained in awe of the filmmaking process, and their involvement in it, but their nervousness over monies spent, and the fact that the major studios were still unwilling to act as an outlet for recuperating their costs, infected a certain degree of tension in their relationship with Donner. "It was kept very much off the set and very much private," Kovács remembered, "[but] every time Dick had a meeting with the producers... when he came back he was very upset."

With Donner's knowledge and agreement, Goodmark Productions eventually cut a deal with the independent outlet AFD (Associated Film Distribution) who would market the film in the U.S., and with Lord Lew Grade's company ITC (Incorporated Television Company), for distribution in Europe. AFD assured the filmmakers that while they could not match the distribution budgets of the majors, *Inside Moves* would be treated with dignity and respect, and promoted as a potential Academy Award winner. With good reviews and strong word of mouth, the film could still have the kind of impact on a wide congregation that Donner and the entire company were hoping for.

As scripted, the final scene of *Inside Moves* called for Roary, Louise, and the regulars at Max's to be waiting at a bus stop, en route to the basketball stadium where Jerry is about to make his professional debut. As Roary locks up the bar, Jerry's prostitute ex-girlfriend approaches and hustles him for $50, before declaring, "You're a sucker, and I'm a whore. That's just the way it is." Such an overtly downbeat finale posed a dilemma for Donner, who preferred something wholly more optimistic by way of conclusion. Thus, an additional scene was filmed; in which Roary and Jerry triumphantly acknowledge one another in the arena of Jerry's pro-basketball debut.

The first version of *Inside Moves* ran in excess of three hours. With more than a third of the film needing to be excised, Donner placed a difficult phone call to Amy Wright. She remembers, "[Donner] says, 'Amy, I have some bad news for you. I've had to drastically cut you out of the film, and I may even be cutting the last scene which is still up in the air.' He didn't cut the last scene, but he had been telling me all along that this part was going to do it for me, [he was like], 'Oh, your life's going change!' and I was like, 'Yeah right.' It was disappointing because the movie was changed to be more 'up.' He had to cut a lot of my storyline out because it was too dark." Despite Wright's understandable disappointment, Donner was jubilant with the final cut of the picture, and delighted with its positive message that he believed would be the key to success. Required to underpin the film's emotional message was a noted composer. A reputable name was needed to join the company of Jerry Goldsmith and John Williams on the Donner list of collaborators. The man chosen was James Bond alumni John Barry, whom the director knew personally from his time living in London during the sixties. Barry traveled from England to Donner's house in California, where a copy of the film was screened. Afterward the composer sat down at an antique piano and played a gentle, romantic thematic that would form the basis of the film's musical accompaniment. With the score inserted, a soundtrack that oscillated appropriately between melancholy and hope, Donner was able to realize his desire that *Inside Moves* be less an exploration of disillusionment, more an experiment with enlightenment.

Inside Moves proved Donner to be operating at the peak of his abilities, flipping genres with ease to deliver back-to-back efforts that were so personal and powerful, one could not imagine them presented by any other director. Liberated from the constraints of big-budget blockbuster filmmaking, free from the distractions of dominating special effects and action-based sequences, *Inside Moves* allowed Donner the opportunity to demonstrate his true virtuosity and range as a filmmaker. If *Superman* was his love letter to his beloved America, then *Inside Moves* was a message for all humanity. The end result is a passionately delivered ode to the triumph of the human spirit, presented with a stylistic bow of Capraesque optimism and hope that reflects his romantic readiness and unerring belief in the American Dream.

The film's distribution was conceived as a throwback to the pre-blockbuster age. AFD opened the movie in the U.S. against Neil Diamond's *The Jazz Singer* on December 19, 1980, in single theaters in New York and Los Angeles, with the intention of nurturing audience anticipation for a wide release early in 1981. Following advanced preview screenings, the nation's critics glowed. *The Washington Post* recommended that *Inside Moves* was "an inspirational comedy-melodrama… [an] artfully old-fashioned morale booster… [that] affirms values that rarely fail to move and unify audiences, for perfectly good reasons: the triumph of love over prejudice, courage over hardship and community loyalty over selfishness." *The New York Times* raved about the "inspirational approach"; noting that the picture contained an energy deriving from "smooth ensemble acting and some excellent performances." Donner challenged preconceptions regarding his range, as noted by the resident critic Janet Maslin, who confessed that his direction possessed "a surprising gentleness." *Newsweek* went further: "*Inside Moves* could easily have turned into a telethon without Jerry Lewis, a tearjerker that jerked so hard it took your eyeballs right out of your head. That this doesn't happen is due to Donner… [He] has directed with a strong, quiet sense of human nuance." The most astute observation came with its summation of the cast contribution. "The actors clearly believe in this film," continued the critic, Jack Kroll, "and they perform as if they really care about each other and didn't simply show up for a day's shooting." It was as Donner intended.

Emboldened by the startling review sheets, and the excited response of exhibitors, AFD quickly amended their marketing strategy and expanded the release. Such a move could have been the catalyst toward a sensational, against-the-odds hit. In retrospect, it was a crucial distribution mistake. Deprived of the opportunity to build positive word of mouth at a pace consistent with its modest advertising budget, the picture drowned in the vast array of studio-backed Christmas hits, which included Sidney Poitier's *Stir Crazy* and the Jane Fonda vehicle *Nine to Five*. With fast openings now the norm, there was sparse flexibility in the new Hollywood system to tolerate independent movie releases that did not perform immediately. Exhibitors suddenly dumped the picture, and *Inside Moves* became an ironic victim of the very blockbuster phenomenon that Donner himself had helped to create. "They should have brought it out [at] a different time," bemoans Steve Kahan, "It just got killed."

Johnny Carson was the host for the fifty-third annual Academy Awards ceremony held on March 31, 1981. The evening's heavy hitters were David Lynch's *The Elephant Man* and the Martin Scorsese tour-de-force *Raging Bull*, both of which enjoyed eight nominations. Donner was again overlooked, although he was fiercely proud of Diana Scarwid's surprise Best Supporting Actress Oscar nomination for her performance as Louise. Although the award would eventually go to Mary Steenburgen for *Melvin and Howard*, the fact that Scarwid was even considered given *Inside Moves'* limited exposure was something of a coup de grâce. The actress herself wasn't surprised when it was announced that she had missed out on the main prize. "I didn't have a studio behind me," she was quoted as saying. "What really disappointed me was that, in this year of gloom and violence on screen, our movie was pulled from release so fast it didn't have a chance."

Scarwid's nomination did, however, offer *Inside Moves* a brief cinematic resurrection. The film was re-launched in theaters two months after its original demise, accompanied by a limited promotional campaign that focused solely upon its spectacular reviews. Again, the film disappeared quickly and without trace. It was a grim reality that for all the advantages of escaping a colossal, high-concept production, there were undoubtedly many serious disadvantages, the most important of which was the formidable support of a studio's publicity and marketing divisions. It was a lesson quickly learned.

In a darkened screening room on the Warner Bros. studio lot, Donner sat alone in nervous apprehension. As the projector whirred into action, he felt an anxious, sickening feeling in the bottom of his stomach. Digesting the images and sounds that he quickly immersed himself into, he didn't like what he saw. "Out of all the shit that has happened to me in the business," he confesses today, "that one really broke my heart." It had been more than two years since the anguish of his firing, but the specially arranged screening of *Superman II* reopened painful wounds. Richard Lester's film included much of his footage from 1977, yet it bore little resemblance to his intended vision for Superman's continuing adventure. Although all of Marlon Brando's scenes were in the can and ready to go, the Salkinds had exorcised the heavyweight star from the sequel. To have not would have cost the producers a percentage of their future takings (rumored to be a gigantic 11% of the domestic gross and 6% internationally). Also replaced for the sequel was renowned composer John Williams, with Ken Thorne stepping in to conduct. Yet perhaps the most noticeable result of the change of directors was a clear degradation of special effects quality. Whereas *Superman: The Movie* had broken new ground in making audiences believe a man could fly, the newly-shot Richard Lester scenes were a giant leap backwards. "We shot cheaply and fast," Margot Kidder complains, "and it was Richard Lester thumbing his nose at the material, getting his money, and being very hip, [but] it takes a much braver man to not worry about being hip and just say, 'I want to believe in this.'"

Through the wonders of editing, the majority of the movie-going public would at least remain blissfully unaware of the film's cinematic bastardry, enjoying as they did seamlessly juxtaposed shots of action that had in many cases been filmed three years apart. The film was an instant smash with both audiences and critics alike, and initially showed tentative signs of breaking the box-office effort of the first installment. Yet despite its positive opening noises, the sequel would not prove to have the financial legs of its forbearer. Nor has it been able to impress the same indelible legacy. Says special effects contributor John Richardson, "I think you can still pick out the scenes in *Superman II* that Dick directed because [they have] that quality feel to it."

At Warner Bros., young producer Lauren Shuler was developing *Ladyhawke*, the medieval tale of two lovers placed under a curse by an evil bishop. Although determined and ambitious, Shuler was young and relatively inexperienced, and she struggled to enlist executive support for the fantasy screenplay by debutant writer Edward Khmara. Ultimately frustrated by Warner's lack of enthusiasm, she secretly smuggled a copy of the script to Alan Ladd, Jr., who, since his acrimonious departure as president of Twentieth Century-Fox, had established his own production unit: The Ladd Company. When Warner Bros. officially put *Ladyhawke* into turnaround, Ladd, Jr. optioned it and advised Shuler to contact Donner.

The director read the screenplay while on a flight from Florida to New York. Although he deemed much of the script unrealistic and disinteresting, he grew intrigued by the notion of an unrequited love story. He was captivated by a passage in which Father Imperius the Monk recalls the tragedy of the lovers' curse. He was so moved that he began to cry. "Can I help you?" a concerned flight attendant asked midway through his flight.

"Just read this page right here," Donner politely asked.

"Oh, this is so beautiful," the stewardess, also close to tears, replied. "Are you going to make this movie?"

"I am now," he smiled.

Shuler quickly consented to script changes. She hired David Peoples to deliver a revised draft of the Khmara screenplay, but only until she discovered his involvement would be postponed due to a looming writers strike. At this point she turned to Australian screenwriter, Michael Thomas, for the task. (When Peoples later submitted his own draft, sections of it were amalgamated with the work of Thomas). This progressive effort succeeded in developing a more cohesive, centralized love story, but the script still lacked humor. Donner again turned to "Dr. Tom Mankiewicz" for medicinal suggestions. Yet no sooner had the writer set to work, and Donner and Shuler begun scouting filming locations in the then-Czechoslovakia, Alan Ladd, Jr. pulled the plug on the project. The Ladd Company was in financial difficulty and was being forced to cut back production output. *Ladyhawke* was one of the vehicles earmarked for divorcement. With a slate that was already full for 1982, including *Blade Runner* and *Night Shift*, Ladd opted to relinquish his interest and returned the project once more entirely into the hands of Lauren Shuler.

As a result of the sudden loss of financial backing, not to mention a crucial industry ally, Donner also put his involvement on hold until further development funds were secured.

Following the controversial departure of Columbia president David Begelman in the mid-seventies, entrepreneurial producer Ray Stark had, in effect, established relative control of the film studio through his Rastar Productions line. In her book *You'll Never Eat Lunch in This Town Again*, producer Julia Phillips described Stark as "a film-making entity within a larger entity... the little man who is really the Big Man." Stark was one of the most powerful men in Hollywood, with one of the more explosive tempers, and it was from his base of control at Columbia that he was developing his latest star vehicle: *The Toy*. A Carol Sobieski-penned remake of Francis Veber's whimsical *Le Jouet*, it featured the tantalizing teaming of comics Richard Pryor and Jackie Gleason in the lead roles. As he completed the fanciful children's fantasy *Annie* with John Huston, *The Toy* appeared to not only fit in perfectly with the Columbia brand of family entertainment, but was of a genre that made Stark feel personally comfortable in commanding complete control of the project.

The main protagonist of the Sobieski screenplay was Jack Brown, an unemployed writer threatened with the loss of his home who reluctantly agrees to become a real-life toy for a week. In becoming the live-in plaything for Eric Bates — a spoilt rich kid, son of the intimidating plutocrat Ulysses Simpson Bates — Jack is forced to live through a variety of indignations and humiliations for his money. Nonetheless, he forms a strong bond with Eric, whom Jack realizes is desperate for the affection of a father figure. The lonely boy learns what it is like to have and to be a friend as he and Jack launch an underground newspaper with a remit to expose corruption at the highest level of Ulysses' company.

Later, the emboldened duo comes to the rescue of Senator Newcomb, an unsuspecting victim of a publicity stunt engineered by Eric's father, in which the devious owner of Bates Industries attempts to photograph the politician shaking hands with the Grand Wizard of the KKK. Finally understanding his offspring's behavior as a desperate plea for paternal love and attention, the senior Bates vows to change his ways, and father and son are eventually reconciled. As a prize for helping to reunite them, Jack wins a job as a reporter for a local newspaper owned by Mr. Bates.

Entering comic legends Pryor and Gleason into such a formulaic tale was, in Stark's eyes, an almost guaranteed recipe for success. But what the project also needed was a mainstream commercial director, a filmmaker who could keep the production firmly on the road toward big box-office numbers.

On a flight out of New York, Donner sat in front of an old friend, former agent Guy McElwaine. An immaculate dresser, with blond hair, perfect features and perhaps the whitest smile in town, McElwaine had first met Donner on the set of *Salt and Pepper*, in London, during the late sixties, at which time he represented Frank Sinatra. Now McElwaine was chairman and CEO of Rastar (by 1983 he would be president and chairman of Columbia). As the Boeing 747 cruised en route to Los Angeles, McElwaine read the latest draft of *The Toy*. "You know, Donner, this is a pretty good script," he cheered from the seat behind, "the kind of stuff you could do real well." McElwaine dropped the script on the empty chair next to Donner and left to enjoy a glass of wine at the first-class bar.

By the time he had turned the last page, the director was certainly intrigued at the possibility of making *The Toy*. It was funny, and the central relationship between Jack and Eric — although sentimental and heavily cliched — offered a framework for an emerging thematic agenda that forcefully promoted love and friendship. Donner also enjoyed the script's light political subtext and the fact that, as a studio picture, it would be guaranteed not to suffer the same marketing demise as that which had befallen *Inside Moves*. Still, he hesitated. How much creative freedom would he be allowed? He reasoned that with Ray Stark — a staunch throwback to the hierarchical mode of production made famous during the old Hollywood studio system — the chance of making substantial changes to the material would lie somewhere between slim and none. Cogitating, he returned the script.

"Pryor and Gleason," McElwaine stated smugly, pearly whites glistening at full beam. Given notice of the involvement of two stars with unrivaled reputations in improvisational comedy, Donner — who enjoyed the shooting process more than any other aspect of film production — could answer only in the affirmative. Any doubts he may have harbored regarding the integrity of the project quickly moved to the back of his mind. Rightly or wrongly, he agreed to direct *The Toy*.

By then an undeniable Hollywood star, Richard Pryor had nonetheless struggled to find cinematic roles worthy of his incredible talent. In films like *Blue Collar* and *Stir Crazy* he had played the part of downtrodden, unemployed black men forced to survive on wisecracks alone. The role of Jack Brown in *The Toy* was no different, but it offered a large salary, and the promise of being involved with what might reasonably have been anticipated to be the comedy hit of 1982.

What made Pryor of such interest to the American public — even more so than his obvious performance skills — was his frenzied, hyper-turbulent private life, haunted as he was by more than one personal demon. A victim of family problems, racism, and drug abuse, and ultimately of fame, his harrowed features connoted an intriguing self-destructive streak.

Jackie Gleason's off-screen excesses rivaled those of Pryor's. The sixties television star dubbed "The Great One" was, in his heyday, the highest paid act on the tube. Since then he had cultivated the persona of a man living the good life to vulgar excess. After enduring a triple heart bypass he continued to drink, overeat and smoke several packets of cigarettes a day. Like Pryor, Gleason had also failed to live up to his cinematic potential. Despite a strong turn in *The Hustler*, the majority of his roles had limited him to undemanding supporting efforts in which he played the clown. What most appealed to Gleason about *The Toy* was that it was offered. It would be easy money in the bank.

Even though he suspected that they were involved primarily for their paychecks, Donner heralded the opportunity to collaborate artistically with two flawed geniuses. *The Toy* would certainly be a chance to test his own abilities, as he would need to strike a careful balance between harnessing moments of magic, and managing the personal eccentricities or extremes of the pair.

Serious problems began almost from the very start of shooting in Baton Rouge, Louisiana, where the production was based. Richard Pryor was depressed, and rarely strayed out of his dressing room. Jackie Gleason drank every afternoon and appeared miserable. "It was not a happy time for [Dick]," says Steve Kahan. "He had a hard time."

Perhaps realizing that he would be testing himself against the newest and freshest kid on the comedy block, and in an effort to appear younger on screen, Jackie Gleason had fast dieted and grown a moustache. He was irritable, disliked working with children, and held an aversion to rehearsal. It was his dependence upon alcohol, however, coupled with Pryor's addiction to drugs, which defined the making of *The Toy*. As Gleason biographer William Henry puts it: "In most of Jackie's past fiascos, he could have at least claimed credit for effort... The first great exception to that craftsmanship is *The Toy*... It is stilted and noisy, lacking in energy and almost totally devoid of imagination. Perhaps he regretted having accepted the script. Perhaps he was slipping into the periodic deep depression that old friends would remark upon as they saw him over the next few years. At least some of the time during filming, he was simply drunk."

On set was James Bacon, a biographer, veteran columnist, and (most importantly) drinking buddy of Gleason's. Donner labeled the journalist an "evil companion" and eventually had him barred from the set. The director remembers, "They used to go to lunch and get drunk, and it bothered me tremendously, but there was nothing I could do about it except yell and scream and rant. I tried to keep him [Gleason] away from this fella… [But] it was rough."

On one occasion Gleason believed he was required for no more than a few reaction shots late in the afternoon, and had proceeded to indulge in his usual six double Scotches with no ice, no soda, no water, and no food, during lunch. When he arrived back to continue filming, the hapless star was bundled into a golf cart by Donner, and ordered to chase Richard Pryor's character across a vast Southern estate — not the pick-up shots he had been expecting. In what Bacon alleges was an unscripted moment, Gleason decided it would be funny to drive the cart into the swimming pool. Although the scene remained in the picture, the journalist contends Donner was furious with his star and malevolent cohort. If Gleason, already in poor health, had been injured during the incident, the whole movie could have been thrown into disarray, and the filmmakers on the receiving end of legal action.

Donner refutes Bacon's interpretation of events, and insists the swimming pool incident was a scripted moment. Either way, it is safe to conclude that Gleason, a man who treasured his independence, was, at the very least, difficult to control. Says Donner, "One of the responsibilities of a director is to control your set. And there are many times you have problems with actors where… personal issues might come up, and you've really got to work your butt off [to] keep it all together and not let it get out of hand, because once it gets out of hand, you've lost it. If it's alcohol you run into that. If it's drugs, you run into that. If it's just personality problems, you quite often face that, but [it's all] part of the job. You've got to know it going in [although] everybody has a different way of handling it. Some turn their back to it totally and allow these things to continue, others face it straight on. I always did. To me, if you were going to have the respect of your actors, you never lost control of them for a second."

Challenging Gleason was easier said than done. The comic enjoyed a long-standing professional relationship with Ray Stark, and a great personal friendship — reasons for which he may have believed that he did not need to pay a great deal of attention to Donner. Suggests editor Stuart

Baird, who did not work on the picture, "[Gleason] was a monster. One of the things about when you're working with a big star actor, they're just monsters. Part of the [director's] job is to be humiliated. You have to do the job and be humiliated by these people. Dick swallowed all that." The cinematographer, László Kovács, concurs, "[Gleason] became very vicious. It was horribly unprofessional. I think he had a lot of mean-spiritedness in himself, and he turned on Dick."

Having dumped the golf cart into the swimming pool, Gleason was still required by Donner for some close-up reaction shots at the huge plantation estate party; although he could not stand up straight long enough to get the footage in the can.

"Put him against the wall!" Donner yelled, frustrated.

In a moment of high farce, the actor required crewmembers to hold him up for his close-up. He refused to do a second take. "I'm not gonna to talk to you," he slurred to Donner. "I'm gonna talk to László."

"Wait a minute," the cinematographer responded. "Don't put me in the middle. Dick is my boss."

"I don't care. I don't want to talk to him. If he wants to find out something, he should ask you and you tell me."

In contrast, Donner found Richard Pryor a joy and developed a great fondness for the actor. At one point during the shoot, Pryor pulled a wad of $100 bills from his pocket, attached them to helium balloons, and then released them into the air to find homes as warm-hearted gifts to some surprised and very grateful Louisiana residents.

On occasion, however, Pryor's erratic behavior got the better of him, too. Shooting a scene opposite a live alligator, he began to suffer breathing difficulties and heart palpitations, and was hospitalized for five days. Although doctors diagnosed Wolff-Parkinson-White syndrome as the source, Pryor was convinced that it was because of his "secret dalliances with the evil white lady." According to at least one biography, Pryor missed filming again on a separate occasion, disappearing without trace for fourteen days, allegedly because of his drug addictions. This second absence is something Donner strongly refutes, "He disappeared for not even a full day. He went to a Willie Nelson concert [and] instead of coming back that night he came back later the following day. It cost me half a day."

Regardless, Pryor's mental state at the time of making *The Toy* was undoubtedly delicate. A year earlier, while in a depressive rage fueled by drugs and the recent death of the grandmother who had raised him, he had attempted suicide by pouring a bottle of rum over his head and lighting a match. He suffered serious burns to the upper half of his body. "I was drunk out of my motherfucking mind," he told his daughter, Rain. "Stoned, too.

And I was feeling sorry for myself. And I wanted to die. So I set my black ass on fire." Pryor and his management team publicized the injuries as the result of an accident, leaving nobody involved with *The Toy* with any idea just how deep the wounds of his mental anguish ran. Some, including László Kovács, dismissed him as a hypochondriac. "He looked very good, but he was so fragile," the cinematographer remembered. "He always felt sick and he was really complaining a lot."

Pryor did at least revel in the company of Gleason, the two men concocting mischief in between takes. As he remembered in his book, *Pryor Convictions and Other Life Sentences*:

"The shit Jackie talked between setups was funnier than anything we got in the movie. He knew about gangsters, gamblers, comics, vaudeville, strippers, and sharks. He'd start talking about something in the 1970s and then suddenly he'd be swirling around the 1920s and '30s, describing people and joints so good I could smell them. One day he asked me to get him some grass. I found some and gave it to him on the bench where we used to sit and talk. It overlooked a lake that had no fish in it. But Jackie didn't like the way I handed it to him. He showed me a sneaky way of handing the exchange, and then he winked. 'That's called a switch,' he said. We laughed. Two stars. Getting paid a few million dollars. And we were practicing dope deals."

Charged with the responsibility of being on set for the duration of the shoot was Ray Stark's protégé, Phil Feldman. A former attorney, Feldman had served in corporate positions at a number of media companies, including CBS, Twentieth Century-Fox, Seven Arts Corporation and First Artists. As vice president of Rastar Films, Feldman knew enough about the "nuts and bolts" of the business to act as a line producer, and was trusted by Stark to keep things in check. Any departure from *Annie* territory, or the riches of the whimsical children's fantasy genre, was not to be tolerated.

As Pryor improvised his way through scenes, however, Sobieski's political subtext came further to the foreground, and certain sequences began to take on a heavier satirical edge. Donner would soon be called to account for the changes, as Stark decided to visit the set to observe shooting himself. After smiling and joking with the crew, and applauding them for their hard work, the producer made it clear that he expected Donner to be able to rigorously defend any changes from the screenplay. As László Kovács recalled, "A couple of times Ray Stark came down on location. He was always very happy, saying, 'Everything's perfect,' and so on, but I know that Dick had some very difficult meetings behind closed doors while he was there... [Donner] likes creative collaboration but you can't expect that from the studio. The barracudas had the power, and especially Ray Stark. He was running the studio behind closed doors."

Outwardly, Donner appeared to be his normal, confident self, but he was living in a dark mental space, tortured by his failure to take charge of events, paranoid that *The Toy* could signal the end of his run at the top. If he believed that when filming wrapped in Baton Rouge his troubles would be over, then he was sadly mistaken. A rough cut of *The Toy* was assembled and a series of test screenings were prepared, as the production readied for a major Christmas release. However, following a series of disappointing previews, Stark brought in his own personal editor, Margaret Booth, to re-edit the film behind Donner's back. Prints were struck for distribution before their color correction was approved.

When he had signed on for the movie, Donner had not been aware of Stark's reputation for assuming control of pictures during the editing stages. "I was an idiot," he reflects. "Ray Stark talked me into not putting in writing my final cut right. He said, 'You can have it, but you'll never need it.' So I went along with everything." It was a disastrous end to a disastrous project.

An addled product of two actors in poor health — both of whom were almost certainly invested in the project primarily for the money — a producer determined to retain creative control of his movie, and a director who, in his heart of hearts, perhaps wished that he hadn't signed on in the first place, *The Toy* was far from a seminal picture. Due to the nature of his employment, Donner was never able to stamp his authority, or his vision, onto the film. Although sporadically funny and cute, for the most part it is confused and disjointed, entirely lacking the singular clarity of *Superman* and *Inside Moves*. Donner concludes, "They [Stark and Feldman] wanted to make a different movie. I don't remember what they wanted to make, but I do remember that if I'd had Guy McElwaine in front of my car I would have run him over."

"I know I am a true romantic.
I don't know what it means, but
I love being it!"

RICHARD DONNER

True Romance

Martin Ritt had insisted to Donner that directing was "80% casting." Logic dictates that if a picture is cast well its chances of success are immeasurably improved. If it is cast badly, it is almost certainly doomed. It sounds simple, but the process is never as easy as the rule. Finding a star whose essential ingredients fit that of a character and who can naturally convince in a role is a complex affair. Finding the appropriate chemistry in an ensemble of actors is even harder. For Donner, the challenge of casting *Ladyhawke* was so severe that it threatened the very existence of the project.

The director dreamt of signing Sean Connery and Dustin Hoffman as his lead stars, but constrained by a moderate $20 million production budget, he chose to pursue just one actor of such stature. He selected Hoffman, and pressed ahead with several meetings aimed at winning the actor's commitment. *The Graduate* star was interested in *Ladyhawke*, but concerned by the prospect of filming in Italy — a country rocked by a series of terrorist bombings, kidnappings and assassinations. Donner gave his personal assurance that the safety of cast and crew was his primary concern, and that extra security would be hired to accommodate someone of Hoffman's celebrity. His fears somewhat allayed, Hoffman gave notice that if he were to sign, he should perform with a French accent. Donner politely considered the request, but feared that, in order to achieve verisimilitude, the rest of the film's cast would have to follow suit. Next, the actor suggested that his friend and noted script doctor, Elaine May, should rewrite elements of his dialogue. As time began to run out and negotiations remained stalled, Hoffman finally confided in Donner that he was struggling to decide how he could play the role of Phillipe "The Mouse" Gaston differently to Ratso — his petty thief character in John Schlesinger's *Midnight Cowboy* who walked with a limp. Exasperated, Donner dryly advised that he should "limp on the other foot."

"I bet you've heard all these stories about me about how difficult I am to work with," Hoffman laughed in reply. "Well, the truth is, sure, I have fights, but only because I want everything to be excellent. At the end of the day my relationship with a director is just like a marriage. We have our fights, but we always end up respecting each other. That always happens to me."

Donner took pause to remember some advice to the contrary, received earlier from his friends and fellow directors, Sydney Pollack and Robert Benton (the latter of whom insisted that "life was too short"), but decided not to comment. Instead, the beleaguered director telephoned *Ladyhawke*'s screenwriter, Tom Mankiewicz, to dissect the problematic casting. "This is going to be such a tough physical shoot," he declared matter-of-factly, "and I'm going to be stuck in the Italian Alps with him worried about getting kidnapped. We'll get somebody else."

He asked Mankiewicz to inquire into the availability of Sean Penn, an up-and-coming brat packer who would soon court tabloid fame and controversy as a result of his relationship with pop star Madonna. To ascertain the actor's potential interest and availability, Mankiewicz placed a call to Penn's agent.

"I can only get in touch with Sean once a week at a phone booth," was the response.

"Why is that?"

"He's on location in Fort Bragg filming *Racing with the Moon*, and his character wouldn't have a phone. So he doesn't have a phone where he is."

"Let me ask you this," the scribe pressed. "Would Sean's character read a medieval love story script?"

"I don't know. I'd have to ask him when I call the pay phone, which will be in another four days."

"I'm terribly sorry," Mankiewicz fumed. "I was under the impression that he was an actor."

Frustrated in their attempts to find an actor to play Gaston, Donner and producer Lauren Shuler briefly turned their attention to *Ladyhawke*'s other lead roles. Although he lacked the broad audience appeal of Sean Connery, the lesser-known Kurt Russell was snapped up to play the dashing Captain Etienne Navarre. With successful turns in John Carpenter's *The Thing* and *Escape from New York* to his credit, the actor had a proven track record in the action-fantasy genre. (Many years earlier, Donner had directed him in episodes of the television series *The Travels of Jaimie McPheeters* and *The Fugitive*.)

Shuler lobbied hard for the part of Isabeau d'Anjou to be awarded to Michelle Pfeiffer, who had recently wrapped opposite Al Pacino on Brian De Palma's remake of *Scarface*. Donner believed the former model to be too inexperienced to play an emotionally demanding role, but Shuler persisted, and arranged for Pfeiffer to complete a screen test. Determined to make her video audition original, the rising starlet arranged for a fade-out to be inserted at the end. When the action faded back in, sitting politely in her place was a confused pet parakeet, accompanied by Pfeiffer's giggling voice, "Dick, this is how I envisioned Isabeau to look." Donner remembers, "It was sentimental. It was emotional. It was very heartfelt. It was cute and charming, and that's exactly who she was." It won her the role.

A strong supporting cast was assembled that included *The Omen*'s Leo McKern. McKern would once again appear as a key narrative propellant: Father Imperius, who — like archaeologist Carl Bugenhagen — was a dealer in curses and a keeper of knowledge highly pertinent to the chief protagonists. Fellow U.K. actors John Wood, Ken Wood and Alfred Molina were also signed.

When it came time to return his attention to the role of Gaston, Donner approached Matthew Broderick on the advice of his sister, Joan, who had seen the actor perform in a theatrical production of Neil Simon's *Brighton Beach Memoirs,* and Shuler, who had read about his performance. The young actor had previously impressed in John Badham's *WarGames* (a movie for which Mankiewicz had also worked as a script doctor) and leapt at the chance to play the part. With cameras set to roll, Donner and Shuler at last appeared to have their cast in place. Or so they thought.

From state to state, coast to coast, critical response to the release of *The Toy* was damning. Vincent Canby of *The New York Times* quipped, "My mind wasn't simply wandering during the film, it was ricocheting between the screen and the exit sign." *Newsweek* concurred that the movie was "shapeless, noisy, vulgar, sentimental and amateurish." Moderate reviews were few and far between, although *Variety* did go as far as to label the comedy "an amusing diversion, even a lot of fun at times."

Despite the critical stink, it was the sweet smell of roses for Ray Stark and the Columbia bean counters. Against such competition as *Airplane II: The Sequel* and *48HRS*, not to mention *E.T.: The Extra-Terrestrial* (still rewriting history in select theaters), *The Toy* opened as the number one film in America. With the support of Pryor and Gleason's loyal fans, and the movie's family-friendly, generic appeal, it eventually collected a domestic tally of $47 million. The financial figures — while never threatening to set the record books alight — did at least ensure that the Hollywood remake of *Le Jouet* would turn a profit. And as one of the more popular releases in the fledgling video rentals market in the U.S., the film would gross further monies in the years to follow.

In early 1983, Donner remained a director in demand. He had rejected many lucrative offers — including the attractive *Warhead* (eventually re-titled *Never Say Never Again*), producer Kevin McClory's unofficial Bond movie starring Sean Connery — in order to recommit to *Ladyhawke*, in development at Twentieth Century-Fox following the unexpected withdrawal of

finance from The Ladd Company. After the debacle of *The Toy*, Donner realized that it was the realm of fantasy and myth, and of romance, that inspired
him the most, and to which his directorial skills were perhaps best suited. It
was not a coincidence that these themes were the creative framework supporting his greatest successes to date: *The Omen* and *Superman*.

While Donner had been filming *The Toy* in Louisiana, Tom Mankiewicz had been granted further license by Shuler to polish Edward Khmara's
screenplay. At Donner's behest, certain action set pieces were eliminated,
and the dramatic focus shifted firmly upon the central love story that had
first captured his attention, and which so aptly reflected his personal belief
in such notions as honor, truth and the sanctity of true love. A boy thief,
Phillipe "The Mouse" Gaston, escapes his execution ordered by the Bishop
of Aquila, fleeing the dictator's dungeon by burrowing through the castle
sewers. While hiding in a small village, he is captured by the Bishop's faithful lieutenant, Marquet, but is saved and befriended by Captain Etienne
Navarre — a mysterious dark knight and fellow fugitive. Gaston learns of a
curse placed upon Navarre by the Bishop. By day, his lover Isabeau d'Anjou
lives in the form of a hawk, while, at night, Navarre exists as a wolf. The
only moments they share in human form are the fleeting seconds at sun-
rise and sunset.

Navarre asks the indebted Gaston — the only man to ever escape the
castle of Aquila alive — to guide him to the Bishop so that he may slay the
instigator of the spell and end the curse. The fearful pickpocket flees the
challenge, only to be captured by henchmen again. Navarre comes to his
rescue once more, but during the course of a fierce battle Isabeau is shot and
wounded by an arrow. Distraught, the Captain orders Gaston to ride his horse
to the home of an old Monk: Father Imperius. Imperius heals the injured
beauty, and the three men move together as comrades in arms ready to seize
Aquila's castle. Evading the pursuant bounty hunter, Cezar, and the forceful
battle skills of Marquet, Navarre kills the Bishop and breaks the curse. He
and Isabeau at last embrace in each other's arms.

One of Mankiewicz's major additions to the screenplay was a series
of humorous monologues — philosophical musings that transformed the
Gaston character into an informal narrator of events. Said the writer, "If
you're stuck in the whole myth and everyone is swallowing it lock, stock and
barrel, then I think you're at a disadvantage telling the story. You don't make
him [Gaston] a cynic, but he's irreverent enough to keep the picture going."
As he had done with *Superman*, Mankiewicz also injected subtle religious
undertones into the screenplay. In a constant state of spiritual crisis, Gaston's
monologues are addressed directly to God. Navarre, too, is written as believing that events are fated by a higher, omnipotent power.

With the script in place and pre-production ready to begin in earnest, complications suddenly arose in Shuler's production deal with Twentieth Century-Fox. Despite originally allowing the property to lapse into turn-around, Warner Bros. was once again interested in the material, and claimed to have a first refusal contract right on all Ladd Company projects, former or otherwise. When complex negotiations reached a stalemate, Fox tabled a motion to share domestic and foreign production and distribution rights. Once confirmed, Donner requested that the executives decide a sole studio that he should report to. It was to be Warner Bros.

Even at such an early juncture of her career, Lauren Shuler's talent was impossible to ignore. Her drive and determination, steely self-belief and keen creative mind had led her to discover the promising project and nurture it through its tortuous development process. Donner, whose contract guaranteed him equal status as a producer and the privilege of final cut, but who had suffered bitter experiences at the hands of Alexander Salkind and Ray Stark, may have felt threatened by her strong opinions.

He was not unhappy to spend time with Shuler, as he had during many months of pre-production, but he was determined to remain in control of his movie. He was also, perhaps, frustrated or even embarrassed that he was unable to manipulate Shuler with his standard artillery of charms.

Donner's nervousness led him to hire Harvey Bernhard as a co-producer, but when Bernhard intimated they should attempt to extrapolate Shuler from proceedings, he found himself defending her. "She brought us the script," he snapped. "Lay off."

In a cramped office on the Warner Bros. studio lot that served as *Ladyhawke*'s pre-production base, sparks flew nonetheless. Shuler rightly refused to be bullied on important decisions, and insisted her views be heard and respected.

On one occasion, Donner's mood of frustration threatened to explode. He was in his office with his cousin, Geoff Howard, who was visiting him from out of state, and with Harvey Bernhard, when he erupted during the middle of a telephone conversation. "What?!" he screamed. "What?!" Are you crazy?! You can't do that!" The discussion, of which the others present in the room could hear only half, had appeared to be going just fine. Suddenly, there was a range of problems to be dealt with. As the level of expletives indicated a disaster scenario, Howard felt increasingly awkward and uncomfortable, while beads of sweat began to literally drip from Bernhard's brow. As Howard recalls, "The executive producer was shitting in his pants. Just going bananas. Then at a point Dick said, 'I can't resolve this. Speak to Harvey,' and thrust the phone in his direction. Of course, there was nobody on the other end — the person had hung up long ago. That was Dick. Ad-libbed, on-the-spot humor. He was always that way. An enormous kidder."

With the success of *Superman* in mind, Donner looked to surround himself with proven collaborators. In addition to Mankiewicz's involvement as screenwriter and creative consultant, and Stuart Baird's role as editor and second-unit director, John Richardson was signed to supervise special effects. While scouting locations in the then-Czechoslovakia, and in the company of Richardson, Donner was involved in a rather embarrassing situation. Remembers the effects wiz, "We'd been driving all day and we got to the hotel and Dick said, 'Oh God, my neck is *really* painful.' I said, 'Do you want me to stretch it for you? Give it a tug?' He said, 'Oh yeah, come on up to the room, we'll have a glass of wine and you can give me a going over.' So I went up to his room, he rang down to room service and ordered some wine. With that Dick laid on the floor. I got on the floor with his head between my legs, my feet on his shoulders and my hands cupped under his chin, and pushed with my feet and pulled with my hands to sort of stretch his neck out. In the middle of this the waiter troops in through the door. The expression on this guy's face, I'm sure he thought we were at some strange sexual position. And I can remember us both laughing heartily over it after the guy had left, because the look on his face was hysterical."

After exploring Czechoslovakia, and briefly contemplating a return to the U.K., Donner found the authentic thirteenth-century locations that he was looking for in Italy. *Ladyhawke* would be filmed in such enchanting locations as the Apennine Mountains, the Gran Sasso range and the Fiora River, with interiors lensed at the famous Cinecittà Studios in Rome. With the decision to base the production in Italy came the services of renowned cinematographer Vittorio Storaro, whose credits included Bertolucci's *1900* and Coppola's *Apocalypse Now*. As befitting his status as the world's premier cameraman, Storaro assumed a heavily involved role in the preparation of *Ladyhawke*, accompanying Donner and Shuler on a month-long preparatory tour of his country, during which time the visual look of the film was established.

"I feel like a fruit," Kurt Russell complained during a costume fitting. With only ten days until the start of principal photography, the actor began to seriously doubt his ability to play the role of Navarre. In rehearsals, he had struggled with the physical rigors of horseback riding and sword fighting. And when he eyed himself in full period attire for the first time, his confidence was all but destroyed. "I don't think I go back in time well," he confessed nervously to Mankiewicz. Donner remembers, "We were all set to go when I got a call from wardrobe saying Kurt Russell refuses to wear a helmet. I said, 'C'mon, you're kidding.' So Kurt came to my office. He said, 'I look terrible in a helmet.' I said, 'Kurt, it's a baseball hat. You play baseball don't you? This is war, you have to have a helmet, and as it is I think you only have to put it on once [for one scene].' He didn't want to, and what I realized is, I guess he wasn't comfortable with the role."

Russell really hated his costume, and confessed to missing his girlfriend, the actress Goldie Hawn, who was still at home in the States. He walked off the production. The threat of the studio pulling the plug on the project had never been a more tangible possibility, and *Ladyhawke* was once more plunged into crisis. Donner telephoned his informal advisor, super agent Michael Ovitz, and pleaded with him to appease nervous executives by informing them that he had a backup plan in place. As soon as Donner put down the phone, he started to think about what his backup plan could be. He first flew to London to meet with Mel Gibson, the star of the low-budget *Mad Max* series. Gibson liked the script, but not the schedule, and passed on the material. Donner then began the arduous task of filtering through a collection of résumés. While doing so he came across a photograph of *Blade Runner* star Rutger Hauer, whose home telephone number was scribbled in pencil on the back. A year earlier, in Los Angeles, Donner and Shuler had offered the actor the part of Marquet, the Bishop of Aquila's faithful lieutenant. Refusing to play yet another screen villain, Hauer had declined the role but expressed interest in the part of Navarre. Donner grabbed a phone and dialed the number. The actor picked up.

"Rutger, we're here in Rome and we'd like to ask you a question."

"Hello, Dick. That sounds nice. How's it going?"

"Well," said the director. "Not so good."

"Oh? Sorry to hear that."

"Lauren and I are on the set of *Ladyhawke*. I'm ten days from the start of principal photography, and we're having some problems. Kurt Russell just left. Remember Navarre?"

"Sure," Hauer replied.

"So what do you think? Are you available, and do you still want to play Navarre?"

"What? Of course. I'll see you in a couple of days," he said. "Make sure they have a parking space for my 55-foot tractor trailer!"

After an epic fifteen hundred mile road trip across Europe, which included a detour around Switzerland (where he had been refused entry at customs), the Dutchman arrived in Italy. The director thought Hauer had been kidding about the tractor trailer, but there it was, a giant eighteen-wheeler parked in front of Cinecittà Studios. "RUTGER, what the…?" Donner boomed. "GODDAMN!"

The actor would eventually find a parking spot for his mobile behemoth, a hillside looking out over Rome, although as the production traveled across the country it provided a constant threat of being visible in the background of a shot.

When the two men lunched together, Donner handed Hauer a glove, asked him to place it on his hand and hold it up in the air. When he did so a hawk screamed into view and rested itself upon the actor's wrist. The director roared with laughter, having arranged the test with the hawk's trainer who was standing outside the open-air restaurant. *Ladyhawke*'s dashing new lead handled the bird with a level of consummate ease that suggested he might have been doing it his whole life. Coupled with the fact that Hauer was a former merchant seaman and army soldier, a skilled fencer and a proficient horse rider, the relieved filmmaker knew that he had made the right casting decision.

Ladyhawke began shooting in the fall of 1983. Donner was relieved to have reached full production and immediately grabbed filming by the scruff of the neck. As always, he invested himself wholeheartedly in the myth, treated it as a reality, and refused to mock or parody the material. His infectious sense of playfulness and fun was also at large, so, too, his enthusiasm for life. His personal management style — crucial to the artistic and commercial success of all his movies — left a motivated cast and crew feeling valued and empowered. John Richardson states, "I've enjoyed working with a good many directors, but if you take it across the board then Dick, for me, wins hands down, because he has all the attributes. He makes it fun, he makes it interesting, he generates enthusiasm, he makes you feel part of the team, and he makes you want to get out there and do it. And he's got a good sense of humor to boot, which, when the going gets tough, a good laugh always helps."

On *Ladyhawke*, Donner's level of enthusiasm was indefatigable. It had to be. As required by the screenplay, the characters Navarre and Isabeau would spend much of the movie in animal form. Four North American wolves had been flown to Italy from California — endangered species that required special permits from the U.S. Department of Interior, a veterinarian with pulmonary and resuscitation equipment, and nurses present on the set at all times. Despite the dedicated attention of their trainers, the wolves proved reluctant to perform on cue. The length of takes featuring the animals was kept as short as possible, meaning that time-consuming, multi-camera setups became the production norm, with Donner desperately seeking to capture the maximum amount of useable footage. Regardless of his efforts, many of the location scenes featuring the wolves would later need to be rerecorded within the controlled environment of a studio soundstage.

The hawks were no more helpful. Numerous takes were required, as the birds demonstrated more affinity for landing on boom mikes than Rutger Hauer's wrist and for spreading wings across the face of the actor while he was in the middle of delivering his lines. Even Othello, the giant Frisson stallion and trained circus performer selected to act as Navarre's loyal steed, proved desperately difficult to predict. Having spent much of his life indoors, the horse was more interested in chasing butterflies than starring in a major motion picture. When Hauer pulled on his reins, Othello rejected medieval battle for a fanciful prance.

Despite the persistent complexity presented by working with animals, it occasionally provided moments of much-needed comic relief. For one scene, Donner needed a simple shot of Broderick on the saddle of the independent-minded Othello, and for the horse to take a few, gentle steps away from camera. "I've been riding my whole life," the actor assured his doubters, "don't worry about it." After receiving an encouraging slap on its rear by Hauer, however, Othello broke into far more than a mild gallop. The horse bolted at high speed into a nearby valley — with the wailing Broderick hanging on for dear life. The pair failed to return for a full, nerve-wracking forty-five minutes.

With the majority of the film lensed on location, Stuart Baird's mobile cutting room served as the production's central nervous system. Donner once more placed complete faith in his "nagging mother-in-law"; the tempestuous team editing dailies together during the evening to assess what additional footage, if any, needed to be shot the following day. Afterward, the bickering duo set up table and chair outside the trailer to enjoy the sunset with a few drinks. Donner also hosted cookouts, so the cast and crew could sip red wine and revel in the stunning Italian landscape. "It was a very good crew," Richardson remembers. "Everybody mixed together; we used to have parties together. We'd all go out to Dick's house on a Saturday night and have a party there... everybody was a family."

Even if the milieu was breathtaking to behold, the complexities involved with filming on location made for rigorous work. At times the temperature was barely above freezing, while in Cortina — an area chosen specifically for its vast snow — the landscape proved dry and barren, prompting producers to fly in fake snow. In order to film Gaston's dramatic escape from the dungeon of Aquila, the mushroom farms that were flooded with water to serve as ancient sewers, offered an unbearable stench.

There were also logistical difficulties. Thirteen sites of historic significance were utilized in order to satisfy Donner's demand for verisimilitude, including three separate cathedrals that — through skillful editing — would appear in the movie as the one walled city, replete with cobbled streets and a moat. Unable to shoot in a real medieval church for the climactic scene of the movie (for fear of damaging precious artifacts), Donner ordered one built. It was 250 feet long, 80 feet high, made out of hardboard, plaster, real stone and tiles.

The set that provided the most complexity was the hilltop abbey of Father Imperius, which required the construction of a funicular railway to safely transport cameras, lights and all related equipment up the side of the cliff. All in all, *Ladyhawke* would overrun its four-month shooting schedule by an entire month.

During filming, Donner invited creative suggestions from each member of the production. He affirms, '[Filmmaking's] not a democracy, but it has to be a collaborative medium. I love to be challenged. It keeps your mind going, it keeps your creative juices going, and if you're smart and you're open-minded it leads you down some wonderful paths you never thought you were going to go down." In his book *Leadership is an Art*, author Max DePree describes participative management as giving everyone "the right and the duty to influence decision making and to understand the results. Participative management guarantees that decisions will not be arbitrary, secret, or closed to questioning. Participative management is not democratic. Having a say differs from having a vote."

Participative management was a cornerstone of Donner's success as a filmmaker, utilized on each and every production helmed, although on *Ladyhawke* the level of influence enjoyed by his cinematographer, Vittorio Storaro, served to create a level of unspoken friction and resentment on the set. The highest paid and arguably the most talented lighting cameraman of his era, Storaro was accustomed to yielding extraordinary power — the stipulations within his contractual deals ensuring him a level of almost complete creative autonomy. Prints could not be struck without his personal signature of approval, and his handpicked, all-Italian camera crew required to answer to him, and only to him. Richardson reflects, "There was a lot of politics surrounding Storaro. Unfortunately, I think the movie got a bit sidetracked because the lighting became more important than anything else. It put Dick in a very difficult position, I think, and it made it uncomfortable for a lot of the rest of us on the movie... The unit would all be there at 7.30am on set [but] Storaro would turn up at 9.00am because he had to take [his] kids to school. Meanwhile, his crew wouldn't put the camera on the set unless Storaro was there. He hired all his own people, he told the lab to have the takes that Dick hadn't printed be printed because he preferred the lighting on them, all sorts of little things like that."

Donner took a bilingual tack in attempting to control Storaro's talkative crew. "Quiet! Quiet, goddamn it!" he pleaded, followed by "Silencio!"

Although it never developed into a serious conflict, a tangible test of strength was fought out between Donner and Storaro. It was a small tension, but a tension nonetheless, perhaps best encapsulated during the lensing of a scene in which Gaston stares lovingly at the wounded Isabeau d'Anjou.

"M-a-t-t-e-w-e," Storaro queried of Broderick.

"Yes?"

"When you lean over to touch her, don't do that."

"V-e-e-e-t-o-r-i-o," Donner chimed in with mock Italian accent.

"Yes, D-e-e-e-k?"

"When you talk to the actors without talking to me first, don't do that."

Officially at least, the producers of *Ladyhawke* refute any suggestion of a difficult working relationship with Storaro. Donner describes him as a "maestro," Shuler as "inspiring." They remain positively in awe of his lavish photography, and highly appreciative of his innovative approach to filmmaking, which included the development of one of the earliest automated lighting boards, utilized for filming on the Aquila cathedral set at Cinecittà.

Michelle Pfeiffer was luminous as *Ladyhawke*'s Isabeau d'Anjou. Donner waxes, "There's a moment [in the film] where she's just a black figure in a big close-up, and she turns very slowly, just moves around gradually to reveal her face. It is so beautiful, she's to die over." Harvey Bernhard concurs, "She was adorable, cute, [and a] wonderful actress… she did a hell of a job."

Although recently married to the actor Peter Horton, Pfeiffer's coruscating beauty ensured that she was a much lusted after object of affection on set. None were more enamored with her than Mathew Broderick, who according to one production insider was "sick in love with her, [but] she didn't give him a tumble." Surprisingly, Pfeiffer was cool with her co-star, Rutger Hauer, likely because of his addiction to Gauloises cigarettes and espresso coffee, habits that lent him medieval-quality breath.

Due to his sheer physicality and strong fencing skills, the dashing Dutchman found restraint during action scenes a difficult concept to master. Stuntmen were often left limping away from bruising encounters. While shooting a climactic swordfight scene, Hauer twisted his ankle and fell awkwardly, suspending shooting for ten days while he walked in a cast.

Richardson reflects, "He was a strange guy, Rutger. I mean I liked him enormously, but he did some funny things. He wanted to drop and fall to his knees in every scene, I remember us joking about it at the time." Donner admired Hauer, even if he was annoyed that having originally declared that *Ladyhawke* was "a perfect script," the actor had begun to suggest changes to the material. On one occasion toward the end of filming, a conversation between the actor and his director became heated. Says producer Harvey Bernhard, "I remember the day he [Hauer] rode up to the castle for the final scene. We had twelve hundred extras and he said, 'I've got shingles and I can't act today.' Dick Donner stood up to him and said, 'You fucking well will act today.' And that was serious. I thought I was going to have to step in between them."

On the last day of filming, Rutger Hauer and Michelle Pfeiffer climbed upon a horse for a publicity photo. When Hauer pulled too hard on the reins,

Othello the Frisson stallion reared up and fell over backward. Pfeiffer was thrown clear, but Hauer was only halfway off when they hit the ground, the horse landing on top of him. Luckily, they had been on grass. If they had been on solid ground, Hauer would have had a broken leg for his trouble.

"I'm in love," Donner confessed over the phone.

"With who, for Christ's sake?" replied Mankiewicz, at home in Los Angeles overseeing production of the television series *Hart to Hart*.

"Lauren Shuler."

"Dick! Dick! When I last left you, Lauren Shuler was the enemy."

"Oh, she's wonderful..."

Unbeknown to anyone on set, Shuler's marriage to Warner Bros. executive Mark Rosenberg had failed. After Rosenberg had visited her on location and the pair agreed to a divorce, she had stared into the abyss of emotional collapse. As Stuart Baird describes, "They'd grown apart, and she was devastated by it. There she was in the middle of nowhere, so to speak, in Italy, with a movie that she had developed and people who weren't being very nice to her. I think that Dick, being a bighearted guy. thought, 'Well, this is terrible. Poor kid.' And it all developed from there."

The independence and resolve that had once irritated Donner now compelled him, camouflaging as it did a clearly sensitive, vulnerable soul. He remembers, "For the first time in two years this girl who was so tough, who had taken on the studios and the producers, I saw her cry for the first time. And my heart opened up, and I fell madly in love." He ended a relationship with a mysterious Italian countess, whom he had dated since filming began, and immediately declared his new feelings to Lauren. Given the collapse of her marriage, the timing was more than a little awkward, but Donner was never one to hide his emotions. He would have burst rather than keep his feelings locked up inside. To his great surprise and relief, Lauren felt the same. The spark of attraction between them had probably always been there, suppressed by their relationships with others and the pressure and level of distrust that comes with collaborating on a major Hollywood movie. Perhaps one reason for the previous tension between them was that, until now, they could not be together.

Donner was an incorrigible romantic, and he had been involved in many a strong relationship over the years, but none of the women he had known could match Lauren. She stood far out above them all. She was beautiful and talented, unafraid to stand up to him, to push him around if he needed it. Yet beneath the bold confidence was a simmering vulnerability that he found simply irresistible. Inside he knew that his life would never be the same again.

Lauren, however, was more cautious. She was as smitten as he, but also fearful of being hurt. At her behest, the new couple attempted to keep their partnership a secret, but to no avail. To their friends it was obvious. "She didn't think much of him when he was being nasty to her," describes Alan Ladd, Jr., "and he didn't think much of her. Then I was in Rome with my wife, we all had dinner, and I said to my wife afterward, 'I think they've got a relationship going.' And sure enough..."

"It's a movie [set]," laughs Stuart Baird. "It's like a little village. Everybody knows what's going on: Who's doing what to whom and how many times... you can't keep anything secret."

At the end of filming, Donner left Italy and returned to his home in Hollywood, which was undergoing renovation. The designer Harry Newman conceived the expansive remodeling, which would ultimately feature a guesthouse on a hill, and a lodgings apartment underneath the property for housekeepers. As he didn't yet employ service staff, Donner turned the housekeeper's quarters into cutting rooms. His garage became a projection room, utilizing two state-of-the-art projectors gifted by Warner Bros. following the success of *Superman*. He felt more comfortable editing *Ladyhawke* in his home, as opposed to on the studio lot, mainly because he feared accusations that the British editor, Stuart Baird, was stealing the job of an American editor. Baird's employment in the U.S. was not against union rules, as the editor had begun working on the project abroad, but Donner decided that he would rather not tempt complaint.

Pouring through the enormous amount of location footage in his makeshift editing suite was an exhausting experience. In order to keep the finished film close to the two-hour mark, the director was pressured by both Lauren Shuler and Stuart Baird to exorcise the many establishing shots he had filmed of stunning Italian vistas, and to trim select action sequences — including much of the dramatic final battle between Navarre and Marquet. To make matters more difficult, the climax of the movie had not been locked down during the scripting process. One draft had Imperius morphing the Bishop into a rat, before transforming himself into an owl. Another draft featured the bishop blowing himself up. In addition to the lover's embrace that was eventually chosen for the final moment, a scene was lensed where — in true fairy tale fashion — Isabeau and Navarre walk out of the cathedral following their showdown with the Bishop, and ride off into the sunset to idolatry cheers. Donner dropped this ending in the editing room as being redundant, maybe even *too* sentimental for his taste.

If the staggering amount of footage slowed the editing process, then so too did the quality of the live audio track. The stormy nature of their partnership may have calmed considerably over the years, but Baird was once more left exasperated by Donner's habit of talking to his actors throughout the course of a take. "If you were an animal, I'd remove your voice box,"

the editor once threatened, despairingly. Also, the concrete floor at Cinecittà Studios had been carpeted with a rubber composite so that Othello,
the giant Frisson stallion, would not slide as he walked. However, the noise
from his hooves driving along the rubber floor sounded contrived. Much
of the dialogue recorded for the film's closing sequence was deemed unus-
able, and Rutger Hauer was required to record additional lines at his home
in Europe.

Blue screen footage of Isabeau's dramatic hilltop fall and transition into a
hawk also proved problematic to edit. At the time of filming (after months
spent on location in the Italian cold) Pfeiffer had developed a serious cold
sore on her lip. Mostly disguised behind heavy makeup, Donner and Baird
nonetheless worked tirelessly to find a shot of the actress that would not
reveal the unfortunate outbreak.

Yet, of all the post-production difficulties, it was the musical scoring of
the film that ultimately caused the most stress and tension.

"No fucking way!" Baird screamed defiantly.

"You've got to listen," the director assured, throwing a dozen albums by
the pop group The Alan Parsons Project on a work desk, "it's going to be
this cool thing."

Donner had spent the entire production listening to albums by the band,
and in his mind, the music had become inextricably linked with the experience of making the film — a production on which he had truly fallen in
love for the very first time. A reluctant Baird cued a rough cut of *Ladyhawke* to music from the assorted albums, and Donner hired Andrew Powell,
a member of the Parsons band, to compose and record an original score.
Just like Spielberg and Lucas, the undoubted kings of the modern entertainment picture, Donner understood the youth of the new core audience
for Hollywood film, and knew that it was crucial that *Ladyhawke* — in
nature a somewhat anachronistic piece — not exclude the vital eighteen-to-
twenty-five-year-old audience demographic. But it remained a controversial
decision taken against the advice of those around him. "Powell went away
and recorded the soundtrack," Baird remembers. "It was not good. With the
beat, nothing seemed cued to the picture. So I said to Dick, 'None of this is
any good.' But he insisted we mix it into the film."

"If ever there was a picture that cried out for Jerry Goldsmith," sighed the
late Tom Mankiewicz with hindsight, "this was it."

The Powell score was dubbed at great expense, but when a rough cut of the
picture tested with preview audiences the worst fears of Baird and Mankiewicz were confirmed. "We previewed it and we realized it wasn't working,"
says the former. "Everyone says, 'Oh it's no good, we'll have to do the music
again.' Yet Dick still insists on going with it."

Even Lauren Shuler, who Baird recalls as originally being in support of Donner's wishes, objected to the final mix. She recalls: "We disagreed, but he was the director. I let him know my thoughts. There's only so much you can do when you're a very young producer as I was, and he was a very established, successful director. I told him my thoughts, I showed him the preview research, and he made his decision."

Donner did not even consider the move a stubborn gamble. He trusted his instinct that the score would ensure that the tone of his movie never slipped into the dangerous realm of taking itself *too* seriously — and could quite possibly make his period drama accessible to a broader audience. A futuristic, electronic sound was thus interwoven into Donner's world of medieval fantasy.

As Donner struggled in the editing room to refine and place the finishing touches to *Ladyhawke*, he perceived a lack of confidence in his work from the Warner Bros. boardroom. He grew disheartened by his meetings with various studio executives, during which attempts to finalize marketing and distribution strategies invariably stalled. Donner grew so paranoid that he feared that the studio might go as far as to bury his film without release. The director was unequivocally proud of the material, and convinced that the picture bore the potential of a dynamic hit, but under such looming doubt he struggled to remain his usual confident and upbeat self.

In spite of the problems with *Ladyhawke*, Richard Donner Productions expanded as it invited a slate of new projects to produce, and Donner soon began scouting for a larger office on the Burbank studio lot. A sprawling space of Southwestern-style design previously occupied by Frank Sinatra quickly captured his attention. The detached bungalow known as "Building 102" offered autonomy as well as history. As of 1984, Steven Spielberg was using the office as a temporary base for the Amblin-produced (but Warner-distributed) *The Color Purple*. When Donner stopped by to venture in, he found Spielberg and his staff packing up boxes.

"Where are you going?" he inquired.

"We're moving to a new lot, a new space at Universal," Spielberg replied.

"Great. Who's got this office?"

"I don't know, but I think they've given it to somebody already."

"Oh really?"

Donner ran back to his more modest workspace, and grabbed a few precious belongings. As Spielberg wheeled out, he motored in. A day later, a stern-faced Warner official arrived to reprimand the opportunistic filmmaker.

"What are you doing?" she demanded. "You can't take this office; we've given it to somebody already."

"I know you did," Donner replied firmly. "You've given it to me."

Unlike his previous headquarters, which were cramped and claustrophobic, this new office space was a vast reflection of the director's premier standing in the industry. Donner decorated it with an assorted collection of toys and gadgets (including model airplanes and a pinball machine), movie posters and other memorabilia. The office was comfortable and relaxed — a funky space more akin to a playhouse than a part of a corporate empire. Rarely inclined to wear suits, Donner's typical attire continued to be casual sweatshirts and battered sneakers.

Donner's salient double whammy of back-to-back seventies blockbusters — *The Omen* and *Superman* — ensured that, as of 1984, he remained on Hollywood's A-list of directors. And it was Steven Spielberg — the friend whose vacated office he had recently assumed, and whose mega-hits *Jaws*, *E.T.* and *Raiders of the Lost Ark* had redefined the measure of a financially successful movie — who sat as the reigning king of modern entertainment cinema.

It hadn't always been that way. The friends had first met in a California sushi bar in 1973, when Spielberg had introduced himself and applauded Donner for his work on *The Twilight Zone* — noting his favorite episode as Donner's "Nightmare at 20,000 Feet." At the time, both men were ensconced in the world of episodic television at Universal, unaware of the future heights their film careers would scale. Yet ever since that first meeting more than a decade earlier, they had continually flirted with the idea of collaborating on a single project, co-producing a movie that one of them would direct. That film began as *The Goon Kids*, a buccaneering quest of adolescent friends searching for the buried treasure of a mysterious pirate named One Eyed Willy, based upon an original idea of Spielberg's and scripted by his protégé, Chris Columbus. Spielberg was content to pass on directing duties, for he yearned to move into "grown-up" filmmaking (in addition to wrapping on an affecting film version of the novel *The Color Purple*, Spielberg was also preparing an adaptation of J.G. Ballard's wartime autobiography, *Empire of the Sun*). As Warner Bros. continued to vacillate over a distribution strategy for *Ladyhawke*, Donner accepted Spielberg's invitation to direct *The Goon Kids*. "Dick gravitated to the screenplay like a fish to water," his former assistant, Jennie Lew Tugend, recalls. "He knew how to make that movie fun."

Both Donner and Spielberg spent hundreds of hours auditioning thousands of eager young hopefuls, constantly searching for the unique blend of innocence and precocity on which the entire production would rest. Even for directors with such established track records, it was a burden of not inconsiderable pressure. In order to relieve some of the anxiety, Spielberg asked Donner to consider hiring two actors with whom he had prior experience of working. Thirteen-year-old Corey Feldman was first to be cast as the wisecracking "Mouth," having previously appeared in *Gremlins*, and Ke Huy

Quan was similarly cast as the technical whiz "Data" — fresh from his turn as Short Round in *Indiana Jones and the Temple of Doom*.

The role of Mikey, the asthma-afflicted leader of the gang who dreams of saving his parents from bankruptcy (and saving his home from the clutches of ruthless property developers), proved more difficult to cast. After much intense auditioning, young Sean Astin arrived to read for the role. He was nervous and repeatedly blew his lines — screaming, "Oh, fuck!" each time that he did so. At first his spewing of profanity made Donner and Spielberg laugh heartily, but after the fourth expletive-laden mistake, the latter got up and excused himself from the room. A devastated Astin thought that he had ruined his chance. Donner instinctually sensed that the boy's nervousness was preventing him from performing to his potential. Astin recalls: "Dick got up and came around from behind the table. He took a knee next to me; he put his arm round me and said, 'Now I know you can do this, I just want you to relax.' He told me what he wanted me to do, and left me with the impression that he really wanted me to do well, that he really cared about me as a person." Throughout his career, Donner had devised many stratagems to bring the best out of his actors, but few ever matched the effectiveness of a comforting arm around a shoulder and a whispered vote of confidence — in particular when it came to child performers. On this occasion it was all that it took to eliminate Astin's anxiety, and he impressed enough to secure the role.

Despite hailing from an acting family, seventeen-year-old Josh Brolin had never performed professionally. But after improvising audition scenes with Donner using general dialogue from the script, he was offered the role of Mikey's screen brother, Brand. At a mere eleven years old, Jeff Cohen became the youngest of all the actors cast for the film, when he was offered the scene-stealing role of Chunk, an overweight kid with a penchant for the odd white lie. Once these core roles were allocated, Kerri Green was cast as the flame-haired love interest, Andy, and Martha Plimpton as her sidekick, Stef. The more experienced Anne Ramsey, Robert Davi and Joe Pantoliano were cast as the villainous Fratellis, the family of bumbling bad guys also in pursuit of the golden doubloons.

Throughout the entire process Donner understood that making the correct casting choices was crucial to the potential success of the project, and once again he sought actors whose "essential ingredients" fit those of the character they were to play. As the director said at the time, "Each of the kids is really his nickname in real life. Jeff is chunky, Key is fascinated with electronics, Corey never shuts up."

Actress Kerri Green agrees that, "Dick was very specific with the casting. He had Josh [Brolin] and I meet before he made a final choice, as he really wanted to make sure that we had chemistry. Martha and I were the only girls and we both came from New York, so we had an immediate reason to bond… and with the boys, I don't know why, but there was definitely [an] instant chemistry like everybody really was that close to one another, and I think that was because of brilliant casting." It had long been a skill of Donner's to audition actors without allowing them to realize that they were being tested. During Kerri Green's test scene, she took her shoes off and put her feet up on a couch. When the scene ended and she looked around, her shoes had vanished. She continues, "I had one of those moments where I didn't know where I had put them, and I didn't want to look stupid, you know, that whole thing. Basically, Dick had hidden my shoes. He is a very playful person, but I think his intention was to see how I would react. He doesn't look at you as an actor, he looks at you as the person that you are. He wants to bring out your personality, because that's what he wants on camera. And to do that he creates an atmosphere high in energy, a lot of silliness and a lot of fun, and I think that definitely comes across in all of his films." Spying Green's natural reaction to not being able to find her shoes gave Donner far more insight into her personality — and thus her suitability for the role — than the mere reading of lines from a page.

Robert Davi and Joe Pantoliano were cast as the squabbling Fratelli brothers, Jake and Francis, based upon their very real, simmering love-hate chemistry. The pleasure they derived in verbally abusing one another during the audition process would spill over during filming. "One minute they'd be joking with each other," Corey Feldman recalls, "and then the next minute they'd want to kill each other." The root cause of the majority of squabbles was Davi's enthusiasm for hiding Pantoliano's toupee.

Before the commencement of principal photography, Spielberg hosted a script seminar week at his Malibu home, developing *Young Sherlock Holmes* with director Barry Levinson in the mornings, and honing the newly-titled *The Goonies* with Donner in the afternoons and evenings. Inspired by his love of Rube Goldberg — the Pulitzer Prize-winning cartoonist, sculptor and author whose inventions made simple tasks amazingly complex — Donner pushed for an elaborate opening sequence that involved numerous such contraptions. The director conceived a front gate opening mechanism for the Walsh household, and introduced the idea that Data should enter by means of crashing through the family room window.

Come week's end, Donner advised Spielberg that the team should approach Tom Mankiewicz to polish a handful of scenes from the script. Having assisted Spielberg in a similar capacity on *Gremlins*, Mank was happy to oblige. A rag-tag bunch of kids (Mikey, Mouth, Data, Chunk, Brand, Andy and Stef) discover a seventeenth-century treasure map, and embark on a quest to capture the buried fortune of a mysterious pirate named One

Eyed Willy, and thus save their homes from the clutches of ruthless property developers. The misfit gang begins their journey in the basement of a run-down restaurant that serves as the hideout for a family of criminals known as the Fratellis. When the Fratellis return, the Goonies, except for Chunk, flee down an underground tunnel. Chunk is captured while attempting to alert the police of the unfolding drama and, after being locked in a cell with a deformed Fratelli son known as Sloth, he divulges the secret of the hidden booty. The Goonies make their way through the tunnels underneath Astoria, avoiding a perilous series of booby traps placed along the path. The kids eventually arrive in a giant cave housing One Eyed Willy's pirate ship and his fabled treasure, but as they start to line their pockets the Fratellis arrive and force them to give up the fortune. They are then made to walk the plank. However, the criminals unwittingly activate a final booby trap, one that causes the cave to crumble and the ship to set sail. All escape the destruction through a hole in the cave wall. Along the shore the Goonies are reunited with their parents, and the Fratellis are arrested (the innocent Sloth is adopted by Chunk and his family). Just as Mikey's father is about to sign a contract releasing the homes of the assembled families to property developers, a maid discovers diamonds hidden in Mikey's marble bag. Witnessing the loot, Mikey's dad tears up the agreement, a move that allows the kids to stay in their beloved Goon Docks.

Filming began in the autumn of 1984, in Astoria, Oregon. Desiring rain for their sleepy suburban town, Donner and Spielberg were delighted when the weather obliged — often raining six days of the week to provide a gray, muddy and cold environment for all involved. The cast and crew were enjoying being part of such a fun movie production that, for most, resembled more a family vacation than grueling film shoot. Although intense in its workload, the entire production adopted a somewhat carnival atmosphere, designed to invigorate and motivate its young cast, and enable their natural energy to be translated into crackling movie scenes. Donner ensured that, throughout shooting, the actors, their parents and guardians — even their teachers — acted as one big Goonie family. Corey Feldman's grandmother, his official production chaperone, baked banana cake for the crew and pumpkin pie for Donner — the director's personal favorite. For the stirring finale, lensed on Oregon's Cannon Beach, Donner insisted that all relatives and chaperones appear in cameo roles. In addition to Feldman's grandmother, Kerri Green's parents and Jeff Cohen's mother and sister would also earn screen time.

Donner also encouraged crewmembers to adorn *Goonies* paraphernalia after his own lead — the larger than life director himself rarely seen on set without his *Goonies* jacket, and a customized cap gifted to him by Spielberg that read "Head Goonie." The director knew that in order to draw the requisite energy from his young charges, filming had to remain fun, and in order to truly behave like kids, they should remain largely blinded to the rigors and demands of the filmmaking process. Says Jeff Cohen, "I remember Dick made it simple for us. If we were hiding behind someone else during a take, he would ask us, 'Who's your best friend?' and we would all have to yell out, 'The lens! The lens!' Then it would be, 'Who's your second best friend?' It was, 'The light! The light!' Then it would be who's your third best friend?' And it would be, 'The director! The director!' Instead of criticizing us because we were not finding our light, or we were missing the blocking, he'd say, 'Who's your best friend?' And he was always positive, he was always happy."

Another key to maintaining energy and enthusiasm was Donner's insistence upon his actors viewing rushes of what was being shot. "He would extend the lunch hour to make us watch what we were doing," remembers Sean Astin, "so that we were aware of what it was we were working on and we stayed connected to it. He was passionately committed to that. Anything that was good about our performances was because we were excited about what he was showing us. He knew how to get us excited about what we were working on."

The secret behind Donner's own unquenchable level of excitement was his inherent Tom Sawyer-like thirst for adventure, and he tumbled wholeheartedly into the myth. "I never saw it as a fantasy or a fairytale," he waxed at the time. "It's a true story [that] we just happen to be documenting the lives of a group of kids in a little town called Astoria, and the kids call themselves the Goonies." Donner's search for verisimilitude had been the creative mantra that guided the grand successes of *The Omen* and *Superman*, and once more with *The Goonies*, it would lend real heart to lighthearted proceedings.

Despite the fun and games, and the familial environment on set, filming *The Goonies* was far from easy. Donner knew that actors, in general, required a great deal of personal care and consideration. Children, too. Child actors, therefore, required an immense deal of attention. Dealing with up to seven of them at any one time, the director's level of patience and understanding was often tested to the extreme. In front of the camera, at least four of the ensemble would be looking the wrong way, while another two would be saying somebody else's lines.

The production was a source of great attention for the Astoria populace, and with the safety of his young actors his principal concern, Donner decided to buy out the local Thunderbird Motor Inn for a month. He turned it into a lockdown base camp. "We lived there," he recalls. "We wanted to try and keep an eye on the kids the whole time, because they were children and we were deathly afraid that they would wander off and get into trouble."

Just like all loving yet dysfunctional families, the Goonies became known for their beautiful chaos. Between the set, the classroom and the Thunderbird Inn, the kids spent so much time together that they quickly started to behave like siblings, which meant not just playing, laughing and joking with one another, but squabbling and fighting, too. "There was a lot of love and hate," Kerri Green recalls. "We were in each other's faces so much that our relationships became very intense. We could be best friends and bitter enemies within the space of an hour. We knew each other's families, and understood the dynamics of how they worked. So it was definitely kids behaving at their very best and their very worst." As patriarch, Donner was needed at all times, but if life was stressful, the director remained secretly delighted by the pandemonium. When production wrapped in Astoria after four weeks of filming and the cast and crew prepared to descend upon Burbank Studios in California, Donner was thrilled by the knowledge that the relationships being developed, and thus played out for the screen, were 100% real.

"There comes a time in every rightly constructed boy's life when he has a raging desire to go somewhere and dig for hidden treasure."

MARK TWAIN, *THE ADVENTURES OF TOM SAWYER*

A Goonie Life
(Hip, Hop! March, March!
Everybody Let's Go!)

When *The Goonies* returned to California and the confines of the sound-stages at Burbank Studios, Donner and Spielberg were often seen in deep discussion, although rumors of friction between the pair are likely wide of the mark. "Obviously, there's tension on any set," describes actor Corey Feldman, "especially when you're dealing with a multimillion-dollar production. But to me they seemed like brothers. They got along famously. They always had their arms around each other, or were huddled together talking."

As the most successful director of his era, Spielberg could not be anything other than a major presence. The auteur mogul filmed a number of sequences for *The Goonies*, far more detailed footage than his billing as a second-unit director gives him credit for (even though many of them ended up on the cutting room floor), but Donner's authority as director in chief was never a matter of dispute. Spielberg did not assume control of any directorial duties. Rather, an addled Donner had requested assistance, in order to capture the material he needed to complete the film on time after Warner Bros. unexpectedly brought forward the film's release date by an entire month. Similarly, Donner also enlisted help from producer Harvey Bernhard and production designer J. Michael Riva.

Jennie Lew Tugend, Donner's assistant at the time, confirms that, "When two filmmakers respect each other, they let each other do their own thing. I don't think Steven ever imposed himself on Dick, or the other way around. During post-production Steven was there a lot more, but when we were actually making the movie it was the Dick Donner show."

Each man was accustomed to being the master and commander of their productions — their track records having earned them the privilege of not having to yield authority — and both Donner and Spielberg understood from the offset that their collaboration invited the prospect of bringing friction to an otherwise smooth friendship. Accordingly, they had taken preventive steps before cameras began rolling. It was cordially agreed that if a creative impasse ever arose between them, then impartial Warner Bros. executive Terry Semel would break the deadlock.

In 1985, Donner made light to the journal *Starlog* that "every once in a while I'll see [Spielberg] talking to one of the kids and I'll grab him by the seat of his pants and tell him: 'Don't mess with my cast.' We start to laugh and have a ball." Spielberg told *Time* magazine that, "I've always been very zealous about directors' rights. I retain final-cut privilege, but I won't exercise it unless the director has a complete nervous breakdown, tries to burn the set down and is found one morning in the corner eating Ding Dongs."

Today, Donner emphatically maintains the line. "From the first day I met that kid, I've respected him," he assures. "I like him very, very much, and I love what his life has turned out to be. I don't think there has been a bad moment between us during the entire time we've known one another."

Donner had chosen to build a life in California, but he remained immensely close to his family in New York. He made a point to attend east coast family events, often wowing the assemblage by arriving with a beautiful Holly-wood woman in tow, such as the likes of Liv Ullmann or Nancy Sinatra. As his cousin, Geoff Howard, puts it, "He didn't slide in the side door. He was wonderful. He was the life of the party."

Carefree and relaxed, Donner seemed to be without a worry in the world. He worked hard, liked to play harder, a soul content to let life's chips fall where they may. His happy-go-lucky persona was honest, but it was not com-plete, for beneath his live-for-the-moment manner was a privately ambitious man, whose hidden focus was a major contributing factor behind his rise to potent Hollywood force. As generous and caring as he undoubtedly was, Donner could also be selfish when he had to be. When it came to his career, he had a bullheaded drive to achieve, and it rewarded him great success. It came, however, at a personal cost, for it undermined and eventually thwarted the majority of his romantic relationships. To Donner, the importance of advancing his filmmaking career always superseded that of cementing an inti-mate long-term connection with a woman. They could never exist in unison, for each demanded such unique, wholehearted attention. And if he could only choose one, he knew which one he wanted more. His career enabled him to express himself artistically, to touch the lives of not one, but millions. On set, directing, he was everything he imagined himself to be at his best: a strong leader, a friend and a father figure, a man whom others admired. And he liked to be in control.

It just so happened that his profession also delivered him financial reward beyond his wildest dreams, including beautiful homes and a collection of classic cars. Nobody was more surprised than Donner, therefore, when for the first time since he arrived in California, nearly three decades earlier, his career ceased to be the first and most important thing on his mind.

"I envy you," he reflected to his sister, Joan, during a family reunion.

"You envy me?" she replied. "What are you talking about, Dick? You've got the world at your fingertips. Everything you want."

"I don't want to do this anymore," he confessed. "I want somebody."

Somebody was Lauren Shuler, the attractive and talented producer with whom Donner had fallen hard in love. When they had first met, he had found her to be brittle and stubborn. Yet it had not taken him long to realize that her toughness was by design and not by nature — a camouflage in a hostile filmmaking world. The real Lauren was graceful, beautiful, generous and nurturing. She was as sensitive as he, a caring and compassionate woman troubled by many of the same social injustices that hurt him so deeply. She shared his love of animals and felt his passionate need to protect them from cruelty. She had been an activist since her college days, and with her help and guidance Donner would learn to channel his dismay over pertinent social issues (ranging from animal rights atrocities, to the tragic injustice of apartheid in South Africa) into dedicated action.

Lauren brought a balance to Donner's life that had otherwise been missing. She helped him to become better organized and more future-oriented. Her appreciation and knowledge of fine food, and her enthusiasm for cultured travel experiences, certainly helped him to develop more of a serious side — although he had traveled to many countries, it was with Lauren that he developed a worldliness he would otherwise not have had.

In the past, Donner was greatly attracted to women who wore vulnerability on their sleeve. He had always been allowed to lead a relationship, to be the man who nurtured and protected his significant other. But if it was Lauren's fragility during the breakdown of her marriage that had first opened Donner's heart to her, it was her independent spirit, confidence, and self-belief that sustained his passion. Her inner strength became the ultimate attraction. Even though they were both far away from the intoxicating romanticism of Italy, he simply could not get her out of his head. She was, as he would frequently describe, "The best thing that ever happened to him."

Yet because of their hectic schedules (he was simultaneously shooting *The Goonies* and editing *Ladyhawke,* she was invested in producing *St. Elmo's Fire,* the cult romantic-drama starring brat packers Emilio Estevez, Rob Lowe, Andrew McCarthy and Demi Moore) the amount of quality time they could spend together was frustratingly far between. This ultimately propelled Donner to view the importance of his career in a whole new light. He remained ambitious, and intended to prolong his stay on the directors' A-list for as long as he could, but with Lauren the first and last things on his mind each day, directing movies was no longer his first love. "He had found an area of work that he loved," recalls lifelong friend Danny Farr. "He was making money and he was successful, [but] he was restless at that time and he hadn't really found himself. He really didn't put his act together until he met Lauren." Donner had not believed in such a thing before, but now he contemplated: Had he met his soul mate? His family and friends would never believe him, but had he finally met *the one*?

"I think the unique thing about working with the kids on this picture is that every night I'm contemplating suicide," Donner joked in 1985. "Individually, they're wonderful, the warmest little things that have come into my life. But in composite form you get them together and it's mindblowing."

Trapping the Goonies within the confines of studio soundstages for several weeks at a time exacerbated the mayhem first witnessed in Astoria. Donner had managed to place his cast at such ease in his company that, more often than not, they would respond to his direction with mischievous, toothy grins, squirt him in the face with a water pistol, and then jump on his back and pull at his neck. Donner secretly loved the boisterous behavior, knowing that in order for the project to succeed they needed to express themselves as kids.

Sometimes, it could be an exercise in patience. Donner worked hard to control his temper if their behavior threatened to run out of control. From time to time he would roll his eyes, rub the bridge of his nose, or shrug his shoulders and throw his arms into the air. Only occasionally would he be forced to snap them back into line with a tentative snarl, for he had learned long before that the secret to developing productive relationships with child actors was to treat them firmly, but respectfully. It had worked for his acclaimed television movie, *Sarah T. — Portrait of a Teenage Alcoholic*, in which he teased a crucial, emotionally-charged performance from *Exorcist* star Linda Blair. For *The Omen*, it had helped him to coax from five-year-old Harvey Stephens a turn of appropriately devilish menace. For *The Goonies*, Donner's approach to handling his rag-tag group of (mostly) pre-teen performers helped induce in them his own one-for-all, all-for-one spirit of fun and adventure. "He was assertive, yet at the same time very understanding," describes Ke Huy Quan, who played "Data." "He listened to what everybody had to say. He respected us. He never talked to us like kids. We talked on the same level... he spent a lot of time with us off-camera when we weren't shooting, and he would just talk to us and hear us out."

Sean Astin remembers a conversation Donner held with him moments before filming an important scene set in the Walsh family attic, during which his character, Mikey, explains to his friends the mythology surrounding the pirate, One Eyed Willy: "In the script it was originally intended for one of the Fratelli brothers to give the speech, but it didn't have the emotional resonance that Dick wanted. Dick came to me literally fifteen minutes before we're going to film it, and he said, 'Sean, I want to tell you a story. I want you to really listen to the story, and when I'm finished, I want you to tell the story back to me.' I said, 'Okay.' He told me this story, and he told it beautifully. It was just like a page and a half of dialogue, but if I'd tried to memorize the whole thing, [when I acted] my eyes would have been shifting back and forth as I tried to remember the lines. [Learning lines] wasn't my particular skill set, but Dick knew that if I heard what was cool about the story then I'd be able to remember it and tell it back."

Such was the importance of the scene, however, that during filming Astin suffered from the same debilitating nerves that had affected him during his audition for the movie. He explains, "I got nervous again, and I kept fumbling it. After a few takes Dick said, 'Okay, everybody stop. Cut. Sean and I are going to go out and go for a walk.' Dick and I were outside, with an entire crew waiting inside. I was so nervous because of all the money that was being spent, and there was a lot of pressure. But he was just like, 'Let's sit down. Let's just hang out. I want you to get some fresh air, I want you to relax, and then we're going to go back in there and we're going to get this. You're going to do it.' He knew I could do it. He believed in me, and I never forgot that level of confidence that he placed in me. We walked back inside [and onto the stage], and I did the scene. He had essentially carried me through it. Dick has such tremendous skill as a director, and that moment was living proof of it."

Throughout his adult life, Donner had professed his intention to never father children. His choice was complicated — a critical dilemma indicative of a man more complex than is first perceived. What is known is that the deaths of his young cousin, Bobby Brauer (who succumbed to illness when Donner was just seven years old), and his great mentor, George Blake (who died from a heart attack at thirty-eight), played a role in his reasoning. "I'm sure it was the reason he didn't have children," confesses his sister, Joan Cohen, "He couldn't handle the idea that they could get sick, or that something could happen. He was petrified of loving that much and something happening to his child." Strangely (given his innate ability to tap into his own inner child), Donner claimed not to "understand" kids. It came as a surprise, therefore, when his young charges started to solicit from him some strong parental instincts. His experience working with *The Goonies* cast had proved him right: Children *were* amazingly deep and unpredictable creatures, but this fact of life no longer struck him with great fear, only enlightenment. As the production wore on, Donner gained immense pleasure from being both a confidante and a friend, a strong figure of male authority to his impressionable ensemble. Says he today, "The relationship I developed with those kids was something I never realized I could have with a child. They were amazing. Such good kids, and so very unique."

Both during production and after the release of the film, the director sustained strong friendships with Sean Astin, Jeff Cohen and Corey Feldman. To Astin, he expressed his fondness by gifting him a series of leather-bound, gold leaf novels — classics by Jack London, Herman Melville, H.G. Wells, and Mark Twain. Says the actor, "I've kept those books everywhere I've gone with me. From my bedroom growing up, to my first condo, to my first house with my wife, everywhere I've moved those books have had a place of importance [because] they represent to me what was important to him when he was a kid."

Donner's relationship with Jeff Cohen was particularly pertinent, as the boy's father had recently abandoned the family home. To an extent, he found himself stepping into the void as a surrogate father figure. Some years later, when an adult Cohen struggled to fight depression induced by his inability to sustain his acting career, it was Donner who would be there for him as a rock-solid pillar of support. He hired him as a production assistant, and encouraged him to explore off-camera opportunities in show business. After Cohen discovered a passion for entertainment law and enrolled in college, it was Donner who stood by his side on graduation day. Today, a partner in his own Hollywood-based legal firm (which ironically represents his Fratelli torturer, actor Robert Davi) Cohen displays but two framed photos on his office desk. The first is a portrait of his beloved mother and sister. The second is of Richard Donner.

Authenticity was integral to the success of *The Goonies*. Donner was interested in capturing the spontaneous, unfettered bedlam of youth over structured performance. He wanted his charges to behave in front of camera as they might in life, and to convey the most natural reaction possible to each outrageous stunt or comedy set piece. His actors were therefore invited to rewrite dialogue and even improvise portions of their scenes. Donner confirms that, "The script was well-written, but if they had an idea that they thought they could do more with than what we had put on paper, then I encouraged them to run with it."

Actor Ke Huy Quan agrees that, "When you read a script, they always have one line at a time per character. But we were kids who were fighting for screen time, and even when we didn't have lines we would speak over one another! Dick let us do it, and that's why he's such a great filmmaker.

He realized that's what kids do. They never talk one at a time, they always overlap."

Donner was not afraid to get tough when he had to. He helped Jeff Cohen achieve real tears, during a scene in which he's interrogated by the infamous Fratellis, by asking the boy to imagine his mother and sister dying. Robert Davi (Jake Fratelli) was also encouraged to intimidate the then-eleven-year-old. He actually pulled the hairs off the bottom of Cohen's neck.

Heavily influenced by the teachings of Stanislavsky, young Josh Brolin believed that the stress of being trapped in an underground cave would lead his character, Brand, to mentally regress to his mother's womb. He believed he should climb the walls of the cave in order to present his emotional descent. He took his idea to Donner, whose response was immaculate. "Yeah, you could do that," he measured to Brolin, "or you could just say the lines."

Despite the pressure of filming to an impossible shooting schedule, Donner's love of improvisation could not be quelled. "Dick doesn't storyboard," says the director's former assistant, Michael Thau. "[On] *The Goonies* [production designer] Mike Riva hired a guy who did three hundred drawings that storyboarded the whole film. Dick had them up on his wall in his office, and he looked at them and said, 'That's interesting.' Then he went and shot something else." Corey Feldman remembers, "Dick likes to see the action come alive on the set. He was the first director that really said, 'Do what you want. Just go for it.' He'd set up the scene for us, and just say, 'Go.'"

In the end, such was the spontaneous nature of the shoot that the finished film contained multiple original jokes created by the young actors.

If improvisation was proving a delight for its director and principal performers, it was less so for its weary editor, Michael Kahn, who was struggling to achieve continuity amongst all the fun. Donner's unique directorial style of talking over actors during a take, chattering instructions, encouraging them to ad-lib over one another, made it unusually difficult for an editor to cut around.

Football player John "The Tooz" Matuszak had been cast as the giant creature "Sloth," a deformed Fratelli locked in chains by his villainous family who is discovered and set free by the Goonies. Matuszak had been the number one choice in the 1973 NFL draft. He went on to play for the Oilers, the Chiefs, the Redskins, the Texans, and for the Raiders, with whom he won two Super Bowl championships. Yet despite his impressive professional achievements, the 6'8", three-hundred-pound-plus former defensive end was perhaps better known for his infamous off-field excesses: booze, out of control substance abuse, parties and fistfights.

Matuszak had been arrested more than once for driving under the influence of alcohol. On one of these occasions a police officer found a bayonet and a .44 magnum packed in his car. However, the most famous vignette from the Matuszak playbook of outrageous behavior was patently false. In his memoir, *Snake*, ex-footballer Kenny Stabler detailed how Matuszak willingly poisoned and killed two of his wife's dogs because they would not stop barking. Matuszak always denied the accusation, and Stabler later admitted the story was based on hearsay, and should not have been included in his book.

Donner had never been one to judge people on hearsay. On the contrary, he positively enjoyed offering opportunities to the misunderstood and the underappreciated, those in need of redemption or a second chance. Donner took people as they came, and rather than see Matuszak's bad guy reputation he found a sensitive, intuitive and humorous man — an underdog who needed little more than a fair shake and someone to believe in him in order to be the best that he could be. Driven by the need to be a positive force, Donner placed his faith in Matuszak.

When the former NFL star had arrived at Donner's office for his audition, the director had taken one look at him and begun jumping up and down with excitement. "This is Sloth, this is Sloth," he repeated, before leading him upstairs to Terry Semel's office.

"Is this Sloth or what?" he asked the studio president.

"Yeah, yeah," Semel agreed. "You're Sloth."

Craig Reardon and Thomas R. Burman's elaborate makeup designs for the deformed character provided many a talking point on set. The finished creation was a face that only a mother could love, with fifteen overlapping pieces and left-eye movement and ears operated by a hidden remote control device. In addition, the tortuous makeup process would have to be repeated from scratch if the actor were to ever get wet, a fact which the other actors would cruelly hold Matuszak to ransom. In his autobiography, *Cruisin' With The Tooz*, the former sportsman revealed: "I would arrive at the set at five in the morning, and it would take them five hours just to make me up. Even then I couldn't shoot my scenes. Because of child labor laws, the children had to be finished with their work and off the set by a certain time. So while they were doing their scenes, I would spend those six to eight hours doing nothing, lying in a trailer, going nuts. There were so many glues and adhesives used that my skin was breaking out all over. One of my eyes was completely covered by makeup, so I couldn't even read. I also couldn't leave the set because a riot would have started if anybody saw me."

Matuszak's occasionally unpredictable behavior on set alienated him from some, in particular producer Harvey Bernhard. Donner remembers Matuszak, who tragically died from heart failure in 1989, somewhat differently. "He put up with such crap from those kids," the director reminisces. "It was a tough shoot... we tried to waterproof (the makeup) for the sequence where they discover the boat and we'd told the kids, 'Whatever you do, don't splash John, because even though we tried to waterproof his makeup we can't guarantee that it is.' They all promised. But when they got in the water, with all their excitement of seeing the boat, they got him so wet that his five-hour makeup job had to be repeated that afternoon. It was a moment where I saw him get frustrated, but he didn't get angry. I can say without reservation that he was a great contributor, and one of the great losses."

As payback for getting him wet, when producers had Kentucky Fried Chicken delivered to the set as a treat for the kids, Matuszak's monster appetite saw him devour three family-sized buckets — leaving little more than scraps and bones for his pre-pubescent provocateurs.

Also causing a stir at the studio were the intermittent visits of various celebrities. Tim Burton and Paul Reubens stopped by during a break from filming *Pee-wee's Big Adventure*. Dan Ackroyd dropped in, as did Harrison Ford, who was keen to explore the underground caves. And then there was Michael Jackson, who at the end of filming presented an enthralled cast with concert tickets for the Jackson 5 "Victory" tour event at the Dodgers Stadium.

As filming entered its final six weeks, the entire production was buoyed by the commencement of shooting on the giant pirate ship, "Inferno," a full-scale model with three separate levels, created by production designer J. Michael Riva and housed in Burbank's largest stage. These scenes were the source of much excitement and anticipation — with Riva's mock-up one of the most impressive and daunting creations ever to grace the famous studio. After filming had wrapped, Donner attempted to persuade numerous theme parks across the U.S. to accept the ship as an attraction. Sadly, come the production's end, the set piece was scrapped.

As had been his approach through the entire shoot, Donner aimed to get only the most natural response from his new stars. He went to great lengths to do so for the movie's climactic scenes. "I never let the kids see the boat. They were banned from the stage from day one, from the start of its construction. The day they were supposed to come out of the shoot and hit the water, turn around and see the boat for the first time, I brought them all in with their backs to the camera. They all knew what they were going to see, but they had no idea what it was going to look like. And so on film when they turn and see the boat for the first time, it's their actual reactions."

With filming complete, Donner faced the daunting task of sixteen weeks of post-production (thanks to the extensive amount of ad-libbing and improvisation, more than a month of dialogue sound looping would be required). Before doing so, however, he was determined to recharge his batteries, and arranged an immediate vacation to Maui. But he could not leave until he had attended the production's official wrap party, the highlight of which was a gag reel that ran for hours. With him in attendance was Lauren Shuler, whom Donner was proud to introduce as his girlfriend.

Throughout the evening Donner was bothered by what he perceived to be the cold and standoffish attitude of the Goonies. In front of Lauren, in whom he had confided his strong feelings for the gang, he repeatedly tried to engage them. His efforts proved to no avail. Now that filming was complete and he had yelled, "Cut!" for the final time, the children appeared to have lost all interest in their director. Believing that he had entirely misread the strength of their bond, Donner left the party disconsolate.

The exhausted director arrived in Maui and slept for the entire day. He woke up the following morning, disturbed by a neighbor whose car had broken down and who needed a ride to the local market. Interested only in basking in the sun, Donner was determined to spend his time free of errands, so he merely offered her the keys to his Jeep. When she protested that she could not drive a stick shift, he reluctantly agreed to serve as chauffeur. By the time the pair returned from the store, such was his rush to hit the beach that he only barely noticed *Goonies* star Josh Brolin hopping around in the sand. "What the hell are you doing here?" Donner queried, shocked.

"Err, remember I told you my mother was taking me surfing after the picture?" the teenage actor stammered.

"Yeah, but this isn't very good surfing here."

The befuddled Brolin wasn't looking at him, but past him. Donner turned around to see that the television set in his family room was on. Confused, he ran back inside.

"Hey, Dick," giggled Jeff Cohen, sitting on Donner's couch with his feet perched up on the coffee table, "don't you have cable in this place?"

"What the hell is this?" the director roared in amazement.

One by one, Sean Astin, Ke Huy Quan, Kerri Green, and Martha Plimpton appeared from various crevices inside the house and ran over to hug him (Corey Feldman would arrive on a flight later in the day). Donner laughed so hard that he dropped to his knees. The motley crew wrenched their stunned director back to the beach, where Spielberg and the Fratellis (actors Anne Ramsay, Joe Pantoliano and Robert Davi) awaited them.

Spielberg had conceived the supersized prank during the final week of filming in California, when each day Jeff Cohen arrived on set dressed as a Hawaiian tourist. Geared up in his vacation shirt and shorts, sun hat and glasses, and carrying a suitcase that read, "Maui or Bust," the portly child star had snuck up behind Donner and cheered, "Hey, Dick, when are we going to Maui, man? What's going on? I can't wait; this is going to be awesome!"

"You know, Jeff, I got an idea," the mischievous Spielberg had smiled afterward. "Wouldn't it be funny if all you kids were there when Dick got to his house in Maui?" Cohen excitedly agreed as his producer colluded with the rest of the ensemble to book them all onto a private plane — complete with parents and guardians in tow — to disrupt Donner's recuperative getaway. The only condition for the prize was that the plan had to remain secret — hence their distant behavior exhibited at the end-of-movie party. "The best acting they ever did in their lives," Donner laughs, "was during that last week of filming, where they all had peanuts in their mouths and couldn't chew them. If one of them had blown it for the others, then they all would have killed them."

Spielberg had planned for his cohorts to stay only half a day, before flying onto a separate island, but when Donner recovered from the shock he insisted that everybody spend the night. He swam with the gang in the ocean, and after buying out the local grocery store, enjoyed "the biggest barbecue in the history of Maui." In the evening he screened a preview copy of *Ladyhawke*, before inviting over another of his neighbors, shock rocker Alice Cooper, to entertain his guests.

Within days of his return from Maui, Donner threw himself into post-production on *The Goonies*. A mere eighteen special effects shots were inserted into the picture, a clear reflection that — for all his delight in painting a canvas vast in action and spectacle — developing engaging, larger-than-life characters remained his first filmmaking priority.

Donner would need to reserve as much energy as possible for one final Goonie task — helming the first two-part movie-themed music video ever. The MTV event for Cyndi Lauper's pop song "The Goonies 'R' Good Enough" was the first to borrow cast members, director and producer of a studio feature. The vignettes would play a pivotal role in the film's promotion.

If Donner's legendary vocal chords had taken a beating during months of shooting the movie, it was nothing compared to what was required to control wild girl Lauper, *The Goonies* cast, and a horde of professional wrestlers. Filming was almost complete pandemonium, amongst which Donner desperately fought to capture more than a hundred shots in just two days of filming. As a result, the finished video would play like it had been conceived on a variety of hallucinogenic drugs.

More than a year since filming had wrapped in Italy, the problematic *Ladyhawke* was still causing consternation for the Warner Bros. executives charged with controlling distribution and exhibition strategies. As of early 1985, Michelle Pfeiffer, Matthew Broderick and Rutger Hauer were not easily recognizable names — thus ruling out star power as a means of selling the picture to the ticket-buying public. It was also less than clear to which genre of film *Ladyhawke* belonged. Was it a period picture? More supernatural fantasy perhaps? Donner stood firm in his belief that *Ladyhawke* was a true romance. Nervous executives, however, were unconvinced that the picture could be sold as such to the (new) key eighteen-to-twenty-five-year-old demographic, and preferred instead to debate the merits of pitching it to this market as an action-adventure flick.

A typically forthright Donner would later air his disgust at what he believed was a chronic lack of energy and creativity within the Warner Bros. publicity department. "They have all these idiots researching it by talking to old ladies at the supermarket," he fumed. "It's bullshit... They had no idea what to do with it. I think they were afraid to say it was a fantasy, or that it was a love story. They tried to turn it into much more of an action piece than it really was. Instead of just saying it was a beautiful, unrequited love story."

Left in despair by the corporate confusion, and in an attempt to inject some momentum into a project whose place on the release schedule was consistently in question, Donner had suggested to Warner Bros. a marketing campaign that implied the film was based upon a famous myth. To complement such an approach, he considered adding a title card to the film claiming that *Ladyhawke* was inspired by a true story. Eventually realizing that this pushed the limits in his quest for verisimilitude, Donner rescinded his concept, although not before the studio had included it in their preliminary promotional materials. The screenwriter, Edward Khmara, was quite naturally irked by the implication that his original idea had been cribbed from a historical truth, and he filed complaint with the Writers Guild of America. The union fined the studio and forced it to phase out the offensive material.

On the eve of *Ladyhawke*'s debut, Donner did his best to remain confident and upbeat. "*Ladyhawke* is a very special, very unusual, very difficult movie to sell and a very difficult movie to earn critical acclaim," he informed one movie publication. "But I will be very disappointed if *Ladyhawke* doesn't really pack them in."

Early reviews of the picture were encouraging. "*Ladyhawke* soars," glowed Sheila Benson for the *Los Angeles Times*. "It is enchanted... a bold, beautiful, marvelous vision." *Variety* called the film "a very likeable, very well-made fairytale," and remarked that Donner "creates a real desire [in the audience] that the duo [Navarre and Etienne] be together after the credits fade." *Newsweek*'s Jack Kroll noted that Donner possessed a "real feeling for the atmosphere of fable."

Vincent Canby of *The New York Times* stood in the opposing corner, decreeing that Donner had "obvious difficulty coordinating the various elements of the overall vision," an opinion shared by *Time* magazine, which concluded the director was "no spellbinder of medieval melancholy." *The Washington Post* insisted Donner "never quite gets the tone right... With these rock anthem guitar solos burning in your ear, you can never enter the movie's world — it just feels like a very expensive costume party."

When the first financial figures were phoned into his Hollywood household a day after *Ladyhawke*'s release on April 12, 1985, Donner found that remaining his usual, deliciously upbeat self was all but impossible. During its first weekend, *Ladyhawke* tolled a meager $4 million in box-office receipts. It was a killer blow for a picture that had opened in more than a thousand theaters. During its entire run, the film would collect just $18 million on U.S. soil.

Throughout the weekend, the mood in the Donner home was one of death. As the director's mood spiraled downward, Lauren became his emotional crutch. Although she too was immensely disappointed by the commercial failure of *Ladyhawke*, she conditioned herself to be pragmatic and levelheaded, to coolly analyze the experience and to learn from it. Her preparedness was helped by having seven projects in development with different studios, and by being poised to put pen to paper on a three-year development deal at Disney. In the end, her strength re-energized Donner and allowed him to focus on the real reasons why *Ladyhawke* had punched so far below its weight at the box-office.

While Rutger Hauer may have possessed the requisite brooding intensity of Navarre, as a leading man, the Dutch actor could not attract the same number of ticket sales as a bona fide Hollywood star. Nobody could know for sure what impact *Ladyhawke* might have made with the name recognition of a Harrison Ford or a Mel Gibson headlining the bill.

In Hauer's defense, he was given little chance to shine by Warner Bros., who chose to omit his image from the standard one-sheet movie poster advertising the film. The finished material instead featured a perplexed-looking Matthew Broderick with an eagle perched above his head, and the stunning Michelle Pfeiffer a less-than-glamorous shadow in the distant background.

Producer Harvey Bernhard believes that *Ladyhawke*'s distribution strategy was primarily to blame for the disaster. Says he, "[Warner Bros.] didn't release the picture right. They should have released the picture as a love story in a handful of theaters and let it build [momentum through positive word of mouth]." In keeping with the times, the studio had opened *Ladyhawke* as an event movie playing on a large number of theater screens, although not necessarily accompanied by the money needed to support such a release.

While each potential reason for *Ladyhawke*'s failure carries a degree of validity, ultimately the film did not succeed because it was a picture out of its time. Donner had been right all along. *Ladyhawke* was an unrequited love story, primarily a passionate throwback to the more-restrained, classically-told romance pictures of the thirties and forties, albeit one seasoned with modernistic, fantasy-based subject matter.

Donner had intelligently combined classic and contemporary form and style on *The Omen* and *Superman*, both of which provided an intriguing mixture of old-fashioned narrative storytelling and slick new Hollywood aesthetic, but somehow *Ladyhawke* fell out of keeping with the cinematic zeitgeist. It is, at times, an awkward clash between myth and modernism that lacked the narrative pace and edge-of-your-seat thrills and spills demanded by audiences of the *Indiana Jones* age.

A few months after *Ladyhawke*'s release, *The Washington Post*'s Paul Attanasio delivered a telling essay entitled "Summer in the Spielburbs." The critic wrote, "After *Raiders of the Lost Ark*, we want 10 thrills a minute; after *Airplane!* the requirements for a density of gags has become almost insatiable. As consumers of pop culture, we've become a nation of speed freaks, without time to think."

Although they were not yet star names, *Ladyhawke*'s cast delivered sincere and engaging performances. Donner's taut direction delivered an effective balance between humor and pathos, and the film's finale was nothing if not rousing and emotionally satisfying. Donner imagined such aspects to be of timeless appeal (Andrew Powell's music score was the only aspect of the picture that would forever date it to the eighties), but in this instant they weren't. For the MTV generation that now made up the crucial majority of the movie-going public, *Ladyhawke* may have appeared overwhelmingly anachronistic.

After the soul-draining experience of making *The Toy*, Donner had found inspiration in the lover's tale of Etienne Navarre and Isabeau d'Anjou. He once said, "I'm very attracted to the notion that love can *always* be resolved. As long as it's *true* love. I mean, *no one* can wish for love to die." For the erstwhile director, *Ladyhawke* was a canvas that reflected his innermost passions — his belief in the power of love and friendship, and the essential goodness of humanity. Like Frank Capra in a way, these feelings charged his every filmmaking move. Regardless of its box-office appeal, or lack thereof, *Ladyhawke* had been the film that *he* wanted to make, the film that *he* wanted to see. He loved the film unconditionally.

Others share his passion. Says former flame Liv Ullmann, "It's so full of dreams and fantasy, and [reflects] so much of what is Dick inside. And at that time it was such a different film and he was so brave to make it." Explains friend Alan Ladd, Jr., "I loved *Ladyhawke*. I would be very, very proud to have my name on it."

Equally, as the years have passed, *Ladyhawke* has become a cult pursuit for fans enamored with its unabashed romanticism.

Warner Bros. *were* fully invested in marketing *The Goonies* — for all intents and purposes the jewel in their forthcoming release schedule. In addition to Cyndi Lauper's two-part MTV video, a host of tie-in products and merchandise were commissioned to publicize the film as a major event. Books, toys, clothes; an entire assortment of ancillary products would be sold in an attempt to turn the months from June through September into one long Goonie summer. To help build anticipation, a theatrical teaser trailer and a series of TV spots would bow several weeks before the release of the movie.

Donner aimed to be centrally involved in the marketing of *The Goonies*, and invited distribution executive Brian Jamieson to his office to discuss how the picture could be positioned for sale. Jamieson was impressed by Donner's enthusiasm and ideas, but even more astounded by Building 102 on the Warner Bros. studio lot. Few corporate figures ever stopped by to visit, and Jamieson was one of the first to discover how Donner had made the office his own. "Other directors had offices on the lot," he remembers, "but Dick seemed to have an entire floor." Donner may have grown more business savvy over the years, remained in tune with the corporate demands of marketing his films, but more than anything his personal space in Building 102 reflected his inner child. Jamieson continues, "It had a room installed dedicated to arcade video games. In many ways it was like walking into a family room. Dick spent so much time there that I guess it was important to give it the feel and the look of what it might have been like back home."

It was the same office Donner had visited more than twenty years before, when he had met Frank Sinatra to discuss set designs on his debut feature, *X-15*. Then it had been a fifties modern space. Donner had since brought in soft couches and "funked it out." He replaced Sinatra's piano with a state-of-the-art sound system, playing the music so loud the building would rock. An outside deck was built and, as a gift, friend and production designer J. Michael Riva commissioned a canvas of the view from his beloved beach house in Maui, replete with palm trees and the ocean. It was just like being at home.

It was agreed with executive Terry Semel that *The Goonies* would be sold as the "Steven Spielberg presentation" of a "Richard Donner film." Donner was no pushover. He understood the mechanics of the business, that to survive one had to learn how to be a solid self-promoter. But if he was not soft, then he was also far from ruthless. Like all great directors, Donner intended to be known and respected for his work. His professional reputation was sacrosanct. But throughout the course of his career, other filmmakers would fight harder than he to ensure that their names entered the realm of public consciousness. The title of "auteur," to walk the path to iconic status, never interested Donner. He was by nature too humble and modest. And, crucially, he was unwilling to give up his semblance of a normal life. Icons became public property, and Donner valued his privacy.

So, too, he knew that to become a universally recognized face of Hollywood took more than just talent and hard work. He had seen others, friends even, choose to envelope themselves within a fabricated aura of mystique, and develop an all-consuming need to protect the enigma. The end result was a life lived in a vicious world of tension, negativity and paranoia. Hollywood agent and studio executive Lew Wasserman once observed that, "Directors, in order to stay in the game, are among the worst people we've got. You have to be absolutely ruthless. Many of them are sociopaths."

Donner enjoyed promoting his movies, but the pandemic craving for attention simply did not exist within him. He shunned nearly everything that went with celebrity status, knowing that if it was afforded him, his life as he knew it would never be the same. At a point during the mid-eighties, he decided that what mattered to him the most were his movies. They could be the icons. For him, this was legacy enough.

The Goonies is irresistible bubblegum entertainment; a Mark Twain-meets-MTV hymn to American boyhood, inspired by love, friendship and the spirit of adventure. Full of crackling dialogue, slapstick humor, and goodies and baddies so clearly defined that you literally want to boo and cheer along with youthful exuberance; it is a sentimental and romantic work that bristles with Donner's unique brand of energy and enthusiasm, and the careful blend of naivety and knowingness he brings to each of his films.

Released on June 7, 1985, the picture grossed $61 million in the U.S. It was a hit but not a sensation, which put paid to a projected string of sequels. Janet Maslin of *The New York Times* reported that it was, "Fast, funny, ingenious, entertaining… there isn't a child in America who won't want to see 'The Goonies' this summer." For *Variety*, the film was, "Consummate filmmaking in service of a fairy tale vision of youth… Donner has elicited fine performances from his young cast and manages to maintain a balance between danger and humor that carefully modulates the action."

Time magazine stood in contrast. "You could say that *The Goonies* is not so much a movie as the kinetic model for a theme-park attraction," wrote critic Richard Corliss. "Dense, oppressively frenetic, heavy on the slapstick and low on the charm meter, the film asks to be experienced, not cherished." Predictably, many approached their analysis of the film by placing *The Goonies* within the context of the Spielberg canon. For *Newsweek*'s Jack Kroll, the picture was an example of how "Steven Spielberg has become the General Motors of kids' movies… it's his sensibility that's stamped on the entire film."

"The best that can be said of Donner is that he knows how to follow orders," damned *The Washington Post*. "The story is credited to Spielberg, and it bears the earmarks of his blockbusters…Joe Dante was able to infuse *Gremlins*, another product off the Spielberg assembly line, with some of his unique perversity, but if Donner has a personality as a director, it's not apparent here."

Such latter perspectives are heavily disputed by those close to the production, in particular by Jennie Lew Tugend, who says, "Dick was the one who invented the idea of going underground and having all these Rube Goldberg contraptions, the idea of being in the cave[s] and the ship and all that. And he loved those characters — there's a piece of his personality in every one of them."

The Goonies was Donner's raging desire to dig for buried treasure. On set, his passion was palpable. He would bellow, "Hip, Hop! March, March! Everybody Let's Go!" in between setups. An even louder "Big Eyes!" just seconds before the roar of "Action!" Enraptured by his giant presence, cast and crew were willing to follow him anywhere.

But *The Goonies* did more than mirror Donner's indomitable energy. It encapsulated almost entirely his personal spirit and the set of values that governed it. Donner lived by the power of positive thinking, the desire to search for the best in everyone and everything. It drove him, enlightened and enriched him, it made him the man he was — it was the secret behind his very real-life Goonie adventure.

"I want this film so badly I'd stab my own mother in the back to get it."

JOEL SILVER TO LAUREN SHULER DONNER
AND JACK RAPKE

10

Lethal Combination

For all Donner's extravagant energy and seemingly carefree attitude to life, there was a side to him he was not as quick to reveal. In a way, he was a secretly solitary man, not a little serious and shy, a closet contemplative of sorts. Actor William Holden once dubbed the director and his group of friends as "the world's most outgoing loners." In the words of Tom Mankiewicz, his good friend simply "wasn't built for marriage." Donner would likely have agreed, had he not met and fallen so deeply in love with Lauren Shuler.

Since Donner and Lauren had met during the making of *Ladyhawke* they had remained entirely committed to one another. He felt in his heart a tremendous trust and respect for her, and he never grew tired of inventing ways to make her laugh. She was a beautiful, intelligent, and talented woman who lived life with integrity. Like he, she possessed a powerful independence and strength that masked a surprising gentleness and simmering vulnerability. Was she the magical missing half he had not previously presumed to need? Just as his movies often searched for and found, had Donner discovered the kind of true love and friendship that, subconsciously at least, he may have always coveted?

While he did not seek fame or celebrity, Donner had undoubtedly made his career the focus of his life. He loved making movies and feared that it could one day stop. Since *The Omen*, he knew he wanted to remain on the roller coaster for as long as possible. In his dedication to his relationship with Lauren, however, he began to enjoy life more away from the production office or the film set. He learned to appreciate the wonders of travel, of fine food, and to channel his natural empathy for social justice and charitable causes into organized action. "[Their relationship] changed his whole life," said the late studio executive Guy McElwaine. "It made him a different person and a better person… [And] he became much more serious about life and the importance of it."

"I wasn't going to get married," Donner explains. "There are people out there that I'd loved and I'd been with for long periods of time, but these weren't the kind of relationships that I wanted the rest of my life to be. I didn't want children. I think that in this town — and I'm not knocking anybody — people just get married because they have nothing better to do on a Saturday. I really wasn't interested."

In the autumn of 1986, the filmmaker's world changed forever. "When I met Lauren, my life turned around. I fell madly in love and I was going to struggle to make that thing work no matter what."

She accepted his surprise marriage proposal, and a discreet wedding ceremony was planned. It was to be held at his home on Thanksgiving Day. Donner explains, "Both of our families were coming to our house for dinner. So we told everybody in the family, 'It's not just going to be Thanksgiving, we're getting married, and we want everyone to celebrate with us.' Everybody was very high about it, but I started to get nervous. We'd decided not to tell anybody but our family and our close friends. And the day before, I went out to get a haircut, and I swear to God, anybody I met I invited them to my house the next day for Thanksgiving Day and my wedding. We had a waiter show up, we had a guy who was an old friend that we hadn't seen in years, but who sure as hell we would not normally have been invited to my wedding. But it was like, 'We're getting married! The world has to know! And they've got to support me!' Then, the morning of the wedding, we were getting dressed and I was taking a shower and I put a bar of soap in my eye. Not a little soap, I put an entire bar of soap in my eye, and it swelled up, and it started to tear, and I couldn't see out of it. I said, 'I can't get married.' In a strange way I probably just panicked and I inadvertently-on-purpose put this bar of soap in my eye to see what would happen to me."

The ceremony fortunately went off without a hitch. Alan Cohen, Donner's brother-in-law who had married his sister after her divorce and whom he loved dearly, served as his best man. (The happy couple received a pair of caged lovebirds as a wedding present, but within a few days they decided that the sight of the animals in captivity was more than they could bear. They set them free.) The union made headlines in New York. "My mother and father were overjoyed when Dick got married," says his cousin, Geoff Howard. "My parents were from a generation that equated marriage with a healthy happiness, and not being married as unhappy. Dick was good looking, successful, but his relationships never stuck. All of a sudden, he had joined the fold. He had found someone he was happy to be with, and he had taken the step, the plunge."

Richard Donner Productions, developing movies at Warner Bros., continued to thrive. Operating under the auspices of Terry Semel, the president and chief operating officer, and Bob Daly, the chairman of the board and chief executive officer, Donner found himself a part of a warm and familial environment that nurtured and invested in major talent. As he recalls, "It was a family. Anybody would do anything for each other, which they did, and everybody was very proud of the process of making movies. It was extremely unique, just extraordinary. They were studio executives who were really caring, passionate lovers of the movies."

Even before Daly and Semel assumed control of the studio, Donner enjoyed only fond memories of the historic company. The relationship had begun on *Superman* — at the time still the highest-grossing film in Warner Bros. history — with Donner reporting to vice chairman Frank Wells, chairman Ted Ashley, and his old friend (and former Filmways employer), the senior executive, John Calley.

When Christopher Reeve had flown into Los Angeles from New York to promote the epic comic book movie, he had called Donner to ask if the studio might arrange a rental car for him to use after his publicity junket. The director communicated Reeve's inquiry to Calley, who replied, "Find out what his favorite color is." When Reeve arrived, he met Calley for lunch at the studio. Afterward, a brand-new, top-of-the-line, red Mercedes-Benz convertible awaited him in the parking lot. Calley handed Reeve the keys. "Here, it's yours."

"Oh, thank you very much, I'll return it in a week," the actor replied.

"No, you don't understand," explained the studio head. "This is yours. It's a thank you from Warner Bros. for being so wonderful in the movie."

Donner enjoyed several options from which to choose his next project after the release of *The Goonies*. Briefly, he explored the possibility of buying the rights to *Inside Moves* and somehow engineering a theatrical re-release. More than five years on, the director was still struggling to come to terms with the commercial failure of his beloved film. Says he, "It was a picture I loved dearly. I hated to see it go down the tube. I did so want it to have the life of its own that was taken away from it. That always bothered me."

During a meeting with Bob Daly and Terry Semel, Donner and Tom Mankiewicz were presented with another tangible opportunity to make history their future. After the underwhelming *Superman III*, starring Richard Pryor opposite Christopher Reeve, Daly and Semel feared for the weakening franchise. "Look," they told Donner and Mankiewicz, "if you guys can resurrect this again, you can write your own ticket." Whatever it took, Warner Bros. would pay it. The offer was flattering and extremely tempting, but Superman had always meant more to Donner than money. After some discussion, the director realized that, for him at least, helming another *Superman* was the equivalent of asking Spielberg to remake *E.T.*, or requesting George Lucas to remake his original *Star Wars*. *Superman* was, likewise, an iconic picture ingrained in space and time as one of the great blockbusters of a magical film era. Overseeing an entirely new adventure would be pointless, for Donner had already given the best that he had. He did agree to offer advice and guidance, should it be requested.

The director came close to making *Shanghai Tango*, the story of an eccentric, off-the-wall U.S. Marine who meets and falls in love with a girl from the American Midwest while in China. When the Japanese suddenly invade Shanghai and capture the capital, Nanjing, the young lovers desperately try to escape so that they may continue their relationship. Producer Harvey Bernhard had established a viable budget and begun scouting locations, actors Debra Winger and Mel Gibson had agreed to headline as the lovers during wartime, and a tentative start date of November 1985 was set. But Donner could not attract a studio to commit the funding. The highly promising project ultimately fell by the wayside.

The director had no such trouble with the teen-vampire script *The Lost Boys*, which he had optioned for development and pitched to Warner Bros. as "*The Omen* meets *The Goonies*" — a scenario that left executives drooling. Sam and his older brother, Mike, move to a sleepy Californian suburb where there have been some strange deaths and rumors of vampires. When Mike starts to disappear at night and sleep all day, Sam teams up with a group of teenage vampire hunters in order to save his brother and rid his new hometown of evil. "I'd just finished reading *Lost Boys*," Donner's former assistant, Jennie Lew Tugend, remembers, "and I pitched it to Dick. He said, 'Wow, that sounds really neat, Kid. Let's look at it.' It fit right in with Dick Donner's sensibilities. The kids were older than the Goonies, but were, nonetheless, an ensemble of cool kids doing cool things, and it just appealed to Dick Donner."

When pre-production stalled, Donner decided to pass the helm onto another director. He would stay with *The Lost Boys* as a producer. "The script went into a series of rewrites," Tugend continues, "but Dick seemed to lose his interest in directing. I think what happens to Dick — and probably other directors — is that the more you develop something it loses its freshness. A lot of directors hate development because in the development process they've already directed the film in their head. It loses excitement. You forget your first impulse." Donner would suffer a similar problem on *Timeline*, a project he could not escape from and which would serve as one of the lowest points of his career.

Lauren Shuler suggested Joel Schumacher for *The Lost Boys*. She had produced his *St. Elmo's Fire*, and the filmmaker was an agreeable factor to then-Warner Bros vice president of production Bruce Berman. Schumacher brought a fresh approach to the film, moving its setting from the suburbs to a coastal town, soothing some of the script's scarier elements, and injecting an aspect of rock 'n' roll cool. Today, the film stands as a bona fide eighties classic.

Donner settled down in the screening room in his garage, a large glass of wine in hand, and fired up the projector to watch a copy of *Rambo: First Blood Part II* — a film which had proved to be an enormous financial success for Sylvester Stallone and Tri-Star Pictures. When the end credits rolled, he turned to an assistant. "I'm going to make one of those," he proffered.

Jennie Lew Tugend remembers, "All of a sudden, one day Dick came in and threw a script on my desk and said, 'I found it, Kid. Here's the one.' It seemed like the antithesis of who I thought Dick Donner was."

Screenwriter Shane Black had conceived *Lethal Weapon* at the tender age of twenty-two. A graduate of UCLA, his first draft script was offered to Donner by Mark Canton, the president of worldwide theatrical production for Warner Bros. Donner at first refused Canton. Emerging producer Joel Silver, a man whom Donner had heard was a hostile presence, was involved with the project. "If you don't want him on the picture," Canton assured, "he'll be off. There's no problem." Donner agreed to read the script.

Aging detective and avowed family man Roger Murtaugh is reluctantly partnered with Vietnam veteran and borderline psychotic Martin Riggs. Murtaugh, who is close to retirement, lives comfortably with his wife and three children, while Riggs slums in a trailer on the beach, whisky in hand, mourning the recent loss of his wife. During their first day together as partners, the explosive Riggs encounters a city worker who is threatening to commit suicide by jumping off the roof of a building. He saves the man by handcuffing himself to him and jumping onto an inflatable crash mat. Riggs' death wish causes the new partners to argue incessantly and violently, but when Riggs saves Murtaugh's life during a bungled arrest and the two men begin to unravel the mystery of Shadow Company — a group of elite military mercenaries importing heroin into Los Angeles — their dynamic relationship starts to shift and evolve.

As a result of their investigation, the partners find themselves and their loved ones in the line of fire. Murtaugh's eldest daughter, Rianne, is kidnapped. Attempting a rescue, the police detectives are themselves taken prisoner and interrogated by the enigmatic leaders of Shadow Company: General McAllister and his chief henchman, Mr. Joshua. Murtaugh and Riggs manage to break away from their captors, killing most of them in the bloody process. Mr. Joshua escapes, however, and heads straight for Murtaugh's home. An intense martial arts street fight ensues between Riggs and Mr. Joshua, in which the former is victorious. Uniformed officers arrest the defeated villain, who then grabs for a gun, but who is shot and killed before he can fire it. The heroic Riggs visits his wife's grave and resolves to move forward in his life. Murtaugh finally accepts his new partner, and invites him to spend Christmas with his family.

The screenplay was full of exciting fights, car chases and explosions, but it was the emotional pull of the relationship between the two main protagonists that really got Donner's creative juices firing. The potential for crafting a strong human story from the conflict and eventual bond between Martin Riggs and Roger Murtaugh made for a tantalizing proposition. "Honey, read this right away," he told Lauren. "I really like this."

Lauren was enthusiastic, too, but wary of her husband involving himself with what he detailed to her as "complications."

Peter Bart described Joel Silver in his book *The Gross* as a "bulky, rough-hewn man whose small head protruded from a large, billowing body." According to Tom Mankiewicz, the billowing body also had a "wild reputation for being maniacally in control of [his] movies." Silver was unashamedly combustive, a dominating, single-minded presence. He would make an unlikely professional bedfellow for Donner, even without taking into account the bitter experiences the director had previously suffered at the hands of Alexander Salkind and Ray Stark. Yet Silver's star was enjoying a dramatic rise in Hollywood. The graduate from New York University Film School had marked the establishment of Silver Pictures in 1985 with the Arnold Schwarzenegger vehicle *Commando*, and the forceful young producer quickly had his eye on becoming the undisputed Crown Prince of the action-adventure genre (a genre threatening to assert itself as Hollywood's dominant formal trend). Although preceded by Spielberg and Lucas's creation of *Indiana Jones*, and the James Cameron action-sci-fi hits *Terminator* and *Aliens*, among others, Silver would dedicate himself to taking hyperbolic feats to a gargantuan level never before witnessed on screen.

Donner went to Mark Canton and told him that he was indeed anxious to make *Lethal Weapon*, but that he would need to take him up on his offer to remove Silver. Canton agreed. Soon after, Donner received a phone call from a friend in Hawaii, music and film producer Shep Gordon. "Dick, you're looking at a project to do and there's a guy who wants to be attached to it named Joel Silver," said Gordon. "Give the guy a chance."

"Really, Shep?" Donner replied.

"Yeah, give him a shot. He wants to be associated with the big boys."

Another call came through. It was film producer Larry Gordon. "Look, I'm calling you because of Joel Silver. Joel became my protégé, I started him in the business, and he called me and told me you have this project he wants to be involved in. Give the guy a shot."

"Oh, jeez," Donner sighed, his conscience now getting the better of him.

When Joel Silver arrived for a face-to-face meeting, he was blown away by Donner's office, Building 102 on the Warner Bros. lot. It was decked out with a candy dispenser, a pinball machine and other assorted toys. (No doubt Silver would have wanted an office just like it one day.) According to Donner,

Silver salivated — perhaps not entirely tongue-in-cheek — that he wanted to be involved in *Lethal Weapon* "so badly I'd stab my own mother in the back to get it." Less vulgar was his assurance that for most of the shoot he would be on location in Mexico on another project, the Arnold Schwarzenegger film *Predator*. Unwilling to be ambushed along the line, Donner protected his position at the top of the film chain by successfully negotiating a lead producer credit (including any sequels), even if his heart was focused almost entirely on directing. Silver was officially onboard, and a decade-long partnership of epic highs and extreme lows began.

During his career in both film and television, Donner had tackled a great many different genres, from horror to fantasy, drama to comedy, and beyond. Until now, he had failed to find a sufficiently interesting action-based project. He would not know it at the time but — for better and worse — he was embarking on a journey that would see his career become inextricably linked to the action-adventure genre.

On *Lethal Weapon*, Donner worked with the young screenwriter, Shane Black, to tone down some of the more graphic aspects of the material. In the original draft, Mr. Joshua tortures Riggs in a bathtub. This was a little too hardcore for Donner, who had the climactic scene rewritten so that Riggs is electrocuted in a shower.

Having been impressed with the visual style of Tony Scott's *The Hunger*, Donner selected ex-London *Sunday Times* stills photographer Stephen Goldblatt to be his director of photography. He informed Goldblatt that he desired to drop the standard 2.35: 1 widescreen aspect in favor of a tighter 1.85:1 ratio — a choice he felt would be better suited to an intimate character study. He also emphasized the need for the film to have a naturalistic feel; he did not want the action to be over lit, as was the case with many other films of the genre. Goldblatt also brought strong ideas of his own to the project. After reading the screenplay, which begins with a drug-induced young woman falling to her death from a high-rise building, he showed Donner a photograph from *Life* magazine of a girl who had jumped from the Empire State Building and landed on top of a car. "Apart from her stocking being a little slipped down around her ankle," says the British cinematographer, "there's no damage to her body. We used that image [because Dick] doesn't like blood and gore. He hates that sort of sadistic thing."

Donner would collaborate with his brilliant but volatile editor, Stuart Baird, for a fourth time. In order to do so he instructed his lawyer to establish a production company in the name of Bronx, Parlor Frames and Sons, a tribute to his late father. (As his father made furniture frames, Donner told stories using film frames.) Baird was placed on the payroll so as to smooth his acceptance into the Motion Picture Editors Guild of America.

Eric Clapton and Michael Kamen were approached to deliver an original music score. They would ultimately deliver a soundtrack less thumping rock, more of the cool jazz that Donner loved so much. A plucky guitar riff motif would be utilized to connote a lightness of tone when and where Donner required it.

Many actors were considered for the role of Martin Riggs, the borderline psychotic seemingly determined to execute a death wish. One of them was Bruce Willis, but he passed, citing his belief that the script was too violent. Ironically, just sixteen months after the release of *Lethal Weapon*, his image would be plastered on billboards around the world as John "Yippee-ki-yay" McClane — star of the bloody *Die Hard* series.

Known for his forceful and emotional performances, thirty-year-old Mel Gibson was at the very top of Donner's wanted list for the role of Martin Riggs. A graduate of the National Institute of Dramatic Arts in Sydney, Australia, Gibson achieved relative fame in 1979 after being cast in the low-budget action flick (and subsequent international cult hit) *Mad Max*. Some acclaimed Australian films followed, notably Peter Weir's *The Year of Living Dangerously* and the Dino De Laurentiis production of *The Bounty*. Yet, as of early 1986, a disillusioned Gibson remained frustratingly on the cusp of major stardom, and he was growing increasingly discouraged in waiting for his breakthrough picture to arrive. After spending a year living in Hollywood, he tired of "Rat Race City" and retreated into semi-retirement.

The actor received the screenplay for *Lethal Weapon* at his farm in Australia's Kiewa Valley, where he resided with his wife, Robyn, and their four children. Enthused, he flew to Los Angeles to meet with Donner at the director's home in Hollywood. They had met once before, when Donner faced a last-minute casting crisis on *Ladyhawke*. Although they did not end up collaborating for that picture, Gibson recalls, "I always kept him [Donner] in my head. I thought, 'He's cool.' He leaves a very strong impression." The pair quickly saw eye to eye over the material, with Gibson believing that he shared many of the character's key traits (the actor was known for his exuberance and for living life on the edge).

Various names were discussed for the role of Roger Murtaugh, an aging detective close to retirement. Joel Silver favored Nick Nolte, with whom he had worked on *48HRS*, until casting director Marion Dougherty suggested Danny Glover for the part. "But the character's not black!" Donner responded. After a pause, he experienced an epiphany. "I realized what a bigoted, narrow-minded person I was," he confessed. "It's not done anymore, thank God, but back then if a screenplay didn't describe a character as 'black' or 'Asian,' you didn't think of a black or Asian actor for the role. I felt really stupid. The moment changed my life."

Glover, a native of San Francisco, and a professional actor only since the age of thirty, had impressed in Peter Weir's *Witness* and in Steven Spielberg's *The Color Purple*. He was delighted to be offered the role in *Lethal Weapon*. "There wasn't any racial casting in the screenplay," he recalled, "the role could have been played by any actor. It didn't have to be a black actor. What really appealed to me was that Murtaugh had a family. In films at that time black protagonists didn't have a family."

After the release of the film, Richard Donner received an NAACP (National Association for the Advancement of Colored People) Image Award for Best Picture of 1987. At the ceremony he humbly told the story of his initial ignorance.

Mel Gibson and Danny Glover had met once before, at the Venice Film Festival, where both were promoting movies. They met for a second time at Donner's house at six-thirty in the morning, in the company of the director and Mark Canton. Donner cooked English bangers for breakfast, before the group embarked upon a full script read-through. When the actors read the script, they clicked immediately, and their characters came to life. As they turned the last page, Mark Canton declared (with proper show-business gusto), "Let's go make a movie!"

Donner ordered Gibson and Glover out to accompany Los Angeles police officers on duty, so that they could sample the lifestyle of the characters they had been hired to play. As the action hero, Gibson entered into a rigorous training regime, lifting weights, taking frequent martial arts classes, and running up to ten miles a day so as to get into shape. His fitness regime was hindered in part by his forty-a-day smoking habit, and his legendary thirst for beer.

Shooting began in August 1986 at Burbank Studios in Los Angeles. Once more the challenge for Donner was to have as much fun as possible with the material, without destroying its credibility. He wanted the characters to be larger than life and humorous, but also realistic. They could be lighthearted, amusing in intense situations, but without winking at the camera and inferring that events were a big in-joke.

In order to extract the very best from his cast and crew, Donner once more went to great lengths to ensure an exhilarating shooting experience. His alchemy with Gibson was immediate. Both men shared a passion for horsing around, and a desire to make the process of filming as much fun as possible. "I figure if you have to work for a living," said Gibson, in an aside eerily similar to his director's ideological approach, "you might as well make fun of it. What I do certainly isn't a cure for cancer. And one of the best things about this job is that you can enjoy yourself at it almost all the time."

"It's such a joy to work with a man who's so funny," says Goldblatt of Donner. "There's always a laugh and an arm around [you]. [Dick's] not a neurotic person. You get a very clear idea of what he wants to achieve, and you're not going around in circles looking for a way to get into the material, and that's fun. It's joyful to be with him and to work for him."

One night, Stephen Goldblatt's wife came to visit him at the *Lethal Weapon* set. Donner spied the pretty lady as she walked across the set. "Mind the hole!" he bellowed. "MIND THE HOLE!" Mrs. Goldblatt panicked, nervously sought to identify the point of danger, before realizing it was a prank as the crew burst into laughter. Her husband would repay Donner in kind. The director of photography recalls, "We were shooting on the back lot of Warner Bros., working all night. We broke for our so-called lunch at one or two in the morning. Dick grabbed some food and went to the cutting room. When he returned, it was quiet. There were no lights on. No crew. Nothing. People were hiding in bushes and behind trees. Dick will be the first to admit that he doesn't have the greatest memory, so for ten to fifteen seconds he was thinking, 'Did I wrap?' The look on his face was priceless!"

During shooting, Donner encouraged both Gibson and Glover to improvise. As the former puts it, "Dick understands that the artistic process has to be organic in everyone. As an actor I was completely charmed by his approach to filmmaking. All of a sudden he was throwing the ball in your court and you're like, 'Let me do some tricks for you.'" Donner's approach resulted in much of the film's zippy banter. It also upped the drama of Riggs' suicide attempt. Gibson continues, "In the script it was sleeping pills and I said, 'C'mon, cops don't use sleeping pills.' So we changed it to make it harder." With a bottle of whisky for company, Riggs stares achingly at a photo of his recently deceased wife. Tears stream down his face. He clutches a revolver and contemplates ending the pain. He grabs for a bullet, loads the gun, and presses it to his forehead, before realizing a better way — through the mouth instead.

Unable to pull the trigger, an angry and frustrated Riggs strikes himself with the gun and clutches the photo of his wife.

Donner remembers, "One day I said to Mel, 'Let's do that scene this afternoon, I think we're up for it.' He looked at me and said, 'Do I have to do it now?' I said, 'No, no. We'll wait until you're happy.' He said, 'Okay.' It was a small set that we had boiled this down to, and we carried it with us, and every once and a while I would say to Mel, 'Hey, are you up for the scene in the trailer?' He was never up for it. I knew I had to do it sooner or later, and he knew he had to do it sooner or later, but it just wasn't happening, and I wasn't going to push him. Then one day we were wrapping and Mel said, 'Hey, Dick, do you have that set with you?' I said, 'Yeah.' He said, 'I think I'd like to do that scene.' I said, 'Super.' We'd had the set with us for so long that we knew how we were going to light it, everybody in the crew knew exactly what his or her job was. So I said, 'Get it ready.' And they got it ready literally in a matter of minutes. I knew it was a tough scene for Mel, so the operator, focus puller and I were the only ones in the trailer. Mel came in and said, 'Let's just do it...' We'd talked it through many times, and so we started to roll. As we're doing it, he started to bring this thing to life. He became so unbelievably real. There's a slight vibration to the camera and if you ever look carefully you'll see that because all of us in the trailer, we were sobbing."

During the course of the scene the actor was only supposed to handle the revolver, but improvised by placing it in his mouth. "I couldn't believe what Mel was doing," Donner reminisced during a publicity interview. "It was so real. I thought, hell, he might have put a shell in the gun... things rushed through my head. Did Mel ask the armourer or special effects guy to, 'Put one in there to give me motivation?' I tell you, I was terrified as Mel started to choke on the barrel, his finger tightening on the trigger. I was torn between rushing in and stopping the scene in case there was a shell in the gun and getting this amazing performance."

Donner could not rush in, for he was glued to the performance, as were the crewmembers watching outside via video screen. The director meekly readied to end the scene, but Gibson kept it going, a few more wails of frustration and the line, "I miss you, Victoria Lynn!"

"It wasn't an easy scene for Mel," says Goldblatt. "It's a difficult scene for any actor to do with sincerity, so that it's convincing to an audience... this was one actor and one camera in a trailer, and to get it to work he had to perform as well as he could. He did, but I don't think it was easy. I remember it was tense on the set, I remember that. It was quiet."

Donner was blown away by Gibson's fraught performance, and concerned for the actor's emotional well-being. Gibson, however, emerged from the trailer wearing a red clown's nose on his face and immediately set about to goof around. If it was clear, in this moment, that he shared Donner's passion for fun and mischief, it was also true that Gibson had a serious side, and the director saw in his charge the foreshadowing of a man who would become a groundbreaking filmmaker in his own right. Throughout shooting Gibson stayed on set even if he were not required for a scene. Quietly, and sometimes not so quietly, the star absorbed Donner's enthusiasm, flair and technique.

Donner had collaborated with many actors, iconic stars even who transcended generations, but this rugged, roguish, cheeky performer dominated the screen like nobody he had directed before. While *Lethal Weapon* was forged on the fictional Riggs/Murtaugh partnership, it was the alchemy between Donner and Gibson that proved the recipe for its success. Their understanding was so intuitive that they would collaborate on five more movies. As Brian Jamieson, who worked in distribution at Warner Bros., puts it, "Dick and Mel really clicked. I think Dick probably looked at Mel as kind of his own son. That first collaboration was about more than just making a movie. I think they both saw in each other a certain strength which they drew upon."

Given their similar personalities and tight, familial bond, perhaps Donner viewed Gibson as an on-screen extension of himself.

Lethal Weapon was a physically demanding shoot. Filming stretched up to eighteen hours a day, often seven days a week — two thirds of it scheduled at night. It became so debilitating that for one scene the director instructed Steve Perry, the production manager, to switch locations from Griffith Park at night to El Mirage by day. Riggs and Murtaugh's failed rescue of Rianne would thus take place in an enormous dry lakebed in the Mojave Desert outside of Victorville, California.

In his biography, *Mel Gibson: Living Dangerously*, author Wensley Clarkson claims that the star was once "so exhausted that he collapsed on set... from that moment on Mel sustained his high-energy antics by being administered oxygen between takes."

The most grueling of all scenes to be filmed was the brutal climax, a street fight with co-star Gary Busey that required four nights of filming martial arts moves while drenched in water sprayed from a fire hydrant. It was so cold the actors could see their breath. "Mel was a happy-go-lucky guy," Stephen Goldblatt recalls. "He had no pretension. He didn't have an entourage. He didn't complain. And he was physically stressed. We shot the fight sequence at the end of *Lethal Weapon* at four in the morning; he was soaked to the skin, wearing just a pair of jeans, shivering and getting hypothermia. I said, 'Mel, you all right?' He said, "I'll do anything for a million dollars!' There are a lot of actors who would have just lost it."

Gibson enjoyed performing many of his own stunts, including a small part of the famous suicide jump from a building rooftop. "The first part of the jump was done by a stunt double," he informed the *Chicago Sun-Times*. "They [Donner and Silver] wanted to show me landing, so you could see it was really me... Standing on the ground, looking up at the cherry picker, it didn't look that high. Then I got up that high and looked down, and I'm glad I remembered to wear my bicycle clips."

The scene in question was shot at the Acme Rug Company building. Shane Black had written the scene set atop a thirty-story building, but Donner didn't feel such a height was realistic. Explains Goldblatt, "I used to have breakfast in the restaurant at the bottom of that building, and I just love that building, and I was new to Los Angeles, and so this was a location I just wanted to shoot. That white deco against the blue sky seemed so Californian, it seemed so great. I suggested to Dick to go up there and have a look at it, because I just liked it photographically. We were standing up there, and he put his arm round me. Coming from other kinds of directors, it was nice. It was so warm. His energy during shooting generated a great comradeship amongst us. He's full of fun, he's always laughing. You love the guy so you want to do well for him."

A film crew shooting in and around Los Angeles was certainly nothing new, but the scene at Acme generated a great deal of attention from spectators. One such passerby was the surprisingly frail Muhammad Ali, the boxing legend who shuffled past on his way for his morning coffee at Barney's Beanery.

Although Donner captured the close-up of Gibson that he wanted, the director still found overseeing stunts to be a terribly stressful experience. While in Long Beach to film helicopter footage for the opening of the movie, a scene in which a young woman falls to her death from a high-rise building, Donner simply refused to come out of his trailer.

Despite the long days, the director shot speedily, determined to put to bed lingering rumors regarding his shooting speed that had plagued him since *Superman*. "Dick was adamant when he did *Lethal Weapon* that he was going to bring it in on time and on budget," says his former assistant, Michael Thau. "He wanted to squash the theory that [he] was a slow director. We came in five days ahead of schedule and under budget."

Contrary to expectations, Donner formed an effective partnership with his co-producer, Joel Silver. "Dick was the big director and Joel was the up-and-coming producer," states Stuart Baird. "They got on, business-wise, very well. It was a very good and very lucrative relationship."

Silver knew only one way to operate: high octane, no holds barred, and never take prisoners. He enjoyed projecting his image of the typical Hollywood monster — irascible, brutish, and deadlier than a ballistic missile. But those who were on set for the original *Lethal Weapon* remember only the slightest of strain in the relationship between the pair. "Initially it was very good and then it got rather bad," Goldblatt remembers, "and then it got good again... When Joel was with him while we were shooting, I just think Dick's concentration was being a little diverted."

Donner did not intend to be a political avatar, but throughout *Lethal Weapon* he took advantage of opportunities to spotlight moral issues that were of importance to him. Says he, "In filmmaking you can get your message in under the guise of entertainment, but if you try and get your message in under the guise of message, you're going to lose the audience." As such, Donner expressed his support for the anti-apartheid movement by strategically placing "Free South Africa" banners and stickers in certain scenes.

Although there are many aspects of *Lethal Weapon* that are rooted in Reagan-era ideology (notably a war on drugs, and the notion of the modern male American as indomitable action hero), the sensitive, liberal Donner has fun throughout the film by intermittently prodding at notions of masculinity. In a particular funny moment, Murtaugh and a fellow detective discuss the veritable merits of "eighties men" and whether or not they should cry in front of a woman: "You know, Roger, you're way behind the times. The guys in the eighties aren't tough, we're sensitive people, show a little of our emotions around women and shit like that."

These were not the only messages Donner snuck into the film. As Riggs and Murtaugh wander Los Angeles during a scene, a movie theater audaciously promotes "Lost Boys: This Year's Hit."

During the editing stages, Donner had a change of heart regarding two pivotal sections of the narrative. He had originally lensed an introduction set in a seedy bar, where Riggs engages in a brawl with three men, breaking one man's arm. While it suitably established his hero as a lethal weapon, Donner now believed it too dark and violent, and feared that audiences might form negative resistance to the character before he was truly established.

Donner was also dissatisfied with his planned ending. He had shot a finale in which Riggs drove off into the sunset, seemingly never to cross paths with Murtaugh again, with the elder detective hinting at imminent retirement. Not for the first time in his career, the director wanted a more upbeat close to proceedings. Thus, a quick pick-up scene was shot that featured Murtaugh and Riggs on the former's front lawn, sharing a warm exchange before reconvening to the house for Christmas dinner. It was more of a celebration of the love and friendship that the characters now shared.

As post-production drew to a close, the director once again became actively involved in the marketing process. Warner Bros. executive Brian Jamieson remembers, "When we had our Japanese exhibitors in town, Dick was the first guy to say, 'How about bringing them up to the house for a dinner?' That's the kind of guy he was. You always looked forward to meeting with him because he was such an 'up' guy, and because he also saw the bigger picture."

Donner's focus throughout filming had been to create characters for an audience to emotionally invest in, to care to see through the roller-coaster highs and lows of the adventure. The U.S. and international one-sheet movie poster, a close-up portrait of Gibson and Glover, reflected the character case study methodology.

Lethal Weapon premiered to instant commercial success on March 6, 1987. It grossed $65 million in the U.S. and $120 million worldwide. The numbers were Donner's biggest figures since *Superman*. Critical notices were also strong. Loudest to rave was Roger Ebert of the *Chicago Sun-Times*, who acknowledged that "Richard Donner has directed a lot of classy pictures...

this time he tops himself." A large section of Ebert's analysis praised Donner's ability to control both story and spectacle. "The plot makes an amazing amount of sense, considering that the action hardly ever stops for it," he extolled.

The Washington Post stated *Lethal Weapon* was a "visceral reminder of how exciting an action film can be... brought to life by a good director and a strong cast... there's none of the idiot's delight in violence that surrounds the muscle-bound police films of Stallone, Schwarzenegger and Eastwood. Donner knows how to keep his film in motion and his actors on edge." *Time* magazine's Richard Corliss advised his readers that with Donner it was "nice to be in such expert hands."

Yet even in the best of times, there were the worst of reviews. As Donner had witnessed throughout his career, his films could not help but inspire sharply polarized views. The cognitive response of *The New York Times* was perhaps tainted by an inherent weariness of the action movies flooding the market (despite the relative youth of the genre cycle). For critic Janet Maslin, Donner's directorial tactics were nothing more than "lurid but effective," although she did confess that the picture "packs an undeniable wallop." Industry bible *Variety* almost delivered its own knockout blow with the claim, "Donner plays his hand well, but in the end it's a bluff... it's style masquerading as content."

Some press coverage profiled the level of violence in *Lethal Weapon*. Donner was offended by the attacks, insisting his picture was full of action, not violence, and argued that there was a distinct difference between the two. He saw his film as an urban western — when someone dies, a bullet strikes him or her, and they fall to the ground with little blood. The director believed that the scene in which Mr. Joshua tortures Riggs would have been shot differently by other filmmakers. Whereas others may have shown a knife slicing off an ear, or bones being broken, Donner showed Mr. Joshua using a sponge to electrocute Riggs.

Critic Roger Ebert came to Donner's defense, agreeing that the focal point of any criticism should not be screen violence. "It's about movement and timing," he observed, "the choreography of bodies and weapons in time and space... we're exhilarated by the sheer freedom of movement; the violence becomes surrealistic and less important than the movie's underlying energy level." Although Mel Gibson's Riggs is shirtless and muscular for the film's climactic scenes, in *Lethal Weapon* there is far less of an emphasis on the hyperbolic body, far less muscle-bound mayhem than in *Commando* or *Rambo*. "There is this stunt and that stunt," said the late Tom Mankiewicz, "and this building blowing up and that building blowing up, but the core of the movie is the relationship between those two guys [Riggs and Murtaugh].

Nobody at the time had ever had a relationship like that [in a movie], between a black man and a white man. A relationship where they bickered at each other, yelled at each other, loved each other, hugged each other... and Dick got the core relationship right."

Although *The Defiant Ones*, *In the Heat of the Night* and *48HRS* pre-date *Lethal Weapon* as bi-racial buddy flicks, for years black actors had struggled to escape roles as downtrodden (often unemployed) men. As Murtaugh, Danny Glover played a career professional who lives with his family in a modern suburban home — a stark contrast to Gibson's rootless loner. In Reagan's America, such a famously conservative time, Donner had dramatically dared to shatter racial preconceptions by reinventing the portrayal of black people on screen.

It was the blockbuster that wasn't supposed to be. Released out of season and with little fanfare, a tribute to the low-budget cop dramas of the seventies became a seminal picture that spawned a billion-dollar series and became the template for a generation of action movies. The love-hate relationship between Riggs and Murtaugh inspired many imitators, including the protagonists in *Tango & Cash*, *Bad Boys* and *Rush Hour*.

The premise for *Lethal Weapon* may not have been as original, but the end result was a movie that was staggeringly so. Donner's humanization of the genre was a crucial factor behind the surprise success. He brought real-life relationships to a tale of spectacular action, creating a template that appealed not just to testosterone-charged young men, but also to women and men of all ages.

As the *Lethal Weapon* phenomenon expanded across the globe, Donner, Mel Gibson, Danny Glover and Gary Busey were invited to take part in a promotional tour of the Far East. It was a torturous trip for Busey, who had recently split from his wife, Judy. Donner kept the star as relaxed and comfortable as he could. Remembers Brian Jamieson, the marketing and distribution executive for Warner Bros. who made the trip to Australia, Japan and Hong Kong, "The camaraderie was really special and there was no question that for these guys it wasn't just a job, that they really enjoyed each other's company. Dick was kind of like the Godfather. We'd be sitting around in a restaurant and Gary would get his guitar out. Dick would always encourage him. He used to call him 'Garth.' Dick's got such a booming voice that, of course, the Japanese people in the restaurant would all be looking over. Dick's voice used to bounce off of the damn wall. He enjoyed a joke, and he liked to have a damn good laugh. People would gravitate towards him."

"Directing Billy is like being a cop at Times Square when all the lights go out."

RICHARD DONNER ON BILL MURRAY

11

Bah, humbug…
Bill Murray

Donner had known Michael Ovitz, the man dubbed Hollywood's most controversial power broker, for almost a decade. They had met after Ovitz had lured Donner's agent, Steve Roth, to his Creative Artists Agency, directly following *Superman*. Since that fateful meeting during the late seventies Ovitz had acted as his informal advisor, at the time encouraging him to helm *Inside Moves* as his follow-up feature. "It's time for you to do a small, intimate picture," Ovitz had assured. "You've done big films. Now let's show them that you are an intimate director, and that your career in film will be as diversified as your television career was." Ovitz had also liaised with Warner Bros. to sooth some of Donner's pre-production woes on *Ladyhawke*. When Kurt Russell walked just ten days before principal photography, it was he who calmed the studio as the director scrambled to find a replacement.

Ovitz was the most important dealmaker in Hollywood, a man whose power and influence had grown to unprecedented levels. Creative Arts Agency, the firm he had formed after leaving the William Morris Agency in 1975, employed close to one hundred agents, responsible for such A-list talent as Steven Spielberg, Tom Cruise, Madonna and Michael Jackson. Such leverage enabled Ovitz to virtually dictate terms to the major studios, to decree that if they desired one of his clients for any given project, they would also have to be prepared to hire others from the CAA stable.

The "super agent" had become an assembler of movie packages, and it was one such deal that he had Donner in mind for during the autumn of 1987. *Scrooged* — a comedy reimagining of the Charles Dickens classic *A Christmas Carol* — was the comeback picture for comedian-turned-actor Bill Murray, of *Saturday Night Live* television fame, a star who had enjoyed a four-year screen hiatus since starring in the blockbuster *Ghostbusters*. Despite the lengthy sabbatical — during which time he had concentrated on raising his two sons with his wife, Mickey, in Upstate New York — Murray was still widely recognized as one of *the* comics of the decade. Paramount Pictures were convinced that he could make *Scrooged* the yuletide hit of 1988, and agreed to pay him a whopping $6 million to stage his name above the marquee. "For each year that Bill didn't work, his fee probably went up," reflected the producer, Art Linson. "... He received more for *Scrooged* than the producer, director and cast combined."

Writers Mitch Glazer and Michael O'Donoghue penned the screenplay specifically for Murray. Linson continued, "Mitch was a respected journalist who had written some excellent unproduced screenplays. O'Donoghue, thin, bald, usually sporting ballet shoes and a woman's diamond evening watch, was notorious, even with this look, for chasing young girls. He didn't start out with any aspirations of being a Hollywood screenwriter. He was the original head writer of *Saturday Night Live*, where his temper was legendary. He was intractable, merciless, self-destructive, but, above all, very talented. The writing team had a yin-yang, good cop-bad cop quality to it."

Frank Cross, the youngest television president in the history of network television, terrorizes all who work for him. Intent on exploiting the Christmas holiday season for all its ratings worth, Cross commissions such dubious programming as *The Night the Reindeer Died, Bob Goulet's Old Fashioned Cajun Christmas*, and the sitcom *Father Loves Beaver*. The jewel in his schedule is an ambitious live-action version of *A Christmas Carol* — a tent-pole event for his IBC network entitled *Scrooge*, which is promoted by a trailer featuring acid rain, drug addiction and international terrorism.

Three ghosts visit Frank in an attempt to make him change his ways. The first appears in the form of a cab driver that takes him back in time to relive a past love affair with a charity worker, Claire. The relationship ends when Frank cynically chooses a dinner date with the president of his network over a holiday commitment to his girlfriend. The second ghost is an energetic fairy with a mean right hook, who ensures that Cross is aware of the painfully impoverished lifestyle of his beleaguered secretary, Grace, and her mute son, Calvin, and of the enduring love felt toward him by his oft-snubbed brother.

While embarked on his ghostly misadventures, Frank is quietly being usurped at IBC by the consultant, Brice Cummings.

When the Ghost of Christmas Future arrives to haunt him, Frank is close to breakdown. Given a glimpse of the imminent consequences of his perennial meanness, he finally sees the error of his ways. He reinstates an IBC employee he had cruelly fired and bursts onto the stage during the live broadcast of *Scrooge*. Frank chastises his viewing audience for watching television on Christmas Eve, instead of spending time with friends and family. Personally redeemed, he confesses his true feelings for his lost love, Claire.

Donner was unsure over the screenplay, but allowed himself to be charmed by Ovitz. "Do me a favor, read it," he had been asked. "It's going to Paramount. I think you'll love it."

A few nights later, at 11.00pm, the phone rang. It was Ovitz again.

"You're not going out, are you?"

"No, why?"

"Because Bill Murray's coming over. Brace yourself. He's got your address."

"No," the director replied. "It's too late."

Donner hated to bring business home, and especially at such a late hour. He liked to be asleep right after the ten o'clock news was over.

Murray arrived, and after an uncomfortable period of small talk the pair began to seriously dissect *Scrooged*. Some two hours later they were in sync, and Donner called Ovitz, a man he found to be insane but irresistible, and agreed to the deal. (Donner had no idea that he had been Ovitz's second choice for *Scrooged*. The dealmaker had spent a great measure of time courting Sydney Pollack to helm, only for Pollack to tap dance his way out of a tentative contract.)

Pre-production on *Scrooged* moved swiftly for Donner, who was joining with a script and a star cemented in place, and a project heavily conceptualized. Cast in the picture as Bill Murray's love interest, Claire, was actress Karen Allen, best known for her feisty heroics as Harrison Ford's girlfriend in *Raiders of the Lost Ark*, and for her tender portrayal of a widow in John Carpenter's *Starman*. Actors John Forsythe, John Glover, Bobcat Goldthwait and Robert Mitchum made for a strong supporting cast. Marlon Brando, however, declined Donner's invitation to appear in a cameo as "Mr. Bah Humbug."

Donner asked Stephen Goldblatt to return as his cinematographer, but he had already signed on to Taylor Hackford's *Everybody's All-American*. The director thus turned to Conrad Hall, who had photographed *Cool Hand Luke*, *Butch Cassidy and the Sundance Kid* and *Marathon Man*, and whose talent he greatly respected. J. Michael Riva, whom Donner had prior experience of working with on *The Goonies* and *Lethal Weapon*, would again serve as his production designer.

Principal photography began on December 7, 1987, on location in New York City. Footage would be lensed at such famous locations as the Rockefeller Center, Saks Fifth Avenue and the Seagram's Building, the latter would serve as the exterior for the corporate headquarters of the fictional IBC network. "Shooting outside in New York at Christmas time with Bill Murray was hysterical," says associate producer Jennie Lew Tugend. "Everybody loved Bill. Car horns would honk; people would be like, 'Hey, Bill!' We had a lot of fun. From my memory the production of *Scrooged* in New York was a blast."

While the atmosphere in New York was warm and friendly, with members of the general public gathering to catch a glimpse of Bill Murray and the production in action, Donner found himself faced with some immediate and complicated obstacles. Just one week into the shoot, he allowed Conrad Hall to leave the picture. He had been frustrated by the pace in which his cinematographer had worked — relatively simple shots that he believed should have been lit within forty-five minutes were taking two and a half hours to set up ("I think he was painting with a finer brush than I did," Goldblatt speculates). In addition, their personalities simply had not gelled; Donner believed Hall to lack a sense of humor. "This isn't going to work," Donner had informed him.

"You're right," Hall happily agreed.

The director failed in a second attempt to extract Goldblatt from his existing contract, so it was Michael Chapman, the esteemed photographer of *Jaws*, *Taxi Driver* and *Raging Bull*, who stepped into the void.

From the offset, Donner's relationship with Bill Murray — to whose manic, energetic mind the entire production was harnessed — was delicate. While Donner encouraged his improvisations, he needed to ensure that the many cutting and sometimes angry ad-libs remained true to the spirit of the script, and did not alienate the audience from his character, Frank Cross. Donner wondered if he had been hired not to direct the star, but to restrain him. "Directing Billy is like being a cop at Times Square when all the lights go out," he proffered. "The challenge was in creating a character whose humor you enjoy even when you're angry with him — someone you'll really care about by the end of the film."

Murray had been involved in all aspects of the *Scrooged* production, including the script development and the casting. He had thrown out pages from the screenplay that he didn't like, and had others retuned to his satisfaction (to his credit this included building up the romantic relationship between Frank Cross and Claire Phillips). Murray's brothers, John and Joel Murray, and Brian Doyle were given supporting roles in the cast, as were several *Saturday Night Live* alumni.

It was Murray's moniker on top of the marquee, his name on the incredible $6 million check. *Ghostbusters* had been an ensemble piece, but the burden for the success or failure of *Scrooged* would rest largely with him. As a result, Murray ensured his influence was near total.

Scrooged was a different type of production to Donner's recent films, upon which he had revisited concepts and stamped his own strong, personal vision. "When Dick decides to come on board it becomes Dick's movie," says Jennie Lew Tugend, "but *Scrooged* became Dick *and* Bill's movie. It was a time in Bill Murray's career where he needed a hit. So I personally think there was a lot of pressure."

Reining in such a powerful influence would prove no easy task, and once the production left New York to be confined in a series of claustrophobic studio stages in Los Angeles, the tension would reach boiling point. "[It] was a miserable gig," Murray confessed to *Starlog* magazine. "... I was trapped on a dusty, smelly and smoky set in Hollywood for three-and-a-half months, having a lousy time by myself, and just coughing up blood from this fake snow that was falling all the time."

Tugend concurs, "When we moved back to Los Angeles we were on that soundstage at Paramount Studios for day after day and week after week. It began to wear on everyone. At the end of that shoot we were all really tired."

A confrontation ensued between Donner and Murray over one scene the star felt passionately about — a fictional television trailer featuring acid rain, suicide and AIDS deaths. *Scrooged* was driven by dark humor, but the director wanted nothing this black. In the end, it was filmed as Murray requested, but Donner ensured the final result was toned down in the editing suite.

Other cast members recalled a happier shooting experience. "We had a ball making this movie," declared actress Carol Kane, the deliciously wild Ghost of Christmas. "... Dick created an atmosphere on the set completely free of tension so that the film — with a timeless message of love — would have a buoyant atmosphere."

The petite star had particular reason to be happy, for she was involved in some of the film's more riotously funny scenes, in which she had the opportunity to physically assault Bill Murray. "Bill did take a fair amount of abuse from me," she remembered. "... I slapped him. I pulled his hair, cheeks and lips. And I tweaked his nose. Bill was very patient because I know it hurt." On one occasion the veracity of Kane's attacks brought filming to a halt. Murray remembered, somewhat mordantly, "There's a piece of skin that connects your lip with your gums and it was really pulled away."

It had been Murray's on-the-spot idea for Kane to get physical during the scene. But it had been the actress's idea not to pull her punches. For Kane, the exchanges took a toll. She claimed to break into twenty-minute crying fits between takes.

Throughout filming Donner remained open to the ideas of his ensemble. When actor John Glover arrived to play west coast producer Brice Cummings, he was disappointed by the business suits that had been selected for him to wear. He believed that a producer from California should dress more casually, and in lighter colors. Donner heartily agreed and allowed Glover to supply his own wardrobe.

Glover's memories of his stint on *Scrooged* are affectionate, and he recalls feeling strongly supported in the creative process. "[Donner] did a lot of takes, and he kept trying [different] things. Very patiently. No pressure. He's one of the good directors — one of the good guys who like actors. He's a wonderful storyteller and just a terrific filmmaker." While improvisation was commonplace, when actor and comedian Buddy Hackett chose to rewrite scenes without seeking approval, it placed Donner in an awkward position. Glover continues, "I did a scene with Buddy Hackett, who I grew up watching and laughing at, and it was an okay scene. In the makeup trailer Buddy Hackett had rewritten the scene and he was giving me all his new cues for his jokes. It was actually quite a good scene for me, but Buddy Hackett's rewrite wasn't. I didn't know what was going to happen, but without missing a beat Dick just dealt with the situation on set and got us right back to the script. He didn't insult Buddy Hackett at all. It just seemed very natural. He kind of made a joke about it. He was very gracious, but at the same time he very cleverly left no air for Buddy Hackett to get in. It was very firm but very generous at the same time."

Scrooged was driven by the performance of Bill Murray, who in his individual brilliance as a comedian also saw the greater value of the ensemble. "Murray was amazing," says Glover. "He was very generous with me. He didn't have to make me look so good, but he did because he knew the better I looked, the better he would be. As funny as he is, he's also a good actor who knows how to tell a story." One scene in particular stands out as a favorite memory. "I had to lead Bill Murray over to an elevator all the way across the two soundstages, and there were only about twenty steps of dialogue written, but Dick seemed to let Bill Murray and me work it out. There was a great line right at the end, right as the elevator doors are closing. 'You got any last tips for me, Frank?' Bill Murray gave it to me right before we started shooting, and I just waited and waited until the elevator door was almost shut and I just said it in his face. It was his line, because I just couldn't come up with anything as good as he could. Ever."

If Bill Murray supplied the ad-libs, it was Donner's presence that Glover drew upon for inspiration. Continues the actor, who would later be known for playing Lex Luthor's father in the television series *Smallville*, "I was basically using him as an image, energy-wise and vocal-wise; I could never get his [deep baritone] because I don't think my balls are as big as his. My voice couldn't go as low. But I was consciously trying to ape him within my body for my character when I acted, because he is so big and fun-loving and open."

Donner ensured on *Scrooged* that a series of personal touches found a way onto the screen. The director utilized many actors who were familiar to him in cameo roles. His cousin Steve Kahan (*Superman*, *Inside Moves* and *Lethal Weapon*) plays an IBC director of live television, Anne Ramsey (*The Goonies*) appears as an elderly homeless lady in search of shelter, and Robert Zemeckis' wife, Mary Ellen Trainor (*The Goonies* and *Lethal Weapon*), enjoys a role as an executive who is possibly enjoying a secret dalliance with Frank Cross.

In the movie, the relationship between Frank Cross and Brice Cummings may also be partly autographical, perhaps a subtle nod to Donner's experience on *Superman*, on which the Salkinds hired Richard Lester to act as a mediator during the notoriously stressful shoot.

When Frank Cross travels back in time with the Ghost of Christmas Past to the set of the television show *Frisbee*, Donner allows the camera to move in on a close-up of a tree, upon which the message "Dick Loves Lauren" is engraved within the shape of a heart. The question, "What's the name of the boat on *Gilligan's Island?*" is asked during a trivia game played by the brother of Frank Cross — a nod to the director's work on the iconic sixties television show.

As in *Lethal Weapon*, Donner displayed his support for the anti-apartheid movement by discreetly placing "Free South Africa" banners around the IBC control room set.

While Donner may have resisted some of the screenplay's darker humor, he embraced the essential narrative message that was entirely in tune with his own thematic agenda: the redemptive power of true love, as especially exemplified by a closing that plays out to the song, "Put a Little Love in Your Heart."

The dialogue for the film's crucial closing scene, in which Frank Cross exclaims his redemption to those on the set of the IBC special, "Scrooge," and to millions of viewers watching the live television event, had not been locked down during scripting. Donner let his cameras roll and relied on Murray's renowned improvisational skills to deliver the goods. And as the star launched into an impromptu skit, the director instructed cast members and production personnel to join him on stage. It was done in the spur of the moment. "[It] came out of nowhere," says Donner. "Singing that song, getting the whole cast and the crew... it just felt right because it's such a seasonal piece and the whole idea of 'Put A Little Love in Your Heart.' Instead of just having it as an end song, I thought we should all just get in and do it."

Even Donner got in on the action, hoisting child actor Nicholas Phillips upon his shoulders and bursting into song. Ten minutes and many sore vocal chords later, he finally yelled 'Cut!' and the cameras stopped rolling. He viewed the dailies that night, and requested the cast and crew return the next day to film a scripted scene based on the improvisation. Ultimately, the spontaneous material was the most effective and would feature in the finished film.

Scrooged was edited by the father-and-son team of Fredric and William Steinkamp. Bill Murray insisted on being present with Donner for the sessions, as did producer Art Linson and the project's uncredited consultant, Sydney Pollack. Also in the room was a young associate producer, Jennie Lew Tugend. She recalls, "There was a lot of guys in there smoking cigars, and there was a lot of testosterone. You've got a director saying, 'I like the scene this way' and you've got an actor saying, 'No, I look better in this other scene.' Mike Ovitz was screaming. Bill Murray was screaming. It was a very stressful time. Everybody had a lot riding on that movie." Donner, who had long since left gun-for-hire status behind, and who was accustomed to being the master and commander of his productions, grew irritable. He stood his ground, but finally became so frustrated with the process that he simply walked out. "At one point at the tail end of *Scrooged* Dick had an ending, and Bill Murray wanted a different ending. Dick Donner said, 'I'm outta here, Jennie. You figure it out. Goodbye.' And he went to take his boat from Florida through the Panama Canal."

Tugend thought Donner was kidding, but he wasn't. He had recently purchased a new boat, and he had a deadline to deliver it from Florida to the west coast. Accompanied by his friend, agent Eddie Rosen, Donner was going to sail through the Panama Canal. Bill Murray was not going to stop him.

Tugend's phone rang relentlessly. "Get me Dick Donner," was the incessant plea.

"He's on a boat," she would reply. "He's only going to be available on a ship-to-shore radio at a certain hour."

As bad luck would have it, Donner and Rosen were caught in a hurricane, and radio communication was limited to once a day at best. All the while, in the editing suite, violent arguments ensued. Bill Murray yelled at Sydney Pollack, as Art Linson attempted to play diplomat. Michael Ovitz, the man responsible for the assemblage, yelled at all of them. Ultimately, under the final cut right he had insisted on being in his contract, Donner got the ending he wanted.

Despite a fraught post-production, expectations were high for the release of *Scrooged*. Paramount had commissioned sneak preview screenings that had garnered a startling 93% rating of audience members who found the film to be "very good." Bill Murray, the headlining talent, was the equivalent to box-office gold. *Ghostbusters*, in which he had starred for Columbia Pictures, had grossed $239 million in the U.S. alone.

The positive buzz amongst Paramount executives was not to last. *Scrooged* made its North American bow on November 23, 1988. It amassed the not insignificant number of $60 million in North American ticket sales, but failed to make the top ten grossing films of the year.

A raft of negative press reviews hindered the release. Vincent Canby of *The New York Times* confessed that the picture had "some very funny things in it," but concluded that the majority of the comedy was "lazily executed." Hal Hinson of *The Washington Post* was positively scathing when he surmised, "As *Scrooged* unspools, you watch with increasing indifference...it plays out as hopelessly as old hat."

Roger Ebert of the *Chicago Sun-Times*, a critic who had barely been able to control his enthusiasm for *Lethal Weapon*, was in this moment powerless to contain his unease. "*Scrooged* is one of the most disquieting, unsettling films to come along in quite some time," he delivered. "It was obviously intended as a comedy, but there is little comic about it, and indeed the movie's over-riding emotion seems to be pain and anger."

Scrooged was a cutting spoof, a satire of a materialistic decade and the ruthlessness of the corporate television media — a crucial point seemingly lost on most who reviewed the picture. Ultimately, the core message of *Scrooged* is the same as in *A Christmas Carol*, the classic novel that loosely inspired it. Behind the rumpled anarchy of Bill Murray is a clear moral theme: united we stand, divided we fall, a selflessness over selfishness message entirely in tune with Donner's own directorial mantra.

As Frank Cross, Bill Murray is magnetic. His splendidly witty one-liners and stinging verbal sparring sessions drive the movie. *Scrooged* is unashamedly high jinks, not high art, and is genuinely very funny for many parts. As Richard Corliss did at least note in his *Time* review, "Nobody tried for a masterpiece here; most people should have a good time." While far from the realm or status of *It's a Wonderful Life* or *A Christmas Story* — America's institutional favorites — through DVD sales and cable showings *Scrooged* remains a popular offering of the festive season.

Donner would nonetheless look forward to 1989 in the knowledge that any select critical favor accumulated on *Lethal Weapon* had been flushed away. There was only one thing for it. It was time to get "Lethal" again.

After *Lethal Weapon*, Donner had contemplated a return to the children's fantasy genre with a live-action version of the Hanna-Barbera cartoon *The Flintstones*. Jim Belushi was penciled in to star as Fred Flintstone. Joel Silver had optioned the rights to the property, along with producer Keith Barish, and was developing a screenplay from Steven E. de Souza and Mitch Markowitz. Donner was intrigued. He knew Hanna-Barbera, having directed episodes of *Danger Island* (a component of *The Banana Splits Adventure Hour*) during the sixties, but he was not impressed with the draft. After toiling for many months to find the requisite *yabba-dabba-doo*, both he and Silver walked. Brian Levant would ultimately direct the picture, starring John Goodman, after a total of thirty-two writers had been paid to work on the screenplay.

As Richard Donner Productions expanded, Donner grew more agreeable to and greater involved in the business side of production. He signed to executive produce and direct several episodes of *Tales from the Crypt*, a new television series for the cable network HBO. Joel Silver, Walter Hill and David Giler had acquired the rights to adapt the gruesome fifties comic book stories. Although the series consisted of episodes just twenty-four minutes in length, each would be lensed on a budget of close to $1 million. Actors such as Whoopi Goldberg, Demi Moore, and Joe Pesci would be persuaded to appear for scale salaries, some of which were to be helmed by first-time celebrity directors, including Michael J. Fox, Tom Hanks and Arnold Schwarzenegger.

Donner's immediate priority, however, was planning a sequel to *Lethal Weapon*. Unfortunately, original screenwriter Shane Black had returned an untenable script for the sequel, one in which Riggs evolved into even more of an anti-hero, more of a tragic figure that again descended into alcoholism and suicidal tendencies, before eventually dying. Donner called in writer Warren Murphy to transform Riggs from a reckless cop with a death wish, to a hero who stops to figure out the odds because he wants to live. Donner also provided a framework for a story idea inspired by his opposition to institutionalized racism and white dominance in South Africa. As Stephen Goldblatt remembers, "He made sure, over the strenuous objections of Warner Bros., that the villain was South African, and that being anti-apartheid was imbedded in the script. He knew he'd lose sale, but he did it from an idealistic point of view. He's a real humanitarian. He doesn't just talk about it, he practices it."

Donner was originally hesitant to helm *Lethal Weapon 2*; he was merely content to co-produce alongside Silver and allow a new director to assume command. His efforts to take a backseat were met by fierce resistance from both Warner Bros. and superstar Mel Gibson. "There's no shortage of action films on the market," the star is quoted as saying, "and you can throw action at an audience until it's coming out of their ears, but that doesn't guarantee success. What made *Lethal Weapon* unique to the genre was that Dick Donner understands that action doesn't mean a thing unless the audience has access to it by really getting to know the characters first. Dick goes to great pains to set up the background in that way before he takes you on a roller coaster ride. There isn't any other director that Danny [Glover] and I would entrust the characters of Riggs and Murtaugh to, except for the man who very much helped to create them — Richard Donner."

Gibson had turned down lead roles in Brian De Palma's *The Untouchables* and Tim Burton's *Batman* in favor of reprising his role as Martin Riggs. Such enthusiastic commitment by a key performer would have been jeopardized had Donner maintained his position. In the end, however, as he became more involved in the pre-production process, and a third writer, Jeffrey Boam, delivered a fresh screenplay that incorporated a noticeable shift from action toward humor, he quickly changed his mind.

The partnership of Riggs and Murtaugh would continue to be tempestuous for *Lethal Weapon 2*. If no longer suicidal, the former would remain an impulsive risk taker, while the conservative Murtaugh would still be looking to play things by the book. Leo Getz, a dishonest tax accountant-turned-government witness, is entrusted into the protection of the two detectives. While on assignment, Riggs and Murtaugh take it upon themselves to investigate corrupt officials from the South African consulate who they suspect of drug trafficking, gold smuggling and money laundering. The duo cannot arrest the malevolent Arjen Rudd and his chief henchman, Pieter Vorstedt, who are protected by diplomatic immunity laws. Instead, the detectives find themselves the target of political mercenaries. Murtaugh finds a bomb strapped to his toilet that will explode if he stands up, but narrowly escapes thanks to the help of Riggs and the police bomb squad. Having fallen for blonde beauty Rika van den Haas, whom he romances at his beachside trailer home, the maverick Riggs finds himself under attack from helicopter gunships.

Soon, Riggs learns from Vorstedt that the hit man had been responsible for slaying his wife four years previous. He is then restrained in a straightjacket and dumped into the sea, where he discovers the lifeless body of Rika (also murdered by Vorstedt). Thanks to a shoulder that he is able to dislocate on command, Riggs miraculously escapes and, along with Murtaugh, turns vigilante in his mission to bring down the bad guys. After destroying the South African consulate home of Rudd, the duo head for a fiery showdown at a shipping port, where millions of dollars in drug money are ready for export to Cape Town. Ferocious gun battles and a street fight ensue. Riggs gains his revenge by killing Vorstedt, but is then shot in the back by Rudd. Fortunately, Murtaugh is on hand to revoke their nemesis' diplomatic immunity — by shooting him in the head. Murtaugh cradles the seriously injured Riggs in his arms as the emergency services draw in.

In order to support Donner's intention that *Lethal Weapon 2* should assume a lighter tone than its predecessor, the development of the Leo Getz character was crucial. Joe Pesci was cast in the role, an actor best known at the time for playing Robert De Niro's younger brother in Martin Scorsese's *Raging Bull*. Pesci possessed a natural talent for improvisation and proved to be an adept comedian. Donner stated at the time, "With Mel and Danny, Joe is the third stooge."

A second twist was the addition of a love interest, Rita van den Haas, played by British actress Patsy Kensit. "She walked into my office," Donner recalled of her audition. "[She] read the scenes, and afterwards we had to resuscitate Mel." In the first *Lethal Weapon* installment there had been no relationship, romantic or sexual, for leading man and international heart-throb Mel Gibson to engage in. Kensit's presence would bring a fresh new dimension to proceedings this time around.

Orchestrating likeable, engaging characters remained Donner's priority, but he privately acknowledged that — given the emerging prevalence of the action-adventure genre — the stunts and set pieces for *Lethal Weapon 2* would need to be bigger and better than ever in order to satisfy audience expectation and demand. As a result he chose to photograph the film in a widescreen 2.35: 1 aspect ratio, switching back from the more intimate 1.85: 1 used for the first film.

Principal photography literally began with a bang, on the normally quiet streets of downtown Los Angeles on November 28, 1988. Donner was reunited with Charlie Picerni, his stunt coordinator on select episodes of *Kojak* during the seventies. Picerni's first job on *Lethal Weapon 2* was to oversee a spectacular car chase in which Riggs and Murtaugh weave in and out of traffic at high speed, trailed by a dozen black and white squad cars, in an attempt to apprehend a red BMW carrying stolen loot. Windscreens are blown out by shotgun fire, cars crash and explode, in the midst of which a helicopter lands on the city streets and flies a gang of machine gun-toting bad guys to safety. It would have been deemed worthy as the main action set piece for any other production, but for *Lethal Weapon 2* it was one of many.

The most audacious stunt of the film would be the destruction of a Hollywood home. Many believed that the only effective way to film it was to use miniature models, but Donner insisted that in order to create a sense of reality, he wanted footage of his actors inside the building. The house, designed by famed architect John Lauter was built twice. The first was constructed on Stage 1 at Burbank Studios, where a system of hydraulics enabled Donner to lens the trembling building with his actors inside (by design the ten-ton structure then collapsed onto the stage floor). A second house was built in Newhall, twenty miles north of Los Angeles. At three fifteen in the morning, Donner gave the command for the spectacular detonation, and the house — which had been built to city ordinance structures and was actually habitable — crashed to pieces. Such moments were bad for Donner's blood pressure, as he constantly worried over the safety of his cast and crew. Alas, they were not the only heart-stopping scenes of the shoot.

For the scene in which his character, Riggs, is placed in a straightjacket and thrown into the sea, Mel Gibson was tied up in a sack and dumped into a water tank. He was supposed to easily untie himself, but the actor frightened crewmembers with the length of time he spent underwater before doing so. Stunt divers were seconds away from launching a rapid rescue attempt when the blue-faced star returned to the surface.

True to form, Donner's shooting experience was memorable for its playfulness and fun, a tone that Mel Gibson found to be highly agreeable. "It was Donner and the boys again," he enthused. "There's a great sense of freedom on these sets with this crew and it's pretty familiar territory, so it's easy to just step into it and feel free to experiment and push it to the edge."

Off-camera, Gibson entertained his crew by wearing a coffee filter on his head like a Jewish yarmulke, and blurting out the song "Edelweiss" from *The Sound of Music*. "He's crazy," Donner confirmed at the time. "He lives on the edge, fully of energy and excitement. If Hollywood was still doing drugs, I'd say Mel was taking lots of drugs, but the truth is that he is crazy naturally."

To prevent his star from becoming bored, Donner gave Gibson a camera and allowed him to record comic sketches in between takes, assorted capers that he would sell to cable network HBO as *Mel Gibson's Unauthorized Video Diary*. The future Academy Award-winning director enlisted cast and crew to accompany him in his high jinks, as well as others of note who happened to be on the Warner lot — including Chevy Chase, Dan Ackroyd and a group of befuddled studio executives. (His comic pseudo-documentary proved such a hit that Gibson would record a follow-up, *Mel Gibson's Video Diary 2: Lethal Weapon 3*, during filming of a second sequel in 1991.)

Despite the pervasive atmosphere of relaxed freedom, and the comfort zone that filming a sequel provided, Donner was not afraid to roughhouse with his stars in order to keep energy levels on set to a maximum. "Now, come on!" he once scolded in his trademark deep octave, after Gibson and Glover had delivered a lackluster take. "You guys are getting fucking millions of dollars. Let's roll!"

While some overly coddled talent may not have responded to such aggressive cajolement, such was the familial relationship Donner fostered with his actors that a proverbial "rocket up the backside" was exactly what was required. "He yells really loud and everybody pops, too," Gibson declares, "but it's a measured explosion. He doesn't lose control when he does it. He's kind of like a good parent — sometimes they have to kick you up the ass."

As *Lethal Weapon 2* evolved it took on a lighter tone than its predecessor. Donner allowed Gibson, Glover, and Joe Pesci to improvise many of the skits. "With Lethal 1 we shot pretty much what was written," says Goldblatt. "With part two it was more of a free for all." Donner's first impulse in life was to find the humor in a situation, but as a director he needed to show restraint. Without such control, scenes could become too "cute" and override the natural drama.

Far from being the perverse horror show anticipated, the professional union between Donner and his frequently apoplectic producing partner, Joel Silver, was amicable, friendly even. They were two bulls in a china shop, but Donner respected Silver's undeniable talent, and he liked the man, whom he found to be a volatile but engaging presence, both interesting and funny. "Joel is another big personality," says Mel Gibson. "He's quite a charmer. I think he wants people to believe he's The King of Schlock, but, in fact, there's a very refined eye and a very discerning artistic talent there." Of the relationship between the two men, the actor remembers, "They were a couple of guys who got each other. They were on the same track. They saw each other's strengths and respected each other's approach. It worked great."

The team was certainly lucrative. The *Lethal Weapon* crew dominated an entire courtyard of the Warner Bros. studio lot, Richard Donner Productions based at one end, and Silver Pictures holding camp opposite. "We owned most of the real estate in between," describes Jennie Lew Tugend. "The studio loved us. It was a very heady time for everybody. We could pretty much do anything. I could pick up that phone at Warner Bros. and get anything I wanted. It was great."

Lethal Weapon was a partnership between Silver Pictures and Richard Donner Productions, but Donner was always in charge and in control. He had insisted to Mark Canton, the president of worldwide theatrical production for Warner Bros., that he receive the lead producing credit on the original *Lethal Weapon*. Both men understood the unspoken seniority in their relationship, designed to insure against tension and instill a sense of harmony. As a result, Donner and Silver worked well in tandem, voicing strong opinions that were respected by the other. Even so, an undeniable sense of competition existed between the two camps. Tugend continues, "When *Lethal Weapon* became a franchise, it raised the profile of Dick Donner as a director, and it made Joel Silver a star. It was a time when egos were flying. There were Dick and Dick's people. There were Joel and Joel's people." In an attempt to keep a lid on vanity, Donner commissioned a sign above the entrance to his office. It read, "Leave Your Ego at the Door."

Just one day after the completion of principal photography on *Lethal Weapon 2*, Donner was behind the camera to direct an episode of his new HBO television series, *Tales from the Crypt*. More than a quarter of a century after he had helmed the classic *Twilight Zone* episode "Nightmare at 20,000 Feet," he once more prepared to prove his undeniable flair for scaring television audiences senseless.

Donner's "Dig That Cat... He's Real Gone" starred Joe Pantoliano. It was the third episode from the first season of *Tales from the Crypt*. Ulric has a cat gland implanted in his brain by a crazed scientist, and then discovers that he has nine lives. His deaths and resurrections sees him become the star of a traveling circus, where he makes his fortune from his freakish immortality, only to see his duplicitous girlfriend steal all his money away from him.

The series was an instant hit in the ratings. *The Washington Post* singled out Donner's effort for praise. "'Dig That Cat' is the best of the three 'Crypt' stories," wrote critic, Tom Shales, "…. The story takes twists you can't foresee. There is relatively little violence, and this episode more than the others has a true comic-booky look."

As he prepared his final cut of *Lethal Weapon 2*, Donner again ensured that subtle messages pertaining to his moral philosophy were ingrained within the text. While the central story of the screenplay was formed from his disgust at apartheid in South Africa, the director also assured that his film carried a positive animal rights message, as exemplified by a dinner scene in which Murtaugh is chastised by his family for eating tuna fish. (Donner was boycotting tuna because fishermen were killing the dolphins they caught in their nets.) As Lisa Lange, a vice president of the organization PETA (People for the Ethical Treatment of Animals), puts it, "[Donner] knows the influence of the medium. And without compromising his storylines and the adventure of his films, he just puts in these messages. It's hugely helpful in our efforts."

Lethal Weapon 2 was an enormous financial success. When it was released into movie theaters on July 7, 1989, it cuffed $147 million on U.S. soil (double the domestic gross of its predecessor), part of a worldwide box-office tally of $228 million. Next to a series of poorly received sequels on offer during the summer of 1989, the picture drew comparatively strong notices. Roger Ebert praised the film for embodying many of the same qualities as the first *Lethal* installment; the critic claiming that it had "the same off-center invention and wild energy as the original." There was special acclaim reserved for Donner: "Unlike a lot of directors specializing in high-tech action comedies, he doesn't seem exhausted or cynical."

"'Lethal Weapon 2' is no artless, autopiloted waste of precocious movie-theater air conditioning," waxed *The Washington Post*. "[It's] playfully escapist summer fare that doesn't make you feel taken advantage of later... [And it] turns out to be more transporting and whole than either 'Batman' or the newest 'Indiana Jones,' and much funnier than 'Ghostbusters II.'" Again, Donner's influence was cited: "What gets you through the all-purpose plot… is Donner's attentiveness to character."

Various institutions attacked the film for its perceived level of violence. Donner was adamant that his film was not violent, merely action-oriented. He would point to the fact that critics would be hard pressed to find much blood visible on screen. Indeed, the tone of *Lethal Weapon 2* is set even before the opening credits roll. As the Warner Bros. logo is presented on screen, it is accompanied by the *Looney Tunes* musical motif, which carries on for a few seconds as a precursor to the film's inventive opening scene (beginning in the middle of a car chase). In Donner's mind, the music suggested a cartoon quality to the action. During this explosive opening sequence, pithy one-liners and comic exchanges abound to make *Lethal Weapon 2* less violent, more a forceful, spirited romp.

In tandem with *Batman*, the box-office juggernaut of 1989, *Lethal Weapon 2* provided Warner Bros. with a double cinematic triumph with which to end the decade. Under the assured leadership of Bob Daly and Terry Semel, men whom Donner felt particularly close to, the entire studio was performing in harmony with marketing, merchandising and international release departments supervised in house. For the first time in years, Warner Bros. was functioning in the manner of a true Hollywood major. "It was like being at a college that had the winning team," Donner declared. "You all want to wear the sweater."

The director reveled in the warm atmosphere of the studio, delighted to be such a valued member of the legendary institution. *Lethal Weapon 2* marked his fifth outing for Warner Bros. There was every indication the partnership would last for years to come. With Daly and Semel's friendship, respect and support of his creative freedom, Donner was now a stronger directorial power in Hollywood than when he had burst onto the A-list scene at the tail end of the seventies.

In his personal life, Donner was fulfilled. In Lauren Shuler he had found the soul mate he never believed existed. He was entirely dedicated to his new wife, and to ensuring that their marriage succeeded. When time permitted, they sought sanctuary at their homes in Maui and on the San Juan Islands north of Seattle, off of Washington State, taking their family of pets with them, as they did on all of their travels across America.

With the nineties around the corner, the director might have been forgiven for feeling on top of the world. Yet as he prepared to enter his fourth decade of moviemaking, a quite staggering achievement, Donner perceived there to be something missing — something he intended to put right.

"My works are like water. The works of great masters are like wine. But everybody drinks water."

MARK TWAIN

12

The Wishing Spot

One of Donner's greatest attributes, as both man and filmmaker, was his ability to see "the bigger picture" — his innate understanding of how to weave multiple elements and arrive at the correct end result. Occasionally, his empathy for the broader directive, and his short attention span and forgetfulness, landed him in trouble. As a young man he would routinely make plans with his friends and forget that he had made them, double or even triple-booking social engagements. When in his twenties, Donner's exhausted best pal, Gene Freedman, had dumped a pitcher of ice water over him in the middle of a crowded restaurant, an act of retaliation for being stood up once too often. When on set, the filmmaker is known to have forgotten the names of his actors — even Marlon Brando, once the world's most celebrated star.

While strolling the lot at Twentieth Century-Fox one afternoon with his friend Stuart Baird, Donner bumped into Art Linson, his producing partner on *Scrooged*. "Hey, Dick, how are you?" Linson inquired.

"Hi, Kid," Donner boomed. "How are ya? How's it going?"

"You haven't a clue what my name is have you?" Linson jested, following some idle chitchat.

"Hey, Kid, of course I know."

"What's my name then?"

"Heh, heh, heh," Donner laughed.

Panicking, the director elbowed Baird for help. The editor, immersed in twisted amusement, refused his request for assistance. "Dick had forgotten his name. He'd probably forgotten he'd worked on the movie with him!"

It was an uncomfortable moment, but far less awkward than a recent experience at a party he had hosted at his house in Maui. Donner retreated early and collapsed onto his bed. After a little while, his wife ran into the room screaming.

"There's a beetle in the living room!" Donner heard. "There's a BEETLE in the living room!" In his tired state, the director bolted out of bed and ran out to remove the pesky bug.

The music suddenly stopped and everyone turned to focus their attention on Donner, sweeping the floor with a broom while dressed only in his underpants. Lauren, who had run after her enthusiastic husband, whispered in his ear what she had really meant.

"There's a BEATLE in the living room," she explained. She was right. Composer Michael Kamen and his wife, Sandra, had arrived at the party, bringing with them iconic singer and songwriter George Harrison and his wife, Olivia. A rather embarrassed Donner decided not to swat the living legend, shook his hand instead, and sat down to discuss the former member of the Fab Four recording a song for *Lethal Weapon 2*.

It had been almost an entire decade, and the wounds inflicted by the disastrous release of his beloved *Inside Moves* had started to heal. Following the box-office death of his favorite picture, Donner had recoiled into the type of mainstream commercial projects that had launched his career. He was now once again ready to throw his hat back into the ring of directing an intimate human drama.

In private, Donner acknowledged that his success on *Lethal Weapon* and (to an extent) his association with *Superman*, had bracketed him as an "action" director. His association with the high-octane genre had brought him personal satisfaction and professional reward, and because of his great success, many exciting and well-paid projects lay before him. But to be bracketed in such a way was both amusing and ironic. Throughout his long career in film and television, Donner had proven adept in a vast array of genres. And since his first experience on the series *Combat!*, he had drawn more anxiety than pleasure from overseeing action scenes.

He held no regret over the film choices he had made during the eighties, but if there was time for an attempt at a change in career trajectory — a chance to truly demonstrate the diverse range of his talent, to build a legacy as a "serious" filmmaker — then it was now.

Radio Flyer was a highly-rated screenplay written by David Mickey Evans, the compassionate and heartwarming tale of two close-knit brothers who build a flying machine out of a red wagon in an attempt to escape from their abusive stepfather. Evans had pitched the premise to Donner before it was complete, but provided enough detail for the director to be deeply affected by it. Evans' idea was a mixture of humor and pathos that forced Donner to nostalgically recall his own childhood, when he had raced his Radio Flyer wagon in and around Mount Vernon, and at Rolling Acres farm in Clinton Corners, New York. He immediately fell in love with the material. "It was the most moving screenplay I'd read in years," he told the *San Francisco Chronicle*. "It was written through the eyes of childhood; it recaptured experiences we've all had as kids. And it spoke of a kind of magic we only have when we're young and alive with this wonderful power of belief."

As he further absorbed himself in the *Radio Flyer* concept, it became clear to Donner that this was a dream project, one that he had waited an entire career for. It had all led him to this point. He said, "The first time I read the script, it was obviously a very special story. I saw it through the eyes of a child, from a point of view way down there close to the ground. I realized that to children the world still has magic, and if I could see a film through their eyes, I could live their magic and make it work. From that moment on, I knew I had to direct this picture."

Donner persuaded Bob Daly and Terry Semel of Warner Bros. to bid on the property. Their tender of $100,000 was submitted to agent Paul Kelmenson (who represented David Mickey Evans), who summarily rejected it and put the screenplay out to bid. A bellicose frenzy ensued. Twentieth Century-Fox and Disney joined the tussle, but it was Columbia Pictures, recently purchased by Japanese electronics giant Sony, but operating under the guidance of American producers, Jon Peters and Peter Guber, who were the most fervent suitors. Peters in particular was determined that nothing would stop him from obtaining the rights to the much talked about property.

Through the production company Stonebridge Entertainment, a unit formed by actor Michael Douglas and based on the Columbia Pictures lot, Peters held the inside track on his rivals. Peter McAlevey, the production vice president of Stonebridge, was a friend of Kelmenson's and negotiated with him the $700,000 purchase of the *Radio Flyer* screenplay. In addition, novice director Evans would be allowed to helm his self-penned work for an additional fee of $300,000.

Donner was shattered when he learned of the deal. He arranged an impromptu vacation to Italy, so that he and Lauren could relive memories of their earlier romance, and put their *Radio Flyer* frustration out of their minds.

When he returned to the U.S. from his escape to Europe, the director was kept busy. In a deal established by Michael Ovitz, Hollywood super agent and long-standing advisor, Donner jetted to Florida to direct his first television commercial in almost forty years. The dramatic advertisement would be no ordinary assignment. The commercial for the new Universal Studios theme park in Orlando, entitled "A Family Adventure," required an eleven-day shoot and a $2 million budget. Donner took the job seriously (he would shoot 25,000 feet of film), bringing in Jennie Lew Tugend to produce, and *Lethal Weapon*'s Stephen Goldblatt to photograph the ninety-second story of a family who encounter an earthquake, a shark, and other characters from movies such as *King Kong, Ghostbusters, The Fly* and *E.T.* A mini movie in itself, it would require all of Donner's experience at meshing live action with grand special effects. In another Ovitz deal, Donner would soon direct singer/songwriter Sting in the music video "It's Probably Me."

Donner's return home to Los Angeles was soured when he switched on the early evening news. He was aghast to witness the arrest of eighteen-year-old Corey Feldman, the young actor with whom he had formed a close bond on *The Goonies*, and whom he had also cast in Joel Schumacher's *The Lost Boys*. Traffic police had stopped Feldman in his car for speeding, during which time law enforcement officers found sizeable quantities of both heroin and cocaine in his vehicle.

The adolescent performer had endured a difficult upbringing. At fourteen he discovered that his parents had spent all but $40,000 of an estimated $1 million he had earned through his successes as a child star. After he was granted legal emancipation from his mother and father, he then married actress Vanessa Marcil, with whom he enjoyed a volatile relationship as his drug addiction worsened.

Donner had known little of Feldman's personal crisis. "I never realized the degree Corey was suffering," he said. "He never let anybody know."

Feldman remembers, "Dick heard about it on the news, and immediately called me with [telephone numbers for] lawyers... [He] said, 'You know, listen, if you need money for rehab, anything you need, I'm there for you.'"

Throughout his adult life, Donner possessed an instinctual desire to help and protect the needy and vulnerable. Seeing Feldman in distress hurt him terribly. The actor continues, "Dick has been there so much for me in my life. I literally would not have made it to become the person that I am today if it wasn't for his help. In some of my darkest hours Dick has always been there for me... whether it be to give the right advice, or to turn me on to somebody that can help me, or whether it be to loan me financial means, he's just always been there. As a matter of fact, he paid for my rehab, because I couldn't afford it. I was so broke."

Donner's stressful start to 1990 continued through March and April, when he was drawn into a legal fight between the family of veteran stuntman Dar Robinson and De Laurentiis Entertainment. The director had collaborated with Robinson on *Lethal Weapon*, only for the stuntman to be tragically killed shortly before the film's release. Donner had dedicated the picture to him.

Robinson's family alleged that the De Laurentiis production group was responsible for their relative's death on the set of the *Million Dollar Mystery* movie, because there was no ambulance or helicopter on set at the time of the high-speed motorcycle accident, and the nearest hospital was sixty-five miles away. Donner was one of many Hollywood names to testify for the Robinson family.

For quite some time, Donner's attention had been focused on the much-sought-after motion picture rights to Michael Crichton's electrifying techno-thriller, *Jurassic Park*. After an astonishing technique for recovering and cloning dinosaur DNA is discovered, creatures extinct for eons roam an island theme park founded by billionaire John Hammond. After an employee of Hammond's attempts corporate espionage on behalf of a rival, power and security features are disabled, and the dinosaurs run amok, killing many at the compound. A group of scientists, consultants, and Hammond's grandchildren, are caught in the mix, all of whom desperately attempt to return power and order to the compound. Such is the level of destruction caused by the dinosaurs that in the end the only viable option is to escape via a supply ship. The island is then violently destroyed by the fictional Costa Rican Air Force.

Donner had read an advance copy of the book before it was published, and was convinced that he was the correct man for the property, although he faced intense competition from all sides of the power spectrum for the film rights. When they were put out to tender, Hollywood's interest reached fever pitch. Twentieth Century-Fox bid, thinking it the ideal vehicle for Joe Dante. Likewise, Universal Pictures submitted an offer for Steven Spielberg. Despite Donner's overwhelming excitement at the book's cinematic potential, Warner Bros. entered the fray instead on behalf of Tim Burton, who had delivered the studio an enormous success with *Batman*. Disappointed, the director turned to the Sony-owned Columbia Pictures to bid on his behalf.

Jurassic Park was a gripping yarn and pertinent allegorical tale, one grounded in the fantasy action-adventure roots in which Donner so excelled. Adapting the book to film would be technologically ambitious, and would require groundbreaking special effects to realize it, but Donner had been here before. *Jurassic Park* could be his new *Superman*, and he wanted the deal badly.

But the competition for the prized material was short-lived. Once Crichton became aware of Steven Spielberg's interest in the property, he vetoed all deals barring that with Universal. In the director's hands, *Jurassic Park* would become a landmark special effects film, and serve as an exemplar text for the study of the marketing of modern Hollywood blockbusters. At the time of its release in 1993, it was the most successful film of all time, hauling in a phenomenal worldwide toll of $915 million.

In June of 1990, David Mickey Evans began filming *Radio Flyer*. The first-time writer-director was under intense pressure, lensing his picture under the ubiquitous scrutiny of producer Jon Peters, who was alleged to have become so involved in the project that he was attempting to direct through Evans. When a horrified Michael Douglas, the head of Stonebridge Entertainment, saw the poor quality of Evans' dailies just three weeks into principal photography, he took the dramatic step of pulling the plug on the entire shoot. Evans was fired from a production that had accumulated an estimated $10 million in costs.

Douglas immediately turned to Donner, a proven hit maker with a genuine passion for the material, to offload the problematic situation. Columbia offered to pay him $5 million to direct, his wife Lauren Shuler Donner $1 million to produce, and a share in any profits to both. It would be the first picture produced by their newly formed company, Donner/Shuler-Donner Productions. As excited as he was, the deal weighed heavily on Donner's mind. He knew from experience what it felt like to have a "baby" taken from him. Only after Evans personally telephoned him and asked him to take over the project did he agree. Donner also insisted to the studio that Evans be allowed to stay with the production as an executive producer.

Even so, his take on *Radio Flyer* would be radically different. As the director, he would need to see the project through his own eyes, to reimagine it in line with his own outlook on life, to mold it into his own vision. He began by dismissing the entire cast and crew, a lineup that had included actress Rosanna Arquette in the lead, the first in a series of changes that prompted staffers at Columbia to unkindly label the new production "Radio Flyer II."

The director attempted to hire legendary cinematographer Vilmos Zsigmond, sending him a copy of the script with a bottle of wine and a handkerchief. An accompanying note read, "The wine is to set you in the mood for the script, and the handkerchief is for after you have read it — for the tears in your eyes."

Zsigmond, however, was otherwise engaged, so Donner turned to his Hungarian counterpart, László Kovács, who had photographed his *Inside Moves*. "Hey, Kid," Donner roared into the telephone receiver. "I have this project that Michael Douglas owns." Underlying the movie's importance to him, Donner emphasized, "This is the kind of project I always wanted."

J. Michael Riva was hired to design the new production, teaming him with Donner for a fifth project in seven years. Dynamic British editor Stuart Baird came aboard for his sixth collaboration. As he had done on *The Omen*, *Superman*, and each of his defining successes, Donner aimed to re-tool the screenplay to his own artistic sensibilities. He asked Evans to complete a revised draft, softening the scenes of child cruelty so that they would be largely inferred, and to adapt a scene in which a pet dog is killed.

In 1969, young brothers Mike and Bobby drive across the U.S. with their mother, Mary, to start a new life in California. In their new hometown Mary marries a man who insists on being called "The King." While their mother works double shifts as a waitress in order to make ends meet, the boys' booze-fueled stepfather begins to threaten Bobby. The intimidation turns to physical abuse. Fearing for their mother's fragile happiness, the brothers do not inform her of the attacks.

Inspired by the local legend of a boy named Fisher, who, it is claimed, once managed to fly his bike from a local landmark named "The Wishing Spot," the boys devise a plan to build a flying machine from a red wagon, so that Bobby can fly away from home and escape his stepfather. Using their initiative to raise funds, Mike and Bobby buy scrap metal to go with an old lawnmower engine, and begin to assemble the machine, known as "The Big Idea." On the night of the intended flight, Bobby pens a heartfelt goodbye note to his mother, which is read first by his drunken stepfather, who races to the Wishing Spot in order to punish the boys. He is too late to stop Bobby's flight, and is arrested at the scene by the town sheriff. As time passes, Bobby sends Mike and his mother postcards from his travels across the globe, as he grows to become a man and fulfill his lifelong ambition to be "a flyer."

Donner cast *GoodFellas* star Lorraine Bracco as Mary and Adam Baldwin as "The King." Nine-year-old Elijah Wood, who would grow up to star as Frodo Baggins in the *Lord of the Rings* trilogy, was cast as Mike. Donner remembered, "I spoke with Barry Levinson, who had just finished *Avalon*, and he could not stop raving about this child. He showed me some footage on Elijah and, when I met him, I knew he would be wonderful in the role."

Seven-year-old Joseph Mazzello was signed as Bobby. "When we got Elijah and Joey together," the director continued, "I just looked at Lauren and said, 'Stop right now,' because we'd found what we were looking for. The chemistry was simply phenomenal."

Donner shifted the main setting for *Radio Flyer* from Los Angeles to a Navy-owned housing development in the city of Novato, just north of San Francisco. Its low population density, and the high amount of open space and parks, provided a rural atmosphere reminiscent of his own childhood, and allowed him to be close to a very special local resident — his ninety-year-old mother, Hattie Schwartzberg.

The cost of David Mickey Evans's abortive effort was rolled into Donner's budget for *Radio Flyer*, which, when added to the fees for new talent, totaled an incredible $33 million. When principal photography began on October 3, 1990, it was Donner's happiest experience behind the camera. "It was one of those pictures where you can hardly wait to get up and go to work in the morning," László Kovács enthused. "It didn't seem to be work at all. It was such an enjoyable experience, because every day was something different, something new. Dick was constantly, constantly into the story, and always had some really great ideas that he wanted incorporated, and our job was really to help him visualize his imagination. It was just really a wonderful experience."

Donner's assistant director, Jim Van Wyck, recalls, "It was like watching a sculptor working with a very fine piece of clay because he loved it so much. He loved the story so much, and he loved the relationship between the kids. He was so great with those two kids, and they loved him. Just watching Dick work with them and the other actors was terrific."

Donner knew the key to potential success on *Radio Flyer* lay in the performances by Wood and Mazzello, and strived to ensure that the shooting process was playful and fun, and would harness their natural energy and bristling imagination. It was not too difficult to make filming exciting, given scenes that featured a pet dog, a turtle, some frogs, and an imaginary buffalo. Says Lauren Shuler, "Once you start filming with any crew and cast, you become a family. This one felt like an especially harmonious family, and a lot of the good feelings stemmed from the way Dick related to the boys. He was very understanding with them. He challenged them, showed patience with them, fathered them. And they loved him."

"He treated them just like his own sons," Kovács concurred. "[Like] his own boys."

Wood and Mazzello, who relentlessly teased and antagonized one another, enjoyed a tangible bond. When not needed in front of camera, they would spend their time playing in a clubhouse with a bunk bed that Donner had commissioned especially for them. The boys were cheered when George Lucas, the director of *Star Wars*, dropped by during filming to meet with the cast and crew.

Lorraine Bracco, however, was less happy, and more than a little frustrated by her emotionally-draining role. Believing herself typecast as "lousy mother" characters, she lobbied for her part to be rewritten as cameras rolled. She remembered, "I'd beg Richard to allow my character some protective spirit. 'She should know what's happening with her sons,' I'd insist. 'She should try to protect them.' But it wasn't in the script."

The screenplay, its subject matter and tone, was an almost impossibly complex beast for a filmmaker to tame. The task of balancing whimsical fantasy with brutal reality was both daunting and difficult. If Donner placed particular emphasis on the script's more magical elements, he could be charged with disregarding the harsh truths of neglect and abuse. If he chose to focus on the latter, it could be a recipe for financial disaster — he would almost certainly neuter *Radio Flyer*'s profitability as a family film. Says Jim Van Wyck, "Dick really tried to capture on the one hand the incredible resiliency that children have in going through something like this, but on the other hand the incredible hurt and pain and difficulty in going through something like child abuse. There was a feeling that we were doing a magical story, and yet it was grounded in such reality — a difficult reality when you're dealing with something like child abuse — but you always felt like there was magic involved in it."

"Dick Donner loved the story," the director's former assistant, Jennie Lew Tugend, reveals, "but Dick Donner had to put it on a canvas that was comfortable for him. His own canvas was not dark, per se. It was more fantastical. Dick struggled with the dark side of *Radio Flyer*. He didn't want to live in that world. That's why Dick doesn't make movies that are too disturbing, because he doesn't want to live in that dark world day after day."

When he first read the screenplay, Donner had intended to shoot in a realistic vein. But he soon realized that he wished the movie to be seen through the children's eyes — for their subjectivity to become totally believable and to transcend reality. He chose to invest in exploring the wonder and magic of childhood within the context of creating an important drama. The director was overwhelmed with an excitement that stemmed from tackling his first "serious" picture since *Inside Moves*. It was a project and an opportunity that he had waited his entire career for. It could be his defining moment. In a telling aside to his cinematographer, László Kovács, he let slip his innermost feelings. "If this picture is going to be a hit," he told his Hungarian collaborator, "[then] I can do other movies like this, and not the *Lethal Weapon*s."

Although he would never openly admit it, the *Radio Flyer* experience provided Donner with such immeasurable pleasure that he hoped it would propel him to leave the action genre firmly behind. "He was hoping that the film would become very successful," Kovács continued. "I think he was really hoping to make great human dramas. He had such a tremendous understanding for that."

In early 1990, a severely depressed David Mickey Evans had just $4 in his bank account, and had been homeless for three years. Thanks to his hard work on *Radio Flyer*, and the generosity of Jon Peters, he was now an instant millionaire. Having failed in his attempt to direct, the aspiring filmmaker was determined to glean as much knowledge as possible from Donner, the man who had made *Superman* — a picture Evans confessed to watching eleven times when it was released in 1978. He rarely left his side during production, observing and learning all that he could, while rewriting dialogue and offering insight into the thought processes behind his script. Donner took his role as mentor seriously, and drew satisfaction from the relationship. He remembers, "I was drawn to him [Evans] because he wrote a truly wonderful screenplay, and he had asked me to be the one to finish it. In so doing I became quite fond of him. He was just a super guy you wanted to hang with."

Donner and Lauren gained pleasure by assuming an environmentally responsible approach to filming. There was no veal on the production's dinner menu. All cans, cups and bottles were recyclable. Under no circumstances was anyone to smoke in front of the children. The production drivers were also ordered to boycott Exxon gasoline — on account of the infamous Valdez oil spill, one of the most heavily publicized environmental tragedies in history.

After six weeks of location shooting, the unit moved base to Columbia Pictures in Culver City, California, where settings were recreated on a soundstage for two weeks of special effects work. To lens the climactic sequence of Bobby flying his red wagon, the director would utilize the very same Zoptic technology that he had helped to pioneer on *Superman*. Afterward, Donner set about with Stuart Baird to edit the picture, while composer Hans Zimmer recorded the music score.

More than any of his films, *Radio Flyer* visibly bore Donner's strong authorial signature. The characters Mike and Bobby embodied his energetic spirit, imaginative drive, and thirst for adventure — their mechanical abilities and entrepreneurial flair a clear tilt to the director's own childhood skill and enterprise. The pet dog, Shane, traipses enthusiastically at the side of Mike and Bobby, a loyal chum just as Hermit had been, Donner's adopted Collie on Rolling Acres farm in Clinton Corners. During a scene in which the brothers frequent a movie theater, as they stroll past a poster advertising a screening of *X-15*, Donner's mother Hattie Schwartzberg appears as a ticket taker, and a voice-over recalls, "In those days, because they never made you leave after the movie was over, we saw two movies twelve times." It was just as Donner remembered of the countless hours spent on 42nd Street and Broadway, when he was supposed to be attending Packard Junior College.

An early shot of young Mike placing his hand outside the window of a moving car, so that it forms the wing of an airplane, is another throwback to Donner's youth. His memory of doing the same while being driven around by his uncle, Herman Brauer, was vivid and enduring. When Mike attempts to lift a car while wearing a star-spangled banner cape, it is a nod to Donner's own childhood love of Superman, and to his 1978 movie.

Donner and Stuart Baird assembled what they presumed to be the final cut of *Radio Flyer*, and were delighted with the finished result. László Kovács remembered, "We all had such high hopes, and when it was put together we really loved the film."

Yet major problems were on the horizon. "The test screening suddenly went very strange," the cinematographer continued. "It didn't get the results we all expected."

Indeed, when the film was screened for a test audience, many parents walked out in disgust at the subject matter. Those who stayed were left perplexed by a confusing dénouement. Donner had deliberately chosen to leave the climax to *Radio Flyer*, in which Bobby soars the sky in his flying machine, deliberately ambiguous, to leave more questions than answers. Did the boy actually fly away? Did he commit suicide? "I wanted it to be up to the minds of the individual," says Donner. "Were there two brothers, or was the story being told by one child who had made up the rest of the story? What was the reality? What do you want to believe?" A similar tactic had worked on *The Omen*, when multiple readings invited audiences to choose which one they believed in, but this approach went against the grain for the majority of Donner's films. He typically took a "death and marriage" approach to narrative, intending to tie up all loose ends for clarity, for the pleasure and satisfaction of an audience.

Tom Hanks, not yet a major star but an actor of stature, was thus hired to perform in two new sequences to bookend *Radio Flyer*, and to narrate the entire film with a voice-over. This, Donner felt, would provide more of an upbeat ending, and help negate some of the ambiguity experienced by test audiences. Fearing that they might be charged with taking the issue of child abuse too lightly, Lauren insisted to her husband that a toll-free 800 number for Childhelp USA's hotline be screened during the end credits of the film.

Tinkering with his preferred cut meant that Donner missed his film's scheduled summer of 1991 bow, and then a subsequent autumn release. It finally made release on February 21, 1992. It recouped just $5 million of its estimated final budget of $35 million at the North American box-office, despite a nationwide release in more than nine hundred theaters. As the test screenings had ominously predicted, *Radio Flyer* failed to connect with audiences, who found the meshing of such fantastic elements as a flying wagon and a talking buffalo, with evidence of a stepfather beating a young child, an impossibly incongruous combination. Donner's directorial trademark of successfully blending fantasy and reality to create a sense of verisimilitude had, on this occasion, drastically failed him. Despite many cut and newly filmed scenes, audiences still found the conclusion to *Radio Flyer* bewildering. The ending worked for him as a filmmaker, and if he could have stood up in every theater in front of every audience, he could have explained it. But Donner acknowledged that he had failed to convey it visually.

The darkest days of the filmmaker's career were to follow. Having admirably striven to achieve a weightiness not seen since *Inside Moves*, the critical response was positively scathing. "Richard Donner's 'Radio Flyer' is one of those infrequent and embarrassing efforts of a perfectly adequate Hollywood director to make the kind of offbeat movie for which he has no aptitude of all," raged Vincent Canby of *The New York Times*. "… Dealing with this delicate material, he is like someone trying to thread a needle while wearing boxing gloves."

"Donner directs the story for effect, not affect," delivered Hal Hinson of *The Washington Post*, "he's not interested in anything beyond getting his audience to jump to his cues." Roger Ebert of the *Chicago Sun-Times* claimed the picture "pushes so many buttons that I wanted to start pushing back... The movie pushes so many fundamental questions under the rug of its convenient screenplay that the happy ending seems like cheating, if not like fraud."

Donner was by now accustomed to generating dismissive reviews. Even his great successes had been written off by some of the film press. Yet this sharp polemic transcended all before it, and was made all the more painful given that *Radio Flyer* was a picture he loved so deeply. "Dick was really heartbroken," Kovács described. "We all were. It was really sad to see all that hard work, all that effort, in a matter of days disappear."

Concurs Jennie Lew Tugend of the release, "It was like a death. It was like a death in the family."

The dissection into one of Hollywood's most shocking and well-publicized failures was immediate. Fortunately, for both Donner and Lauren, the consensus appeared to be that — rather than laying the blame with the shell-shocked pair — the film industry itself had to accept ultimate culpability for the mess. Excitable studio bosses had, in all likelihood, been so caught up in the fervent atmosphere of competition that, when multiple suitors began courting the *Radio Flyer* screenplay, few actually stopped to ask themselves if it was a project that should have been made. "Even if this film worked, how do you get an audience?" questioned an insider, interviewed on condition of anonymity by *The New York Times*. "If you tell an audience it's about child abuse, they won't come. So you tell them it's about childhood. So an audience shows up and sees the movie, and they say, 'Hey, wait a minute. This is not what we paid seven bucks for. A kid is being beaten.' They walk out. They feel betrayed. They hate you!"

When invited to contribute to the same article, Donner declined to comment. Instead, Lauren provided the newspaper with notes from her Hollywood friends — letters that congratulated her and her husband on their bravery, and described their film as "wonderful," "inspirational," and "beautiful." (Donner had also received a letter from David Mamet, whom he did not know, praising the film.)

As an ode to childhood wishes and dreams, *Radio Flyer* succeeds handsomely. Donner coaxes affecting performances from his leads, spirited efforts that perfectly capture a sense of honor and integrity, of love and promises, which can only exist in the world of one's early youth. At points the story grips, even if, ultimately, it is flawed. Although Donner deliberately intended his direction to reflect a story as told through the eyes of a child, the many close-up shots of watery eyes and saccharine features appear to remain, at times, heavy-handed. Other shots and frame composition lack delicacy, be it the close-up of a hand that pulls beer out of a fridge, or the eyes of the stepfather forever hidden behind dark glasses.

Does *Radio Flyer* morally fail when it portrays children who do not tell of abuse, even when given multiple opportunities to do so? Donner would argue that although Mike and Bobby never share their dark secret with an adult, they are anything but passive, as they set about solving the problem in the only way they know how.

What harms *Radio Flyer* the most are the more unsettling moments of the story that detract from its functionality as a family film. If Donner had made a film that concentrated on the magic of childhood, made purely for kids, it would likely have succeeded, just as it might if he had mastered the screenplay's mature themes and concentrated them only for adults. Actress Margot Kidder believes her friend should have adopted the latter mantra. "Here he had some pretty serious subject matter, and he just couldn't resist glossing it up. You wanted to scream at him, 'Hey, you're talking about child abuse. This is serious shit. Don't try and make a commercial movie out of it.' There is so much more in that man… he should have gone full pelt boogie from the absolute depths of his big old complicated heart and left his comfort zone."

In challenging a middle ground, one that meshes all the elements, the production is diluted, somewhat ineffective. The end result is a film that does not deliver broad satisfaction, it is rather a fascinating but perplexing picture, beguiling yet frustrating — a complex prism of interpretation. "It was very, very difficult subject matter," Jim Van Wyck concludes. "I'm not sure that there's ever been a movie that deals so directly with child abuse, and ultimately deals with the death of a child. I think it was a difficult thing for people to want to go and see."

Donner was married to a beautiful and brilliant woman. He remained without dispute one of the most successful filmmakers in Hollywood history. But for a moment it meant nothing, as the black cloud of *Radio Flyer*'s apocalyptic release formed a shadow above him, consuming his every thought. Donner was personally destroyed by the failure, the disappointment far greater even than that caused by the release of *Inside Moves*. He felt anxious, depressed, frustrated and afraid — torn inside and out. He could not mention the film by name. As he sank, it was his wife who rescued him. "As hurt as Lauren was by the reaction to that film," he later revealed, "she helped me through it. We never like to use the expression 'It's only a movie' because it never is; it's a year out of your life. But there was a point at which Lauren said to me: 'It's only a movie. We've got to move on.' And she was right." It was one of the few intensely bleak periods in Donner's life, and his emotional recovery would take time. Professionally, he would never be the same again.

During the harrowing post-production period of test screenings and re-edits on *Radio Flyer*, the childhood drama that he loved so much, Donner was rumored to be developing a Shane Black script inspired by the television series *The Wild Wild West*, to star Mel Gibson. In truth, he had already privately agreed with Warner Bros. executives, Bob Daly and Terry Semel, to return to the proven riches of the action-adventure genre and helm a third *Lethal Weapon* picture. Screenwriter Jeffrey Boam, one of the hottest com-modities of the moment, was contracted to pen a script inspired by Donner's vision for the sequel. Troubled by the news of escalating gang violence in Los Angeles, the increasing number of young black males murdered from gun crime, and the revelation that armor-piercing bullets dubbed "Cop Killers" were being sold on the streets of Los Angeles, the director insisted the issues be spotlighted on screen in *Lethal Weapon 3*. Donner believed when he was young that the "NRA [National Rifle Association] was really an important thing, because they taught you gun safety as a child living on a farm." He had since formed the opinion that the group had evolved into a "right-wing political phenomenon." This belief was to be a focal point of his bi-racial buddy sequel, and from this moment forth the director would inject anti-NRA slogans into the background scenery of his films. (In *Lethal Weapon 4*, a poster bearing the message "A Child a Day Is Killed by a Handgun" is clearly visible at the police station set.)

Riggs and Murtaugh arrive at the scene of a suspected car bomb. Rather than wait for the arrival of the bomb squad, Riggs drags his partner — who is just eight days from retirement — into an underground car park to diffuse it. When the wrong wire is cut, the two men race away as the bomb dramati-cally explodes behind them. Demoted to patrol duty for their efforts, Riggs and Murtaugh learn of Jack Travis, a brutal former police lieutenant, who disciplines subordinates by burying them alive in concrete and who is ped-dling armor-piercing "Cop Killer" bullets. Riggs and Murtaugh's subsequent investigation is impeded by the presence of internal affairs officer Lorna Cole, who assumes control of the case. Leo Getz, the former corrupt accountant and government witness, returns reinvented as a bleached-blond real estate agent who is helping Murtaugh to sell his home.

After narrowly missing out on arresting Travis, a despondent Riggs and Murtaugh are drawn into a violent firefight as they bust a drug deal being conducted by a group of young black males, during which Murtaugh shoots and kills a friend of his son, sending the veteran officer into a drunken depres-sion. Riggs and Lorna Cole become romantically involved as they assist one another in their pursuit of Travis.

Travis kidnaps Captain Murphy. Riggs, Murtaugh and Cole give dramatic chase, closing in on the antagonist and his henchman at a remote housing development. During a fierce gun battle, Lorna is shot and injured, but saved by Riggs, who kills Travis with his own armor-piercing bullets. Murtaugh is surprised when his family presents him with a retirement cake. He confesses that he has reversed his decision to retire. He and his partner Riggs live to survive another day.

In developing *Lethal Weapon 3*, Donner put to use his "Whammo Chart," a narrative system he had started to develop on *The Omen*, which he had adapted for action screenplays, so that they possessed an explosive set piece every ten pages in order to hold attention.

In *Lethal Weapon 3*, the previous hard edges of the series were softened, as Donner set his sights on developing the comic nuances of his main characters that would lend the formula a jolt of levity. Mel Gibson's inner rapscallion would be allowed to shine like never before, the star allocated a hefty quota of amiable one-liners. As a result, the script would be slightly less coherent than its predecessors; more of a collection of eclectic scenes that Donner, Joel Silver, and the series' stars desired to be filmed. For the veteran filmmaker such an approach was justified — people would go and see the movie not necessarily for the story but because they loved Riggs and Murtaugh, and wanted to spend time with them.

Lauren Shuler had suggested the addition of a female character "as wild and fearless as Mel [Gibson]." Thus, Rene Russo, a native Californian and former fashion model who had made her acting debut in 1989's *Major League*, was cast as Lorna Cole. Upon her hiring, the actress began training with Cheryl Wheeler, a former U.S. kickboxing world champion, and was schooled in martial arts. Also on the advice of Shuler, *Star Wars* actress Carrie Fisher was invited to contribute some uncredited dialogue, including the memorable Riggs line (to Cole): "You're supposed to grow old *with* someone, not *because* of them."

Donner was content to return to the laughter and excitement of the action-adventure genre. Although not entirely without stress and strain, the surroundings were familiar, and with two previous outings behind him, he was comfortable that he knew what to expect from the shoot ahead. It was to be business as usual, albeit without two major contributors to prior installments. The editor, Stuart Baird, and the cinematographer, Stephen Goldblatt, had declined to return for part three. Robert Brown and Battle Davis would thus cut the picture, while Jan de Bont, the future director of *Speed* and *Twister*, was hired to photograph.

Filming began on location in Orlando, Florida, at the city's Soreno Building Town Hall. The abandoned eight-story property had taken two years to build in 1959. It would need just thirteen seconds to implode during a controlled demolition, part of the film's dramatic opening scene. A special effects team had spent two months fitting the building with fifty-five-gallon drums containing debris and explosive powder that would cause four thousand pounds of glass, cork and paper to blow out. In front of an estimated crowd of fifteen thousand curious Floridian onlookers, Mel Gibson and Danny Glover nervously stood on the building's entry steps ready to run from the explosion. As the former recalled, "When they said...'You're on a countdown [until] the building blows up,' we took off, Danny and I both. Our feet did our duty and we boogied out of there as fast as we could because we knew it was going to get a little hot."

Donner used the stunt, which was not directly linked to the plot, as a bold, attention-grabbing opening to his movie, borrowing from his television experience to lend the sequel an episodic feel.

Donner had allowed Mel Gibson into the line of fire for the famous shot, a fact that the mischievous star believed entitled him to complete his own stunts. Prepping a scene in which Riggs races through a thick wall of steam on a motorcycle, Donner was pleased to see Mic Rogers, a stunt double, climb aboard the bike. Yet when the cameras rolled and the motorcycle came roaring through the cloud, it was a grinning Gibson who sped toward a precipice seventy feet in the air. Fuming, Donner assigned a team of production staffers to keep an eye on his star, but eventually turned to the actor's wife to protect him — and his own stress levels — from harm. When Robyn Gibson served her husband with the ultimatum that he should not return home if he continued to take unnecessary risks, his enthusiasm for stunt work quickly waned.

Improvisation took a vice-like hold on the *Lethal Weapon 3* shoot. More than ever the film's fictional characters were exaggerated reflections of the cast's own larger-than-life personas — the line where Gibson and Glover ended and Riggs and Murtaugh began was becoming blurred. "They [the actors] feel very safe with Dick because they've done so many films with him before," explained Joel Silver to the U.K. press, "and they know the characters very well so they really feel it is a familiar situation. Not only the people in front of the camera are the same, but those behind the camera are the same, the same prop guys, the same special effects guys, the same sound co-coordinators. There is this feeling that we can do whatever we want because we have a great team and we know the kind of movie we want to make. It's really old-fashioned filmmaking; it's a consistency of people, consistency of ideas."

Lethal Weapon 3 was indeed an organic product of consorted informality. In addition to his cousin, Steve Kahan, returning as Captain Ed Murphy, Donner persuaded his wife, Lauren Shuler, to film a cameo appearance as a hospital nurse attending to Leo Getz. Donner's hearty leadership, a straightforward desire to entertain, and to have fun while doing it, governed the shoot.

As a result, the tone of the series shifted further away from its edgy, urban western tag, and toward the comic territory of *The Three Stooges*. "I think we've shown the further development of that friendship and a whole new series of antics," Gibson stated toward the end of filming. "We've had fun playing these characters in all three pictures and hopefully that's reflected in the finished product." Whenever possible during a scene, Donner encouraged stars Gibson and Glover to bash Joes Pesci around the head, the director's playful catchphrase becoming, "Hurt him!"

Lethal Weapon 3 premiered in the U.S. on May 15, 1992. It destroyed all competition at the box-office. The movie grossed $145 million domestically, the foundation to a worldwide total of $322 million. Barely three months after hitting rock bottom with the release of *Radio Flyer*, Donner had a number one hit on his hands. It was the highest grossing film of his career. Yet if audiences around the world fell in love with Riggs and Murtaugh once more, Donner's association with them, and the action-adventure genre, was used as rope to hang his filmmaking credentials by. Hal Hinson of *The Washington Post*, who continued his apparent pattern of destruction when it came to Donner and his films, delivered a testy diatribe which included his verdict that "Donner still hasn't learned the first thing about directing action so that it has any coherence or beauty."

"The back-and-forth banter is now so fast-paced that the overlapping dialogue may be more unintelligible than intended," offered Vincent Canby of *The New York Times*. "The movie isn't going anywhere, but it goes in circles at top speed." Even Donner's staunchest defender, Roger Ebert, confessed that *Lethal Weapon 3* "shows signs of settling down into a formula... [It lacks] the sense of invention that brightened the earlier movies." He did acknowledge, however, that the picture remained a cut above "the routine movies in this genre."

Nonetheless, Donner saw movie theaters jammed full to capacity, and he knew that he had gotten it right. Entertaining the masses was an incredible, highly addictive pleasure, and he reveled in the success of his latest project. He disregarded the polemic. In his heart and in his mind he firmly believed that *Lethal Weapon 3* was a socially-conscious film, a multi-ethnic film with interesting roles for women, a film that possessed an interesting subtext that profiled important social issues, namely gang violence and gun crime. *Lethal Weapon 3* was both entertaining and meaningful.

The media-fueled furor surrounding screen violence surfaced yet again. Donner resolutely defended his film, as he had others in the hit series, although he oversimplified the debate when he contended, "These are action movies, like westerns, with good guys and bad guys. The good guys win. What's the difference between Mel jumping on a stagecoach and jumping on a car? It's just that we don't use horses."

Lethal Weapon 3 was a deserved hit. Its characters and their quick-witted humor are endearing, the action set pieces suitably exciting, pleasures that are part of an established buddy-cop formula, punctuated and reinforced throughout by Michael Kamen's playful, jazz-influenced score. It was two hours of undeniable good fun, just the way Donner had intended. With his third element of the trilogy, Donner created a new isotope for big-budget, action-comedies.

Warner Bros. valued the standard it had set and pulled out all the stops to reward those responsible for the success. When the film broke the all-important $100 million barrier in the U.S., Donner, Silver, screenwriter Jeffrey Boam, as well as Gibson, Glover, Joe Pesci, and Rene Russo, were summoned by Bob Daly and Terry Semel to convene in the studio boardroom. As a large cake was rolled out decorated with a Hollywood trade ad declaring the landmark figure, Daly drew an envelope from his pocket. As he opened it, seven sets of car keys fell to the table. The executive later recalled, "Out in front of our building were parked seven Range Rovers, in all different colors. They went out and chose the color they wanted."

Donner clearly possessed the magic touch of delivering highly profitable blockbusters, a talent that kept his studio financiers very happy indeed. His industry stock had always been better than good, although never had it been better than now. Few, if anyone, knew of the dark professional demons he was fighting inside.

Donner with Sean Astin at the time of The Goonies. RICHARD DONNER

Wet and wild on The Goonies. RICHARD DONNER

Donner directs a scene from The Goonies *featuring the giant pirate ship "Inferno."*
RICHARD DONNER

The Donners with close family on their wedding day. RICHARD DONNER

The Donners were married in 1986. RICHARD DONNER

Actors Mel Gibson and Michael Shaner get ready to jump in a signature scene from Lethal Weapon. WARNER BROS/THE KOBAL COLLECTION

Donner joins his *Lethal Weapon* stars on a promotional tour of the Far East.
RICHARD DONNER

Donner and Bill Murray compete to direct Scrooged. AUTHOR'S COLLECTION

Donner with Robert Zemeckis and Walter Hill, the directors of the first three episodes of Tales From The Crypt, *which debuted as a 90-minute trilogy on HBO.* AUTHOR'S COLLECTION

Mel Gibson with Danny Glover in Lethal Weapon 2. RICHARD DONNER

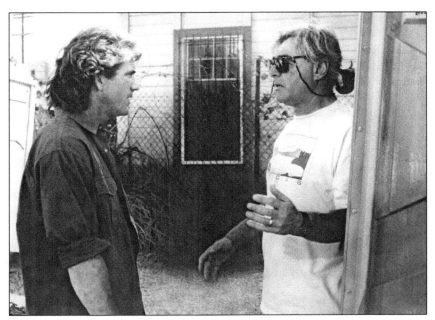

Donner and Mel Gibson on the set of Lethal Weapon 3. *The two men formed a familial bond and collaborated on six movies.* WARNER BROS/THE KOBAL COLLECTION

Donner poses with Warner Bros. executive Bob Daly, who gifted brand new Range Rovers as Lethal Weapon 3 *surpassed $100 million at the U.S. box-office.* WARNER BROS.

Donner directs Joseph Mazzello and Elijah Wood in Radio Flyer. AUTHOR'S
COLLECTION

Donner directs Radio Flyer. AUTHOR'S COLLECTION

The Donners joke with young star Elijah Wood while filming Radio Flyer. AUTHOR'S COLLECTION

The Donners celebrate the release of Radio Flyer *with Rita Wilson and Tom Hanks.*
RICHARD DONNER

On the set of Maverick, *Donner reviews script pages with James Garner and Mel Gibson.* RICHARD DONNER

Donner, Jodie Foster and Mel Gibson pose aboard the "Lauren Belle" on Maverick. The paddle steamer was named after Donner's wife. RICHARD DONNER

Donner directs Maverick. RICHARD DONNER

Donner with Lauren on the set of Maverick. RICHARD DONNER

Donner with Mel Gibson at the time of Maverick. RICHARD DONNER

Sylvester Stallone as Robert Rath in Assassins. AUTHOR'S COLLECTION

The crew of Assassins. RICHARD DONNER

The Donners in Hawaii with music and film producer Shep Gordon, recording executive Jerry Moss and his wife, Anne. RICHARD DONNER

Julia Roberts and Mel Gibson in Conspiracy Theory *formed one of the strongest star headlines of the nineties.* WARNER BROS/SILVER PICTURES/THE KOBAL COLLECTION

Donner and Warner Bros. executive Terry Semel celebrate the release of Conspiracy Theory.

Donner with Bruce Willis and Mos Def on location for 16 Blocks. AUTHOR'S COLLECTION

Donner directs Bruce Willis in 16 Blocks. AUTHOR'S COLLECTION

Donner with Mel Gibson in 2009. PETER ZACHARY/TILT PHOTOGRAPHY/AMERICAN CINEMA EDITORS

Donner laughs with Frank Urioste, Stuart Baird and Mel Gibson, who presented him with his Golden Eddie Filmmaker of the Year Award at the 59th Annual American Cinema Editors Awards. PETER ZACHARY/TILT PHOTOGRAPHY/AMERICAN CINEMA EDITORS

"I knew if I really believed and made it happen, hell then that [was] nothing short of magic."

MEL GIBSON AS BRET MAVERICK

13

Lights, Camera…
Action!

Donner was awash with film choices during the summer of 1992, a year that had begun so disastrously for him with the fraught and devastating release of *Radio Flyer* (which only later developed a passionate following). One promising option was *Free Willy*, the uplifting tale of a street kid placed in foster care who befriends a captive killer whale and helps return it to the open sea. The script was the brainchild of actor Keith A. Walker, who after appearing in *The Goonies* as Mikey's father, Irving Walsh, had been inspired to pen his own screenplay set in Astoria, Oregon. *Free Willy* was the pet project of Donner's former assistant, Jennie Lew Tugend, who actively developed the idea and oversaw its eventual journey to film, assisted by Jim Van Wyck. Both operated under the auspices of Lauren Shuler, who nurtured the screenplay through to a final draft, as she did for each of her pictures.

The material resonated strongly with Donner, who was philosophically opposed to the capturing of wild animals for exhibition in zoos, aquariums, circuses or theme parks, even if the institutions were non-profit organizations, educational centers, or both. *Free Willy*, the third feature film for the fledgling Donner/Shuler-Donner Productions unit, was a movie full of childhood wonder and magic, the script an adept blend of fantasy and reality that seemed perfectly tailored to Donner's expertise. Surprisingly, perhaps, the director and passionate animal rights activist remained non-committal.

Donner had no such doubts in regard to the lucrative relationship he had established with producer Joel Silver. By nature both men were the most powerful presences in any room — two giant personalities who had defied the odds of expectation and established not only a solid business association but also a personal friendship. They enjoyed a mutual sense of playfulness and fun, of mischief and prank, and a joint enthusiasm for entertaining the masses with their epic brand of entertainment. Donner drove the creative side, while Silver delivered the promotional force. Both were perfectly in tune with the public zeitgeist. After Donner gifted his producing partner a customized pinball machine that emitted explosions, gunfire, and curse words instead of the usual audio sound effects, the pair made public their plans to adapt their HBO television series, *Tales from the Crypt*, into a mystery-suspense-thriller movie franchise for the nineties. Donner, Walter Hill, and Robert Zemeckis would each helm a film in the projected trilogy. Donner chose the full-length feature script *Witching Hour*. Cameras were scheduled to roll in North Carolina in January 1993, after Michael Ovitz had mapped out a strategy to secure the $30 million investment required for the three pictures. Ultimately, a deal for the aspiring franchise failed to materialize.

Although Donner had multiple fires to burn, he was finding it difficult to focus his energy on any one in particular. The director announced that he would not direct *Free Willy*, a vehicle he appeared perfectly suited to. The reason for his rejection of the picture lay deep within him.

After *Radio Flyer*, he was, to an extent, unwilling to commit to material he could become too emotionally involved with, or that presented itself as somewhat of a commercial risk. *Free Willy* was both — a movie inspired by a cause dear to him, and a picture whose potential success rested largely on the shoulders of a child performer (it would be without a star name or a plethora of special effects to pull in audiences). For a director who was thrilled to entertain the masses, who had gotten such a kick out of seeing lines form around the block to see his *Lethal Weapon 3*, Donner's appetite was now exclusively for blockbusters — high-concept pictures with major stars attached. He had founded his reputation on the blockbusters *The Omen* and *Superman*, cemented it with his *Lethal Weapon* trilogy. These were the type of films that made studios money, and paid him a great living to do so. *Inside Moves* and *Radio Flyer* would always be his dearest, most important films, pictures that provided him with the strongest sense of fulfillment, but such a passion of feeling may now have become a secondary factor for Donner as he made crucial career choices.

He lensed two lucrative, high-profile commercial spots for the Coca-Cola Company and negotiated the sale to Twentieth Century-Fox Television the network rights to episodes of *Tales from the Crypt*. Following a successful run on the cable station HBO, the syndication of episodes edited for nudity and or profanity would see it air in millions of households across the U.S.

For a while Donner appeared set to helm *Dragonheart*, an ambitious fantasy epic of a disillusioned dragon-slaying knight. But the director's interest was conditional. Universal Pictures would need to supply a hefty special effects budget for Charles Edward Pogue's screenplay to be realistically brought to life, and superstar Harrison Ford would need to turn his cautious curiosity in the project into a firm commitment to headline. Donner would get his first wish, but not the second, and thus withdrew his own interest in proceedings. *Dragonheart* was released in 1996, starring Dennis Quaid. Rob Cohen directed.

Lauren Shuler hired the Australian director Simon Wincer to helm *Free Willy*. Donner visited the set during filming and became a champion for the film and its star — Keiko, the killer whale. On the last day of principal photography on location in Mexico City, Keiko leaped out of the water several times without prompting from his trainer. "They were really beautiful breaches," Donner commented, "and he did them all on his own. He knew, I really think he knew that we were about to leave. There were certainly a lot of wet eyes when we pulled out of there."

While all suffering broke Donner's heart, he found something particularly torturous in cruelty to animals. Perhaps it was the countless hours spent as a child on Rolling Acres farm in Clinton Corners, New York, where he and his sister named every single cow and chicken, and endlessly begged their father not to sell them to the local butcher. Maybe it was because his best friend then had been "Hermit," an adopted collie that traipsed enthusiastically by his side — a loyal chum who was there with him through every adventure, no matter how great or how small. Whatever the root cause of his pain and concern, Donner cared deeply for all animals, believed them to enjoy an intangible sense of purity, and was drawn to protect them from harm. With great passion he focused his activism on the plight of marine mammals.

Keiko had spent eleven years imprisoned at the amusement park in Mexico. He was distressed and in poor health from being confined to a shallow pool of water. His muscle had turned to flab, he was lethargic, and he suffered from severe skin lesions. Donner and Lauren were shocked and infuriated by the plight of the seven-thousand-pound orca and were moved to learn more. As a result of his research he would threaten to lead a boycott of the Olympic Games because of whaling practices. Said he, "I do not understand someone who puts on a costume, picks up a sophisticated weapon and kills a living thing — just for sport. I think it's about the same as the killings on the streets of Los Angeles. Man is inhumane, even to himself. When we learn to live with animal life, maybe we can live with ourselves."

In a move that formed headlines and drew international media attention, Lauren Shuler, Jennie Lew Tugend, and Dave Phillips of the Earth Island Institute, arranged for Keiko to be flown on a UPS plane (the use of which was donated free of charge) and moved to a privately owned pool at the Oregon Coast Aquarium, where Keiko would be taught to hunt live fish in preparation for his hard-earned freedom. The Donners agreed that the end credits for *Free Willy* should list a toll free telephone number for viewers to call and express their support for organizations opposed to the capture of marine mammals. When the movie was released in the summer of 1993, nearly eight hundred thousand calls were received. Lisa Lange, an executive with PETA (People for the Ethical Treatment of Animals), reflects that, "What was important about *Free Willy* was that it was geared — without excluding the adult viewership, because it certainly didn't — to the younger audience that is so key to our campaign. It really is the next generation that's going to dictate how many animals are captured, how many animals are bred in captivity."

As Donner achieved more and more of his professional goals, a passionate sense of humanitarian responsibility began to take center stage in his life. Quietly and without fanfare, he embarked upon secret charity work, helping to raise millions of dollars for a variety of causes. Throughout the late eighties and early nineties, he and Lauren became actively involved in Lupus Research, Johansson Research, NRDC (Natural Resource Defense Council), NRDA (Natural Resource Damage Assessment), Planned Parenthood, and many children's health and welfare organizations. They were highly motivated to raise money and awareness to aid the causes about which he cared so passionately, and, in the end, his philanthropy rewarded him a level of excitement that rivaled that of making movies.

Free Willy earned a highly respectable $78 million in the U.S., part of a $154 million haul at the global box-office (it would later become a record-breaking release for Warner Home Video). More importantly, it raised awareness of Keiko's plight, whose rehabilitation the Donners and Tugend had taken it upon themselves to facilitate. They solicited financial contributions from Warner Bros., UPS, the Humane Society of the U.S., and the cell phone tycoon Craig McCaw to do so. As a result, the environmental group Earth Island Institute was able to fly Keiko in an ice-filled crate to a new home in Newport, Oregon — a $7 million pool four times the size of his Mexican tank filled with seawater deep enough for the whale to dive in. Within months of arriving in Oregon, Keiko gained just short of a ton of muscle weight. His skin disease healed and he began to catch his own fish. Meanwhile, the whale's story continued to capture the public imagination — he was even featured on the cover of *Life* magazine. Not satisfied, the Donners continued their support, assisting in relocating Keiko to Iceland and a new pool the size of a soccer field. When he eventually joined the company of wild whales and swam nearly a thousand miles to the Norwegian coast, the moment stood as one of the proudest of the couple's life.

Toward the end of 1993, Donner's activism saw him embroiled in a bitter media dispute with Tom Fetter, the president of Kettenburg Marine, a company that had captured three Pacific white-sided dolphins near Santa

Catalina Island in San Diego, where they awaited transportation to the Shedd Aquarium in Chicago, a venue Donner believed held a reputation of "death," in regard to its captive whales and dolphins. Quick to support such groups as the Whale Rescue Team and San Diego Animal Advocates, he and Lauren attended a carefully organized protest, for which the couple flew in two planeloads of celebrity supporters. Chevy Chase, Victoria Principal, Tony Dow, and the entire cast of the television show *Full House* were among those invited by the Donners to express their support for the cause. "I'm not a reactionary," the filmmaker and activist told the *San Diego Business Journal.* "I just got excited about this. I want to tell the folks in San Diego, including Tom Fetter, that they made a mistake."

In response, Fetter accused Donner of being a publicity seeker. He seethed, "I think the media and public are being manipulated by a couple of publicity-seeking Hollywood types. And I'm not certain it's not for self-serving purposes."

Donner's response was firm. He proclaimed, "Fetter is out of step with the '90s."

Mel Gibson was editing his directorial debut, *The Man Without a Face,* when he paused to shoot the breeze with his producer partner, Bruce Davey. The western genre had recently been reinvigorated and reinvented through the Academy Award-winning successes of *Dances with Wolves* and *Unforgiven,* and, remembering what fun the fifties television show *Maverick* had been, Davey pitched to Gibson the idea of updating the famous series for the big screen. Favoring a lighthearted adventure tale with which to follow his rather serious *The Man Without a Face,* the mega-star was immediately sold. He promptly arranged a meeting with Terry Semel of Warner Bros., who having reviewed the recent success of *The Fugitive* — another television series reimagined as a major motion picture — agreed to the commission.

Development was placed on a fast track. Legendary screenwriter William Goldman, of *Butch Cassidy and the Sundance Kid* fame, was hired to pen the screenplay. Donner was approached to direct. "Bill [Goldman] turned in a great cake," remembered Gibson with irreverence. "We took the cake over to Donner's place. He took a bite and bought it. It just all kind of fell in." Donner was the logical choice to direct the movie, given not only his previous, hyper-successful partnerships with Gibson, but also their deep friendship. With both men on the wagon trail, a Goldman script that was a riotous mixture of action and comedy, and the overall revival of the western genre, *Maverick* had hit written all over it. Certainly, Bob Daly and Terry Semel predicted it should be the highlight of the 1994 blockbuster season.

Fast-talking gambler Bret Maverick dangles from a hangman's noose. He recalls the misadventures that led to his predicament. In an attempt to raise enough money to enter the Three Rivers Poker Championship, he had ridden into the town of Crystal River and joined a game of poker.

Maverick had upset a group of players, including the villainous Angel, by winning handsomely. After a fight, the vivacious Annabelle Bransford had visited Maverick in his room. The sexy con-woman stole both a kiss and Maverick's wallet, which he later recovered. The next day, while in the town bank, the ladies man was robbed for a second time. Maverick had left Crystal River on a stagecoach, accompanied by Annabelle and the Marshal Zane Cooper.

Indians, who demanded a human sacrifice, had apprehended them. Luckily, the tribe chief was Joseph, a friend who owed the cunning cardsharp money. The pair schemed Maverick's release, and he headed toward the poker championship. It was at this point that he had encountered Angel, who unbeknown to him had been hired to ensure that he never made it to Three Rivers. Maverick was strung up and left for dead.

Maverick escapes the hangman's noose. In Three Rivers he again meets Angel, and reunites with Annabelle. He cons a Russian archduke into funding him in the tournament run by Commodore Duval, and emerges as the winner.

Angel draws a gun, but is shot down by Cooper and Maverick. Cooper's moment as hero is short-lived, as he decides to steal the jackpot. He had been in cahoots with the commodore the entire time, but when the two men meet later that night, the greedy commodore pulls a gun. Maverick appears and steals the money back.

Maverick and Cooper are revealed to be father and son. As they quibble over the course of events, Annabelle appears and snatches the cash prize. Maverick confesses that half the money is hidden in his boot, and that he expects to enjoy retrieving the rest.

The Shrine Auditorium hosted the 1994 Academy Awards ceremony. Steven Spielberg stood at the podium to receive his long overdue award, collecting best picture and best director statuettes for the masterful World War II epic, *Schindler's List*. His win in the directing category was at the fourth time of trying. He had previously been nominated for *Close Encounters of the Third Kind, Raiders of the Lost Ark* and *E.T.: The Extra-Terrestrial*. *Schindler's List* finally proved that the master fabulist, with an innate sense of the language of film, was also serious artist.

Donner was thrilled for Spielberg, and took pause to recall memories from careers that had so often intertwined. In the early seventies, Donner was the television veteran at Universal, Spielberg the apprentice eager to learn all that he could. By the end of the decade both men had ascended to the realm of A-list filmmakers, delivering between them some of the more indelible blockbusters of a golden era for mainstream Hollywood. For Donner, *The Omen* and *Superman*, like *Jaws* and *Close Encounters of the Third Kind*, touched generations of moviegoers. Both men immersed themselves in their spectacular fictional worlds, and established themselves as great cinematic illusionists.

Donner had been the first to lend his artistic ability to an important human drama, when he delivered the strongly acclaimed, but ultimately unprofitable, *Inside Moves*. Spielberg, too, yearned to balance his directorial résumé with vehicles that could showcase his abilities as a serious filmmaker, and he followed a feature adaptation of Alice Walker's novel *The Color Purple*, and J.G. Ballard's *Empire of the Sun*.

As the nineties had dawned, both directors faced junctions in their careers. They had both amassed enormous success, but both again chose to invest their efforts into less commercial projects that carried personal meaning. The films they chose to make would play a strong part in defining their legacies. For Donner, his best efforts could not avert the intimate *Radio Flyer* from being a disaster — a failure that left him badly shaken. Contrastingly for Spielberg, *Schindler's List* was a crowning achievement, one that confirmed him as critical darling and filmmaker of the utmost historical importance. "Dick has done a number of very seminal movies," declared the late Guy McElwaine, the former president of Morgan Creek Productions, during a review of Donner's career. "[But] he's never done that one *Schindler's List*, or that one *Godfather*. *Godfather* and *Godfather II* are two of the best movies ever made. Francis [Ford Coppola] has made some movies that weren't quite so great, but he'll always be recognized for making two of the greatest movies of all time."

In truth, Donner did not really care to worry about recognition or awards. Certainly, he never thought for a second about competition with his contemporaries or rivals. He wished to be respected for his work, but did not worry about his legacy. His place in Hollywood history was a dilemma for others to cogitate over. He would rather go fishing.

Having achieved all that he had in his professional life, what was important to Donner was to select projects that would be enjoyable to shoot, that bore the potential to excite and uplift an audience. Mel Gibson's *Maverick* provided him the opportunity to do exactly that.

Armed with the presence of bona fide superstar Mel Gibson, the foundation of a stellar William Goldman script (albeit one likely to be deviated from during the course of shooting), and the full power and support of the Warner Bros. hierarchy, Donner was greatly excited.

Stuart Baird would return to edit the picture, while esteemed cinematographer Vilmos Zsigmond, of *Deliverance* and *The Deer Hunter* fame, Oscar winner for *Close Encounters of the Third Kind*, was contracted to photograph. The Hungarian was no stranger to the western genre, having also served as director of photography on *McCabe and Mrs. Miller* and *Heaven's Gate*.

Donner and Gibson hired production designer Tom Sanders, who strove to establish an authentic western setting. A primary focus for the team was to create muddy and dusty streets, as few frontier towns had enjoyed the convenience provided by sidewalks.

Maverick reunited Donner with Jim Van Wyck, his DGA (Directors Guild of America) trainee assistant on *Inside Moves*. A graduate from the University of Oregon, Van Wyck had played professional baseball for eight years before he started a filmmaking apprenticeship in 1980. He had fast become one of the most highly rated assistant directors in Hollywood. Bright, witty, creative, and tenacious, for more than a decade Donner would depend upon him for each of his films. They would become firm friends.

The role of Marshal Zane Cooper had originally been envisaged as being the same age as Maverick, but when Paul Newman expressed a desire to join the cast, Goldman rewrote the role as an aged character, one far more intrinsic to the basic plot. Then, suddenly, Newman withdrew his interest. For Donner and Gibson, the iconic actor's decision to appear instead in the low-key *Nobody's Fool* was likely a blessing in disguise. "Mel and I love to improvise," Donner told *Entertainment Weekly*, "and I know Paul Newman is very rigid — you shoot the script. If we had cast somebody rigid in this, we would've been against the wall."

The answer to the casting lay in revisiting the roots of the original *Maverick* television show. "I think in our hearts we didn't want to go to Jim Garner for risk of offending him," Donner reflected. "Here's the guy who created the role, what else could we ask him to play except Maverick, but Mel's gonna play that. Mel and I were talking: Should we go to Garner? All he can do is get angry at us, so we sent a script."

A veteran of the Korean War awarded the Purple Heart, Garner was a $500-a-week contract performer until Bret Maverick made him a television star in 1957 (he later starred in *The Rockford Files*, ensuring he remained a household name in the U.S. for many years). When approached, Garner cheerfully agreed to meet. Donner observed him sitting next to Gibson on a couch, teaching incredible one-handed card tricks. The actor possessed a certain kind of energetic glow, and established an instant rapport with the star of the movie. When he arrived home, a voicemail message awaited confirming his hiring.

It was Meg Ryan and Kim Basinger who initially appeared favorites for the scene-stealing role of Annabelle Bransford. When those deals could not be struck, Terry Semel suggested Jodie Foster, a double Academy Award winner, for the part. Donner did not perceive Foster to be a sultry sex siren. It took the viewing of a set of provocative stills from a recent photo session, and Semel's persistent lobbying, for him to accede. Foster accepted the challenge of a first comedic role just three weeks prior to the commencement of shooting.

Next to her, the main cast would also include Graham Greene, Alfred Molina, and James Coburn. Donner insisted upon hiring familiar western heroes in various supporting roles, including stars from such classic television series as *Laramie* and *The Virginian*.

Maverick was lensed on location at the High Sierras near Lone Pine (the scene for more than two hundred-and-fifty westerns), Yosemite, Lake Powell in Arizona, and the Columbia River in Oregon, where filmmakers restored a paddlewheel tug, around which they built the façade of the "Lauren Belle" (a surprise for his wife, Lauren). The riverboat interior was filmed on a soundstage at Warner Bros. in Burbank, California. Further sets, including the Crystal Palace gambling hall, were built in Arizona.

Maverick set a new standard for the amount of time devoted to ad-libbing and improvisation on a Donner set. The director routinely hectored and cajoled his actors throughout the course of a take, nattering enough multiple instructions to leave script supervisor Cynnie Troup on the verge of collapse. Some of the film's scenes would be filmed as the screenplay demanded. Others veered loosely from the written word. A few would be improvised almost entirely.

When the script called for Gibson and Garner to relax in a steaming Turkish bathhouse in San Francisco, so as to recover from their money-earning exploits, Foster was urged to substitute her line, "It's the splendid similarities that tip you off," — a thinly veiled nod to the size of both men's manhood — with the more mischievous, "It's the little things that tip you off." The line didn't make it into the movie, although the surprised facial expressions of her co-stars did. (Lauren played a bathhouse maid in this scene.)

Donner's bold instructions, coupled with his sense of playfulness and fun, were crucial to the natural energy of the movie, and to extracting enjoyable, spirited performances from his cast. Garner, for one, was particularly impressed with Donner's forthright style of filmmaking, and rarely wished to leave the set. When not required, he could be found in a corner laughing at proceedings, or making others giggle with his own dirty jokes. "Actors get it right away that he knows what he's doing," observed Donner's friend and colleague, the late Tom Mankiewicz. "I remember when he was shooting *Maverick* Jim Garner said to me, 'What a refreshing change to work with a director who really knows what the hell he wants and what he's doing.'" Vilmos Zsigmond was similarly enamored and inspired. He told *Variety* that

Donner had "a great sense of humor, a terrific mood around him. I've never worked with anyone who had such a great time."

But Donner was more than just a good time guy. Zsigmond quickly discovered a talented artist who was able to communicate a vast technical knowledge and expertise. "It was interesting working with Donner," he informed *American Cinematographer*. "We had very good communications and discussions, including one on how to compose close-ups in anamorphic [lenses]. He wanted more chin and less head, but personally, I don't like the eye being so close to the frame line. I'd rather see them closer to the middle of the frame. That is what makes this a collaborative process. Everyone has an opinion, but in the end it is always the director's film."

In a more recent interview, Zsigmond added that, "Dick gives you so much freedom. He leaves it up to you how you light, how you set up the camera. And he appreciates [you]. When he sees dailies, he always tells you if you did a good job."

Donner insisted upon using multiple cameras to capture spontaneous reactions. The director intended to draw his audience into the humor by emphasizing the reactions in the eyes, and the facial expressions, of his actors.

Zsigmond desired to shoot the night interiors in natural light with high-speed lenses, which was not possible due to Donner's insistence on an active camera, going from wide shots to tight close-ups. He would occasionally ask Zsigmond to slide into a zoom during tracking shots, although his enthusiasm for camera movement is best exemplified by the Steadicam sequence that captures the climactic riverboat card game. After a master shot establishes that James Garner is walking around the hall, the audience is treated to a four-minute point-of-view experience, as the camera operator makes 360-degree circles around all three tables, at one point stopping to peer over the shoulder of an actor, who holds his cards in front of the lens. The subjective viewpoint, a result of painstaking rehearsal, effectively captures the excitement and tension of the scene.

The final poker game was a critical moment in the film. Donner employed a third camera to ensure maximum coverage. "The actors were doing a lot of ad-libbing with body language and facial expressions," Zsigmond recalled, "and Dick wanted to capture spontaneous reactions that are difficult to repeat. Sometimes, we had both medium and close-up lenses on Mel at the same time."

Jodie Foster was not as quick as Mel Gibson and James Garner to embrace the ubiquitous, fun-loving mood on set. When she arrived ten days into the production following a business trip to France, she was overwhelmed and somewhat concerned. "I don't know what the hell you guys are doing here," she informed her director, "but I'm in your hands, so don't ruin my career."

Starring in a comedy was a baptism of fire for Foster, who initially struggled with Donner's method of communicating instructions to her mid-perfor-mance. "He doesn't apologize about it at all," she explained. "If I was in a drama and in the middle of a scene, and he said, 'Turn right! Open your mouth! Hurry!' maybe I would want to kill him."

Donner enjoyed teasing Foster, and in unison with Gibson, his frequent cohort, he set up an audacious prank. "I don't think we have enough back-ground," he informed the actress one afternoon. "The audience is not going to understand the relationship between you and Mel. We just wrote this little scene, let's see if you like it or not." Donner then handed her and Gibson the new script, and invited them to do a read-through. The scene began gently, tenderly, then quickly delved into the world of the bizarre. "Whoa! Whoa! Whoa!" she screamed over the revelation that her character, Annabelle Brans-ford, had been raped. Within seconds of Donner's first loud guffaw, she realized that this was not an exercise designed to explore character context, rather a simple gag designed to make her feel loved. It was her birthday, and the surprise was revealed with banners, balloons, and singing.

Throughout shooting, Mel Gibson was mischief personified. He routinely attached paper clips to Foster's costumes, and arranged for a bucket of feathers to be dumped on Jim Garner's head during the middle of a scene — the video playback of which kept cast and crew entertained for days. While Donner normally saw fit to beat anyone's joke, on the very first day of filming he too was a victim, as a team of cohorts surreptitiously conspired to ambush him.

Knowing of the director's famous ability to confuse fellow Hungarians Vilmos Zsigmond and László Kovács, Gibson and company arranged for the latter to be flown on location in the El Mirage desert.

On a dry lakebed, in blistering heat, the director prepared to film a scene in which Mel Gibson dangles precariously from a tree in a hangman's noose, hovering a few feet above a clump of snakes. Donner sat in his director's chair, while Kovács stood with his back to him, lighting the shot. "C'mon, Vilmos," the filmmaker boomed, eager to get proceedings underway. "We haven't got all day long." Kovács did not say a word, merely continued to adjust his light-ing meter. "C'mon, let's go!" Donner continued.

"Dick," Kovács replied as he turned, "these mechanical snakes are not working."

Donner saw, but he did not believe it. His jaw fell open wide. For once, he was speechless. "László?" he queried, paralyzed by confusion.

"Yes?" replied the cinematographer, deadpan.

After several seconds of uncomfortable silence, Donner turned behind him, and witnessed Zsigmond and assembled crewmembers smiling back. The entire set roared with laughter.

Donner did at least get even with a camera operator, Ray De La Motte, whom he knew to be terrified of snakes. For the rest of the day the director crept up behind the anxious technician and clamped his hand on his ankle to simulate snakebite.

Donner drew further giggles when he ordered T-shirts to be handed out to everyone on set. Printed on the front of each was a list of the top ten "Donnerisms" heard during filming. They read:

> 10. *This is the slowest crew I've ever worked with!!*
> 9. *I don't want to hear your life story.*
> 8. *Why are you looking at your watch, are you a producer?*
> 7. *Come on, Jimmy, why aren't we rolling?*
> 6. *Who's on the good camera?*
> 5. *Energy, energy, get it up, get it up!!*
> 4. *Who's not ready? I want names.*
> 3. *Kick ass!*
> 2. *Hip hop, hip hop, hip hop.*
> 1. *Huh, huh, huh, huh, huh, huh, huh...*

After a tentative start, Jodie Foster acclimated to the infectious irreverence on set. With fears regarding her reputation and career allayed, her final evaluation of the filmmaking process was overwhelmingly positive. She confessed of her time on *Maverick*, "It was the most fun I've ever had. With Donner, you get the feeling that it's just haphazard, but he knows what he's doing better than anybody I've ever worked with." It was a strong compliment from an Academy Award winner, who had previously collaborated with filmmakers such as Martin Scorsese and Jonathan Demme. The actress acknowledged the intricacy of Donner's approach. Said she, "In comedy, you have to follow a different god, because it doesn't matter if it matches, and it doesn't matter if it's elegant. What matters is if it's got life. And you can't buy that, no amount of film school's gonna tell you how to get there. It means that your biggest priority is to make sure there's always a laugh on the set, that nobody's under undue pressure, or in a bad mood. Or it will never produce that spark."

"He likes to have fun on the set," concurs Zsigmond. "He likes to have everybody feeling good... everybody loves him on the set and everybody does [their] best. This is really especially true when we did *Maverick*. I enjoyed it so much."

When Mel Gibson sat down at a table to film a scene with James Coburn, he belched loudly, before blowing a few smoke rings from a cigar. It was not an unusual occurrence, and in the end Foster nicknamed her co-star "the king of tastefulness." When it came time for cameras to roll, Gibson hid his cigar in an ashtray under the table.

"People are going to wonder why there's a fire coming from between your legs," Foster heckled.

"That's subtext," was Gibson's roguish response.

Off-camera, Gibson, Foster, and Alfred Molina regularly initiated their own high-stake games of poker with their respective assistants. The Hollywood talent was more than a little chagrined, however, as the staffers continuously walked away with the pool.

The centerpiece stunt for *Maverick* required the film's hero to climb out the window of a runaway stagecoach, maneuver to the driver's bench, leap onto a horse's back and edge his way to the front of the team — all the while as the horses race toward the edge of a cliff with a 1000-foot sheer drop overlooking the Colorado river. During the course of the stunt Maverick falls underneath the stagecoach carriage. The feat had been committed to film once before, by Yakima Canutt for John Ford's *Stagecoach*. More than fifty years later, it was the responsibility of stunt coordinator (and Gibson double) Mic Rodgers to duplicate the event. Rodgers ascended from the stage, and jumped three pairs of galloping animals. As he arrived to the lead pair, however, one of the horses stumbled and began to fall. Rodgers literally pulled the animal back to its feet, stopping the careening stagecoach, and avoided a brutal disaster. It was a truly remarkable sequence.

The production's second unit designed the sequence using doubles for Gibson and Foster. The main unit then shot it again with Gibson conducting 90% of the stunts himself. He would be photographed underneath the moving carriage, supported by a wooden board and a rope around his waist. When it came time to lens the complex moment, it was in the presence of executives Bob Daly and Terry Semel — who had flown in to witness the event. As Donner prepared to holler, "Action!," Gibson spotted a possible continuity error. "I would have had to go down to bring the body back," he said.

"Save that stuff for your personal life," Donner chortled. "We'll do the reverse tomorrow, when the horses are in front of you."

The horses then bolted, dragging their multimillion-dollar commodity down a quarter mile of rocky road, with Donner and his crew eagerly chasing the action alongside.

Maverick had been a relatively stress-free shoot, one filled with hard work but driven by fun and laughter, the end result of which was a highly entertaining movie to which audiences greatly responded. Surrounded by supremely talented individuals who also happened to be friends, it was, in many ways, the most enjoyable project Donner had ever been a part of. But for all his apparent confidence, Donner was not immune to the type of inner turmoil and anxiety that afflicts all artists. As he then expressed to a London journalist, "I do anything just to keep on going to the next one. You never know if you're going to get hired again, and you always think that this is the last job you're ever going to have. I swear to God, you get so insecure, you think they'll forget your name... It's a very strange business. You put a year of your life into making a movie and you're scared stiff when it opens up. The audiences are very fickle, and you don't know whether you've found the right pulse. And if it's a comedy, when you have that first screening and the first joke comes up, if they don't laugh at it you think 'Oh dear God, I'm dead!' And then they laugh at something you never thought was funny, and you realize that you are totally in the hands of the world, that you didn't make the movie for yourself but for an audience, and then your start to evaluate yourself a little differently."

Donner's relationship with Mel Gibson provided him with a certain comfort. A tacit agreement existed between the two men, one that served to remove some of the pressure and uncertainty that came with making a major motion picture. Gibson trusted in Donner's skill and experience, was faithful that he would draw from him his strongest performance and craft the best possible film. The director believed in the undeniable talent of his screen icon, and was confident that his star power would bolster the picture's commercial prospects.

As the theatrical release of *Maverick* neared, Donner remained nervous. Screenwriter William Goldman had delivered his first draft screenplay on March 12, 1993, since which time the director had been informed by Bob Daly and Terry Semel that his film would open, absolutely without fail, on May 20, 1994.

It had been a riotous shoot, one on which Donner convinced numerous friends, family members, and colleagues to appear in cameo roles, including his wife Lauren Shuler, his cousin Steve Kahan, actors Corey Feldman (*The Goonies*), Danny Glover (*Lethal Weapon*) and Margot Kidder (*Superman*). In a personal aside, Donner named the grand paddleboat tug (turned floating casino) the "Lauren Belle," after his wife.

Miraculously, less than two months before its scheduled official bow, a test screening was scheduled. Two hundred people gathered in a theater on the Warner Bros. studio. It was a hot afternoon and the air conditioning system failed. After a while, some lost interest and simply walked out. Donner feared the movie was too long, and returned to the editing suite to exorcise more than thirty minutes from an original run time of more than two and a half hours. Eliminated entirely from the movie was a sequence that reunited Gibson with Linda Hunt, his co-star in *The Year of Living Dangerously*. This section of the plot saw Hunt play a magician who saves Maverick from the hangman's noose, nurses him back to health, and then provides him with money to enter a poker game. As a major chunk of film was being removed, some minor reshoots were quickly arranged.

When the opening weekend approached, the exhausted filmmaker escaped Hollywood to his home on Puget Island, off of the Washington State coast.

Donner refused to answer his phone until the early financial figures were faxed through to him. Fortunately, when they arrived, they made for happy reading. Over Memorial Day weekend *Maverick* galloped to $17 million in theater ticket sales, more than double the earnings of any of its rivals. In three days it became the biggest film opening of 1994, and the biggest non-sequel, non-holiday weekend opening ever. Quite naturally, Donner was ecstatic. His film eventually earned $102 million in the U.S., part of a world-wide box-office haul of $183 million. It was a second consecutive smash hit for the veteran helmer.

Maverick's success was helped in part by some favorable press reviews, a luxury Donner had rarely been able to rely on in the past. *The New York Times* applauded that the film was, "Fast, funny, full of straight-ahead action and tongue-in-cheek jokes... [It] sets the summer-film season off to an unbeatable start." *Time* decreed that the picture allowed the audience "to spend a perfectly agreeable evening without making you feel completely stupid or totally conned."

Donner responded, "These reviews — it should happen to me for the rest of my life. A lot of people see this movie for what it is. It's really a road picture. Like Bob Hope, Bing Crosby and Dorothy Lamour. Here we have Mel, Jodie and James Garner. What are we trying to say? We're just trying to say, 'Come out of the theater and feel good.' It's not Shakespeare. It's light entertainment."

Maverick is indeed a comfortable, undemanding pleasure, but one that rises well above generic mediocrity. Thanks to Tom Sander's authentic production design, and Vilmos Zsigmond's stunning photography, a luscious environment and atmosphere is created. Randy Newman's accompanying music score perfectly embodies the balance of comedy and thrills to which the picture carefully conforms. And for Donner's part, he once again mastered both story and spectacle, overseeing the development of characters that snap and crackle — that perform to make an audience really care to see through the adventure to the end. The entire picture reflects both his fun-loving spirit, and his insistence on verisimilitude. While he may softly jab at every western cliché in the book, he simultaneously "plays it straight" throughout. Says Zsigmond, "Dick's sense of humor comes out in the movie. *Maverick*, I think, is one of his best movies. I don't think there's another western that's funnier."

Yet above and beyond all else, *Maverick* thrives due to the irresistible charm, charisma, and comedic talent of Mel Gibson (and his engaging chemistry with co-star Jodie Foster). As Bret Maverick, the actor pulls his audience wholeheartedly into the fantasy. Be it in winning a gun draw during the opening poker match, or predicting a card in the tense final tournament battle, he urges a faith in the fantastic. "I knew if I really believed and made it happen," he says in the movie, bringing his audience with him, "hell then that [was] nothing short of magic." It was the essence of Donner's craft, to start with the believable, to skillfully achieve a verisimilitude that would enable his audience to invest in the ride, in the grandest tradition of silver screen entertainment.

Assassins, the pulp fiction tale of an aging hit man whose livelihood is threatened by the presence of a younger rival, penned by future *Matrix* creators Andy and Larry Wachowski, was being developed by quick-tempered producer Joel Silver. A resurgent Sylvester Stallone, making headlines once again thanks to the hits *Cliffhanger* and *Demolition Man*, was courted to star, and the project sold to Bob Daly and Terry Semel of Warner Bros. Donner was urged to direct.

At this point in his career, *Assassins* should have appealed strongly to Donner. As *Lethal Weapon 3* and *Maverick* were before it, the picture would be a Warner Bros. showpiece event, backed by a $50 million budget and a major Hollywood star. But Donner declined Silver's overtures. He was wary of Stallone, whom he did not believe he would have much in common with, and he felt little emotional connection to the screenplay. To the director, a natural empathy for the material remained the most important factor in choosing his next project, regardless of the level of commercial potential. Still, Donner did agree to give audience to the Wachowski brothers, a meeting that did not go well. The filmmaker inadvertently caused offence when he suggested to the screenwriters that they rewrite a central character as a police officer. "No," one brother interjected, "you can't have the police. The only good cop is a dead cop."

"No," Donner replied, shocked.

"That's what we believe."

"C'mon, you're so full of shit," the director hit back.

"No, no. We were brought up on the tough streets of Chicago."

Donner really doubted that they were, and was offended enough by the conversation to extinguish any nominal interest he may have harbored. He had already begun negotiations with Joseph Barbera (whose *The Flintstones* he had failed to bring to the big screen in 1987) over adapting the *Jonny Quest* cartoon into a live-action feature. He was also busy lending his support as an executive producer to an expanding number of projects, including

Demon Knight (a movie spin off from *Tales from the Crypt*), Gil Adler's television show *W.E.I.R.D. World*, and *Free Willy 2: The Adventure Home*. Each demanded a percentage of his interest and attention. There were rumors of a *Maverick* sequel, talk that was only quashed when Mel Gibson committed to directing and starring in *Braveheart*, the epic tale of Scottish warrior William Wallace, who leads his country to rise up against English rule.

Joel Silver, however, refused to take no for an answer on *Assassins*, and pressured Warner Bros. to offer his friend and frequent business partner the biggest payday of his career. His lobbying succeeded. When Bob Daly and Terry Semel promised Donner a multimillion-dollar fee to direct, plus further monies to produce and a share in the film's profits, the golden carrot proved too tasty to refuse. (Donner later confessed of his acceptance, "I was a little bit of a whore.") The financial offer — then a record fee for a director — was gigantic; more than double his regular retainer, a deeply flattering show of faith and appreciation from the studio. Despite his reservations, Donner did an immediate about turn, determining in his mind that he would somehow, after all, give *Assassins* his full, enthusiastic attention.

Donner was enthusiastic that the picture be a "pre-action" suspense film, and not just a fast-paced action thriller. He liked action, but he was deeply concerned at the violence and level of killing in the Wachowski brothers' screenplay. The director did not wish to dwell on bullet holes or blood, did not desire to recycle the graphic mayhem of other action pictures. As he had done with *The Omen*, for which he had insisted the script be altered so that it did not simply repeat the formula of other genre films, on *Assassins* Donner wanted something more — a pervasive honesty and sincerity. In his vision, Donner would insist that Stallone be allowed to flex his muscles — but he would do so with his shirt on.

The director imagined taking the project in a more emotionally charged route. His intention was clear: as his original *Lethal Weapon* had focused on character relationships over the hyperbolic feats and explosions that defined the likes of *Commando* and *Rambo*, *Assassins* would focus upon the ever-evolving dynamic between the three characters (Rath, Bain and Electra) to create a tension and suspense reminiscent of classic thrillers. The first step in his plan was to contract young writer Brian Helgeland to redraft the script, instructing him find a gentler soul in the lead character, Robert Rath — to create a pistol-packing hero with a heart who wants to protect the innocent. "*Assassins* was a movie that I think Dick worked really hard on," says Jim Van Wyck. "He wanted it to be the best dramatic performance that Sly [Stallone] had ever given."

The role of Robert Rath was a more complex character than some of the strictly action types he had played in the past, a precursor of sorts to his excellent performance as Sheriff Freddy Heflin in James Mangold's *Copland,* released in 1997.

When methodical gunman Robert Rath receives a commission to assassinate an FBI witness at a funeral, another hired executioner, Miguel Bain, beats him to the kill. Rath engages Bain in a gun battle and gives chase. When his rival escapes the scene, he steals a taxicab and scours the streets of Seattle in search of him. When Bain identifies Rath, they fight once more, only for Bain to escape again.

From a faceless employer who communicates via text on a computer screen, Rath is issued a $2 million contract to retire a female surveillance expert named Electra, who is peddling stolen software information to a group of Dutchmen. Rath must kill both the buyers and the source, and recover the software disk, before he can collect the money that will finally allow him to give up his profession.

Rath follows the Dutchmen to a hotel where Electra has hired two rooms connected by an air duct. It is Bain who bursts into the room, killing all but Electra, who flees accompanied by Rath. Agreeing to become partners, Rath and Electra negotiate with Rath's boss for money to be deposited in a Caribbean bank in exchange for the coveted software. Knowing that Bain will surely be hired to kill him, Rath devises a plan. He aims to stay inside the bank long enough to drive the rival assassin mad with frustration, and force him to leave the ruined hotel building where he is staked out. This would allow Electra to steal his weapon and make Bain the target. Yet Electra falls through the floor of the burnt out building before she can do so, forcing a final firefight to ensue during which Rath realizes that Nicolai — a man whom he believed he had murdered many years earlier, is his unnamed employer — has been manipulating him, seeking revenge the entire time. Both Nicolai and Bain are shot and killed.

From *Maverick*, Donner retained Tom Sanders as production designer, Vilmos Zsigmond as director of photography, and Jim Van Wyck as producer and first assistant director. He then set about casting *Assassins*.

Although over the years Stallone's popularity in the U.S. had declined, he remained a phenomenally attractive worldwide draw, as evidenced by some of his recent successes, including *The Specialist*, which he headlined alongside Sharon Stone. He remained one of the most powerful actors in Hollywood, long accustomed to wielding enormous influence on set, and, as an accomplished director, he was used to calling many of the shots himself. Indeed, Stallone often handpicked his own directors — likely basing his decisions less on the talent of those he hired, more on their capacity to capitulate. Donner was not one of these, but he was sensitive to the actor's desire to control his image, and empowered him in the creative process by allowing him to be involved in all aspects of production, without ever yielding his power of the final say. Donner invited Stallone to be active in hiring his co-stars. Together they considered Woody Harrelson for the role of the villainous Miguel Bain, although the part was eventually offered to Christian Slater. When the latter declined, Spanish actor Antonio Banderas accepted. Julianne Moore won the role of information thief Electra.

Stallone and Banderas were put through intense firearms training, while Moore was familiarized with the electronic surveillance devices her character would expertly use. All were clearly excited by the script's potential. Stallone later explained the film to be "a character-driven thriller; it shows the lifestyle that these people live in a way that's never been portrayed before. Robert Rath is someone who believes in doing his best at anything he attempts, but he realizes at a sudden point in his life that he is going to be just like the assassin who came before him, and the best will always be topped by the new, hungrier young lion. When he confronts this realization, he knows he has to find his way out of a nearly airtight system — and that will be his greatest test."

To satisfy Donner's neo-noir ambitions, he carefully weighed appropriate locations in which to film. In the end the director chose to make the Pacific Northwest his base, an area rich in shading (a metaphor for characters who live their lives in the shadows), and a place full of unexpected light and darkness. *Assassins* would be lensed primarily on location in Washington State (scenes were filmed at the base of Seattle's famed Space Needle, a nighttime chase sequence lensed on the wet streets of Alaska Way and the Viaduct, and a cemetery scene was filmed in Everett, just outside of Seattle), in Portland, Oregon, but also in San Juan, Puerto Rico, where — in direct contrast to the Pacific Northwest — everything appears white against a flat blue sky.

The making of the movie was defined by Donner's trademark openness to collaboration, and his prioritization of narrative over spectacle. "What Dick Donner instills in you is an openness so that you're free to express your own creative ideas," waxed Conrad Palmisano, the stunt director and second assistant director on the film. "It's an open working relationship. Maybe the first idea won't be used. But one idea may key another idea. There are few people in the industry as open as he is. For me, one of the great joys is to be allowed to be able to bring out the best in yourself."

Palmisano continued, "One of the good things about Dick is that it's not that the fireball has to be bigger or that the car rolls over more times than the last one. It's how he ties it all in with actors."

There would be crashes, explosions and gunfire galore, but Donner dissuaded his camera operators from bathing in it. Gunshots would be captured by the pop of a silencer, a whistle — the actual violent end result masked by shadow.

The production schedule was tight (*Assassins* would be filmed in less than eighty days), but Donner allowed plenty of time to improvise scenes. He refused to bring storyboards or a shot list to the set, preferring instead to rehearse with his actors and allow scenes to organically evolve. When it came time to holler "Action!," up to five cameras could be in use, recording from opposing angles, capturing the maximum amount of coverage.

Donner worked closely with Vilmos Zsigmond to establish a visual thematic. Rejecting the homogeneity of the contemporary action film, the director wanted something different, a stylized movie and an artistic film. *Assassins* would be lit like a classic Hollywood film, utilizing an exaggerated but realistic sense of light and dark — a *film noir* look but in color. "You always learn from a good director and I was amazed by what I learned from Dick," said Zsigmond, "... He'll look at a shot and say, 'Oh, this is so boring, can't we do something else?' For example, there is a shot where the two assassins (Stallone and Banderas) are side by side on the road — Stallone sitting in a car — and each is unaware of the other's identity. Now I would usually have shot Stallone through an open window. It's easier to light, to see the face. But Donner said, 'Why don't you close the window?' I said, 'But what about the reflections? You will hardly see the face.' And he said, 'Oh, I love the reflections — that's great, wonderful!'"

In addition to emphasizing shadows and contrast, throughout shooting the director would incorporate his love of slow zooms as a tool by which to build suspense.

Stallone appeared to value Donner, a director he found to be able and confident, principled and firm. "Sylvester just needs someone he respects," Donner confirmed to the *Los Angeles Times*. "Someone with a point of view he buys into and to whom he can delegate the responsibility of ensuring that he stays in it. In the past, he probably had to protect himself. Now, he's leaving that protection in my hands."

And the director appeared to be enamored with his star. "Sly's presence is so overpowering," he continued. "If I could bottle it I'd be rich. Rub on a little Stallone." Throughout filming Donner allowed Stallone's son, Sage, who harbored a desire to direct, to assist him on set, and to absorb the mechanics of the craft.

Yet despite this public proclamation by Donner, issued during promotion of the film, there was indeed a tangible tension between the two men, as revealed by the director of photography, Vilmos Zsigmond. "I think there was a conflict between him and Stallone, for whom the role was difficult." In truth, the iconic action star was not entirely confident in Donner's intentions for the material, or in his own ability to pull them off. He likely felt frustrated, likely believed that his character should be less passive in the face of such a clear and present danger. Nonetheless, Donner insisted to Stallone that he continue to trust him, and be prepared to try something different.

Banderas, on the other hand, proved a delight to work with, and Donner and Lauren became good friends with both him and his girlfriend, Melanie Griffith.

During post-production, Donner made it clear that he disliked the music score recorded by his friend and frequent collaborator, Michael Kamen. He wanted something more up-tempo than the moody, atmospheric composition delivered. The beleaguered filmmaker turned to Mark Mancina for a new soundtrack, which was rushed through in a mere five weeks. Regardless, Donner and the Warner hierarchy quickly realized that *Assassins* was not the picture they had hoped it could be. Compared to Luc Besson's stylish low-budget thriller *The Professional*, starring Jean Reno, Gary Oldman, and Natalie Portman, it was neither fresh nor original. A summer release was abandoned in favor of a less competitive fall date. Donner fought to delay the release further, citing the fact that *Miami Rhapsody*, in which Antonio Banderas starred, and Stallone's *Judge Dredd*, had only recently failed.

On October 6, 1995, *Assassins* died the death of a mark, recouping just $30 million of its budget in the U.S. Further monies would be earned internationally, but the numbers were the cause of massive disappointment. *Assassins* looked and sounded like a conventional thriller, but it was a strangely empty, soulless affair. If Stallone's efforts were overtly bland and uninteresting, Banderas played to an opposite extreme, littering his performance with an array of frenzied facial expressions. The screen chemistry between the pair, so vital to the production, was virtually non-existent.

There were elements of *Assassins* that Donner truly enjoyed. He was proud of a complicated sequence involving a car chase through the streets of Seattle. In the scene, Stallone's Robert Rath has stolen a taxi and Banderas' Miguel Bain is trapped in the backseat. The cab's bulletproof Plexiglas divider splits the pair. A wild gunfight ensues. It was a terrifically tense, expertly crafted moment — sadly a rare exception, not a rule, for the movie.

Ultimately, *Assassins* had Donner's full attention and professional commitment, but it did not have his heart. The film had made him the highest paid director in the world, but if he signed up for the money, it was at an artistic cost. The hunger, passion, and humanity that infused *Superman* and *Inside Moves* was so clearly missing.

The failure troubled Donner, rattling his legendary reserves of self-confidence. He had enjoyed the presence of a major star and full studio backing. As director, the burden of any shortcomings fell squarely on his shoulders. There were few mitigating circumstances that could be blamed. He had found the original screenplay to be fairly ludicrous, but he had been given every opportunity to have it rewritten, as indeed he had done so. To rework the screenplay, he had brought the greatly talented Helgeland on board.

"[*Assassins* is] noisy, shallow and glibly violent... simple and improbable," chimed Hal Hinson of *The Washington Post*. Some critics had word for Donner again sneaking into his movies a number of political statements, including anti-fur and pro-choice messages. It was his anti-NRA message, in a film about professional hit men in which shootings abound, which was deemed too ironic by Janet Maslin of *The New York Times*. "Until a better definition of the word chutzpah comes along," she wrote, "that one will do."

Although he had attempted to make character dynamics the focus of his attention, and not the pervasive action, on *Assassins* Donner's guiding mantra, the attainment of verisimilitude, was not achieved.

"I do not believe *Assassins*," wrote Roger Ebert of the *Chicago Sun-Times*, "because this movie is filled with such preposterous impossibilities that Forrest Gump could have improved it with a quick rewrite."

On May 27, 1995, *Superman* star Christopher Reeve suffered a tragic accident while competing in a horseback-riding event in Culpeper, Virginia. His animal had suddenly refused a jump, and the actor had been thrown from his horse. With his hands tied by the bridle, the bit, and the reins, Reeve landed headfirst, causing a cervical spinal injury that paralyzed him from the neck down. It was reported he was not breathing during the three minutes it took paramedics to arrive.

The stunning news, which made headlines around the world, left Donner reeling. He describes, "It was one of the worst shocks to my system I've ever had in my life. I just knew I had to get on an airplane as fast as I could."

However, the University of Virginia Medical Center, where Reeve had been flown, rebuffed Donner's effort to see his friend, under strict instruction from the Reeve family to refuse all requests. The actor was in no condition to see visitors. In the five days it took him to regain consciousness he suffered from ICU (Intensive Care Unit) psychosis. When he did fully wake up, he was informed that his first and second cervical vertebrae had been destroyed, that his head had become detached from his spine, and that his lungs were filling with fluid. Reeve contemplated suicide, but was dissuaded by his wife, Dana.

After enduring complicated surgery to reattach his head to his spinal column, Reeve was taken to the Kessler Rehabilitation Center in West Orange, New Jersey. Donner and Lauren flew out as soon as they were allowed to, and were devastated by what they saw. "It was horrible," Donner recalls. "Just plain, God damn horrible... It was a mission to keep him alive."

After recovering from multiple blood transfusions and breathing tube malfunctions, Reeve entered into an intense period of occupational, physical and respiratory therapy. By the end of the year he was able to breathe without a respirator for up to thirty minutes.

Donner maintained communication with Reeve and his family. He was in awe of the actor's spirit, by his campaigns to improve life for the victims of spinal cord injuries, and by his remarkable medical progress. He had convinced himself that he would live to see Reeve walk again. Sadly, Reeve died on October 10, 2004, from complications arising from an infected pressure wound.

In early 1996, Donner and Joel Silver formed Decade Entertainment (named after the length of time that they had known one another) with a remit to focus solely on the creation of action-thrillers budgeted in the $6-$10 million range. Representatives for the duo traveled to the Cannes Film Festival, and successfully negotiated a deal with The Kushner-Locke Company to produce four action films in two years.

Kushner-Locke would be one of three main backers for Decade. The German-based company had acquired many of the rights to international distribution, while HBO (Home Box Office) would enjoy domestic pay television rights, and Republic Pictures the American home video rights. The business savvy Donner and Silver had also managed to retain ownership of the negatives and all domestic television syndication rights. The following year at Cannes, Decade would mark the anniversary of the deal by announcing a major, multimillion-dollar arrangement with Helkon Media for the German distribution rights of the company's first five pictures. Although *Made Men* — an ensemble piece featuring Denis Leary and directed by Scott Kalvert — was scheduled to be the outfit's debut film, it would instead be *Double Tap* — produced by both Donner and Silver and starring Stephen Rea and Heather Locklear — that would be the first offering from the new unit.

Donner saw the creation of Decade as a wise business investment, one to contribute handsomely to his retirement annuity. Yet as a filmmaker he found himself conflicted. According to some, including then-*Variety* editor-in-chief Peter Bart, he was growing increasingly frustrated with the proliferation of mega-star, mega-budget pictures. He wished Hollywood studios would make more films in the $10 million arena. Yet he had turned down the helm of the low-budget *Free Willy*, and never expressed his intent to direct any of Decade's output. Rather, he continued to pin his career on summer-season tent-pole fair. Until such a suitable project came along, he was happy to divide his time between the arms-length producing of *Bordello of Blood* — another spin-off from *Tales from the Crypt* — and his increasing activism.

Doctors Without Borders, the prestigious international medical organization dedicated to aiding disaster victims worldwide, had honored the

Donners. A year later the couple received the James Herriot Award from the Humane Society of the United States. As he grew older, Donner's natural propensity for championing the underdog, coupled with a passionate devotion to animal welfare, meant that he was unable to distance himself from certain plights once they had come to his attention. He and Lauren were still heavily involved in trying to free Keiko, the Orca whale turned celebrity. They had worked hard to assist in the rehabilitation of the ailing mammal, and were attempting to free him back into the wild off the coast of Iceland. Other causes also earned his attention. When he learned that gaming officials in New Mexico had been issued licenses to shoot seven aged bulls, he immediately threw his influential weight behind a campaign to save the animals from termination. Perhaps more fired up than by any recent movie project, he was joined in his cause by Lauren, and by filmmaker Oliver Stone, among others. Those whom they were campaigning against were quick to respond, and with a familiar argument. "If you see some of the carnage these guys put on the screen," a New Mexican economic official offered, somewhat sarcastically. "It is surprising they would take such a stance on this issue."

In Donner's own words, "The poor soul did not know the difference between the fantasy of movies and the reality of killing domesticated animals."

"Love gives you wings.
It makes you fly."

MEL GIBSON AS JERRY FLETCHER IN
CONSPIRACY THEORY

14

Fun with Dick and Mel

Extreme measures were required in order to successfully cast *Conspiracy Theory*, an edgy, offbeat thriller about a paranoid New York City cab driver who publishes a newsletter alleging multiple government conspiracies, and who is madly in love with a woman he can never have. Donner was eager to helm the promising Brian Helgeland script, and set about to cast his great friend, Mel Gibson, an actor whom he considered to be the finest screen talent of his generation, in the lead role.

On March 26, 1996, *Braveheart* had been awarded the Best Picture Oscar at the sixty-eighth Academy Awards ceremony. On stage with Gibson to accept the award was his friend and business partner, Bruce Davey, and Alan Ladd, Jr., whose Ladd Company had stepped up to partly fund the epic picture after Terry Semel of Warner Bros. declined. Donner felt great pride in the moment, delighted to see two of the men to whom he was closest in the business bestowed with such an honor. The night was made more special when Gibson collected a second Oscar for Best Director.

Seemingly at the pinnacle of his power and fame, Gibson faced options galore. If he hadn't before, he now had the world at his fingertips, and having recently wrapped on Ron Howard's highly rated thriller *Ransom*, he could afford to procrastinate over *Conspiracy Theory*. Donner gamely decided that his friend needed a little shove for persuasion. The director, Joel Silver, and a team of carpenters walked over to the Icon Pictures office on the Warner Bros. lot, and threatened to nail him inside a room unless he agreed to star in the movie. Gibson gauged the carnivorous stares, and decided that his friends were not joking. After ninety minutes of pressure he found the situation so bizarre that he finally cracked. "I couldn't believe how it worked on me," says the star. "It was really weird. It was so hilarious and charming at the same time I just said, 'Okay, let's go.'"

The filmmakers considered Julia Roberts, a superstar enjoying a sudden resurgence since her late eighties/early nineties heyday, to play Gibson's leading lady, Alice Sutton. Gibson had long coveted to play opposite her. Busy filming the romantic comedy *My Best Friend's Wedding*, Roberts, too, was reluctant, although she was at least interested. Donner, Silver, and Gibson flew to New York and invited her to Donner's hotel suite, where they hoped to deliver a charm offensive. When she arrived for her scheduled appointment, the surreal atmosphere took her aback. Donner did most of the talking. Silver paced frantically back and forth around the room. Gibson, meanwhile, stood quietly in a corner.

"What are you doing?" Roberts asked him anxiously.

"I'm a lamp," he instructed. "Ignore me."

Just as before, Roberts was told she would not be allowed to leave the room until her participation had been confirmed. She pleaded with Donner that she needed to contact her agent before accepting any offer, but he was unrelenting. Overwhelmed by the pressure, her resistance ultimately broke. "What the hell," she spluttered.

Once confirmed, a brass band burst into the room and performed a victory march. Donner typically reserved such celebrations for on-set birthdays, but he had planned ahead in order to appropriately welcome Roberts into the production family. Fervent staffers appeared out of different crevices in the suite, descended upon the bewildered actress with their measuring tapes, and began readying her costumes. Roberts sighed, figuring she had at least made a decision that her life was not going to be boring for a few months. Joel Silver left no doubt over what was on his mind. "I can just *smell* the money," he enthused as he strutted out of the room and into the hallway.

At first, Donner had been reluctant to direct *Conspiracy Theory*, a vehicle he believed to be better suited to a television series format. For a while it had appeared that his next picture was to be *The Sea Kings*, a pirate adventure penned by William Goldman. Set in the early 1700s, the tale of lethal pirate Blackbeard and wealthy planter Stede Bonnet was perfectly in tune with the director's creative sensibilities. Essentially it was the story of two men, both of whom were the other's dream. Bonnet was rich beyond counting, but miserably unhappy and desperate for an adventure-filled life. Blackbeard was sick of adventure and yearned for a sweet death in bed.

Binary opposites were the lifeblood of Donner's movies — the idea of an "unlikely couple" was a dominant theme in his work, from his very first television episode, "The Twain Shall Meet" on *Wanted: Dead or Alive*, where much of the drama was sourced from the contrast between real-world gunslinger Josh Randall and Harvard-educated newspaper reporter Arthur Pierce Madison, to *Lethal Weapon*, which paired the risk-taking loner Martin Riggs with conservative family man Roger Murtaugh, and beyond.

Despite its strong appeal, *The Sea Kings* would ultimately sail away from Donner's film horizon. Producer Joe Levine had been attempting to fund the picture since 1979, and with the high-profile sea adventure duds *Waterworld* and *Cutthroat Island* strong in Hollywood memory, his near-twenty-year odyssey to fund the high-cost production was not likely to bear fruition anytime soon.

Donner instead prepared to develop the sports drama *Playing Hurt*. Jim Van Wyck was instructed to begin scouting locations for a movie that centered upon the adventures of a professional football team. Yet as Helgeland continued to retool his *Conspiracy Theory* screenplay, it was the mystery-suspense-thriller that captured Donner's attention the most. (*Playing Hurt* would eventually be made as *Any Given Sunday*, starring Al Pacino and Cameron Diaz, produced by Lauren Shuler, and directed by Oliver Stone. Donner would retain credit as an executive producer.)

A conspiracy theorist, Jerry Fletcher, visits Justice Department lawyer Alice Sutton and lobbies her to investigate a perceived plot to kill the U.S. president. Soon afterward, he is abducted and tortured. Jerry fights back, biting the nose of his persecutor and kicking his way to safety.

Concerned, Alice visits Jerry in hospital. There, she meets Dr. Jonas, a shadowy intelligence agent with bite marks on his nose. When Jerry goes missing, she discovers him attempting to escape the hospital through a linen chute. She decides to help.

At Jerry's apartment, the chatty New York cab driver says his life is in danger because of the newsletter he publishes: "Conspiracy Theory." An armed team then storms the building. Jerry and Alice disappear through a secret trap door in his bedroom.

Jerry is tracked by government agents and flees inside a movie theater. He creates a bomb scare and vanishes in the ensuing pandemonium. Alice traces "Conspiracy Theory" subscribers and learns that all but one of them has recently died. She locates the surviving subscriber, Henry Finch, who is actually Dr. Jonas. He reveals that Jerry is the victim of a secret government-sponsored mind control experiment, a trained assassin who killed Alice's father, a Judge, and that he has been obsessed with her ever since.

Working for Dr. Jonas, Alice meets Jerry, and travels to the place of her father's death. Once there he admits to being trained for the assassination, but claims that Judge Sutton became a friend who tried to help him.

Jonas's men again swoop in by helicopter and abduct Jerry. He is held at a disused power station. Jerry and Alice embrace, and begin to fall in love. Jonas intervenes and admits to killing Alice's father. During a struggle Jonas shoots Jerry, but he is shot and killed by Alice in return.

After visiting Jerry's grave, Alice goes horseback riding. She finds a pin that she had placed on his grave, and realizes that he is still alive.

While not a uniquely American phenomenon, elaborate conspiracy theories — particularly those that implied that governments withhold the *real* truth behind certain historic events — have long gripped a raw public nerve, arresting the imagination of the U.S. populate, a fact that in addition to the selling power of Gibson and Roberts made the film a highly commercial prospect. To Donner, however, this appeal was secondary to the opportunity presented by the script's unusual love story. Although in his screenplay Jerry and Alice did not kiss, or in fact barely held a clinch, Brian Helgeland had nonetheless crafted a unique, off-the-wall romance that was surprisingly devoid of cynicism. "Love gives you insight," proclaims Jerry to Alice in the movie. "Love lets you see things you wouldn't normally. I just know that I've loved you since the first time I ever saw you."

Such dialogue won Donner's heart, and the project was set in motion. The director would make *Conspiracy Theory* not as a thriller, nor as an action film, but as an unconventional, unrequited love story. (The parallel to *Ladyhawke* is clear. In the finished movie Donner's medieval fantasy plays in a theater in which Gibson and Roberts hide while on the run from Jonas.)

After assembling the tantalizing dream ticket of Mel Gibson and Julia Roberts for *Conspiracy Theory*, Donner hired John Schwartzman, Francis Ford Coppola's nephew, as director of photography. Production designer Paul Sylbert was contracted for his expert knowledge of New York. The film would be edited by Kevin Stitt and Frank J. Urioste, and scored by Carter Burwell.

Filming on location in the Big Apple presented many logistical challenges. To capture a dramatic car chase on the Queensboro Bridge, the historic 59th Street location was closed for several hours early on a Sunday morning, as Donner descended with his crew and six state-of-the-art motion picture cameras to record an action-packed scene featuring fifty stunt cars and two helicopters. When he needed a helicopter to land in Manhattan's Union Square, it was the first such landing in the densely populated area for more than twenty years. Fortunately, Jim Van Wyck was on hand to co-ordinate the technical effort and to help contain the production's vast $75 million budget in order that Donner could concentrate on working closely with his actors.

The moment of her casting should have served as forewarning, but Julia Roberts was shocked nonetheless by some of the on-set antics of Mel Gibson, just as Jodie Foster had been on *Maverick*. On the first day of shooting, the actor harangued an assistant into presenting her with a lavish gift box, tied in beautiful bows, a warm gesture to welcome her on board. When the actress opened it, she found a freeze-dried rat inside. Her shriek captured the attention of the on-set security and two police officers. In another instance, before a scene in which the star duo was to shake hands, Gibson mixed a dead cockroach and hair gel into his palm. Ever the crowd pleaser, he ensured that the entire crew knew about the joke beforehand, raising a giant roar as Roberts's confusion morphed into sheer horror. And it wasn't just Gibson conspiring against the star actress. In a scene in which she was required to peer nervously around a bathroom, Roberts pulled back a shower curtain and was startled by the imposing figure of Joel Silver, who promptly screamed "Bleeeeeeh!" right into her face. Gibson this time keeled over from his laughter.

The actress finally earned revenge when she crept into her co-star's trailer and saran-wrapped his toilet bowl. The non-diligent star was in for a shocking surprise. "An old trick but effective," he later admitted. "… I was tap-dancing like Gene Kelly singing in the rain… I was thankful it was just number ones."

Such high jinks were one of the many reasons why Donner loved to work with Gibson. A mischievous sense of playfulness was an intrinsic part of Donner the man, and a vital creative tool for Donner the director. "Mel and I have learned to trust each other," he explained. "There needs to be trust between an actor and a director but it has become increasingly difficult to achieve. Humor is so important. Everything's so explosive on a movie set. When you lose your sense of humor about what you're doing, you become very linear and defensive."

Despite the time crunch presented by a strict twelve-week shoot, an air of relaxed freedom to improvise pervaded, even though the approach wasn't always productive. "There were moments where I just had diarrhea of the mouth — the words just burst out of me," Gibson admitted.

In Mel Gibson and Julia Roberts, Donner arguably possessed the strongest headline of any picture of the decade. *Conspiracy Theory* was proof that, in the words of author and former *Variety* editor-in-chief Peter Bart, he had become the "master at the care and feeding of movie stars." Donner's reputation as an "actor's director" was unrivaled. He had tremendous respect for them, and trusted in them to make correct decisions. If they needed help along the way, then he was there for them, encouraging them to do something different, surprising them into doing something unexpected. He could love and be supportive of their efforts. He could also bully and shove.

When Roberts struggled with an emotional scene set at a graveside, the filmmaker encouraged her to remember her father, who died of cancer when she was just nine years old. As she had knelt over a real grave, memories of her father came flooding back. Roberts broke down uncontrollably during the moment. Donner insisted cameras continued rolling, instead of calling a halt to the scene. Only once the footage was in the can did he rush over to the grieving actress and embrace her with a consoling hug.

Donner and Julia Roberts interpreted the relationship between Jerry Fletcher and Alice Sutton differently. The director wanted their romantic bond to be quirky and unsure, while his leading lady lobbied hard for more obvious intimacy. "Put me and Mel in a movie," she insisted, "and people are going to be waiting for a little smoochie." Donner greatly admired Karel Reisz's *Morgan: A Suitable Case for Treatment*, an eccentric British comedy drama from 1966. He may have subconsciously used aspects of this film as a template for the romantic thread of *Conspiracy Theory*. Just like David Warner's character, Morgan Delt, the mental condition of Jerry Fletcher is "seriously illegal!" His love for Alice defined not through typical displays of affection, but by his obsessive-compulsive personality (in effect, he stalks her throughout the movie). Like Vanessa Redgrave's character in *Morgan*, Leonie, the true feelings of Alice Sutton are ambiguous. Fleetingly, she is receptive to Jerry's fantasist behavior, in other moments she is cold and distant. Exhibition time would tell if director or star was right in their approach.

Against all predictions, Donner reveled in his role as dedicated husband. Lauren Shuler was the woman he adored, his best friend, a person of incredible strength and tenderness with whom he shared himself completely and trusted in entirely. Being married to her was the most wonderful feeling he had ever experienced. "Lauren has enlightened me in so many ways," he told *Variety*. "... She has opened my eyes."

Although, as partners in Donner/Shuler-Donner Productions, life wasn't always easy, especially when one wanted to invest in a project that simply didn't interest the other. At times they could make each other angry, although they each insisted on never bringing conflict home with them. They drove in separate cars, and when they arrived home they would forget where they just were. What Donner did struggle to overlook was his wife's treatment at the hands of film legend Warren Beatty. During the making of *Conspiracy Theory*, he was distracted by new twists in Lauren's six-year conflict with the acclaimed actor, producer, and director.

Many years earlier, Lauren had successfully negotiated with the estate of Jules Verne for the film rights to his story *The Trials and Tribulations of a Chinese Hitman*, on behalf of the director Francis Veber and herself. She had developed the project, based on the idea of a man hiring his own killer, with Tom Cruise in mind to star. She had sold her efforts to Roger Birnbaum, while he was president of worldwide production at United Artists, and he took the idea with him when he became executive vice president of Twentieth Century-Fox. It was at this time that Barry Diller (who was the chairman and chief executive officer of parent company Fox, Inc.) mentioned the project to Beatty during a formal dinner, at which the actor proclaimed his delight at the idea. *He* knew exactly how to make it work. All of a sudden, Lauren was instructed that she must co-produce with Beatty, and an impossible relationship was born. Whichever screenwriter she suggested for hire, Beatty vetoed, making it clear that not only was he unwilling to accept input from her, but that he desired to take over the project in its entirety. In the end he went to Diller to stake his solo claim, which was approved by the corporate head. Beatty would produce, direct, star in, and script the project to be ultimately known as *Bulworth*. Lauren was out.

It took many years for Beatty to develop his vision for the material, and by the time he readied to shoot a different regime presided at Twentieth Century-Fox. When Bill Mechanic and Peter Chernin, who had replaced Roger Birnbaum and Barry Diller respectively, learned of *Bulworth*'s troubled origins, they insisted Lauren's producing credit and fee would be honored. Beatty seethed. As Peter Bart describes in his book, *The Gross:* "Beatty said he'd go along provided she [Shuler] not involve herself in the production in any way. Reacting to this prohibition, she opted instead to be listed as executive producer, a credit that implied a more distanced role, but Beatty suddenly protested. 'Warren threatened to 'kill me in the press' if I received executive producer credit — that he'd spread the word that I had absolutely nothing to do with the picture,' she said.

"In the end, Beatty relented. When Shuler Donner saw the finished picture, however, she discovered that her credit was on screen for a fraction of a second. 'That move was pure Warren,' she said ruefully." ("It's the sickness of this town," Donner reflects, "and in my eyes, Warren is one of the sickest.")

Conspiracy Theory was originally to be released on July 25, 1997, until word had spread of extremely favorable exhibitor screenings of Harrison Ford's *Air Force One*, from Columbia Pictures, which was scheduled to bow on the exact same day. After Donner wrapped on February 7, 1997, he was informed that Warner Bros. were to postpone the release of his picture by two weeks in order to avoid a bloody battle between properties. The new August 8 release date would give Donner's movie a prime summer weekend all to itself.

The director enjoyed a luxurious amount of post-production, during which time he considered (and reconsidered) various elements of his film's construction. He had shot largely to the Helgeland script, which was stylish and moody. In parts the film was violent, its scenes of torture dark and disturbing (although, as befitting Donner's moral framework, Jerry and Alice always apologize for striking "an innocent").

Donner had filmed two different endings. In one conclusion, filmed verbatim to the screenplay, Jerry Fletcher dies moments after he confesses that he did indeed murder Alice Sutton's father. In the other, as Alice rides her horse Geronimo, she finds a pin on the saddle — the same pin that she had earlier placed on Jerry's grave. Jerry is alive, watching from a car, where he is now living under protection. He cannot be with Alice. She will be safe as long as he is believed to be dead.

Donner tested both endings with preview audiences, and was pleased that the latter proving more favorable. The director's perennial enthusiasm for upbeat endings is well documented. The death of a hero was unpalatable to a man whose traditional storytelling principles called not only for Jerry to live, but to be completely exonerated from the charge of murder.

On August 8, 1997, *Conspiracy Theory* punched somewhat below its weight with a $19 million opening weekend. It was just shy of the $20 million it had been expected to clear, but more importantly, it was only slightly ahead in the battle for number one film in the country against *Air Force One*, which was in its third weekend of release. Given the trend of big openings and fast drop offs at the box-office, and with only a few weeks left of the crucial summer season, it was a nervous, shaky start for Donner's event picture. The film would eventually toll $76 million in the U.S. and $137 million world-wide; numbers that were not unimpressive, although once distribution costs were added to the sizeable budget, the reality was that *Conspiracy Theory* barely crept into profit. The home entertainment market would be required to comfortably extend this margin, a crutch Donner was not accustomed to relying on.

The nation's critics were nonplussed. "It is one of those soap bubbles of a film," observed *The Washington Post*, "fleeting, ephemeral, seemingly there when it is not... [Donner is] somewhat off his game here; he never comes close to the intensity of action that marked his original *Lethal Weapon*."

"Implausible and unsatisfying," damned the *Los Angeles Times*. "...The film's exposition is listless and the tentative feelings between Fletcher and Sutton are unconvincing." For Roger Ebert of the *Chicago Sun-Times* a good film was "buried beneath the deadening layers of thriller clichés and an unconvincing love story." *Variety* labeled it "a sporadically amusing but list-less thriller." The *Boston Herald* called it "soulless." In a rare respite, *Newsday* deemed the picture "a welcome breeze in one of Hollywood's most arid sum-mers." Donner cheered, "*Newsday* always gets it right!"

Conspiracy Theory is Hitchcockian in flavor, an almost postmodern homage to *North by Northwest* with perhaps just a gentle tilt of the hat to Scorsese's *Taxi Driver*. The narrative is full of twists and turns, no one is who they seem, and the audience is entirely restricted to the knowledge enjoyed by the lead characters.

Ultimately, however, the picture functions mostly as an alternative love story. Donner was never afraid to wear his romantic nature on his sleeve, in his films as in life. He had crafted endearing love stories from movies as diverse in genre as *Superman*, *Inside Moves*, and *Ladyhawke* — even if, on this occasion, the paranoid nature of Gibson's character sometimes threatens our engagement with him as a romantic lead.

Throughout Donner's career he had strived to cast actors in his movies whose "essential ingredients" matched that of the character they were to play. Casting against type was always a box-office risk. Audiences had cheered Mel Gibson's manic intensity as Martin Riggs in *Lethal Weapon*, embraced his roguishness as Bret Maverick in *Maverick*. Jerry Fletcher in *Conspiracy Theory* left them confused. Says the star, "People wanted to know what they were buying, and I think that that one made them scratch their heads a little [and say], 'What is that about?'"

He continues, "It was so unusual. It was an odd concept. [My character] was such a strange man... an odd guy. He's like a stalker or something. Perhaps that was a little odd, that whole dynamic with the relationship. He's kind of stalking her. It's a little weird. He really is kind of a loser."

Despite its meek triumph, Gibson remembers *Conspiracy Theory* as one of his favorite collaborations with both Donner and Silver. He continues, "Nobody ever really knows how something is going to fair when you go out there, what the mind and the mood of the public will be. That's one of my favorites with those guys just because of the oddness of it. We took a risk. We didn't go with convention."

"The studio's in trouble," confessed Lorenzo Di Bonaventura, then Warner Bros. joint president of worldwide theatrical production. "We're in trouble. It's as simple as that." In 1997 a series of high-profile, expensive flops, including *Batman and Robin* and *The Postman*, had rocked the historic film studio and its dynamic leadership team of Bob Daly and Terry Semel. So much so that when the estimated budget for *I Am Legend*, a giant sci-fi extravaganza set to star Arnold Schwarzenegger, reached $120 million, the pair ordered the screenplay into turnaround. (A decade later the film would become a huge hit for the studio starring Will Smith.)

1997 was a dire time for Daly and Semel, two of Donner's staunchest allies and supporters. A bitter lawsuit lost to filmmaker Francis Ford Coppola to the tune of $80 million, the result of a legal wrangle over an intended live-action version of *Pinocchio*, had placed a stain on their otherwise impeccable reputations. To make matters worse for the pair, when director Tim Burton and actor Nicolas Cage left the stuttering *Superman Lives* project (a controversial reimagining of Donner's franchise based on "The Death of Superman" comic book line), a staggering $40 million was lost through talent guarantees, script development, and completed sets.

With a giant Man of Steel-sized hole in their production slate, Warner Bros. needed a new tent-pole event for the summer of 1998. But what would it be? Confidence was low for future output, a product list that included the eventual flops *The Avengers* and *Quest for Camelot*. Daly and Semel needed the closest thing to a guaranteed blockbuster smash in order to salvage a chunk of the most lucrative film season, their total year finances, perhaps even their careers.

Six years had passed since the last installment of the *Lethal Weapon* property, and if Warner Bros. desired a fourth film in the series to be its fiscal savior, enormous obstacles would need to be overcome. Would all of the talent be available at such short notice? Would they be interested in making a fresh sequel? Could the movie be developed, filmed, and marketed within the necessary time frame? Donner was not dismissive, but resistant to overtures without a credible screenplay. The director commissioned four screenwriters to work on independent visions for a sequel inspired by his own premise. Writers Channing Gibson, Jonathan Lemkin, Alfred Gough, and Miles Millar separately imagined the return of Riggs and Murtaugh, this time on the chase of human traffickers smuggling slave families into Los Angeles by sea.

As with previous sequels, Donner desired important news subjects to ground proceedings with a semblance of honesty, and to spotlight an issue of concern to him. Inspiration this time came from a frightening news story he had read in *The New York Times*, one that detailed the smuggling of Chinese immigrants into Long Island. It affected him enough to insist that it be the focal narrative point of any new *Lethal Weapon* picture.

Of the four scripts that were returned, the strongest elements from each were pooled into a new, second draft from Channing Gibson. The screenplay was still unpolished, not where it needed to be, but Donner was encouraged enough to accede and to sign a contract to direct and produce *Lethal Weapon 4*. Superstar Mel Gibson remained uncommitted — despite tentatively approving the premise of the movie. His once excellent relationship with the Warner hierarchy had cooled somewhat over the years, especially after Terry Semel refused to partly fund his epic *Braveheart* without a contract committing him to pictures of the studio's choice. Gibson was offended by the suggestion of a secondary deal, and in the end Semel's move proved a glaring error. Gibson took *Braveheart* to Twentieth Century-Fox and Paramount Pictures. The studios would benefit from an eventual worldwide gross of $210 million and the prestige of Academy Award victory.

Therefore, even though Gibson had a gap in his schedule, Warner Bros. could not assume his involvement with *Lethal Weapon 4* as a given. If the studio wanted him, they would have to pay big. In the end, they did. Gibson would not receive the $40 million salary reported in the press, but a sizeable $20 million fee plus a large chunk of the film's profits (rumored to be an amazing 17%). Gibson committed his signature to the contract a mere seven weeks before the commencement of shooting.

Gibson's inclusion gave the project the momentum it needed. Danny Glover and Rene Russo signed to return, as did Joe Pesci, who held out until the very final moment in order to negotiate the largest possible wage, forcing Warner Bros. to succumb to his demands. He would earn $3 million for three weeks' work.

Requiring a villain with broad international appeal, Asian icon Jet Li was asked to audition in Los Angeles. He chatted with Donner and improvised a scene with Gibson, who admitted to him, "I saw your pictures, I like your fights. Just decide how to beat me up." Li was retained to play the villain Wah Sing Ku. His personal choreographer, Yuen Kwai, was also hired.

During pre-production, Donner arranged several sit-down conferences with his principal cast and crew to exchange ideas for the movie before a roll of film was shot. During these meetings he grew frustrated with Jet Li's lack of input. Little did he realize that Li's silence was less an unwillingness to collaborate, but a reflection of the fact he spoke barely a word of English.

Before shooting began, the cast budget for the film was alone rumored to be in excess of $50 million. There were also to be sizeable fees for Donner and Joel Silver. In addition, just to get the picture made, Daly and Semel had agreed to relinquish 40% of all box-office profit to members of the production. If there was a saving grace for the studio, it was the relatively low physical production costs. The majority of the film would be shot locally in Los Angeles, across the state of California, with a brief spell in Las Vegas, Nevada. Money would be needed for elaborate stunts and spectacular pyrotechnics, but there was no requirement for budget-draining computer graphics work.

Lethal Weapon 4 was officially green-lit by Warner Bros. in December 1997. Shooting would begin on January 16, 1998. So began the daunting task of putting together a major Hollywood blockbuster in just six months. It was to be a bumpy ride.

"I'm confident I will have a finished script by the end of principal photography," Donner desperately quipped. Indeed, much of *Lethal Weapon 4* would be conceived — and reconceived — as filming progressed. The end result would be a new adventure that still depended on the chemistry between Riggs and Murtaugh, and their unique style of zippy banter.

During a shootout with an arsonist, Roger Murtaugh reveals to his partner, Martin Riggs, that Riggs's girlfriend, Lorna, is pregnant. In turn, Riggs announces to Murtaugh that Murtaugh's daughter, Rianne, is pregnant, the father unknown.

Almost nine months later, the two men are fishing in Los Angeles harbor when they hear gunshots emanating from a passing ship. Riggs boards the vessel and discovers gunmen smuggling Chinese immigrants into the U.S. After a gunfight, Murtaugh allows a slave family, the Hongs, to live in his home.

Riggs and Lorna discuss marriage. In the process, she reveals that Rianne is secretly married to a cop, Detective Lee Butters, and that she is too afraid to tell her father. The mischievous Riggs proceeds to convince Murtaugh that Butters is gay.

Riggs and Murtaugh interrogate "Uncle Benny," a Chinatown crime boss, and meet a mysterious triad gang leader, Wah Sing Ku. Soon afterward, Wah Sing Ku arrives at Murtaugh's home and steals the Hong family. Riggs and Murtaugh are beaten up and bound next to their loved ones on the floor. The house is set on fire. Ping, a young Chinese boy who had been hiding, cuts them loose, and they escape.

At U.S. customs, Wah Sing Ku meets with a corrupt Chinese general, whom he intends to bribe for the release of his gang members from Hong Kong. He intends to pay in counterfeit currency produced by the Hongs.

At the point of exchange, Riggs and Murtaugh arrive and expose the scam. A violent shootout ensues. Riggs and Wah Sing Ku wrestle underwater. The latter is shot and killed, but Riggs becomes trapped underneath some debris. Murtaugh dives in to rescue his friend.

Riggs and Lorna decide to marry, just before she gives birth (coincidentally at the same time as Murtaugh's daughter). Long-standing friends, Ed Murphy, a police captain, and Leo Getz, a private investigator, arrive to join the celebrations. The whole group comes together not as friends, but "family."

A night shoot in Long Beach, California, marked the start of shooting on *Lethal Weapon 4*. Donner lensed a pre-credit scene largely unconnected to the plot of the movie, one in which Riggs and Murtaugh attempt to stop an armored arsonist wielding an array of assorted weaponry, including an imposing flamethrower. The sequence embodied the evolution of the franchise — lighthearted, comedic banter between engaging performers, set amongst an exciting, edge-of-your-seat, action set piece. The formula borrowed somewhat from the famous openings of the James Bond series, and, to a lesser extent, perhaps, to Donner's early background in episodic television. Once this footage was in the can, Warner Bros. used elements to craft a teaser trailer, which they were anxious to release into theaters as soon as possible.

On weekends, Donner called intense production meetings in an attempt to complete the script and establish solid shooting schedules. The last-minute addition of comedian Chris Rock, cast as Detective Lee Butters, brought a new vitality to the mix, but meant that Channing Gibson would be present on set every day, writing and rewriting scenes due to lens the next day or, in some instances, scenes that were to be filmed in all but a few hours.

Filming without a locked down screenplay made for a messy four-month shoot. On *Lethal Weapon 4* Donner found many of the scenes were simply being made up on the spot. He consistently embraced improvisation as a vital creative tool, a hallmark of his career, but before he had always enjoyed the foundation of a script that he approved of.

Donner felt the glare of external forces, especially Bob Daly and Terry Semel, who were vitally dependent upon him to deliver the goods, and whom he did not want to disappoint. Within himself he felt a heavy burden, coming as he was off the back of successive pictures that had underperformed at the box-office. The sheer scale of the task, the many different factors he needed to manage in an incredibly short space of time, was mindboggling. The pressure was intense, but he strove not to let it show. His confidence and effervescence would matter greatly, even if it were sometimes false. (Donner's state of mind was not helped when he contracted bacterial asthma, the result of filming the finale in a filthy industrial complex rife with oil, metal shards and other debris.)

At this time actor Ke Huy Quan, who had starred for Donner in *The Goonies,* stopped by to visit his former director. He was nervous about doing so, for he had not seen him in many years. Says the actor, "I thought that he wouldn't recognize me. I showed up on the set [and] I saw him sitting there looking over storyboards. I went up to him and said, 'Hi, Dick.' He turned around and said, 'Oh my God! How are you?' He gave me this big hug. With a lot of people [such emotion is] on the surface — like a lot of Hollywood — but even after we'd sat down and he'd got busy with his stuff setting up the shot, he was screaming out, 'Hey! Where's Ke? Where's Ke?' I felt very important."

When another Goonie dropped in, he encountered a different Donner, one exhibiting signs of the stress he was undoubtedly under. "I was actually there to pitch him something," Corey Feldman recalls. "We were hanging out on the set and watching a scene get shot and everything was cool. Then we went into his trailer, and I started the pitch. During the pitch for whatever reason he just kind of snapped and started telling me how it wouldn't work. 'What? Are you crazy?! That's never going to work! It's the worst thing I ever heard!' He laid into me I guess like a father would but, in a way, I don't think he was aware of the way he was acting."

Few would dare to contemplate that such a major Hollywood movie could be completed in such haste, and Donner's anxiety was likely not helped by the rumors of an imminent shift in power at Warner Bros. — consistent signals that held potentially serious ramifications for his continued tenancy. "There is a conscious effort to expand the family and make it more diverse," Lorenzo di Bonaventura told *Variety.* The paper continued to report "one top industry agent points to the expensive older deals with Weintraub, Peters and the Donners as close to extinction."

Donner found comfort, as always, in the close relationship he enjoyed with his cast. His first rule of filmmaking had always been to develop characters that invoke a strong emotional response, to pull an audience into believing the action, and this process again provided him with the great pleasure. With so many experts surrounding him, the action would take care of itself. The true heart of *Lethal Weapon 4*, as had been the case for the entire series, was the intrinsic, natural chemistry that Donner enjoyed with his ensemble. He was particularly close to Gibson and Glover, actors whom he believed to possess a special kind of screen magic. They were simpatico, giving individuals who understood and appreciated each other both on and off screen. Of the many screen icons he had collaborated with over the years, none held as dear a place in his heart as Gibson.

Jet Li kept Donner's headlining star on his toes. Before filming began, Li had been warned of Gibson's penchant for practical jokes, and had decided to launch a pre-emptive strike. "I bought this trick ring that gives you a shock," confessed the martial arts expert, "and I walked over and did it to Mel. Mel jumped and said, 'Hey! Wait a minute. I never did anything to you!' I got him good."

Wary of Li's martial arts prowess, Donner urged some restraint from the Hong Kong-based star during their many action-packed fight scenes. Although Li pulled his punches, Gibson still had a great deal of difficulty in responding to his artful swiftness. As Li put it, "If I punched [Gibson] seven times, he saw maybe two."

Li was eventually ordered to slow down his moves, which Gibson had to memorize, in order for the camera to properly capture them.

Production wrapped in the middle of May, and a finished cut screened for an assembled test audience just three weeks later. "We really hadn't had the proper amount of time to develop the action sequences," Van Wyck remembers, "and we had to do that on the fly, whilst shooting, which is always hard to do. So you're shooting and prepping at the same time and trying to shoot in continuity as much as possible. Dick literally had to work with the editors and turn over reels before we'd even finished principal photography."

Despite being beyond down to the wire like never before, on July 7, 1998, a gala premiere was held at Mann's Chinese Theater, for which two blocks of Hollywood Boulevard were closed off. Donner and his stars began the hard promotional sell for the movie, completing interview junkets with up to seventy reporters a day. On July 10 — a mere thirty-seven days since the end of principal photography — *Lethal Weapon 4* was released across the U.S. It debuted in over three thousand theaters nationwide.

"In the current climate of big movies with low entertainment quotients," offered *Variety*, "[*Lethal Weapon 4*] will stand out because it delivers the goods." *The New York Times* was impressed that the picture utilized "pre-MTV storytelling logic that some of us still find helpful, and the story actually has a few substantial ideas in mind." The critic Janet Maslin also noted in her review that the "characters remain funny and likeable… [and] the formula still has some zip."

Maslin's west coast counterpart wasn't so charitable. "A fourth-generation copy of a distant original," pitied the *Los Angeles Times*. "…it makes a fetish of familiarity, featuring the usual faces doing one more time what they've done repeatedly in the past… The result is a calculated, cynical piece of business that epitomizes the creative bankruptcy and contempt for the audience that infects so much of the blockbuster side of Hollywood." The author of the polemic — the critic Kenneth Turan — had never been kind to Donner, but some of the director's strongest supporters were left equally as cold and unimpressed. "[It] has all the technical skill of the first three movies in the series, but lacks the secret weapon, which was conviction," wrote Roger Ebert of the *Chicago Sun-Times*. "… This time, we're watching an exercise… it's all kind of hollow. By the numbers."

When pressed over such negative criticism, Donner's response was quick and forthright. "The public disagrees with those critics," he informed *USA Today*. "And if the public disagrees with a critic, it's better for me. They're going to go to the movie!"

The public did disagree. *Lethal Weapon 4* was a hit, grossing $130 million in the U.S. and $285 million worldwide. The figures fell short of the series benchmark set by *Lethal Weapon 3*, and the installment had certainly cost Warner Bros. significantly more than its predecessor, but Daly and Semel's investment was fully justified — the picture easily proved to be the studio's highest grossing film of 1998.

Of all the episodes in the series, *Lethal Weapon 4* offered the most impressive visual spectacle. The explosions were undeniably bigger, the action even faster-paced. Although computer-generated imagery was by then the industry's dominant mode of special effect, Donner had insisted that his production utilize traditional physical effect techniques. He steadfastly believed that keeping the actors within the heart of the action, part of a real scenario (instead of later creating such an environment on a computer), created an honesty and integrity that actors performing in front of a green screen could not achieve. For the film's spectacular opening involving the exploding of a gas station and a fuel tanker, Gibson and Glover were literally part of the shot, their involvement captured by sixteen cameras.

"Audiences have lived with these guys for a long time," Donner decreed. "They're characters that audiences have fallen for — people have a relationship with them. Out of a relationship come moments and out of those moments comes the action in the movie."

Donner had approached *Lethal Weapon 4* as he had each of his pictures. His energy and enthusiasm were undimmed, his mindset undiminished. Yet due in part to this picture's quick conception and muddled gestation, the end result was drastically different to past productions. Donner knew as he made the picture that it lacked cohesion, and, as if to compensate or distract from this, the energy level in most scenes is cranked to the maximum — at points the overlapping yelling of the actors matches the decibels of the gunfights and explosions. Indeed, with performances ad-libbed more than ever before, the once-vibrant characters of Riggs and Murtaugh are this time less dimensional, teetering upon caricatures, and the movie as a whole almost a parody of previous adventures. Nonetheless, while not as whole or transporting as previous entries, for the most part the exchanges between the actors remain a lot of fun, and the movie has a feel-good ending that doesn't leave you feeling cheated — a fact clearly reflected by the box-office numbers. *Lethal Weapon 4* may have been flawed, but it thrilled the masses. Illusory entertainment, making an emotional connection with an audience, remained the name of the game, and against almost impossible odds; Donner had gotten it right yet again.

In the fall of 1999, Bob Daly and Terry Semel retired from their posts at Warner Bros. They bid farewell to stars and leading industry figures at a reception outside Mann's Chinese Theater in Hollywood. The two men had started their tenure as deputies to the great Steve Ross, widely considered to be the last great mogul. For sixteen of their nineteen years Warner Bros. enjoyed a top three share of the market (leading the field for eight of those success-filled years). Their reign coincided with a period of great professional stability for Donner, and he lamented the loss. He confirms, "I would say their legacy is this: They continued the history of the great American studios. They never let that down... they were true studio executives who loved film and the filmmakers who made them. They will be desperately missed."

The wind of change was blowing, and not in the right direction for the venerable helmer. Without Daly and Semel, Donner was isolated and under threat from a new guard determined to rid Warner Bros. of its perceived air of "cinema du papa."

Daly and Semel's time in power had been defined by their flair for combining big name stars with big name filmmakers, attaching both to big-budget blockbusters. It was a policy that had reaped huge rewards, although expensive flops such as *The Postman*, *Mad City*, *The Avengers* and *Wild Wild West* meant the ideology was simply no longer sustainable.

On October 4, 1999, Alan Horn became the new president and chief operating officer of Warner Bros. He would oversee new franchises, including *The Matrix* and *Harry Potter* series, but in an attempt to minimize cost and reduce risk he would look to co-finance pictures with other major studios.

Unlike his predecessors, Horn was unconcerned when it came to keeping a grip on the studio's marquee talent. Thus, Mel Gibson took his production company Icon Pictures to Twentieth Century-Fox, as did *The Fugitive* producer Arnold Kopelson.

During *Lethal Weapon 4* the relationship between Donner and Joel Silver had unraveled. "Shut up," Donner pleaded to him during a recording session, attempting for quiet. "Or you'll lose the last friend you have in the world."

"I have friends I haven't even used yet," Silver snapped back.

On a separate occasion, "a Silver minion" handed Donner a legal paper. The director refused it. "Sign it or I'll never speak to you again," Silver demanded.

"Is that a threat or a promise?" Donner chided in return, not quite sure if his co-producer joking.

Under instruction from his attorney, Donner would not sign the paper — a request for a loan that required only his signature. So began a series of events that prompted the end of their prolific partnership, including Donner's assertion that Silver retained $250,000 in profits from their *Tales from the Crypt* series due to him. Says he, "When I confronted him he admitted it. He said he had just needed it for the moment, but it took many months of prodding and legal action to get it repaid."

The aftermath to the split with Silver, a volatile yet calculative man whom Donner had allowed himself to believe in, was a painful time. "To tell you the truth," the director confesses, "I liked him. I thought he was a real hustler. He was bright."

Donner thought back to when he and Silver first met, the moment when "everyone in the business tried to warn me… [But] I thought I was smarter than everybody." Soon afterward, Donner was served an eviction notice for his office at Warner Bros. Building 102, the bungalow that had once belonged to the likes of Frank Sinatra and Steven Spielberg, was being re-allocated. After fifteen pride-filled years, the director's professional tenure at Warner Bros. unraveled in a matter of hours. To add insult to injury, as he moved out, it was Joel Silver who cheerily wheeled in. (Silver's assistant, Dan Cracchiolo, had once confided to Donner that his boss coveted the office — and what Joel Silver wanted he usually got. Cracchiolo was killed in a motorcycle accident in 2004, while trying to recover from a drug dependency. Donner saw the motorcycle as "a deadly gift" — for whoever gave it to him "must have known the dangers.")

Donner believed that Silver had conspired not only to have him ejected from the studio, but to steal his office, too. "Joel doesn't give a shit about people," said the director's cousin, Steve Kahan. "He's a rough, insensitive kind of guy. He's not worried about being gracious at all. He'll just push past you."

Some infer Silver bore a quiet cross of antagonism toward Donner for many years, that he secretly resented the credit the director received for his work on *Lethal Weapon*.

Beyond all of the speculation, Donner reveals a perceived disloyalty as the ultimate cause of the break up. "I always thought I was his true friend. Unless I wasn't, because the two other couples that were his friends I would hear terrible stories about them. Someone close to me said, 'Don't ever say anything to Joel Silver that you don't want to hear back.' So then I'm saying to myself, 'If I'm hearing these stories about these people, what are they hearing about me?'" (The director insists he was always "extremely careful not to say anything about anyone to him [Silver].")

The two men had only recently inked a fresh studio deal to launch *Tales from the Crypt* onto the big screen. Despite the poor performances of *Demon Knight* and *Bordello of Blood*, two previous attempts Donner produced at a distance, both still believed in the cinematic potential of their cult television series. Suddenly, the staggeringly successful partnership collapsed under the weight of colossal ill feeling.

"Because in the late twentieth century, you couldn't seriously ask other people to think that you believed in honor and truth, the defense of women, the sanctity of true love, and all the rest of it."

MICHAEL CRICHTON, *TIMELINE*

15

Out of Time

Having overseen three high-profile pictures in the space of four years, Donner took time for a new millennium pause. He and his wife hired Thomas A. Kligerman of the New York and San Francisco-based firm Ike Kligerman Barkley to complete a new retreat in Hawaii. (Kligerman had previously designed the Donners' home in the San Juan Islands off the coast of Washington in 1996.) The director kept his instructions simple and straightforward. "I don't want anything fancy," he explained. "I want the sort of place where if I don't wash the sand off my feet when I come up to the house from the beach, I don't have to worry about it." Rather than inhabit a large house that occupied an entire lot, the couple preferred a smaller home on a larger lot, with plenty of space for Lauren's love of flowers and greenery. The finished property featured stone floors, high ceilings, and oversized windows for extra light. A horizontal band of glass surrounded the master bedroom, providing an uninterrupted panoramic view overlooking West Maui, Lanai, and Molokini, a crescent-shaped volcanic crater.

Lauren enjoyed her study, which faced the cooler, eastern side of the property and featured a ceiling fan and wood louvers for a gentle breeze, but it was the outdoor life that rejuvenated her husband. He spent most of his time in a hammock on the ocean front, surrounded by palm trees. He would stare intently at the thatched roof of his new home, which he imagined to be "the hull of a boat that you might turn upside down and float away into the Pacific."

Despite the allure of the peace and tranquility, Donner's sabbatical from the business of moviemaking was to be brief.

In 1995, the iron-fisted talent agent Michael Ovitz left his Creative Artists Agency to sign on as president of The Walt Disney Company. His reign as head of all things mouse lasted just fourteen months, and the resulting split, particularly Ovitz's astronomical $125 million severance package, sent waves across the entertainment and business worlds. Such was his rapid fall from grace that the man once considered the most powerful figure in Hollywood was turned into a virtual industry pariah.

Donner was sympathetic to a person who had served as an informal advisor since the late seventies. When Ovitz, through his new company, Artist Production Group, asked him to become involved with the screen adaptation of *Timeline*, the newest, as-yet-unpublished novel from *Jurassic Park* author Michael Crichton, he respectfully considered.

For many years Donner had intended to collaborate with Crichton. He greatly admired the prolific writer's talent, especially his ability to take an impossible idea and create a believable reality. *Timeline* was no different. The forthcoming book about a group of archaeology students who travel back in time to rescue their history professor from fourteenth-century France was an entertaining romp, exactly the kind of thrilling, fantasy adventure that Donner so greatly enjoyed.

After he and Lauren read a galley proof of the book, and following further intense lobbying from Ovitz, they committed themselves to the project.

Ovitz intended his pet project to be a groundbreaking deal. The price of the property would be free, if a studio accepted an accelerated development schedule, paid the $3 million producing fee of Donner, Crichton, and Ovitz, and Donner's directorial wage, plus a large end (rumored to be 15%) of the eventual first dollar gross.

In September of 1999 *Timeline* entered the market for studio bidding. On October 25, 1999, *Variety* reported that — in the face of interest from Warner Bros. and Disney — Paramount Pictures had won the unusual "nothing down" arrangement. *Timeline* was placed in active development while a script was prepared. Shooting was scheduled to begin in the summer of 2000.

Meanwhile, Donner/Shuler-Donner Productions morphed into The Donners Company, a new unit based in Beverly Hills. Donner looked set to produce *The 28th Amendment*, a $70 million action movie assembled by Michael Ovitz, financed by Warner Bros, and helmed by *Speed* director Jan De Bont. He planned to start work on the movie about a young U.S. president who discovers a shadow government operating against him once his commitment to *Timeline* was fulfilled.

The Donners had hired newcomer George Nolfi to adapt the Crichton novel into a screenplay. The writer submitted several drafts across a period of several months, none of which proved satisfactory. Jeff Maguire, a second screenwriter, was contracted. Although an $80 million budget had tentatively been approved by Paramount, executives were in no mood to rush forward given the obvious scripting difficulties and the looming threat of a writers strike. Come October 2000 — a full year since the deal with the studio had been clinched — a project intended for accelerated development was yet to be set a date for filming to begin.

In 1997 George Lucas had digitally restored and enhanced his original *Star Wars* trilogy, which when re-released into theaters demonstrated the incredible resonance of blockbusters from the late seventies and the vast amount of box-office wealth they were capable of accumulating. Other film-makers quickly began work on revisionist projects. Francis Ford Coppola would assemble *Apocalypse Now Redux*, which would include an incredible forty-nine minutes of previously unseen footage. Steven Spielberg readied to offer an expanded cut of *E. T.: The Extra-Terrestrial*, to coincide with its twentieth anniversary.

With *Timeline* temporarily in limbo, Donner revisited *Superman*, which had been commissioned by Warner Bros. for a lavish restoration. The director sanctioned the inclusion of previously deleted scenes that added eight minutes to the picture's run time. The film was re-mastered and a new surround sound mix created, although Donner proudly declined to use modern computer graphic technology in order to update what were once ground-breaking special effects.

The restoration was a technical triumph, and Donner's expanded edition of *Superman: The Movie* landed for a special, one off screening in San Antonio, Texas, in March of 2001. Thanks to the Internet, fan interest around the world was fever pitch. If the single showing was a success, a wider, perhaps even nationwide, re-release could follow (a brand-new trailer advertising as such had already been cut and printed, and was ready for shipment to theaters across the U.S.). The weekend, however, turned out to be a cruel, non-event. The night before the premiere, a decision was taken to show the film in not one but multiple theaters, which, when the numbers were analyzed, slammed the brakes on *Superman* taking flight once more. Donner was livid. He explains, "[Someone] didn't want that picture to go out and be successful. [In San Antonio] the entire box-office was totally dissipated and analyzed per theater screen rather than what it did in one little town. It was really disrespectful. There had to be a reason, and I assume it had something to do with the people that were involved with the remake."

A successful re-release of *Superman: The Movie* may have reinvigorated public interest in a new movie franchise. Alternatively, such was the importance of Donner's iconic film, of Christopher Reeve's indelible portrayal; there is the possibility that it may have adversely harmed the chances of a future Superman movie being publicly accepted. Donner suspected that producers Jon Peters and Lorenzo di Bonaventura — still haplessly attempting to conceptualize the comic book property for the new millennium — were of the latter way of thinking. He believed they might have actively sabotaged the re-release.

Following years of rumor and conjecture, and some hardcore petitioning from dedicated fans, Donner took another retrospective step and readied to develop a sequel to *The Goonies*. While it had always been one of the more fondly remembered, persistent cult pictures of the eighties, in recent years the popularity of his 1985 film had boomed — striking a chord with an entirely new generation of kids, effectively establishing the picture as the children's classic it always yearned to be. "*The Goonies* is one of those enigmatic pieces of film that lives on for its own reason," waxes Corey Feldman, who starred as Mouth. "It has lived on in the hearts and minds of children. Kids come up to me today that are only four or five years old. They say, [sounding awe-struck] 'Were you in *The Goonies*?' It's one of those films that just takes a piece of time with it."

Talk of a sequel was not entirely new. Actress Kerri Green, who played flame-haired love interest, Andy, remembered speculative chatter at the point of filming the original. Warner Bros. interest in a franchise apparently cooled after the theatrical release delivered financial numbers that were less than had been hoped, although the studio remained keenly aware of the potential revenue that could be generated from a new movie. Before the decade was even out, some cast members, including Ke Huy Quan and Jeff Cohen, had been invited to Warner Bros. for an informal screen test of sorts, but although the proposition was mooted, no official contracts were offered to the actors. The latter recalls, "[The studio] was just seeing what we looked like then."

After *Timeline*, Donner was firm that *Goonies Never Say Die* would be his next directorial assignment. Penned by *X-Men* writers Michael Dougherty and Dan Harris, a new gang of pre-teen pals would embark upon a fresh Goonie adventure set on a runaway train, assisted in part by original cast members.

Fans were hopeful for the project, but as months passed there was no official statement with which to prop up their optimism. Spielberg continued to assemble multiple new projects, as did Donner. In October 2001, he suddenly announced that *Sam and George*, a movie exploring the emotional and psychological elements of a friendship between two men, was to be his post-*Timeline* picture. The film, underwritten by Paramount, would reunite Donner with Mel Gibson, pending script approval from the pair. After *Sam and George*, Donner was expected to direct *Crazy Taxi*, a movie based upon a Sega video game in which amateur taxi drivers take to the sidewalks, pick up unwitting customers and take them on daredevil drives across the streets. Although Donner was to direct and produce through The Donners Company, no distributor was announced.

Desperate for information on *Goonies Never Say Die*, Sean Astin went to meet with Donner. Says the actor, "When I went in to ask him what was happening with the sequel, he wasn't ready to do it." Many believed that it was a skeptical Warner Bros president Alan Horn who had nixed the project, but Donner claims that a once serious proposition was ruined by the lack of a storyline to match the first. "We tried to beat it," he says. "But [a sequel] is very difficult to delve into if you're not going to pull off something as good."

Astin and Corey Feldman refused to give up. The latter launched a campaign on his personal website, hoping to garner one hundred thousand signatures. He earned the attention of *Entertainment Weekly*, which ran a feature on his efforts.

Timeline spent two years in development before Donner was ready to shoot. Such a lengthy preparatory period was not healthy for his level of creativity. As a filmmaker he was driven by instinct. If pre-production stumbled, he suffered a propensity to overanalyze that would inevitably lead to a loss of clarity and self-doubt. It had happened before, on *The Lost Boys* and *Any Given Sunday*, when he had so exhausted himself in preparation that he lost all his enthusiasm and eventually allowed others to assume the helm.

On *Timeline* there would be no such escape. Donner's friend, acclaimed producer Alan Ladd, Jr., confesses that, "We were in Hawaii together just before he started the movie and he said, 'I want out of this picture.' I don't think he ever really believed in the project."

Donner had sought to extricate himself by asking Paramount Pictures for the impossible. "He put up a demand," continues Ladd, Jr., "[and] they'd meet it. He'd say, 'They're not going to go for this.' They'd say, 'Oh, okay.'" (Lauren, in her role as producer, also searched for an escape.)

For Donner, what might have been a tantalizing return to the fantasy-adventure genre had become an albatross around his neck. The complicated legal mechanics of his deal were such that there was simply no way out for the disillusioned helmer, even if he wanted to quit.

Adapting the novel *Timeline* into a workable screenplay had required an enormous effort. It had taken an entire year to develop a draft that he was even partly satisfied with. "They had a hell of a time getting going," says the director's cousin, Steve Kahan. "I don't think they ever got the script they wanted."

For the movie, many characters were rewritten, downsized, or eliminated completely. For reasons of narrative pace, Donner was adamant that he did not want the screenplay to be bogged down by expository scenes that explained the "science" of time travel. Explained the director, "It's a rough book — most books are. [And] this one in particular, because it had so much science. I didn't want to make a time-travel film, per se. I wanted to make it something that if you bit into it, you could believe it was possible — that it wasn't a fantasy."

Archeologist Professor Johnston heads an excavation in the Dordogne Valley, France. His son, Chris, a student Kate Ericson, an assistant professor Andre Marik and a physicist, Josh Stern, assist him.

After the professor vanishes suddenly, a scroll bearing his handwriting and the broken lens from his eyeglass are discovered in an underground cave. The items are determined as being hundreds of years old.

Chris and his colleagues are summoned to New Mexico by ITC, the technology corporation financing the team. It is revealed by company chief Robert Doniger that — during previous experiments conducted by scientists at the site of the dig — ITC had stumbled across a wormhole in time to 1357 France. Upon discovering the secret, Professor Johnston had traveled back in time and become lost in the past. With the exception of Stern, Chris and his friends agree to travel back in time and rescue his father.

Caught in the middle of hostilities between the English and French, an ITC bodyguard is killed and another wounded. The injured guard returns to New Mexico, where a grenade explodes and destroys the laboratory. The wormhole will close in just a few hours.

In a race to return to the future, Chris and Kate recover Professor Johnston, but are captured by Lord Olivier, the leader of English forces. Marek, meanwhile, rescues and falls in love with the beautiful Lady Claire, before Olivier also captures him.

The hostages are forced to aid the English in preparation for combat with the French. During a fierce battle, Marek destroys Olivier's weapons arsenal, opening a secret passage to the castle and inspiring a French victory.

In the present day, Stern repairs the damaged laboratory, allowing his friends to return home, only for Doniger to attempt to sabotage the rescue. During the melee, Doniger is transported through time and is killed on the battlefield, just as Stern's friends are returned to the present day (with the exception of Marek, who decides to stay in the past to marry Lady Claire).

For filming, Donner surrounded himself with as many familiar faces as possible. Jim Van Wyck was once more contracted to serve as first assistant director and as co-producer. Richard Marks, an editor on *Assassins*, was rehired for *Timeline*, as was Daniel Dorrance, promoted from art director to production designer. Caleb Deschanel, with whom Donner had not previously collaborated, was signed as cinematographer. Renowned composer Jerry Goldsmith was confirmed to provide the music score.

In assembling the majority of his principal cast, Donner signed up-and-coming British talent as opposed to contracting named Hollywood stars. Chief among these was Gerard Butler, who won the part of the dashing Andre Marek. Donner found the young actor to be bright and articulate, to possess a strong sense of humor, as well as a winning, movie star smile. For the part of Professor Johnston, he chose the more established Billy Connolly. The director had recently seen him star in the acclaimed drama *Mrs. Brown*, and offered him the role without as much as an audition. He was, however, shocked when they first met. The jovial actor had dyed his gray beard purple for the occasion (it had originally been green, but Connelly felt it looked too much like he'd spilled spinach on it). Frances O'Connor, an actress who had starred in Steven Spielberg's *AI: Artificial Intelligence*, was cast as the vivacious Kate Ericson. Fellow Brits David Thewlis and Anna Friel also joined, to play villainous ITC boss Robert Doniger and the attractive Lady Claire respectively.

The casting of Chris Johnston, the professor's son who instigates the search for his lost-in-time father, came down to a choice between two actors: the young American Paul Walker and the promising New Zealander Martin Henderson. The former — with the surprise success of the action film *The Fast and the Furious* behind him — edged a close decision. Walker was delighted. "I grew up on Dick Donner's movies," he explained. "I've seen *The Goonies* probably 200 times and I also loved *Ladyhawke*. When I got the offer, there was no way I was going to refuse."

Each member of the main cast would enter training regimes in horse riding, archery and swordplay.

Donner originally intended to lens *Timeline* on location in France, but was quickly dissuaded by the economic cost of such a move and by the growing modernization of the areas he had preliminary scouted. The director settled upon a return to the U.K., the production base of his great film triumphs, *The Omen* and *Superman*. Yet no sooner had sets of the period towns and castles been built in Wales, and studio space booked in England for interior scenes, the production suffered a major setback. In February 2001 it was exposed that the devastating livestock "foot and mouth" disease was ravishing Britain's countryside. In an attempt to manage the epidemic, the U.K. government introduced several control measures, one of which was a severe restriction on travel throughout the land. Faced with being unable to shoot outside of the studio, Donner and his production were forced to look elsewhere. In an instant, preparatory work worth $4 million was written off.

Donner's next base was a federal park outside of Berlin, Germany. Then, just as he readied to recreate his medieval sets, the devastating news of the 9/11 terrorist attacks in New York reached him. Donner was greatly distressed by the events, particularly as he still had many dear friends who lived in the city. With the highest concentration of Al-Qaeda members in Europe reported to be in Berlin, Donner and his team were enthusiastic to secure an alternate location for filming. Donner would shoot in Québec, Canada, allowing him to retain his British cast members and save approximately $7 million in comparison to shooting in the U.S. (Some limited filming would later take place in Prague, in the Czech Republic, and in Los Angeles.)

"*Timeline* had a few difficulties," reflects Jim Van Wyck over an uneasy shoot. "The Michael Crichton book was very dense and not a lot of fun to script. And for the first time in years Dick was really working with a fairly inexperienced cast. That requires an enormous amount of patience. He loved the kids. He adored Paul Walker and Frances O'Connor, and Gerry Butler and Anna Friel. Really adored them. It was just a more difficult project for all of us because we were really trying to develop characters. It required a lot of time and a lot of effort on Dick's part."

Donner had famously reversed time at the end of *Superman: The Movie*. If he could turn back the clock now, he would likely have sent himself to the exact moment he accepted the *Timeline* offer from Michael Ovitz — the point of which he now recognized to be the biggest mistake of his career. He would have walked off the project, were it not for what he believed was his "stupid, misplaced loyalty." Says Donner of his relationship with Ovitz, "I felt sorry for him. Here he was being dumped on by everybody, and I knew that probably some of it he earned or deserved, but he had gotten me the opportunity to work with Crichton that I always wanted. I was not going to let him down. And I wasn't going to let Crichton down." Donner later believed he had been misled. "Ovitz told me that I was first choice. After I signed I ran into Steven [Spielberg]. He said to me, 'I don't know how you're going to beat that [referring to the screenplay].' So I knew right away that he'd been offered it!"

Later he received a phone call from his lawyer, notifying him that Paramount executives, Sherry Lansing and Jonathan Dolgen, were pulling their deal with the Donners (and with Michael Crichton). They were to pay only half of the financial arrangement originally agreed. Donner was dumbstruck, although he soon discovered he was not the first to suffer such a fate. He believed Paramount preyed on "filmmakers who were so deeply committed to the project, they couldn't in good conscience pull out with so many people already involved."

Once on set the project had his full attention, but it was a hard struggle. The director continues, "I had to generate an artificial energy for all the people there. I couldn't let them in on what was going on inside me, because I wanted to try and get the best out of them regardless. It was a killer. It took a lot of years off my life."

It was more than a difficult screenplay and an inexperienced cast that caused him anxiety. In Québec he missed Lauren, who spent much of the shoot in Vancouver filming *X2: X-Men United*. Their professional relationship did, however, create tension in their marriage. Afterward they would vow not to collaborate as director and producer again. "It's just not healthy in our case," Lauren told the *Chicago Sun-Times*. "It's very difficult to work. What's nice is when he makes a movie and I make a movie, and we can advise each other. That's much more fun."

On one occasion it appeared Donner's misery had finally spilled over on to the set. The director abruptly snapped when he spotted a French Canadian gaffer lugging a set of lights across the way. He charged up to him with a face like thunder. "What are you doing?!" he bellowed. "What are you doing?!" A blanket of shock descended onto the set. Donner was always loud, but he never yelled directly at someone. What could have caused him to boil over so spectacularly?

The barrage continued, "What the hell is wrong with you?! What is your problem?!" The gaffer, who believed he had been doing his job correctly, squirmed until the moment the cause of Donner's anger was revealed. "Doesn't your kid have a soccer game today?"

"Oh, jeez," responded the staffer, relieved. "Yes."

"What are you doing here? Get out of here. Go! Your kid has a game."

"But what about the work?"

"We'll be fine without you for five hours. We'll live. Get out of here. Go see your kid's game."

Donner would not take no for an answer. The next day, he spotted the same gaffer, lugging two sets of lights across the way. "Hey, boss!" he yelled. "They didn't win the game, but I got to see him score a goal." Donner likely smiled. It was important to be a good filmmaker, but more important to be a good person.

At the director's decree, the fourteenth-century time period was meticulously researched to ensure that 1357 France was represented as accurately as possible on screen. So too, Donner insisted that the use of computer-generated imagery be kept to an absolute minimum. He wanted his actors to feel the reality of the situation, and not merely emote in front of a high and wide green screen backing.

The fortress La Roque was built as a full-size castle, measuring 60 feet high, set on an old farmyard outside of Montreal, Canada. As Jim Van Wyck put it, "Everybody's mouths dropped when they first saw it. You had to go over and touch the walls to realize that it wasn't actually stone. It looked as if it had been there for centuries."

"I certainly respect other filmmakers who use special effects and computer graphic imaging (CGI)," Donner explained, "but it's not the way I work. I'm a holdout from the old school, and it's important to me to give actors something with which they can interact." In his pursuit of verisimilitude, the director hired mediaeval re-enactors as extras to bring a strong sense of believability to *Timeline*'s intense battle scenes. And in addition to the La Roque castle, the entire village of Castlegard was built. The set comprised of ten buildings, including a grand manor house and a monastery. For those locations set in the present day, the most dramatic set was that of the time machine — a circular drum with pivoting mirrors.

A seventy-five-day shoot wrapped in July 2002, which meant Paramount's desired Thanksgiving holiday release date was an impossible deadline to meet. Donner convinced the studio to delay their planned release and allow him to hone *Timeline* to its maximum potential. He suggested Christmas 2002, itself an unrealistic date.

Although the film was eventually theater ready in April 2003, the lack of confidence in the final cut was palpable. Nobody, from Donner to the disappointed studio executives, believed the project was weighty enough for the spring, let alone the prime summer season, and its launch was again postponed, on this occasion to November.

Anxious to try and make *Timeline* as successful as it could be, Donner lensed additional scenes in Montreal and in Los Angeles. In the cutting room, he slashed first act exposition, and, surprisingly, chose to reduce the narrative emphasis on the love affair between Andre Marek and Lady Claire. Extra focus was instead placed on developing fearsome action sequences. As a measure of *Timeline*'s final dilution, Donner's new edit was so drastically different to his original cut that the music score by Jerry Goldsmith needed to be replaced. A faster-paced soundtrack from the composer Brian Tyler was inserted.

When making *The Omen* and *Superman*, Donner had directed by the seat of his pants. He was governed by his innate film sense, driven by a strong empathy for actors and for a good story. In subsequent decades, as he and his industry matured, he was far from averse to second-guessing himself. He could pander to his internal struggles and to the influence of others — be it test audiences, studio executives, or trusted colleagues. As he puts it, "It's nothing more than growing older. I think you question things a little more than you normally would. You run a little less instinctive than you would normally. [But] the day you're not insecure is the day you're so overconfident you're going to make some terrible blunders." Could he craft a time travel film as charming as *Back to the Future*? An archeological adventure as spirited as *Indiana Jones*? Only time would tell if Donner had been right to amend his vision this time around.

Timeline was released on November 26, 2003, in close to three thousand theaters nationwide, although — as if with the wave of a white flag before battle had even begun — it was accompanied by little in the way of promotion from Donner or any of the film's stars. The project collected a mere $19 million on U.S. soil and $44 million worldwide.

The New York Times cited the film for lacking "a genuinely human moment" and ridiculed it for being "so verbally stingy it feels as though it were written with a stopwatch." To *The Washington Post*, the picture resembled "A 'Star Trek' episode by way of 'Scooby Doo.'" Donner's direction was labeled "middlebrow hackery."

Roger Ebert of the *Chicago Sun-Times* could not defend the filmmaker he had so often praised. "The movie follows the modern formula in which story is secondary to action," he noted, "and the plot is essentially a frame for action scenes."

Throughout his distinguished career Donner prided himself on developing engaging characters that pulled an audience through the many stunts, explosions, and visually spectacular feats of the modern blockbuster. So where had he gotten it so wrong? Ultimately, *Timeline* would raise more questions than answers.

Persistence and determination had taken Donner far, but it was instinct — a word synonymous with success in all walks of life — that had driven him to the very top of his profession. An innate impulse enabled him to see *The Omen* as a chilling mystery-suspense-thriller, a powerful intuition envisaged *Superman* as an affecting love story. Instinct drove him to treat the whimsical adventure tale of *The Goonies* as fact, not fiction, just as it drove each of his major successes. So did Donner fail to trust his instinct on *Timeline*? Or did his instincts fail him?

The root cause of the failure was a multi-faceted source novel that proved a nightmare proposition to adapt. And having begun filming with a script he did not truly believe in, Donner was immediately placed on the back foot. *Timeline* was a complicated mixture of science fiction and medieval drama, both a spirited action-adventure and a romance. In condensing the four-hundred-and-sixty-four-page story into a two-hour motion picture, the director chose to omit much of the science-fiction aspect, refusing to dwell on the "science" of time travel. Confesses Van Wyck of Donner's original cut, "At the end of the day Dick felt that what we had put together in the beginning was a little too heavy and a little bit too complex."

The result of some vast editing is a movie that hurtled through the bare bones of a first act, as Donner sought to propel his protagonists (and his audience) well away from scientific exposition and into medieval drama as fast as possible. Characters were under developed, our ability to empathize with them severely reduced, and narrative suspense all but eliminated. In direct contrast to *Superman*, where a methodical narrative pace invoked a sense of mythic grandeur, *Timeline* moved at such hyper-speed that an audience was not allowed to enjoy a sense of wonderment over the fantastic premise. For Rod Serling, creator of the iconic *Twilight Zone* television series on which Donner had once worked, success came by asking viewers to "unlock this door with a key of imagination." *Timeline* never asked, so the audience never gave.

With an unhappy director who wished he'd never signed onto the project, one responsible for leading an inexperienced cast for the first time in years, the film was perhaps doomed from the very start. Donner blamed himself for "not quitting when the time was right. I should have walked away when we couldn't beat the script, or when Paramount pulled the 'bait and switch.' I should have trusted my instincts."

Donner's strong association with the comic book hero Superman continued into the new millennium. During the promotional tour for the movie *X2*, director Bryan Singer had pitched to him an idea he had for resurrecting the dormant *Superman* movie franchise. Singer believed that a new movie should mirror the Man of Steel's hiatus from the big screen. As such, his premise would be inspired by the notion that the Kryptonian hero should return to Earth after a five-year deep space mission searching for remnants of his home planet, where he would find that the world has moved on without him. Singer believed a new Superman film should retain such easily identifiable characters as Lex Luthor, Jimmy Olsen and Perry White, and keep the famous John Williams theme music. The tone of a new movie should not be one of incessant postmodernism, as pursued in recent years, but rather the same traditional reverence of Donner's original picture, that it should rigidly adhere to its romance/action template.

Donner was impressed by Singer's eagerness and flattered to be sought for his opinion. His enthusiasm encouraged Singer to take his idea forward, which he did. The director of *The Usual Suspects, X-Men* and *X2* successfully lobbied Alan Horn of Warner Bros for a tilt at committing his vision to film. The homage-infused *Superman Returns* would fly into theaters into 2006, fueled by the utmost respect for Donner and his classic 1978 film. It incorporated much of Tom Mankiewicz's dialogue and unused footage of Marlon Brando as Superman's father, Jor-El. These creative decisions by Singer would help pave the way for a separate, groundbreaking project for Donner — one that he would never have imagined possible.

Donner had shot most of *Superman II* in 1977, before he had to concentrate solely on finishing *Superman The Movie,* which he had been told "had to make a [release] date." Even though the film was a major hit, personal differences between the filmmaker and his producers (Alexander Salkind, Ilya Salkind and Pierre Spengler) had become irreconcilable, and he was fired from returning to complete his sequel. When Richard Lester was hired to finish the project, both he and the producers chose to make major changes to the film, the most famous of which was their decision to exorcise all of Marlon Brando's completed footage so that they did not need to pay him — even though the star's commitment to the project was the reason it was able to be made in the first place. These scenes were replaced with new film featuring Susannah York as Superman's mother, Lara. Keeping Brando would have cost the producers an enormous percentage of their future takings (the figure is believed to be 11% of the domestic gross of both films, and 6% internationally). As a result of this and some additional tinkering, only remnants of Donner's concept would appear in the version of *Superman II* that was ultimately released in the U.S. in 1981.

At the time, few would have known of the film's controversial origins. It took the Internet explosion of the nineties to make thousands of fans across the world fully cognizant of its cinematic bastardry. For years a number of websites campaigned for the unearthing of lost Donner footage from *Superman II*, which many believed would offer a more authentic continuation of the tone established by the fondly remembered and highly regarded original film.

First came the online sharing of copies of obscure television airings from Australia and Denmark, which had featured limited unseen Donner footage in their broadcasts of *Superman II*. Then there was the ambitious "Restored International Cut," a fan tribute featuring the same footage, albeit professionally restored and distributed on DVD. It became a bootleg phenomenon. Finally, a group of the most powerful comic book movie webmasters colluded in a bold attempt to rattle the branches of power, writing directly to then-Warner Home Video president Jim Cardwell to demand an official *Superman II* special edition DVD.

A number of complicated factors had stood in the way of such a path. It was not known for sure if the lost footage still existed. Was it in the vaults at either Shepperton or Pinewood Studios in England, where the film had been made? If so, why had it not been discovered during the deluxe restoration of *Superman: The Movie* in 2000? Most of all, it was the legal implications presented by the Brando footage that provided the single greatest stumbling block. In the end it was the reasonable price for which Warner Bros. paid the Brando estate for material to use in *Superman Returns* (and the persistence of producer Michael Thau) that convinced the studio that a Richard Donner *Superman II* could be cost-effective, that it was a project worth pursuing.

After years of concerted campaigning, the announcement fans had almost given up hope of hearing was made toward the end of 2005. As part of its "Year of Superman" Warner Home Video would release a new version of *Superman II* in November of 2006.

After his dark experience on *Timeline*, a truly gripping story with intriguing characters would be needed to lure Donner back behind the camera — something special to fire up his passion. It arrived in the form of the screenplay for *16 Blocks*, by writer Richard Wenk.

Police detective Jack Mosley is told to escort a witness, Eddie Bunker, to a courthouse. When Mosley stops at a liquor store, he exposes Bunker (whom he locks inside a police vehicle) to a group of hit men, only for the limping cop to violently intervene. The pair flees to a nearby bar.

Mosley's former partner and several police officers arrive. Detective Frank Nugent warns Mosley, whom he knows to be accustomed to looking the other way, that Bunker is due to testify against a corrupt colleague. Nugent implores Mosley to let him and his men deal with Bunker.

Mosley surprises his old partner and himself when his conscience clicks into gear. He wounds one officer and hurries out of the bar. While on the run across New York, the detective learns that the chatty, well-meaning criminal in his company intends to move to Seattle and start a new life managing a bakery.

Mosley and Bunker jump onto a city bus and a hostage crisis ensues. When Mosley releases passengers, Bunker sneaks off in the confusion. But rather than escape he rushes back to help his new friend. The pair force their way out of the dead end, but Bunker is shot in the process. Mosley contacts his sister, who is a paramedic. As an ambulance pulls up to the courthouse, Nugent stops it. But Diane Mosley had placed Bunker on a different ambulance, tended by a different paramedic.

Mosley admits to his new friend that he has also been a corrupt cop, but that he wishes to come clean. At the courthouse he confronts Nugent and secretly records a discussion of their past crimes. Nugent allows Mosley to enter an elevator in the knowledge that one of his team is preparing to shoot him, only for a SWAT sniper to kill Nugent's man. Mosley presents his evidence to a prosecuting attorney.

Two years later, Mosley celebrates his birthday in a restaurant. A cake arrives from Bunker, one decorated with the message "People Can Change."

Donner was greatly excited by Wenk's pitch, delivered to him at his home in Hollywood. The characters fit the "unlikely couple" profile Donner so enjoyed; one that he believed created truly interesting drama. Once they find themselves in a life-or-death situation, Mosley and Bunker are forced to work together. They are forced to take action, make decisions, and begin a path to redemption. Once again, the tale is essentially a story of the healing power of love and friendship.

So began two years of intense maturity. "It was a very involved development process," describes co-producer Derek Hoffman. "Richard Wenk would come to the office for a meeting and sometimes he would just stay in the office and write after we'd talked. It evolved. Dick would be sitting there, and he'd be like, 'Hey, man, how come they just don't quit at this point in the movie? Why isn't the movie over right now?' And you'd really have to work in order to satisfy Dick with a good reason why the movie should go on after that."

Donner cast Bruce Willis as chief protagonist Jack Mosley and began to raise the finances necessary to fund the picture. He found independent support from Alcon Entertainment, Millennium Films and Nu Image Entertainment. Glen MacPherson was hired as director of photography and Arvinder Grewal as production designer. Steven Mirkovich would edit the picture. Klaus Badelt would provide the music score.

Willis suggested that Donner should consider the rapper Ludacris to play the role of Eddie Bunker, but the director decided upon rising talent Mos Def instead. David Morse was cast as Frank Nugent, reuniting Donner with an actor who received his very first screen role as Jerry Maxwell in *Inside Moves*. "David is an amazing actor and an amazing partner [in the collaborative process]," Hoffman continues. "Dick had given him his first movie role on *Inside Moves*. So they went way back. Mos had this real infectious energy and you could see he was like, 'I'm working with Dick Donner! I'm working with Bruce Willis!' It was really cool."

16 Blocks was filmed on location in New York and in Toronto and Ontario, Canada. In the former, Donner reminisced over his time as a young man working for George Blake Enterprises, so many years before. He could still recall the address of every place he ever worked, remembered fondly each of the city's great pubs and restaurants he used to frequent with Danny Farr and Gene Freedman. In the movie he paid homage to both friends, allowing his camera to linger on a sign for the fictional "Farr Freedman Kosher Butchers, Mount Vernon, NY."

If not quite reaching the gold standard set by *Maverick*, the *16 Blocks* shoot was nonetheless defined by a warm mood of playfulness and fun. When north of the border, while filming the bus hostage standoff, a mischievous crewmember snuck the CD "Rock Swings" by Paul Anka (one of Canada's favorite sons) into a sound system that blasted music around the set. Bruce Willis and Mos Def were quickly in full swing, joining in with Anka's somewhat comical lounge version of "Eye of the Tiger."

Because the picture was devoid of major studio support, Donner suffered little in the way of outside interference. On set he was gracious and in good spirits. "One day, four of my friends came up to visit," Hoffman remembers. "We all went to Indiana University, and one of them was wearing an I.U. shirt. We were just about to start shooting so I told them, 'Hey, just tuck away in a corner there. I'll be right back.' Dick must have seen it. He just stopped and kind of glared at me. He got up and he stopped shooting. He was like, 'Hold the roll.' He ran over and grabbed my friends out of the corner and sat them right in front of the camera. He said, 'Jesus, Derek, you're a bad host! What are you doing?'"

Bruce Willis invested totally in his role, a gasping, out-of-shape antithesis to his iconic action hero, John "Die Hard" McClane, and was driven to deliver a remarkable performance. He appeared to develop a noticeable paunch (which Donner later admitted was mostly padding) and grew a mustache. When investors saw the facial growth, they went ballistic. "That's not Bruce Willis!" they screamed.

"You're right," Donner replied assuredly. "That's Jack Mosley."

Although determined to portray the mental anguish of a man who has long given up on life, Willis was most concerned that — while caught up in the action of a scene — he might forget that his character walked with a limp. A simple remedy was conceived, as he spent the entire shoot walking around with a stone wedged in his shoe.

Donner liaised with cinematographer Glen MacPherson, establishing a strong visual style that invoked a feeling of claustrophobia. He wished to avoid handheld camera shots, which he believed to be overused. As Mosley and Bunker feel the world closing in on them (as they are hunted down by Nugent and his rogue officers), Donner positioned his cameras in places that captured realistic perspectives. In a bar scene, the director lensed through chairs placed on tables. Later, during a scene set on a bus, an actor's shoulder leans across camera, creating an obstacle. Donner refused to roll down car windows, capturing Jack in his police car beneath the reflections of city buildings.

Donner lensed two finales for *16 Blocks*. The first was filmed as scripted by Richard Wenk, and a second was improvised on set. Originally, it was the new ending that was preferred and Donner intended to incorporate it into his final cut. As Mosley enters the courthouse elevator, Nugent calls his men — who await upstairs, ready to shoot — and commands them to stand down. With only moments until the jury's tenure ends and the case goes away, Mosley presents himself to the district attorney as the new witness in their witness tampering investigation. He claims he can provide names, dates and incidents of extortion and manslaughter, incriminating himself in the process. All he wants in return is for Eddie Bunker's criminal record to be expunged. As this is quickly agreed, one of Nugent's men moves to shoot Mosley regardless of his orders. Nugent attempts to throw his body in the line of fire, to protect his old partner, but it is too late. As Mosley is dying, the voice recorder upon which his evidence is stored plays. A birthday cake decorated with the message "See Jack — People do change" is sent to Mosley's sister, accompanied by a letter from Bunker thanking him for his bravery.

This ending presented a different, more layered character in Nugent, and worked well as a whole, but at the last minute Donner decided to go back to his original dénouement, one less weighty perhaps, but stronger in feel-good factor.

An energetic Donner was to be found in the editing room for each day of post-production, his demeanor so very different to the worn-down helmer of

Timeline. Such excitement bore through in the finished film. The director's action-thriller was a triumphant return to form, easily his most entertaining, most standout picture since *Maverick*. For the genre, Jack Mosley and Eddie Bunker, played by Bruce Willis and Mos Def, were remarkably nuanced characters, as noted by Kevin Crust of the *Los Angeles Times*, who wrote that their chemistry "allows the movie to work on the level of a buddy picture, with Jack's cynicism no match for Eddie's belief that anybody is capable of changing. But the relationship also provides a foundation for the meatier theme of redemption, and the film's depiction of a defeated man summoning the moral courage to address his past is, satisfyingly, more '70s than '80s."

Variety called the movie "closer to a compact film noir than to the many gimmicky entertainments of the vet director's past" and applauded Donner's "commitment to driving the film constantly forward but within the bounds of logic."

Roger Ebert, writing as ever for the *Chicago Sun-Times*, described Donner as "a specialist in combining action, chase sequences and humor," and praised the film for being "more of a character study… [driven by] good performances."

It was Warner Bros. that purchased the U.S. distribution rights, and in keeping with Donner's animal rights beliefs a gala premiere for the film was held in New York City on February 27, 2006, that was strictly a "no-fur" event. The picture was released in close to three thousand theaters on March 3, 2006. In terms of box-office grosses, it was narrowly beaten into second place by *Tyler Perry's Madea's Family Reunion*, although Donner handsomely won out against competition presented in the form of other new releases, including the action-horror *Ultraviolet* and family-comedy *Aquamarine*.

16 Blocks grossed $37 million in the U.S. and $66 million worldwide. The financial return was vastly disappointing. Reminiscent of his experience on *Assassins*, Donner partly blamed Warner Bros. for releasing the picture over the weekend of the Academy Awards ceremony (traditionally a weak weekend at the box-office), and on the very same day as *Dave Chappelle's Block Party* — which also featured his star actor Mos Def. He also believed that Alcon Entertainment had not invested the necessary funds to advertise the movie with a national poster campaign spotlighting the number '16.' He was told the group did not believe in "outdoor advertising," an approach that changed before the company found success with *The Blind Side*. "It was just really hard for Dick," says co-producer Derek Hoffman, "…to put a really good movie out there that people responded to, and to then have it handled that way I think really bummed him out."

Michael Thau, the producer and editor who had been hired by Warner Bros. to assemble the "new" *Superman II* project, wanted Donner to be strongly involved in overseeing the reconstruction of his lost footage, which would include the moment Marlon Brando's Jor-El commits suicide in the Fortress of Solitude in order to return his son's super powers, and an opening sequence in which Lois Lane leaps from the top of the Daily Planet building in an attempt to unveil Clark Kent as Superman. Donner's favorite "blank bullets" scene, set in a Niagara Falls hotel suite, when the cape is finally lifted on Clark's alter ego, could not be found. Instead, it would be recreated by editing together separate screen test footage of Christopher Reeve and Margot Kidder.

After more than six tons of film had arrived in California from Technicolor in London, and the necessary organization and restoration of materials had been accomplished, Donner was invited to review some of the footage. When he arrived at the studio, he found 1977 a difficult time to return to. He struggled to accurately recall and regenerate his mindset of the day, was even slightly embarrassed by some of the footage he had shot early on during the production, and which he would likely have reshot if he had been given the opportunity. Donner also found the scenes allowed much of his bitterness toward the *Superman* producers and the director Richard Lester to resurface. While holed up in an editing suite, the film served as a hefty jab, a fresh reminder of the heartache his firing had caused him — a full, Kryptonian-style shove of what might have been. In the brief number of interviews he would later grant to promote the film, he could not bring himself to mention Richard Lester's name, referring to him only as "the other director."

The project would be known as *Superman II: The Richard Donner Cut*. For commercial reasons it was crucial that his name be lent to the project, and in the days leading up to the release of the film, Donner — who was not being paid for either his consultation or his endorsement — could not help but notice advertisements and packaging with the words "Richard Donner Cut" in a type setting almost as large as the word "Superman." Ever so slightly aggrieved, he approached Warner Bros. and inquired as to his compensation. He was surprised to be told that he "should have made a deal before we started." Donner, in his excitement to complete (as best he could) his work on *Superman II*, had never thought to negotiate with the studio. In hindsight, he believes that president and chief operating officer, Alan Horn, whom he felt was "cut from the same cloth as Daly and Semel," must not have been notified.

The groundbreaking special edition garnered vast media intention. The press was fascinated with the controversial back story, by the magic of the lost Brando footage, and intrigued by the notion that a director could re-cut a picture he was fired from almost thirty years later. Billed as "The Version You Have Never Seen," the film received a world premiere at the famous

Hollywood Directors Guild Theater on November 2, 2006. Many original cast and crewmembers were present, as well as stars and key personnel from the new *Superman Returns*. At the event, Donner and Ilya Salkind appeared to reconcile, which would be more in line with a statement the director gave in 2004. He said then, "I don't hold any grudges because although I didn't get along with them [the Salkinds], they had the sense and the good taste to make the film, and even better sense to hire me. I think sometimes of some of the frustrations I had with them, but I also think that, hey, they were pretty smart people to have gotten that property away from Warner Bros. They were smart, really smart. I mean Warner Bros. owned [the property] and were sitting on it. The Salkinds went to Warner Bros., bought it away from them, sold the picture, and then sold it back to Warner Bros. That makes Warner Bros. not too smart, but it sure makes the Salkinds smart. So even though there were massive problems, in hindsight I have a lot of respect for them."

The DVD release was a spectacular success for Warner Bros. While an exact revenue figure is not known, it is believed to be as high as tens of millions of dollars.

"I've never experienced any great struggle or anguish, because I've always thought myself the luckiest son of a bitch alive to be doing what I'm doing."

RICHARD DONNER

16

Post-Credit Sequence

Richard Donner exhibits few signs of slowing down. He retains several movies in development, including a promising western scripted by Brian Helgeland (based on an original idea from Donner), the successful outcome for which appears to be linked to the director's ability to assemble actors of appropriate stature in lead roles.

The filmmaker may not be at the helm of *Lethal Weapon 5*, should a mooted fourth sequel in the long dormant franchise ever materialize. In 2008, the original screenwriter of the series, Shane Black, submitted a treatment to producer Joel Silver that was subsequently approved by Warner Bros. Silver then in turn invited Black to direct the new movie, which was dependent upon Mel Gibson being persuaded to participate. The actor dodged his way out of delivering a firm yes or no, side stepping Silver's overtures to help Donner (whose own premise for a fresh sequel was not optioned by Warner Bros) escape from being aced out of a series that many consider to be his signature work.

As the only director of the *Lethal Weapon* films, Donner found the speculation surrounding a new sequel to be a source of great irritation. The latest move by his former partner turned adversary felt like yet another turn of the knife.

If Donner chooses to retire as a director, then there should be little dispute as to his filmmaking legacy. The director of *Superman* is the putative author of the comic book movie — a man without whom we would likely never have witnessed such epic franchises as the *Batman*, *Spiderman* and *X-Men* series. With his iconic *Lethal Weapon*, he brought a previously marginalized genre into the mainstream, created a billion dollar series, and set the template for a generation of supersized action movies that defined nineties cinema. His breakthrough smash *The Omen* — widely recognized as one of the most popular horror films of all time — has inspired three sequels, a television special and a 2006 theatrical remake, while his cult classics *The Goonies* and *Lady-hawke* continue to resonate around the world.

If Donner's career has had a guiding mission — more than simply selecting projects based upon his emotional reaction to the source material — then it has been, in his own words, "the ability to lift people, people you don't know, total strangers... to see them happy and joyous." Such a drive is similar to that of the legendary American director Frank Capra, whose pictures were infused with a sense of optimism and hope, brimful with irreverent oddball characters and wonderful incidental moments, and propelled by messages underlining the basic goodness of human nature — just as Donner's are.

Crucially, no matter the story Capra told, he would always end a movie on a positive note. Donner in turn employs a likewise approach. "I just like to feel good at the end of a movie," he states. "My feeling is that if you want to be depressed you turn on the news."

Capra famously won four Academy Awards. There may be no such statuette in Donner's trophy cabinet, but for more than a decade the amount of institutional appreciation leveled at the director has clearly accelerated. He has received multiple awards to spotlight his achievements, most notably from groups such as the Casting Society of America and the American Cinema Editors. On October 19, 2008, he and Lauren received a long overdue double star on the "Walk of Fame" on Hollywood Boulevard. Among many others, childhood friend Gene Freedman and his wife, Claire, were there to witness the event.

And given the ascent of a new wave of critics, many of whom grew up on his movies, Donner's films — once noted for their impressive box-office largesse but generally dismissed in terms of true value and relevance — are now seen as vitally important components in the history of blockbuster cinema. (Prime examples of modern Hollywood's unique brand of epic entertainment *done right*.)

Donner's forceful personality, so evident since his early youth, wins others to him. As Christopher Reeve once described, "The more I worked with Dick Donner, the more he seemed like a fifty-year old kid in a candy store. With his deep, booming voice and infectious laugh, you wanted to follow him anywhere."

More recently, while standing in for his wife, Lauren, to perform producing duties on the Sydney, Australia set of Gavin Hood's *X-Men Origins: Wolverine* (Lauren was committed to overseeing *Hotel for Dogs* and *The Secret Life of Bees* in the U.S.), Donner bonded with the film's star, Hugh Jackman. "Dick kind of reminds me of an Aussie," the actor later told the *Hollywood Reporter*. "He's just a nonstop practical joker. He rings me sometimes pretending to be other people, pretending to be Mel [Gibson]. He's an example of what we'd call in this country a 'stirrer,' in the best sense of the word."

Music executive Jerry Moss, best known as the co-founder of A & M Records, has been a close friend of Donner's since the mid-sixties. He knows only too well the lengths the director will go to in the name of mischief and prank. One of his favorite memories of Donner is when, during a family vacation to France during the mid-seventies, his friend flew in to visit. The pair would often pass the time by indulging in a game of cards by the pool. Moss recalls, "We weren't playing for money or anything, it was just a funny little game to play while we were having a conversation, but he beat me, and he knew it bothered me. I don't like to lose. Dick excused himself for a minute or so, and I see my little daughter is angling toward me with a funny look on her face. She said, 'Daddy, who won the game?' I said, 'If you must know, Dick won the game.' She said, 'Okay,' gave me a look, and walked away. Pretty soon my little boy came over. He could barely get the words out, but he said, 'Hey Dad. Who won?'

'Dick won. Thank you. Dick won.'

This continued everywhere we went. Strangers would come up to me on the streets of France and ask me, 'Who won sir, you or Mr. Donner?' Finally, when we went out to dinner that night, we walked in the restaurant and the Maître d' said, 'I have your table ready, but one question please...' Before he could finish, we all just fell down laughing."

Donner's sense of humor is intrinsic. At times, however, the forever playful personality, the persistently upbeat manner, has distracted critical attention away from his forceful talents — namely his instant, intuitive understanding of actors, of narrative, and his keen sense for the artistic possibilities provided by film. For an entire career, the larger than life persona has masked a quiet yet fierce determination to succeed.

Donner may offer the impression of a man who has been content to let life's chips fall where they may, but — if not necessarily a laser like focus — those who know him understand that once he discovered his path in life, he channeled an absolute commitment to it. Under the tutelage of his great mentor, the filmmaker George Blake, and then later during his tenure in television, Donner tirelessly absorbed every aspect of production, learning all there was to know about cameras, their available lenses, of certain types of film stock, and lighting techniques. He spent hours reading scripts, and lived on film sets and in editing suites. He never lost sight of his dream to successfully direct for the silver screen.

Donner is noticeably indebted to Blake, as he is to others, including Martin Ritt and Alan Ladd, Jr. (the latter of whom, on *The Omen*, placed faith in his friend without which his big break in movies may never have occurred). And Donner's dedication to the term "verisimilitude" — in a way the foundation of his unique success — is a mantra likely introduced to him by his original acting coach, David Alexander, those many years ago.

It is Donner's intention to find the reality in the farce, to balance naivety and knowingness without straying too far either side, that stands as his most beguiling trait as a filmmaker. Even the most fantastic of ideas, he believes, must to be played straight, for the risk of insulting both the source material and an audience. Despite his famous forays into the action genre, he has always insisted that the spectacle should complement the narrative, and not vice versa. As Mel Gibson once said of *Lethal Weapon*, "Dick Donner understands that action doesn't mean a thing unless the audience has access to it by really getting to know the characters first."

This mantle is one being assumed by emerging blockbuster directors, including Christopher Nolan, who retrieved Donner's comic book movie standard through his reinvention of the *Batman* franchise. Nolan's buzzword for both *Batman Begins* and *The Dark Knight* was verisimilitude — the tricky multi-syllable term Donner had painted outside his office during the production of *Superman*, and which defines a career. (After Donner was screened a copy of *Batman Begins* in the summer of 2006, he was moved to write a letter to Nolan, applauding him for his work.)

Donner understands well the mechanics of his industry. He has always served as a tremendous promoter of his movies, clearly revels at being a part of the intoxicating world of showbiz. Yet, perversely, when the spotlight falls directly upon him, as it invariably has, it is the source of tremendous discomfort. He has long since mastered the art of avoiding the personal question, detracting attention well away from himself, of employing his enormous energy and lightning quick humor as a sleight of hand designed to draw one from ever probing too far. As a result, little is truly known of the private side of one of the world's most successful filmmakers.

What can be assumed is that, for most of his adult life, Donner was a lone soul who lived vicariously in a series of "surrogate family" relationships.

Of the early friendships he formed once he arrived in California, Donner speaks not of movie stars or celebrities, but of a man, Ronnie Buck, a real estate businessman responsible for building the first home he purchased on Mulholland Drive. He says that it was Buck, his wife, Anne, and their children, Leanne and Mark, who became "my dearest friends out here." (Buck later became a partner in Donner's famed nightclub, "The Factory.")

Despite his need to be a part of such family units, Donner lived fast and loose, consuming countless romantic dalliances throughout his young adulthood and beyond. Few would have dared to use the words "Donner" and "marriage" in the same sentence, right up until the moment he famously exploded the incongruity when he fell in love with Lauren Shuler, whom he wed in an intimate ceremony conducted on the lawn of his Hollywood home. It was Shuler who changed his life completely. Says Jerry Moss, "Outside of Liv [Ullman], all those other women were really just 'fun.' I hate to relegate them to that, but whenever I saw him I never sensed anything serious. It didn't seem like there was going to be a 'forever' scene for Dick. But Lauren, obviously, was a woman of quality. I'm not saying the others weren't, but she was very beautiful and very smart, and there was a lot to love about her. She had her own career that she was very serious about. For Dick 'the business' became a little more interesting because he could go home and discuss certain things at night with someone who was keen and sharp and had her own opinion. They became a team."

Producer and friend, Alan Ladd, Jr., concurs that, "The ladies he went out with before were all passive women, and I think why their marriage is so successful is that she's totally different from the [type of] people he went out with before. She's very strong, very independent. After he and Lauren got married, he still had his own outgoing personality, but he became a more responsible human being, certainly more than he was before. It's been a great marriage to watch. They're obviously very much in love. They like to travel, they like to do things together, and he's settled down to become a really good husband."

Lauren is the focus of Donner's life, the continued strength of his twenty-four year marriage his clear and overriding success.

Donner has been reluctant to approach the darker side of life in his films, to expose his own inner demons, whatever they may be. *Superman* and *Inside Moves* undoubtedly showed us his heart, but he has never truly revealed the complexity of his soul. It was Robert Paul Smith, one of the director's favorite authors, who wrote that, "People who don't have nightmares don't have dreams." Donner has proven himself to dream, so what is his nightmare? What is the suffering that leads to his undoubted compassion? "I will be in love with him until the day I die," says the actress, Margot Kidder, "[but] his biggest secret is his dark side, and he's just guarding that with his life. I think it's time for him to stop. It's time for him to get brave enough to show human pain in his movies, rather than just the great dance of life."

Despite the open persona, there is much to Donner that is not easily revealed. Beyond the broad confidence and warmth exists a man who is also introspective, solitary, shy even. As he is strong, he is also fragile. In rare moments, a soft morbidity dwells. Although he has given no open indication of it, one imagines his perennial optimism and his atheism can create moments of confliction. Donner blames religion for causing "almost all of the suffering in life." His rejection of organized faith might be a lead taken from his family. In the words of his cousin, Geoff Howard, "I don't know if I can really speak for every person [in the family]. But I think by and large there was a very marginal link to being Jewish. I don't know one of the cousins who turned out to be what I would call religious. Nobody repudiated being

Jewish in any way, but there was not a religious connection — a cultural connection, an ethnic connection, but not religious."

Donner shares much with his family, including what might be considered a tacit agreement not to reveal pain, to expose despair, as if it should spread like a disease. It was not until a moving family dinner in Novato, California, held on the eve of her ninetieth birthday, that Donner's mother, Hattie Schwartzberg, finally revealed a startling secret about her mother, Ida Harowitz.

Ida Harowitz had been born Ida Epstein, the second eldest of six Jewish daughters raised in Bereza Kartuska, a small village in the landlocked country of Belarus (at the time annexed by Russia). Not quite at the dawn of the twentieth century, extensive violence against Jewish people was commonplace. It had been many months since her father had traveled to America in an attempt to secure a life for them all, and he had yet to meet his youngest child, the baby Annie.

When the Cossacks inevitably stormed Bereza Kartuska, Ida's mother and older sister were killed. It is not known how the twelve-year-old or her younger sisters escaped the pogrom, but somehow Ida and her siblings, the youngest of whom was barely four or five months old, left the village. They traveled by foot for two days, bustled their way onto a train to the shipping port, where they would find passage to New York in the hope of reuniting with their tragic father.

In steerage, clean drinking water was likely given grudgingly, barely edible food only doled out. Some relief would have come through a friendship Ida formed with a young husband and wife, traveling with two small infants of their own, a man and woman who, like her, dreamed of a new life in America. But sickness was rife, and the hope of a better tomorrow could of itself be deadly. The parents ultimately succumbed to pneumonia. The irrepressible Ida vowed to raise and protect their children, in addition to her own sisters.

This newly formed family survived to reach New York, and — as if a scene from a Hollywood movie — as they cleared Ellis Island an emotional Ida rushed to the embrace of her awaiting father, trailed by the orphans and her siblings, the youngest of whom, Annie, she held aloft in her arms.

When Hattie finished relaying her mother's story, her brother, George, turned to his son, Geoff, who remembers, "My father [who was eighty-three] turned to me and said, 'You know, that's the first time I've heard that story…'"

In telling it, Hattie could only draw from sporadic parts of conversations that she had secretly overheard growing up. Why had Ida chosen never to openly disclose this amazing tale to her children? Why did Hattie then wait an entire lifetime to reveal what she had ascertained? Donner's mother and grandmother were forces of emotion, like he. Also like he, they were irrepressibly vibrant and optimistic, but appeared to struggle greatly in processing emotional pain, and seemed unwilling to share it.

As Donner is happy, he is radiantly so. As he is angry, he is volcanic. When he is pained, he routinely shuts down — as he did during a trip to Europe in the early nineties, when he visited the Dachau concentration camp outside of Munich, Germany. Barely ten minutes into his tour of the site, he abruptly pulled back. Donner was taken to an office, where he soberly educated a site official on some private family history. He explained that his father, Fred Schwartzberg, had arrived in America as an infant at the turn of the century, after his grandfather had decided to escape the persecution of Jewish communities in Minsk, the Polish-Lithuanian commonwealth annexed by Russia.

As he sipped at a cup of coffee in an attempt to regain his composure, the official to whom he was speaking pulled at a large draw of printed files, and uncovered documents charting more than sixty Schwartzbergs — some potentially connected to Donner — who had perished at Dachau. Donner was devastated by what was revealed to him.

Donner will forever be remembered as the director of *Superman*, the first comic book movie, a sweeping epic that won the hearts of children aged eight to eighty. In his picture he promised, "You'll Believe A Man Can Fly!"

We did. Yet as *Superman* — and subsequently Donner's career — soared, the director never allowed his feet to leave the ground. After fifty years in Hollywood — a passage of time that might leave many exhausted or profoundly compromised — he is famous for his optimistic, and remarkably humble and generous nature. Donner may act impatiently, in haste, or in temper. At a point, as each of us have done, he will have inflicted hurt or pain. But beyond these universal orders of mankind it is clear that there is an essential kindness to the man, that he is willing to see the best in everyone, and, if he can, lend a helping hand.

Donner was a little older when his first great film success arrived with *The Omen*. At forty-six, he may have been more mentally prepared for, or at the very least less susceptible to, some of the damaging temptations that Hollywood can offer. Today, after countless collaborations with some of the biggest stars in film history, two of his best friends remain Danny Farr and Gene Freedman; pals with whom he formed a determined bond while in the third grade at William Wilson Elementary School in Mount Vernon, New York, those many years ago. Described his friend, the late Tom Mankiewicz, "Dick has very few friends in the business. Dick doesn't pal around with actors. Dick never palled around with executives. He's always had his own life. He has a house north of Washington and a house in Hawaii, and he loves his animals and he loves his wife. It's not that it's so impossible to get Dick out to a party or something, or a gathering, or a dinner. He just doesn't want to go. If you went over to Dick's house he'd be in a torn pair of pants fixing his pool, or cooking stuff, or serving the dogs their meals. Dick has no sophisticated pretensions. He's very, very honest. Dick doesn't bullshit people."

Mankiewicz continued, "The Dick Donner people see is a Captain Bluster who is really quick and funny, and loud and brash, who knows how to verbally roughhouse with people, but the Dick Donner inside is somebody with an unbelievable belief in humanity and goodness. He cares. If the lowest ranking member on the crew has a child that's sick and he finds out about it, he makes sure the child has the right doctor. Yet he's the same man who'll walk over in the morning and say, 'What the fuck is everybody doing?! Why am I waiting?!' He's just a wonderful combination and very much unique. I've never seen somebody with that kind of bluster and that kind of huge heart."

In the end, Donner sees life as George Blake did, that it is to be found in the relationships he forms with others. Concludes Stuart Baird, who edited eight of Donner's films and who has known the filmmaker for more than thirty years, "Dick will be remembered in the history of American cinema because he loves people. And there ain't too many people making movies that love people."

Notes

Any comprehensive biography requires an enormous level of research. Although primarily dependent upon a series of interviews with Richard Donner, his friends, family members, and many of those who have worked with and for the filmmaker, additional information and quotes were obtained from a variety of sources.

Books quoted are mentioned here only by title. Publication details can be found in the select bibliography.

Chapter One: Taking a Shot

All quotes from Sean Astin, Stuart Baird, Jeff Cohen, Joan Cohen, Richard Donner, Danny Farr, Mel Gibson, Steve Kahan, Margot Kidder, László Kovács, Lisa Lange, Kathy Liska, the late Tom Mankiewicz, David Morse, David Petrou, Diana Scarwid, Lauren Shuler Donner, Liv Ullman, and David Warner are, unless otherwise cited below, taken from interviews with the author. "Neverland had been" from J. M. Barrie's *Peter Pan*. "a disgrace…" from Don Shay's interview with Richard Donner, *Cinefantastique*, vol. 8, no. 4. "I never saw" from the documentary *The Making of The Goonies*, Amblin Entertainment/Nice Guy Productions, 1985. "The public-address" from *The Goonies Souvenir Magazine*. "One day we" from Tom Weaver's "When The Omen First Was Spoken," *Fangoria*, August 1991. "I found myself" from "Learning not to kid a kidder," *Variety.com*, posted July 31, 1997. "Mr. Donner has" from David Thomson's *The New Biographical Dictionary of Film*.

Chapter Two: Early Years

All quotes from Joan Cohen, Richard Donner, Danny Farr, Gene Freedman, and Steve Kahan are from interviews with the author.

Chapter Three: New York City

All quotes from Joan Cohen, Richard Donner, Danny Farr, Gene Freedman, Bob Gilbert and Steve Kahan are, unless otherwise cited below, from interviews with the author. The quote "Black Sheep Uncle" is from David W.

Samuelson's "Behind the Scenes of 'Superman,'" *American Cinematographer*, January 1979. "The appearance of being true or real" from *The New Oxford Dictionary of English*. "I have my" from Jeff Goldsmith's "Richard Donner pioneered superhero genre," *Variety.com*, posted October 15, 2008. "Humanity. He was" from Beverly Walker's "Vet helmer's long and boffo road," *Variety. com*, posted July 31, 1997.

Chapter Four: King of the Pilots
    All quotes from Harvey Bernhard, John Calley, Richard Donner, Danny Farr, Gene Freedman, Bob Gilbert, Alan Ladd, Jr., Guy McElwaine and Liv Ullmann are, unless otherwise cited below, from interviews with the author. "You're the director," "If you can," "He's an actor" and following, "I gotta talk" and following, and "Come on, Steve" and following from Neile McQueen Toffel's *My Husband, My Friend*. "Every conceivable hassle" from Christopher Sandford's *McQueen: The Biography*. "Stay up late" is from Steve Winbaum's interview with Richard Donner, *SF Movie Land* 29, May 1985. "I used to," "the biggest director's" and "fought very strongly" from John Heitland's *The Man from U.N.C.L.E. Book*. "I remember once" from Craig Reid's interview with Richard Donner, *Cinefantastique*, October 1999. "86 is that" and "endless footage" from Donna McCrohan's *The Life & Times of Maxwell Smart*. "Liked to hop" from Gary Fishgall's *Gonna Do Great Things: The Life of Sammy Davis, Jr.* "It was terrible" and "There was a" from Sammy Davis, Jr. and Gerald Early's *The Sammy Davis, Jr. Reader*. William Rice reviewed *Salt and Pepper* in *The Washington Post*, October 3, 1968. A.H. Weiler reviewed *Salt and Pepper* in *The New York Times*, September 19, 1968. Roger Ebert reviewed *Salt and Pepper* in the *Chicago Sun-Times*, October 25, 1968. "You never see" from Mason Wiley and Damien Bona's *Inside Oscar: The Unofficial Story of the Academy Awards*.

Chapter Five: Death, Destruction, and a Kick in the Balls
    All quotes from Stuart Baird, Harvey Bernhard, Richard Donner, Alan Ladd, Jr., John Richardson, and David Warner are, unless otherwise cited below, from interviews with the author. "He was a" from the documentary *666: The Omen Revealed*, Twentieth Century Fox Home Entertainment, 2000. "Things were going" and "He [Munger] warned" from Susan King's "Those 'Omen' Memories Still Haunt," the *Los Angeles Times*, October 30, 2001. "I never regarded" and "We used a" from Gary Arnold's interview with Richard Donner, *The Washington Post*, July 25, 1976. "What if the" from Tom Weaver's "When The Omen First Was Spoken," *Fangoria*, August 1991. "All those rip-offs" and "To me, the" from Bart Mills' interview with Richard Donner in the *Guardian* (U.K.), October 13, 1976. "The script held," "Well,

Harvey [Bernhard]" and "David [Seltzer] and" from Don Shay's "Filming
The Omen," *Cinefantastique*, vol. 5, no. 3. "Who is he?" and following from
Michael Freedland's *Gregory Peck*. "The legs were" and "I'll do it" and fol-
lowing from *The Omen* DVD Audio Commentary, Twentieth Century Fox
Home Entertainment, 2000. "I can remember" from the documentary *The
Omen Legacy*, Prometheus Entertainment, 2001. "You may choose" and fol-
lowing from Gary Fishgall's *Gregory Peck: A Biography*. "Just before he" and
following from Lee Goldberg's interview with Richard Donner, *Starlog* 93,
April 1985. Parts of this chapter reference the author's own "Bad Omens,"
Hotdog (U.K.), February 2005.

Chapter Six: Brando, Bagels, and the Man of Steel

All quotes from Stuart Baird, John Calley, Richard Donner, Bob Harman,
Steve Kahan, Margot Kidder, Peter MacDonald, the late Tom Mankiewicz,
David Petrou, John Richardson, Ilya Salkind, and Liv Ullmann are, unless
otherwise cited below, from interviews with the author. "[Kids] don't want
science" from Robert Paul Smith's *"Where Did You Go?" "Out." "What Did You
Do?" "Nothing."* Richard Schickel reviewed *The Omen* in *Time*, June 28, 1976.
Richard Eder reviewed *The Omen* in *The New York Times*, June 26, 1976. Tom
Shales reviewed *The Omen* in *The Washington Post*, June 26, 1976. "It's nice to
be on top" is from Bart Mills' interview with Richard Donner in the *Guardian* (U.K.), October 13, 1976. "The day *The Omen* came out" and "You don't
jack" are from Skip Press's interview with Richard Donner, *Premiere*, February 1980. "What's Superman?" "Ilya and Pierre" and "The management regrets"
are from David Petrou's *The Making of Superman: The Movie*. "This is Alexander Salkind" and following, "It was a well-written script" and "Spengler was
the liaison" are from Don Shay's interview with Richard Donner, *Cinefantastique*, vol. 8, no. 4. "Among the scenes" is from Julius Schwartz's *Man of Two
Worlds*. "Whatever Jimmy Carter" appeared in *Time*, August 1, 1977. Quotes
"didn't like to work" and "delivered the Polonius-like adages" are from Peter
Manso's *Brando*. "You know, I was thinking" and "Are you going" are from
Superman: The Movie Expanded Edition DVD Audio Commentary, Warner
Home Video, 2001. "We had this" is from *American Film*, May 1981. "*Star
Wars* and" appeared in *American Cinematographer*, January 1979. "Hey, you
in tights!" from Lorna Luft's *Me And My Shadows: A Family Memoir*. "Hey,
everyone, look" and following is from Larry Hagman's *Hello Darlin': Tall (and
Absolutely True) Tales About My Life*. "He [Superman] is" from the documen-
tary *The Making of Superman: The Movie*, Alexander Salkind/Dovemead Films/
Film Export A.G./International Film Production, 1980. Parts of this chapter
reference the author's own "Close Encounters of the Salkind," *Hotdog* (U.K.),
August 2004.

Chapter Seven: American Dreamer

All quotes from Stuart Baird, John Calley, Richard Donner, Steve Kahan, Margot Kidder, László Kovács, Alan Ladd, Jr., the late Tom Mankiewicz, Guy McElwaine, David Petrou, John Richardson, Ilya Salkind, Diana Scarwid, Liv Ullmann, and Amy Wright are, unless otherwise cited below, from interviews with the author. "It was an" from F. Scott Fitzgerald's *The Great Gatsby*. Richard Schickel reviewed *Superman* in *Time*, November 27, 1978. James Harwood reviewed *Superman* in *Variety*, December 13, 1978. Jack Kroll reviewed *Superman* in *Newsweek*, January 1, 1979. "I'm just totally" and "misplaced loyalty" from Don Shay's interview with Richard Donner, *Cinefantastique*, vol. 8, no. 4. "If he's [Spengler]" from the documentary *You Will Believe: The Cinematic Saga of Superman*, New Wave Entertainment, 2006. "I'd love to" appeared in *Variety*, January 30, 1979. "I started to" appeared in *American Film*, May 1981. Gary Arnold reviewed *Inside Moves* in *The Washington Post*, December 18, 1980. Janet Maslin reviewed *Inside Moves* in *The New York Times*, December 19, 1980. Jack Kroll reviewed *Inside Moves* in *Newsweek*, January 5, 1981. "I didn't have" from Mason Wiley and Damien Bona's *Inside Oscar: The Unofficial Story of the Academy Awards*. "a film-making entity" from Julia Phillips's *You'll Never Eat Lunch in This Town Again*. "In most of" from William A. Henry III's *The Great One: The Life and Legend of Jackie Gleason*. "An evil companion" from James Bacon's *How Sweet It Is: The Jackie Gleason Story*. "Secret dalliances with" and "The shit Jackie" from Richard Pryor's *Pryor Convictions and Other Life Sentences*. "I was drunk" from Rain Pryor's *Jokes My Father Never Taught Me*.

Chapter Eight: True Romance

All quotes from Sean Astin, Stuart Baird, Harvey Bernhard, Jeff Cohen, Richard Donner, Corey Feldman, Kerri Green, Geoff Howard, Alan Ladd, Jr., Jennie Lew Tugend, the late Tom Mankiewicz, John Richardson, and Lauren Shuler Donner, are, unless otherwise cited below, from interviews with the author. "I know I" from Skip Press's interview with Richard Donner, *Premiere*, February 1980. Vincent Canby reviewed *The Toy* in *The New York Times*, December 10, 1982. David Ansen reviewed *The Toy* in *Newsweek*, December 13, 1982. *Variety* reviewed *The Toy* dated December 1, 1982. "Rutger, we're here" and "Quiet! Quiet, goddamn" from Rutger Hauer's *All Those Moments*. "Each of the" from *The Goonies Souvenir Magazine*. "I never saw" from the documentary *The Making of The Goonies*, Amblin Entertainment/Nice Guy Productions, 1985.

Chapter Nine: A Goonie Life (Hip, Hop! March, March! Everybody Let's Go!)

All quotes from Sean Astin, Harvey Bernhard, Jeff Cohen, Richard Donner, Danny Farr, Corey Feldman, Geoff Howard, Ke Huy-Quan, Brian Jamieson,

Alan Ladd, Jr., Jennie Lew Tugend, Lauren Shuler Donner, Michael Thau, and Liv Ullmann are, unless otherwise cited below, from interviews with the author. "There comes a" from Mark Twain's *The Adventures of Tom Sawyer*. "every once in" from Lee Goldberg's interview with Richard Donner, *Starlog* 93, April 1985. "I've always been" from Richard Corliss's "I Dream for a Living," Time, July 15, 1985. "I think the" and "I never let" from the documentary *The Making of The Goonies*, Amblin Entertainment/Nice Guy Productions, 1985. "Yeah, you could" from Justin Kroll's "Goonies cast reflect on life-changing film," *Variety*, October 15, 2008. "This is Sloth" and following, and "I would arrive" from John Matuszak's *Cruisin' With the Tooz*. "They have all" and "*Ladyhawke* is a" from Lee Goldberg's interview with Richard Donner, *Starlog* 99, August 1985. Sheila Benson reviewed *Ladyhawke* for the *Los Angeles Times*, April 12, 1985. *Variety* reviewed *Ladyhawke* on April 3, 1985. Jack Kroll reviewed *Ladyhawke* for *Newsweek*, April 22, 1985. Vincent Canby of *The New York Times* reviewed *Ladyhawke* on April 12, 1985. Richard Corliss reviewed *Ladyhawke* for *Time*, May 13, 1985. Paul Attanasio reviewed *Ladyhawke* for *The Washington Post*, April 15, 1985. "After *Raiders of*" from Paul Attanasio's "Summer in the Spielburbs," July 21, 1985. "I'm very attracted" from James Burns'"Ladyhawke," *Starburst* 81 (U.K.), May 1985. "Directors, in order" from Peter Biskind's *Easy Riders, Raging Bulls*. Janet Maslin reviewed *The Goonies* in *The New York Times*, June 7, 1985. *Variety* reviewed *The Goonies* on June 5, 1985. Richard Corliss reviewed *The Goonies* for *Time*, July 1, 1985. Jack Kroll reviewed *The Goonies* for *Newsweek*, Jun 10, 1985. *The Washington Post* reviewed *The Goonies* on June 7, 1985. Parts of this chapter reference the author's own "Goon But Not Forgotten," *Hotdog* (U.K.), March 2004.

Chapter Ten: Lethal Combination

All quotes from Stuart Baird, Richard Donner, Mel Gibson, Danny Glover, Geoff Howard, Brian Jamieson, Jennie Lew Tugend, the late Tom Mankiewicz, Guy McElwaine and Michael Thau are, unless otherwise cited below, from interviews with the author. "bulky, rough-hewn man" from Peter Bart's *The Gross*. "I figure if,""I couldn't believe" and "so exhausted that" from Wensley Clarkson's *Mel Gibson: Living Dangerously*. "The first part" from Roger Ebert's interview with Mel Gibson and Danny Glover, the *Chicago Sun-Times*, March 15, 1987. Roger Ebert reviewed *Lethal Weapon* for the *Chicago Sun-Times*, March 6, 1987. Richard Harrington reviewed *Lethal Weapon* for *The Washington Post*, March 6, 1987. Richard Corliss reviewed *Lethal Weapon* for *Time*, March 23, 1987. Janet Maslin reviewed *Lethal Weapon* for *The New York Times*, March 6, 1987. *Variety* reviewed *Lethal Weapon* on March 4, 1987. Parts of this chapter reference the author's own "Lethal Weapon," *Total Film* (U.K.), May 2007.

Chapter Eleven: Bah, humbug... Bill Murray

All quotes from Richard Donner, Mel Gibson, John Glover, Stephen Goldblatt, Steve Kahan, Lisa Lange, and Jennie Lew Tugend are, unless otherwise cited below, from interviews with the author. "Directing Billy is" from Clarke Taylor's "A Scrooge for the '80s," the *Chicago Tribune*, November 20, 1988. "It's time for" and "Do me a" and following from Robert Slater's *Ovitz*. "For each year" from Timothy White's "The Rumpled Anarchy of Bill Murray," *The New York Times*, November 20, 1988. "Mitch was a" from Art Linson's *A Pound of Flesh*. "The challenge was" and "We had a" from the *Scrooged* Handbook of Production Information press kit, Paramount Pictures Corporation, 1988. "[It] was a" and "There's a piece" from Ian Spelling's "Bill Murray Ain't Afraid of No Ghosts!" *Starlog* 140, March 1989. Vincent Canby reviewed *Scrooged* for *The New York Times*, November 23, 1988. Hal Hinson reviewed *Scrooged* for *The Washington Post*, November 23, 1988. Roger Ebert reviewed *Scrooged* for the *Chicago Sun-Times*, November 23, 1988. Richard Corliss reviewed *Scrooged* for *Time*, November 28, 1988. "There's no shortage" and "With Mel and" from the *Lethal Weapon 2* Production Information press kit, Warner Bros Publicity, 1989. "She walked into" appeared in *People Weekly*, July 31, 1989. "It was Donner" and "He's crazy," from Wensley Clarkson's *Mel Gibson: Living Dangerously*. Tom Shales reviewed *Tales from the Crypt* in *The Washington Post*, June 10, 1989. Roger Ebert reviewed *Lethal Weapon 2* for the *Chicago Sun-Times*, July 7, 1989. Roger Piantadosi reviewed *Lethal Weapon 2* for *The Washington Post*, July 7, 1989. "It was like" from Corie Brown's "The Years Without Ross," *Premiere*, January 1996.

Chapter Twelve: The Wishing Spot

All quotes from Richard Donner, Corey Feldman, Margot Kidder, László Kovács, Lauren Shuler Donner, Jennie Lew Tugend, and Jim Van Wyck are, unless otherwise cited below, from interviews with the author. "It was the" from John Stanley's interview with Richard Donner, the *San Francisco Chronicle*, February 22, 1992. "The first time," "I spoke with" and "When we got" from the *Radio Flyer* Production Information press kit, Columbia Pictures Industries, 1992. "I never realized" from Julie K. L. Dam's "Back in Tune," *People Weekly*, November 13, 2000. "The wine is" from David E. Williams' "Shooting to Kill," *American Cinematographer*, November 1995. "I'd beg Richard" from Lorraine Bracco's *On the Couch*. Vincent Canby reviewed *Radio Flyer* in *The New York Times*, February 21, 1992. Hal Hinson reviewed *Radio Flyer* in *The Washington Post*, February 21, 1992. Roger Ebert reviewed *Radio Flyer* in the *Chicago Sun-Times*, February 21, 1992. "Even if this" from Bernard Weinraub's "Tracking A Tailspin, Script to Screen," *The New York Times*, March 9, 1992. "As hurt as" from Bernard Weinraub's interview with Richard Donner, *The*

New York Times, May 24, 1994. "When they said" from the documentary *Pure Lethal!: New Angles, New Scenes, and Explosive Outtakes*, Incue, 1998. "They [the actors]" and "Our movies are" from Philip Thomas's "No ordinary Joel..." *Empire* 39 (U.K.), September 1992. "I think we've" from the *Lethal Weapon 3* Production Information press kit, Warner Bros Publicity, 1992. Hal Hinson reviewed *Lethal Weapon 3* for *The Washington Post*, May 15, 1992. Vincent Canby reviewed *Lethal Weapon 3* for *The New York Times*, May 15, 1992. Roger Ebert reviewed *Lethal Weapon 3* for the *Chicago Sun-Times*, May 15, 1992.

Chapter Thirteen: Lights, Camera... Action!

All quotes from Richard Donner, László Kovács, Lisa Lange, the late Tom Mankiewicz, Guy McElwaine, Jim Van Wyck, and Vilmos Zsigmond are, unless otherwise cited below, from interviews with the author. "They were really" appeared in *People Weekly*, August 9, 1993. "I do not" from Beverly Walker's "Vet helmer's long and boffo road," *Variety.com*, posted July 31, 1997. "I'm not a" and following from Larry M. Edwards's "Kettenburg hit by protest wave over dolphins," the *San Diego Business Journal*, December 13, 1993. "Bill [Goldman] turned" from Jeff Simon's "Aces Up Their Sleeves," the *Buffalo News*, May 22, 1994. "Mel and I," "With Donner, you," "the king of" and following from Bruce Fretts' "Funsmoke," *Entertainment Weekly*, May 6, 1994. "a great sense" from "Donner's professionalism, warmth infectious," *Variety.com*, posted July 31, 1997. "It was interesting" and "The actors were" from Bob Fisher's "Zsigmond Shows Strong Hand on Maverick," *American Cinematographer*, November 1994. "I don't know," "*Maverick* was the" and "I do anything" appeared in *What's On In London* (U.K.), July 1994. "He doesn't apologize," "I would have" and following, and "In comedy, you" from Fred Schruers' "How the West Was Fun," *Premiere*, June 1994. "It was the" from Martha Sherrill's "The Rein Of Jodie Foster," *The Washington Post*, December 25, 1994. Caryn James reviewed *Maverick* for *The New York Times*, May 20, 1994. Richard Schickel reviewed *Maverick* for *Time*, May 30, 1994. "These reviews – it" from Bernard Weinraub's interview with Richard Donner, the *Chicago Tribune*, June 23, 1994. "a character-driven," "What Dick Donner" from "Stunts a blast for cast & crew," *Variety.com*, posted July 31, 1997. "You always learn" from David E. Williams' "Shooting to Kill," *American Cinematographer*, November 1995. "Sylvester just needs" and following from Elaine Dutka's "Summer Sneaks," the *Los Angeles Times*, May 14, 1995. Hal Hinson reviewed *Assassins* for *The Washington Post*, October 6, 1995. Janet Maslin reviewed *Assassins* for *The New York Times*, October 6, 1995. Roger Ebert reviewed *Assassins* for the *Chicago Sun-Times*, October 6, 1995. "If you see" from Nancy Miller's "Well, someone has to stand up for old bison," the *St. Louis Post-Dispatch*, March 10, 1996.

Chapter Fourteen: Fun with Dick and Mel

All quotes from Richard Donner, Corey Feldman, Mel Gibson, Ke Huy Quan, Steve Kahan, and Jim Van Wyck are, unless otherwise cited below, from interviews with the author. Part of Julia Roberts casting in *Conspiracy Theory* sourced from James Spada's *Julia: Her Life*. William Goldman recalled the plot to *The Sea Kings* in *Which Lie Did I Tell?*. "Bleeeeeeh!" and "An old trick" appeared in *USA Today*, February 7, 1997. "Mel and I" and "Lauren has enlightened" from Beverly Walker's "Vet helmer's long and boffo road," *Variety.com*, posted July 31, 1997. "There were moments," "master at the," "Beatty said he'd" and "The studio's in" from Peter Bart's *The Gross*. "Put me and" from Corie Brown's "A buddy picture," *Newsweek*, August 11, 1997. Stephen Hunter reviewed *Conspiracy Theory* for *The Washington Post*, August 8, 1997. Kenneth Turan reviewed *Conspiracy Theory* for the *Los Angeles Times*, August 8, 1997. Roger Ebert reviewed *Conspiracy Theory* for the *Chicago Sun-Times*, August 8, 1997. Todd McCarthy reviewed *Conspiracy Theory* for *Variety*, August 4, 1997. James Verniere reviewed *Conspiracy Theory* for the *Boston Herald*, August 8, 1997. Jack Mathews reviewed *Conspiracy Theory* for *Newsday*, August 8, 1997. "I saw your" from James Robert Parish's *Jet Li: A Biography*. "There is a" and following from Dan Cox's "WB to roll back output, cut down on event pix," *Variety*, May 4, 1998. Leonard Klady reviewed *Lethal Weapon 4* for *Variety*, July 8, 1998. Janet Maslin reviewed *Lethal Weapon 4* for *The New York Times*, July 10, 1998. Kenneth Turan reviewed *Lethal Weapon 4* for the *Los Angeles Times*, July 10, 1998. Roger Ebert reviewed *Lethal Weapon 4* for the *Chicago Sun-Times*, July 10, 1998. "The public disagrees" from Andy Seiler's "'Lethal' math: More is merrier," *USA Today*, July 10, 1998. "Audiences have lived" from the official Warner Bros. website for *Lethal Weapon 4*.

Chapter Fifteen: Out of Time

All quotes from Sean Astin, Jeff Cohen, Richard Donner, Corey Feldman, Derek Hoffman, and Jim Van Wyck are, unless otherwise cited below, from interviews with the author. "Because in the" from Michael Crichton's *Timeline*. "I don't want" and "the hull of" from Jeff Turrentine's "Richard Donner & Lauren Shuler Donner," *Architectural Digest*, November 2008. "It's a rough" from Edward Gross's interview with Richard Donner, *Cinefantastique*, December 2003/January 2004. "I grew up" and "Everybody's mouths dropped" from the official Paramount Pictures website for *Timeline*. Stephen Holden reviewed *Timeline* for *The New York Times*, November 26, 2003. Ann Hornaday reviewed *Timeline* for *The Washington Post*, November 26, 2003. Roger Ebert reviewed *Timeline* for the *Chicago Sun-Times*, November 26, 2003. "It's just not" from Mike Thomas's "This Hollywood couple knows how to keep it together," the *Chicago Sun-Times*, November 23, 2003. Kevin Crust reviewed *16 Blocks* for the *Los Angeles Times*, March 3, 2006. Robert Koehler reviewed *16 Blocks* for *Variety*, February 25, 2006. Roger Ebert reviewed *16 Blocks* for the *Chicago Sun-Times*, March 3, 2006.

Chapter Sixteen: Post-Credit Sequence

All quotes from Stuart Baird, Richard Donner, Geoff Howard, Margot Kidder, Alan Ladd, Jr., the late Tom Mankiewicz, and Jerry Moss are, unless otherwise cited below, from interviews with the author. "I've never experienced" from Robert Martin's interview with Richard Donner, *Rod Serling's The Twilight Zone Magazine*, July 1981. "The more I" from Christopher Reeve's *Still Me*. "Dick kind of" from Todd Longwell's "Separate but equal", the *Hollywood Reporter*, October 16, 2008. "Dick Donner understands" from the *Lethal Weapon 2* Production Information press kit, Warner Bros Publicity, 1989. "People who don't" from Robert Paul Smith's *"Where Did You Go?"* *"Out." "What Did You Do?" "Nothing."*

Filmography

1960

"The Twain Shall Meet" *(Wanted: Dead or Alive)*
    Starring Steve McQueen.
"So Young the Savage Land" *(Zane Grey Theater)*
    Starring Claudette Colbert, John Dehner, Chris Robinson, Harry Dean
    Stanton, Roy Barcroft, Lee Kross, Perry Cook.

1961

"The Last Retreat" *(Wanted: Dead or Alive)*
    Starring Steve McQueen.
"Bounty on Josh" *(Wanted: Dead or Alive)*
    Starring Steve McQueen.
"Quiet Desperation" *(Letter to Loretta)*
    Starring Michael Burns, Byron Morrow, H.M. Wynant, Loretta Young.
"The Voice of Silence" *(Wanted: Dead or Alive)*
    Starring Steve McQueen.
"The Choice" *(Letter to Loretta)*
    Starring Jean Gillespie, George Nader, Richard Ney, Loretta Young.
"When Queens Ride By" *(Letter to Loretta)*
    Starring Leslie Barringer, Jennie Lynn, John Milford, Lois Smith, June
    Vincent.
"The Preliminaries" *(Letter to Loretta)*
    Starring James Drury, George Macready, Lory Patrick, Katherine
    Squire, Vaughn Taylor.

Entries with an asterisk (*) are uncredited.

"Woodlot" *(Letter to Loretta)*
  Starring Charles Bronson, Ellen Burstyn, John Clarke, Ted Stanhope.
"Barney's Bounty" *(Wanted: Dead or Alive)*
  Starring Steve McQueen.
"The Piano" *(Have Gun — Will Travel)*
  Starring Richard Boone, Kam Tong.
"A Bridge Across Five Days" *(Route 66)*
  Starring Martin Milner, George Maharis.
"A Drop of Blood" *(Have Gun — Will Travel)*
  Starring Richard Boone, Kam Tong.

1962
"Gunfire" *(The Rifleman)*
  Starring Chuck Connors, Johnny Crawford, Paul Fix, Ross Elliott, Joe
  Higgins, Bill Quinn, Grant Richards, William Bryant, Preston Price,
  Lon Chaney, Jr.
"Deadly Image" *(The Rifleman)*
  Starring Chuck Connors, Johnny Crawford, Paul Fix, Leonard Stone,
  Robert Bice, Bill Quinn, Gloria Moreland.
"The Debt" *(The Rifleman)*
  Starring Chuck Connors, Johnny Crawford, Paul Fix, Hank Patterson,
  Keith Andes.
"Never the Twain" *(The Detectives Starring Robert Taylor)*
  Starring John Chandler, Mark Goddard, Enid Jaynes, Laurie Main,
  George Matsui, Ed Nelson, Bob Okazaki, Robert Taylor, Adam
  Williams.
"Guilty Conscience" *(The Rifleman)*
  Starring Chuck Connors, Johnny Crawford, Paul Fix, Lee Patrick, Tom
  Nolan, Argentina Brunetti, Chubby Johnson, Billy Cerone.
"The Day a Town Slept" *(The Rifleman)*
  Starring Chuck Connors, Johnny Crawford, Paul Fix, Lawrence
  Dobkin, James Best.
"Milly's Brother" *(The Rifleman)*
  Starring Chuck Connors, Johnny Crawford, Paul Fix, Joan Taylor,
  Richard Anderson.
"Outlaw's Shoes" *(The Rifleman)*
  Starring Chuck Connors, Johnny Crawford, Paul Fix.
"Cream of the Jest" *(Have Gun — Will Travel)*
  Starring Richard Boone, Kam Tong.
"The Target Over the Hill" *(Sam Benedict)*
  Starring Edmond O'Brien.

1963

"Not Even the Gulls Shall Weep" *(Sam Benedict)*
    Starring Edmond O'Brien.

"The Boiling Point" *(Sam Benedict)*
    Starring Edmond O'Brien.

"Advice to the Lovelorn and Shopworn" *(The Eleventh Hour)*
    Starring Harry Guardino, Ruth Roman, Natalie Trundy.

"Some Fires Die Slowly" *(Sam Benedict)*
    Starring Edmond O'Brien.

"Accomplice" *(Sam Benedict)*
    Starring Edmond O'Brien.

"Of Rusted Cannons and Fallen Sparrows" *(Sam Benedict)*
    Starring Edmond O'Brien.

"I Feel Like a Rutabaga" *(The Eleventh Hour)*
    Starring Eddie Albert, James T. Callahan, Richard Gautier, Joan
    Tompkins.

"No Trumpets, No Drums" *(Combat!)*
    Starring Rick Jason, Vic Morrow, Pierre Jalbert, Jack Hogan, Dick
    Peabody, Tom Lowell, Steven Rogers, Jean Del Val, Peter Balakoff, Billy
    Beck, Nicky Blair, Andrea Darvi.

"The Two Star Giant" *(The Lieutenant)*
    Starring Gary Lockwood, Robert Vaughn.

"Nightmare at 20,000 Feet" *(The Twilight Zone)*
    Starring William Shatner, Christine White, Ed Kemmer, Asa Maynor.

"The Helping Hand" *(The Nurses)*
    Starring Shirl Conway, Zina Bethune.

"X is the Unknown Factor" *(Mr. Novak)*
    Starring James Franciscus.

"A Thousand Voices" *(Mr. Novak)*
    Starring James Franciscus.

1964

"The Private Life of Douglas Morgan, Jr." *(Mr. Novak)*
    Starring James Franciscus.

"Interlude" *(The Lieutenant)*
    Starring Gary Lockwood, Robert Vaughn.

"The Death of a Teacher" *(Mr. Novak)*
    Starring James Franciscus.

"From Agnes — with Love" *(The Twilight Zone)*
    Starring Wally Cox, Ralph Taeger, Sue Randall, Raymond Bailey, Don
    Keefer.

"The Day of the Picnic" *(The Travels of Jaimie McPheeters)*
  Starring Dan O'Herlihy, Kurt Russell.
"One Way to Say Goodbye" *(Mr. Novak)*
  Starring James Franciscus.
"Sounds and Silences" *(The Twilight Zone)*
  Starring John McGiver, Michael Fox, Renee Aubry, William Benedict,
  Penny Singleton.
"The Jeopardy Room" *(The Twilight Zone)*
  Starring Martin Landau, John Van Dreelen, Bob Kelljan.
"The Brain Center at Whipple's" *(The Twilight Zone)*
  Starring Richard Deacon, Paul Newlan, Ted de Corsia, Thalmus
  Rasulala, Shawn Michaels, Bert Conroy.
"Come Wander with Me" *(The Twilight Zone)*
  Starring Gary Crosby, Bonnie Beecher, John Bolt, Hank Patterson.
"Moonlighting" *(Mr. Novak)*
  Starring James Franciscus.
"The Case of the Missing Button" *(Perry Mason)*
  Starring Raymond Burr.
"Two on a Raft" *(Gilligan's Island)**
  Starring Bob Denver, Alan Hale, Jr., Jim Backus, Natalie Schafer, Tina
  Louise, Russell Johnson, Dawn Wells.
"The Iowa-Scuba Affair" *(The Man from U.N.C.L.E.)*
  Starring Robert Vaughn, David McCallum, Leo G. Carroll, Katherine
  Crawford, Margarita Cordova, Slim Pickens, May Heatherly, Shirley
  O'Hara, Dorothy Neumann, Vincent Deadrick, Charles McDaniel,
  Byron Morrow, Ollie O'Toole, Ted White, John Herman Shaner.
"Home Sweet Hut" *(Gilligan's Island)*
  Starring Bob Denver, Alan Hale, Jr., Jim Backus, Natalie Schafer, Tina
  Louise, Russell Johnson, Dawn Wells.
"The Quadripartite Affair" *(The Man from U.N.C.L.E.)*
  Starring Robert Vaughn, David McCallum, Leo G. Carroll, Jill Ireland,
  Anne Francis, Richard Anderson, Roger C. Carmel, John Van Dreelen,
  Robert Carricart, Sherwood Keith, Jay Della, May Heatherly, John
  Garwood, Stuart Nisbet, John Richards.
"President Gilligan" *(Gilligan's Island)*
  Starring Bob Denver, Alan Hale, Jr., Jim Backus, Natalie Schafer, Tina
  Louise, Russell Johnson, Dawn Wells.

"The Giuoco Piano Affair" *(The Man from U.N.C.L.E.)*
   Starring Robert Vaughn, David McCallum, Leo G. Carroll, Jill Ireland,
   Anne Francis, John Van Dreelen, James Frawley, Gordon Gilbert, Jon
   Silo, Martin Garralaga, John Garwood, Norman Felton, Sam Rolfe,
   Joseph Calvelli, Dick Donner.
"The Case of the Tragic Trophy" *(Perry Mason)*
   Starring Raymond Burr.
"Beyond a Reasonable Doubt" *(Mr. Novak)*
   Starring James Franciscus.
"The Terbuf Affair" *(The Man From U.N.C.L.E.)*
   Starring Robert Vaughn, David McCallum, Madlyn Rhue, Albert
   Paulsen, Jacques Aubuchon, Michael Forest, Kurt Kreuger, Alan
   Caillou, George Margo, Rex Holman, Gigi Verone.

1965
"St. Gilligan and the Dragon" *(Gilligan's Island)*
   Starring Bob Denver, Alan Hale, Jr., Jim Backus, Natalie Schafer, Tina
   Louise, Russell Johnson, Dawn Wells.
"The Case of the Gambling Lady" *(Perry Mason)*
   Starring Raymond Burr, Barbara Hale, William Hooper, William
   Talman, Ray Collins, Wesley Lau.
"The Loneliest Place in the World" *(12 O'Clock High)*
   Starring Paul Burke, Chris Robinson, Frank Overton, Andrew Duggan,
   Robert Colbert, Claudine Longet, Paul Carr, William Arvin, Jack
   Raine, Chris Howard, Ken Baechel, Leo Gordon.
"The Night of the Inferno" *(The Wild Wild West)**
   Starring Robert Conrad, Ross Martin, Suzanne Pleshette, Victor
   Buono, Nehemiah Persoff, James Gregory, Tom Reese, Walter Woolf
   King, Phil Chambers, Warren Parker, Alberto Morin, Clint Ritchie,
   Bebe Louie.
"R/X for a Sick Bird" *(12 O'Clock High)*
   Starring Paul Burke, Frank Overton, Chris Robinson, Gia Scala, J. D.
   Cannon, Tige Andrews, Don Quine, Tom Stern, Eric Braeden, Charles
   Kuenstle, James Brolin, John Crowther, Paul Comi.
"The Hot Shot" *(12 O'Clock High)*
   Starring Paul Burke, Frank Overton, Chris Robinson, Warren Oates,
   Jill Haworth, Andrew Duggan, Jill Ireland, Walter Brooke, George
   Brenlin, William Bryant, Charles Kuenstle, Seymour Cassel, Tom
   Symonds, Gunnar Hellström.

"Washington 4, Indians 3" *(Get Smart)*
>   Starring Don Adams, Barbara Feldon, Anthony Caruso, Adele Palacios, Willis Bouchey, Bill Zuckert, Donald Curtis, Monroe Arnold, Armand Alzamora, Barry Russo, Roberto Contreras, Edward Platt.

"Show Me a Hero, I'll Show You a Bum" *(12 O'Clock High)*
>   Starring Paul Burke, Chris Robinson, Frank Overton, Lois Nettleton, Lloyd Bochner, Burt Reynolds, Barney Phillips, Anne Whitfield, Michael McDonald, Steve Bell, Lee Farr, Ira Barmak, Mike Doherty, Shawn Michaels, Charles McDaniel.

"Our Man in Leotards" *(Get Smart)*
>   Starring Don Adams, Barbara Feldon, Michael Pate, Robert Cornthwaite, Robert Carricart, Nestor Paiva, John Stephenson, Edward Colmans, Fernando Roca, Robert Stevenson, Edward Platt.

1966

"Wife Killer" *(The Fugitive)*
>   Starring David Janssen, Janice Rule, Kevin McCarthy, Barry Morse, Stephen Roberts, Bill Raisch, Lloyd Haynes, Steve Wolfson, John Luce, Charles McDaniel.

"The Spy-Master" *(The F.B.I.)*
>   Starring Efrem Zimbalist, Jr., Philip Abbott, Stephen Brooks, Patrick O'Neal, Whit Bisell, Kevin McCarthy, Marian Thompson, Keye Luke, Nelson Olmsted, Lloyd Haynes, Ed Deemer, William Wintersole, Robert Gibbons, Greg Mullavy, Richard Wendley.

"The Night of the Bars of Hell" *(The Wild Wild West)*
>   Starring Robert Conrad, Ross Martin, Arthur O'Connell, Indus Arthur, Paul Genge, Milton Parsons, Chet Stratton, Jenie Jackson, Shawn Michaels, Elisha Cook, Jr.

"The Night of the Murderous Spring" *(The Wild Wild West)*
>   Starring Robert Conrad, Ross Martin, Michael Dunn, Jenie Jackson, Phoebe Dorin, Bill McLean, Leonard Falk, William Fawcett.

"In a Plain Paper Wrapper" *(The Fugitive)*
>   Starring David Janssen, Lois Nettleton, Michael Strong, Kurt Russell, Pat Cardi, Michael Shea, Mark Dymally, Barry Morse, Arthur Malet, Wolfe Barzell, Bing Russell, Kay Riehl.

"And Then I Wrote Happy Birthday To You" *(It's About Time)*
>   Starring Frank Aletter, Jack Mullaney, Imogene Coca, Joe E. Ross, Cliff Norton, Mike Mazurki, Mary Grace, Pat Cardi.

"Upbeat and Underground" *(Jericho)*
>   Starring Jacqueline Beer, Horst Ebersberg, Don Francks, John Leyton, Marino Masé, Nehemiah Persoff, Gia Scala.

"A Date with Terror" *(Felony Squad)*
 Starring Howard Duff.
"The Night of the Returning Dead" *(The Wild Wild West)*
 Starring Robert Conrad, Ross Martin, Sammy Davis, Jr., Peter Lawford,
 Hazel Court, Ken Lynch, Alan Baxter, Frank Wilcox.
"Death of a Dream" *(Felony Squad)*
 Starring Howard Duff.
"A Penny Game, A Two-Bit Murder" *(Felony Squad)*
 Starring Howard Duff.

1971
"Casualty" *(The Interns)*
 Starring Stephen Brooks, Broderick Crawford, John Davidson, Mike
 Farrell, Hal Frederick, Elaine Giftos, Pat Harrington, Jr., Skip Homeier,
 Diana Hyland, Ron O'Neal, Sandra Smith, Christopher Stone.
"Ring Out, Ring It" *(Sarge)*
 Starring George Kennedy.
"Crisscross" *(Cade's County)*
 Starring Glenn Ford, Edgar Buchanan, Taylor Lacher, Peter Ford.
"Conqueror's Gold" *(Bearcats!)*
 Starring Rod Taylor, Dennis Cole.
"Bitter Flats" *(Bearcats!)*
 Starring Rod Taylor, Dennis Cole.
"A Gun for Billy" *(Cade's County)*
 Starring Glenn Ford, Edgar Buchanan, Taylor Lacher, Victor Campos,
 Peter Ford.
"Death Is a Double Cross" *(Cannon)*
 Starring William Conrad.
"Flight Plan" *(Cannon)*
 Starring William Conrad.

1972
"The House That Cried Murder" *(The Sixth Sense)*
 Starring Gary Collins.
"Blackout" *(Cade's County)*
 Starring Glenn Ford, Edgar Buchanan, Taylor Lacher, Peter Ford.
"The Old College Try" *(Banyon)*
 Starring Robert Forster, Joan Blondell, Richard Jaeckel, Julie Gregg.
"The Concrete Captain" *(Ghost Story)*
 Starring Sebastian Cabot, Stuart Whitman, Gena Rowlands, Walter
 Burke, Eugenia Stewart, Glenn R. Wilder, Lloyd Gough.

"Who'll Cry for My Baby" *(Ironside)*
    Starring Raymond Burr, Don Galloway, Don Mitchell, Elizabeth Baur,
    Tisha Sterling, Johnny Seven, Titos Vandis, Don Pedro Colley, John
    Quade, Gwenn Mitchell, Ted Cassidy, Charles McGraw, Jan Arvan,
    Val Bisoglio, James Oliver.

1973

Hernandez
    Starring Henry Darrow, Desmond Dhooge, Dana Elcar, Ronny Cox,
    G.D. Spradlin, Amapola Del Vando.

Nightside
    Starring John Cassavetes, Alexis Smith, Mike Kellin, June Havoc,
    Joseph Wiseman, Richard Jordan, Seymour Cassel, Joe Santos, Seth
    Allen, F. Murray Abraham, Dick Cavett.

Stat!
    Starring Frank Converse, Michael Delano, Marian Collier, Casey
    MacDonald, Henry Brown, Monika Henreid, Peggy Rea, Marcy Lafferty.

"He Who Digs a Grave" *(Cannon)*
    Starring William Conrad, Anne Baxter, Barry Sullivan, David Janssen,
    Murray Hamilton, Tim O'Connor, Louise Troy, Lee Purcell.

"Memo from a Dead Man" *(Cannon)*
    Starring William Conrad, Martin Sheen, Sheila Larken, Robert Webber.

"One for the Morgue" *(Kojak)*
    Starring Telly Savalas, Roger Robinson, Art Metrano, Dan Frazer,
    Kevin Dobson, Anthony Charnota, Arnold Williams, Joseph R. Sicari,
    Ji Tu Cumbuka, Richard Lawson, Bart Burns, Borah Silver, Jerry Leon,
    Michael de Lano, Larry Watson.

1974

"Commitment" *(The Streets of San Francisco)*
    Starring Karl Malden, Michael Douglas.

"A String of Puppets" *(The Streets of San Francisco)*
    Starring Karl Malden, Michael Douglas, Claude Akins, Lola Falana,
    James J. Sloyan, Hari Rhodes, Ben Frank, Robert F. Simon, Roger E.
    Mosley, William Bramley, Sam Edwards, James Oliver, Reuben Collins,
    Don Rizzan.

Senior Year
    Starring Gary Frank, Glynnis O'Connor, Barry Livingston, Debralee
    Scott, Scott Colomby, Lionel Johnston, Jay W. MacIntosh, Michael
    Morgan, Jan Shutan, John S. Ragin, Dana Elcar, Chris Nelson,
    Christopher Norris, Randi Kallan, Teresa Medaris.

Lucas Tanner
> Starring David Hartman, Rosemary Murphy, Kathleen Quinlan, Ramon Bieri, Joe Garagiola, Nancy Malone, Michael Baseleon, Robbie Rist, Alan Abelew.

"Wall Street Gunslinger" *(Kojak)*
> Starring Telly Savalas, Dan Frazer, Kevin Dobson, Demosthenes, Alan Feinstein, Bernard Barrow, Zitto Kazann, Ann Coleman, Vince Conti, Mark Russell.

"Death in High Places" *(Petrocelli)*
> Starring Barry Newman, Susan Howard.

"The Best War in Town" *(Kojak)*
> Starring Telly Savalas, Mark Shera, Norman Burton, David Doyle, Dan Frazer, Kevin Dobson, Demosthenes.

"A Covenant with Evil" *(Petrocelli)*
> Starring Barry Newman, Susan Howard.

1975

A Shadow in the Streets
> Starring Tony Lo Bianco, Sheree North, Dana Andrews, Ed Lauter, Jesse Welles, Bill Henderson, Dick Balduzzi, John Sylvester White, Lee de Broux, Lieux Dressler, Richard Keith, Sherwood Price, Jack O'Leary.

Sarah T. — Portrait of a Teenage Alcoholic
> Starring Linda Blair, Larry Hagman, Verna Bloom, William Daniels, Michael Lerner, Mark Hamill, Eric Olson, Laurette Spang, M. Emmet Walsh, Steve Benedict, Richard Roat, Marian Collier, Hilda Haynes, Jessica Rains, Sheila Larken.

Bronk
> Starring Jack Palance, Joseph Mascolo, Henry Beckman, Tony King, Dina Ousley.

1989

"Dig That Cat… He's Real Gone" *(Tales from the Crypt)*
> Starring John Kassir, Joe Pantoliano, Robert Wuhl, Kathleen York, Gustav Vintas, Steve Kahan, Michael Bower, Dorothy Neumann, Jack O'Leary, Paul Tuerpe, Rick Zumwait, Al Maines.

1990

"The Ventriloquist's Dummy" *(Tales from the Crypt)*
> Starring Don Rickles, Bobcat Goldthwait, John Kassir, Shelley Taylor Morgan, Symie Dahut, Steve Susskind, April Clawson, Joycee Katz, Courtney Mellinger, Jacqueline Jacobs, Robert Katims, Mindy Rickles.

1992
"Showdown" *(Tales from the Crypt)*
> Starring Monty Bass, Mel Coleman, Roderick Cook, Thomas F. Duffy, Neil Gray Giuntoli, John Kassir, David Morse, Paul T. Murray, Tommy Townsend.

In addition to his credit as director, Donner is listed a producer of *A Shadow in the Streets* (1975), and as a producer or executive producer on all episodes of *Tales from the Crypt* (1989-1996). He is credited as an executive producer of *Two-Fisted Tales* (1992), *The Omen* (1995), *W.E.I.R.D. World* (1995), the series *Perversions of Science* (1997), and *Matthew Blackheart: Monster Smasher* (2002).

He appears by proxy through the credit "Donner/Shuler-Donner Productions" on *Cameo by Night* (1987).

FEATURE FILMS AS DIRECTOR

1961
X-15
> Produced by Tony Lazzarino and Henry Sanicola. Story by Tony Lazzarino. Screenplay by Tony Lazzarino and James Warner Bellah. Music: Nathan Scott. Cinematographer: Carl Guthrie. Editor: Stanley E. Rabjohn. Art Director: Rolland M. Brooks.
>
> Starring David McLean (Matt Powell), Charles Bronson (Lt. Col. Lee Brandon), Ralph Taeger (Maj. Ernest Wilde), Brad Dexter (Maj. Anthony Rinaldi), Kenneth Tobey (Col. Craig Brewster), James Gregory (Tom Deparma), Mary Tyler Moore (Pamela Stewart), Patricia Owens (Margaret Brandon), Lisabeth Hush (Diana Wilde), Stanley Livingston (Mike Brandon), Lauren Gilbert (Col. Jessup), Phil Dean (Maj. McCully), Chuck Stanford (Lt. Cmdr. Joe Lacrosse), Patty McDonald (Susan Brandon).

1968
Salt and Pepper
> Produced by Milton Ebbins. Written by Michael Pertwee. Music: John Dankworth. Director of photography: Ken Higgins. Editor: Jack Slade. Production designer: Bill Constable.

Starring Sammy Davis, Jr. (Charles Salt), Peter Lawford (Christopher Pepper), Michael Bates (Inspector Crabbe), Ilona Rodgers (Marianne Renaud), John Le Mesurier (Col. Woodstock), Graham Stark (Sgt. Walters), Ernest Clark (Col. Balsom), Jeanne Roland (Mai Ling), Robert Dorning (Club secretary), Robertson Hare (Dove), Geoffrey Lumsden (Foreign Secretary), William Mervyn (Prime Minister), Llewellyn Rees ('Fake' Prime Minister), Mark Singleton ('Fake' Home Secretary), Michael Trubshawe ('Fake' First Lord).

1969
Twinky

Produced by Clive Sharp. Story by Norman Thaddeus Vane. Screenplay by Norman Thaddeus Vane. Music: John Scott. Director of photography: Walter Lassally. Editor: Norman Wanstall. Art director: Michael Wield.

Starring Charles Bronson (Scott Wardman), Orson Bean (Hal), Honor Blackman (Mummy), Michael Craig (Daddy), Paul Ford (Mr. Wardman), Jack Hawkins (Judge Millington-Draper), Trevor Howard (Lola's grandfather), Lionel Jeffries (Solicitor), Kay Medford (Mrs. Wardman), Robert Morley (Judge Roxborough), Susan George (Lola), Peggy Aitchison (Mrs. Finchley), Tony Arpino (New York Judge), Eric Barker (Scottish Clerk), Erik Chitty (Lawyer's Elderly Client).

1976
The Omen

Produced by Harvey Bernhard. Written by David Seltzer. Music: Jerry Goldsmith. Director of photography: Gilbert Taylor. Editor: Stuart Baird. Art director: Carmen Dillon.

Starring Gregory Peck (Robert Thorn), Lee Remick (Katherine Thorn), David Warner (Jennings), Billie Whitelaw (Mrs. Baylock), Harvey Stephens (Damien), Patrick Troughton (Father Brennan), Martin Benson (Father Spiletto), Robert Rietty (Monk), Tommy Duggan (Priest), John Stride (The Psychiatrist), Anthony Nicholls (Dr. Becker), Holly Palance (Nanny), Roy Boyd (Reporter), Freda Dowie (Nun), Sheila Raynor (Mrs. Horton).

1978
Superman

Produced by Alexander Salkind, Ilya Salkind and Pierre Spengler. Superman created by Jerry Siegel & Joe Shuster. Story by Mario Puzo. Screenplay by Mario Puzo, David Newman & Leslie Newman and Robert Benton. Music: John Williams. Photographer: Geoffrey Unsworth. Editor: Stuart Baird. Production designer: John Barry.

Starring Marlon Brando (Jor-El), Gene Hackman (Lex Luthor), Christopher Reeve (Superman/Clark Kent), Ned Beatty (Otis), Jackie Cooper (Perry White), Glenn Ford (Jonathan Kent), Trevor Howard (1st Elder), Margot Kidder (Lois Lane), Jack O'Halloran (Non), Valerie Perrine (Eve Teschmacher), Maria Schell (Vond-Ah), Terence Stamp (General Zod), Phyllis Thaxter (Martha Kent), Susannah York (Lara), Jeff East (Young Clark Kent).

1980
Inside Moves

Produced by R.W. Goodwin and Mark M. Tanz. Screenplay by Valerie Curtin and Barry Levinson, from the novel by Todd Walton. Music: John Barry. Cinematographer: László Kovács. Editor: Frank Morriss. Production designer: Charles Rosen.

Starring John Savage (Roary), David Morse (Jerry Maxwell), Diana Scarwid (Louise), Amy Wright (Anne), Tony Burton (Lucius), Bill Henderson (Blue Lewis), Steve Kahan (Burt), Jack O'Leary (Max), Bert Remsen (Stinky), Harold Russell (Wings), Pepe Serna (Herrada), Harold Sylvester (Alvin Martin), Arnold Williams (Benny), George Brenlin (Gil), Gerri Dean (Hooker).

1982
The Toy

Produced by Phil Feldman and Ray Stark. Written by Carol Sobieski, from the book by Francis Veber. Music: Patrick Williams. Cinematographer: László Kovács. Editors: Richard Harris and Michael A. Stevenson. Production designer: Charles Rosen.

Starring Richard Pryor (Jack Brown), Jackie Gleason (Ulysses Simpson 'U.S.' Bates), Ned Beatty (Sydney Morehouse), Scott Schwartz (Eric Bates), Teresa Ganzel (Fancy Bates), Wilfred Hyde-White (David Barkley), Annazette Chase (Angela), Tony King (Clifford), Don Hood

(O'Brien), Karen Leslie-Lyttle (Fräulein Hilda Hans), Virginia Capers (Ruby D. Simpson), B.J. Hopper (Geffran), Linda McCann (Honey Russell), Ray Spruell (Senator Newcomb), Stocker Fontelieu (D. A. Russell).

1985

Ladyhawke

Produced by Harvey Bernhard, Richard Donner and Lauren Shuler. Story by Edward Khmara. Screenplay by Edward Khmara, Michael Thomas, Tom Mankiewicz and David Peoples. Music: Andrew Powell. Cinematographer: Vittorio Storaro. Editor: Stuart Baird. Production designer: Wolf Kroeger.

Starring Matthew Broderick (Phillipe Gaston), Rutger Hauer (Captain Etienne Navarre), Michelle Pfeiffer (Isabeau d'Anjou), Leo McKern (Father Imperius the Monk), John Wood (Bishop of Aquila), Ken Hutchison (Marquet), Alfred Molina (Cezar), Giancarlo Prete (Fornac), Loris Loddi (Jehan), Alessandro Serra (Mr. Pitou), Charles Borromel (Insane Prisoner), Massimo Sarchielli (Innkeeper), Nicolina Papetti (Mrs. Pitou), Russell Kase (Lieutenant), Don Hudson (Guard on Cart).

The Goonies

Produced by Harvey Bernhard and Richard Donner. Story by Steven Spielberg. Screenplay by Chris Columbus. Music: Dave Grusin. Director of photography: Nick McLean. Editor: Michael Kahn. Production designer: J. Michael Riva.

Starring Sean Astin (Mikey Walsh), Josh Brolin (Brand Walsh), Jeff Cohen (Lawrence 'Chunk' Cohen), Corey Feldman (Clark 'Mouth' Devereaux), Kerri Green (Andy Carmichael), Martha Plimpton (Stef Steinbrenner), Ke Huy Quan (Richard 'Data' Wang), John Matuszak (Lotney 'Sloth' Fratelli), Robert Davi (Jake Fratelli), Joe Pantoliano (Francis Fratelli), Anne Ramsey (Mama Fratelli), Lupe Ontiveros (Rosalita), Mary Ellen Trainor (Harriet Walsh), Keith Walker (Irving Walsh), Curtis Hanson (Elgin Perkins).

1987

Lethal Weapon

Produced by Richard Donner and Joel Silver. Written by Shane Black. Music: Eric Clapton and Michael Kamen. Director of photography: Stephen Goldblatt. Editor: Stuart Baird. Production designer: J. Michael Riva.

Starring Mel Gibson (Sergeant Martin Riggs), Danny Glover (Sergeant Roger Murtaugh), Gary Busey (Mr. Joshua), Mitchell Ryan (General Peter McAllister), Tom Atkins (Michael Hunsaker), Darlene Love (Trish Murtaugh), Traci Wolfe (Rianne Murtaugh), Jackie Swanson (Amanda Hunsaker), Damon Hines (Nick Murtaugh), Ebonie Smith (Carrie Murtaugh), Bill Kalmenson (Beat Cop), Lycia Naff (Dixie), Patrick Cameron (Cop #1), Don Gordon (Cop #2), Jimmie F. Skaggs (Drug Dealer #1).

1988

Scrooged

Produced by Richard Donner and Art Linson. Written by Mitch Glazer and Michael O'Donoghue. Music: Danny Elfman. Cinematographer: Michael Chapman. Editors: Fredric Steinkamp and William Steinkamp. Production designer: J. Michael Riva.

Starring Bill Murray (Frank Cross), Karen Allen (Claire Phillips), John Forsythe (Lew Hayward), John Glover (Brice Cummings), Bobcat Goldthwait (Eliot Loudermilk), David Johansen (Ghost of Christmas Past), Carol Kane (Ghost of Christmas Present), Robert Mitchum (Preston Rhinelander), Nicholas Phillips (Calvin Cooley), Michael J. Pollard (Herman), Alfre Woodard (Grace Cooley), Mabel King (Gramma Cooley), John Murray (James Cross), Jamie Farr (TV Jacob Marley), Robert Goulet (Robert Goulet).

1989

Lethal Weapon 2

Produced by Richard Donner and Joel Silver. Story by Shane Black and Warren Murphy Screenplay by Jeffrey Boam. Music: Eric Clapton, Michael Kamen and David Sanborn. Cinematographer: Stephen Goldblatt. Editor: Stuart Baird. Production designer: J. Michael Riva.

Starring Mel Gibson (Martin Riggs), Danny Glover (Sergeant Roger Murtaugh), Joe Pesci (Leo Getz), Joss Ackland (Arjen 'Aryan' Rudd),

Derrick O'Connor (Pieter 'Adolph' Vorstedt), Patsy Kensit (Rika van den Haas), Darlene Love (Trish Murtaugh), Traci Wolfe (Rianne Murtaugh), Steve Kahan (Captain Ed Murphy), Mark Rolston (Hans), Jenette Goldstein (Officer Meagan Shapiro), Dean Norris (Tim Cavanaugh), Juney Smith (Tom Wyler), Nestor Serrano (Eddie Estaban), Philip Suriano (Joseph Ragucci).

1992

Radio Flyer

Produced by Lauren Shuler Donner. Written by David M. Evans. Music: Hans Zimmer. Cinematographer: László Kovács. Editors: Stuart Baird and Dallas Puett. Production designer: J. Michael Riva.

Starring Lorraine Bracco (Mary), John Heard (Daugherty), Adam Baldwin (The King), Elijah Wood (Mike), Joseph Mazzello (Bobby), Ben Johnson (Geronimo Bill), Sean Baca (Fisher), Robert Munic (Older Fisher), Garette Ratliff (Chad), Thomas Ian Nicholas (Ferdie), Noah Verduzco (Victor Hernandez), Isaac Ocampo (Jorge Hernandez), Kaylan Romero (Jesus Hernandez), Abraham Verduzco (Carlos Hernandez), T.J. Evans (Big Raymond).

Lethal Weapon 3

Produced by Richard Donner and Joel Silver. Story by Jeffrey Boam. Screenplay by Jeffrey Boam and Robert Mark Kamen. Music: Eric Clapton, Michael Kamen and David Sanborn. Cinematographer: Jan de Bont. Editors: Robert Brown and Battle Davis. Production designer: James Spencer.

Starring Mel Gibson (Martin Riggs), Danny Glover (Roger Murtaugh), Joe Pesci (Leo Getz), Rene Russo (Lorna Cole), Stuart Wilson (Jack Travis), Steve Kahan (Captain Ed Murphy), Darlene Love (Trish Murtaugh), Traci Wolfe (Rianne Murtaugh), Damon Hines (Nick Murtaugh), Ebonie Smith (Carrie Murtaugh), Gregory Millar (Tyrone), Nick Chinlund (Hatchett), Jason Meshover-Iorg (Young Cop), Alan Scarfe (Herman Walters), Delores Hall (Delores).

1994

Maverick

Produced by Bruce Davey and Richard Donner. Written by William Goldman, from the television series by Roy Huggins. Music: Randy Newman. Cinematographer: Vilmos Zsigmond. Editors: Stuart Baird and Mike Kelly. Production designer: Tom Sanders.

Starring Mel Gibson (Bret Maverick), Jodie Foster (Annabelle Bransford), James Garner (Marshal Zane Cooper), Graham Greene (Joseph), Alfred Molina (Angel), James Coburn (Commodore Duvall), Dub Taylor (Room Clerk), Geoffrey Lewis (Matthew Wicker / Eugene), Paul L. Smith (The Archduke), Dan Hedaya (Twitchy), Dennis Fimple (Stuttering), Denver Pyle (Old Gambler on Riverboat), Clint Black (Sweet-Faced Gambler), Max Perlich (Johnny Hardin), Art La Fleur (Poker Player).

1995

Assassins

Produced by Richard Donner, Bruce A. Evans, Raynold Gideon, Andrew Lazar, Joel Silver and Jim Van Wyck. Story by Andy Wachowski and Larry Wachowski. Screenplay by Andy Wachowski, Larry Wachowski and Brian Helgeland. Music: Mark Mancina. Cinematographer: Vilmos Zsigmond. Editors: Lawrence Jordan and Richard Marks. Production designer: Thomas E. Sanders.

Starring Sylvester Stallone (Robert Rath), Antonio Banderas (Miguel Bain), Julianne Moore (Electra), Anatoly Davydov (Nicolai Tashlinkov), Muse Watson (Ketcham), Stephen Kahan (Alan Branch), Kelly Rowan (Jennifer), Reed Diamond (Bob), Kai Wulff (Remy), Kerry Skalsky (Buyer with Remy), James Douglas Haskins (Buyer with Remy), Stephen Liska (Cop), John Harms (Cop), Edward J. Rosen (Cemetery Caretaker), Christina Orchid (Dowager).

1997

Conspiracy Theory

Produced by Richard Donner and Joel Silver. Written by Brian Helgeland. Music: Carter Burwell. Director of photography: John Schwartzman. Editors: Kevin Stitt and Frank J. Urioste. Production designer: Paul Sylbert.

Starring Mel Gibson (Jerry Fletcher), Julia Roberts (Alice Sutton), Patrick Stewart (Dr. Jonas), Cylk Cozart (Agent Lowry), Stephen

Kahan (Mr. Wilson), Terry Alexander (Flip), Alex McArthur (Cynic), Rod McLachlan (Justice Guard), Michael Potts (Justice Guard), Jim Sterling (Justice Guard), Rich Hebert (Public Works Man), Brian J. Williams (Clarke), G.A. Aguilar (Piper), Cece Neber Labao (Henry Finch's Secretary), Saxon Trainor (Alice's Secretary).

1998

Lethal Weapon 4

Produced by Richard Donner and Joel Silver. Story by Jonathan Lemkin and Alfred Gough & Miles Millar. Screenplay by Channing Gibson. Music: Eric Clapton, Michael Kamen and David Sanborn. Director of photography: Andrzej Bartkowiak. Editors: Frank J. Urioste and Dallas Puett. Production designer: J. Michael Riva.

Starring Mel Gibson (Martin Riggs), Danny Glover (Roger Murtaugh), Joe Pesci (Leo Getz), Rene Russo (Lorna Cole), Chris Rock (Detective Lee Butters), Jet Li (Wah Sing Ku), Steve Kahan (Captain Ed Murphy), Kim Chan (Benny 'Uncle Benny' Chan), Darlene Love (Trish Murtaugh), Traci Wolfe (Rianne Murtaugh Butters), Eddy Ko (Hong), Jack Kehler (State Department Man), Calvin Jung (Detective Ng), Damon Hines (Nick Murtaugh), Ebonie Smith (Carrie Murtaugh).

2003

Timeline

Produced by Richard Donner, Lauren Shuler Donner and Jim Van Wyck. Screenplay by Jeff Maguire and George Nolfi, from the novel by Michael Crichton. Music: Brian Tyler. Director of photography: Caleb Deschanel. Editor: Richard Marks. Production designer: Daniel T. Dorrance.

Starring Paul Walker (Chris Johnston), Frances O'Connor (Kate Ericson), Gerard Butler (Andre Marek), Billy Connolly (Professor E.A. Johnston), David Thewlis (Robert Doniger), Anna Friel (Lady Claire), Neal McDonough (Frank Gordon), Matt Craven (Steven Kramer), Ethan Embry (Josh Stern), Michael Sheen (Lord Oliver), Lambert Wilson (Lord Arnaut), Marton Csokas (Sir William De Kere/William Decker), Rossif Sutherland (Francois Dontelle), Steve Kahan (Baker), David La Haye (Arnaut's Deputy).

2006

16 Blocks

Produced by Randall Emmett, Avi Lerner, Arnold Rifkin, John Thompson and Jim Van Wyck. Written by Richard Wenk. Music by Klaus Badelt. Director of photography: Glen MacPherson. Editor: Steven Mirkovich. Production designer: Arvinder Grewal.

Starring Bruce Willis (Det. Jack Mosley), Mos Def (Eddie Bunker), David Morse (Det. Frank Nugent), Jenna Stern (Diane Mosley), Casey Sander (Capt. Dan Gruber), Cylk Cozart (Det. Jimmy Mulvey), David Zayas (Det. Robert Torres), Robert Racki (Det. Jerry Shue), Patrick Garrow (Touhey), Sasha Roiz (Kaller), Conrad Pla (Ortiz), Hechter Ubarry (Maldonado), Richard Fitzpatrick (Deputy Commissioner Wagner), Peter McRobbie (Mike Sheehan), Mike Keenan (Ray Fitzpatrick).

Superman II: The Richard Donner Cut

Produced by Alexander Salkind, Ilya Salkind, Pierre Spengler and Michael Thau (2006 reconstruction). Superman created by Jerry Siegel & Joe Shuster. Story by Mario Puzo. Screenplay by Mario Puzo, David Newman & Leslie Newman. Cinematographers: Robert Paynter and Geoffrey Unsworth. Editors: Stuart Baird, Michael Thau (2006 reconstruction) and John Victor-Smith.

Starring Gene Hackman (Lex Luthor), Christopher Reeve (Clark Kent/Kal-El/Superman), Marlon Brando (Jor-El), Ned Beatty (Otis), Jackie Cooper (Perry White), Sarah Douglas (Ursa), Margot Kidder (Lois Lane), Jack O'Halloran (Non), Valerie Perrine (Eve Teschmacher), Clifton James (Sheriff), E.G. Marshall (The President), Marc McClure (Jimmy Olsen), Terence Stamp (General Zod), John Ratzenberger (Controller #1), Shane Rimmer (Controller #2).

FILMS AS PRODUCER

In addition to his credit as producer of films he directed, Donner received producer or executive producer credit on *The Final Conflict* (1981), *The Lost Boys* (1987), *Delirious* (1991), *Free Willy* (1993), *Demon Knight* (1995), *Free Willy 2: The Adventure Home* (1995), *Bordello of Blood* (1996), *Free Willy 3: The Rescue* (1997), *Double Tap* (1997), *Made Men* (1999), *Any Given Sunday* (1999), *X-Men* (2000), *Ritual* (2001) and *X-Men Origins: Wolverine* (2009).

Donner appears by extension in films that carry the credit "Donner/Shuler-Donner Productions" or "The Donners' Company": *Dave* (1993), *Volcano* (1997), *Out Cold* (2001), *X2* (2003), *Constantine* (2005), *She's the Man* (2006), *X-Men: The Last Stand* (2006), *Unaccompanied Minors* (2006), *Semi-Pro* (2008), *The Secret Life of Bees* (2008) and *Hotel for Dogs* (2009).

Select Bibliography

Bacon, James, *How Sweet It Is: The Jackie Gleason Story*, St. Martin's Press, New York, 1985

Bart, Peter, *The Gross*, St. Martin's Press, New York, 1999

Baxter, John, *Steven Spielberg*, HarperCollins, London, 1996

Bruck, Connie, *Master of the Game: Steve Ross and the Creation of Time Warner*, Simon & Schuster, New York, 1994

Crichton, Michael, *Timeline*, Alfred A. Knopf, New York, 1999

Clarkson, Wensley, *Mel Gibson: Living Dangerously*, Thunder's Mouth Press, New York, 1993

Davis, Jr., Sammy and Early, Gerald, *The Sammy Davis, Jr. Reader*, Farrar, Straus and Giroux, New York, 2001

DePree, Max, *Leadership is an Art*, Doubleday, New York, 1989

Fishgall, Gary, *Gonna Do Great Things: The Life of Sammy Davis, Jr.*, Scribner, New York, 2003

Fishgall, Gary, *Gregory Peck: A Biography*, Scribner, New York, 2002

Freedland, Michael, *Gregory Peck*, William Morrow and Company, New York, 1980

Goldman, William, *Which Lie Did I Tell? More Adventures in the Screen Trade*, Pantheon Books, New York, 2000

Griffin, Nancy, & Masters, Kim, *Hit & Run*, Simon & Schuster, New York, 1996

Hagman, Larry with Gold, Todd, *Hello Darlin': Tall (and Absolutely True) Tales About My Life*, Simon & Schuster, New York, 2001

Haney, Lynn, *Gregory Peck: A Charmed Life*, Carroll & Graf, New York, 2003

Hauer, Rutger with Quinlan, Patrick, *All Those Moments*, Harper Entertainment, New York, 2007

Heitland, Jon, *The Man From U.N.C.L.E. Book*, Titan Books, London, 1987

Henry III, William A., *The Great One: The Life and Legend of Jackie Gleason*, Doubleday, New York, 1992

Linson, Art, *A Pound of Flesh: Perilous Tales of How to Produce Movies in Hollywood*, Grove Press, New York, 1993

Manso, Peter, *Brando*, Hyperion, New York, 1994

Matuszak, John with Delsohn, Steve, *Cruisin' With the Tooz*, Franklin Watts, New York, 1987

McCrohan, Donna, *The Life & Times of Maxwell Smart*, St. Martin's Press, New York, 1988

McQueen Toffel, Neile, *My Husband, My Friend: A Memoir*, Atheneum, New York, 1986

Parish, James Robert, *Jet Li: A Biography*, Thunder's Mouth Press, New York, 2002

Petrou, David Michael, *The Making of Superman: The Movie*, Warner Books, New York, 1978

Pryor, Richard with Gold, Todd, *Pryor Convictions and Other Life Sentences*, Pantheon Books, New York, 1995

Quirk, Lawrence J. and Schoell, William, *The Rat Pack*, Harper Paperbacks, New York, 1999

Reeve, Christopher, *Still Me*, Random House, New York, 1998

Rossen, Jake, *Superman vs. Hollywood*, Chicago Review Press, Chicago, 2008

Sandford, Christopher, *McQueen: The Biography*, Taylor Trade Publishing, New York, 2003

Schwartz, Julius, *Man of Two Worlds: My Life in Science Fiction and Comics*, Harper Entertainment, New York, 2000

Seltzer, David, *The Omen*, Signet, New York, 1976

Slater, Robert, *Ovitz: The Inside Story of Hollywood's Most Controversial Power Broker*, McGraw-Hill, 1997

Smith, Robert Paul, *"Where Did You Go?" "Out." "What Did You Do?" "Nothing."* W. W. Norton & Company, New York, 1957

Spada, James, *Julia: Her Life*, St. Martin's Press, New York, 2004

Walton, Todd, *Inside Moves*, Doubleday, New York, 1978

Weatherby, W.J., *Jackie Gleason: An Intimate Portrait of The Great One*, Pharos Books, New York, 1992

Wiley, Mason, and Bona, Damien, *Inside Oscar: The Unofficial Story of the Academy Awards*, Ballantine, New York, 1988

Williams, John A., and Williams, Dennis A., *If I Stop I'll Die: The Comedy and Tragedy of Richard Pryor*, Thunder's Mouth Press, New York, 1991

About the Author

James Christie is a contributor to *BBC News Entertainment*, *DVD Review*, London's *Guardian* newspaper and *Total Film*. He lives with his family in Orlando, Florida.

JESSICA PONTIER

Index

A. B. Davis High School 37, 41

Academy Awards 18, 65, 73, 83, 97, 104, 145-6, 149, 154, 156, 237, 289-92, 296, 311, 320, 347, 352; nominations 11, 13, 14, 17-8, 45, 46, 65, 73, 146, 156

Ackroyd, Dan 197, 237

Adams, Don 66-8

Adamson, Ed 53, 55

AFD 153-5

Air Force One 317-8

Alcon Entertainment 345, 347

Alexander, David 14, 44, 62, 353

American Cinema Editors 20, 282

American Cinematographer 107, 294

Anka, Paul 345

Anna Christie (theatre) 107, 113

Annie (film) 158, 163

Any Given Sunday 313, 335, 389

Arnaz, Desi 53

Assassins 20, 25, 277-8, 300-6, 336, 347, 386

Astin, Sean 7, 18, 183, 186, 193-4, 198, 263, 334-5

Astoria 19, 185-7, 285

Auschmen, George 43

Australia 24, 214, 222, 343, 352

Avengers, The (film) 319, 326

Bacon, James 161

Baird, Stuart 7, 12, 21, 24, 85, 89-90, 95, 100, 107, 116-7, 120, 143-4, 148, 150, 162, 172, 175, 178-81, 213, 219, 243, 248, 252, 257, 282, 291, 358

Ballard, J.G. 182, 291

Ball, Lucille 53

Banderas, Antonio 303-5

Banyon 78, 377

Barry, John (composer) 154

Barry, John (production designer) 18, 100-1, 143, 146

Bart, Peter 212, 307, 315, 317

Batman (film) 234, 239-40, 247; franchise 17, 351, 354

Batman (television) 15, 98, 144

Batman Begins 354

Baton Rouge 160, 164

Bearcats! 78, 377

Beatty, Warren 74, 104, 316-7

Bernhard, Harvey 7, 12, 15, 72, 77, 79-90, 95-6, 171, 177, 189, 196, 201, 210

Bertolucci, Bernardo 97, 172

Birnbaum, Roger 316-7

Black, Shane 211, 213, 218, 234, 256, 351

Blade Runner 158, 173

Blair Academy 41-2

Blair, Linda 78-9, 192

Blake, George 14, 46-8, 113, 123, 193, 353, 358

Boam, Jeffrey 235, 256, 260

Bordello of Blood 307, 328, 389

Boyd, Jimmy 64

Bracco, Lorraine 249-50

Brando, Marlon 13-4, 17, 44, 61, 74, 97, 100-7, 116, 132, 148, 156, 227, 243, 342-43, 348

Brauer, Bobby 22, 193

Brauer, Herman 22-3, 252

Brauer, Tess 22-3

Braveheart 301, 311, 320

Britain *see* United Kingdom

Broderick, Matthew 18, 140, 169, 175-7, 199, 201

Brolin, Josh 183, 195, 198

Bronk 63, 379

Bronson, Charles 56, 58, 70-1, 73, 129

Bronx Parlor Frames and Sons 30, 43, 213

Buck, Ronnie 71, 354

Bulworth 317

Burbank Studios 181, 187, 189, 197, 215, 236, 293

Burns, Ronnie 64

Burns, Sandra 64, 74

Burton, Tim 197, 234, 247, 319

Butch Cassidy and the Sundance Kid 227, 289

Butler, Gerard 336, 338

Byrnes, Edd 61

CAA 147, 225, 331

Cabaret 73, 83

Cade's County 78, 377

Calley, John 7, 50, 58, 72, 97, 101, 103, 113, 148, 209

Cameron, James 84, 212

Canby, Vincent 169, 200, 233, 253, 259

Cannes Film Festival 97, 147, 307

Cannon 78, 377-8

Canton, Mark 211-12, 215, 238

Capra, Frank 149, 202, 352

Carpenter, John 168, 227

Carter, Jimmy 100, 146

CBS 53, 59, 60, 63, 66, 126, 163

Chase, Chevy 237, 289

Chasin, George 82

Chicago 289, 300

Chicago Sun-Times 70, 218, 220, 233, 254, 306, 318, 325, 338, 341, 347

Christmas Carol, A 225-6, 233

Cinecittà Studios 172-3, 177, 180

Cinefantastique 82, 98, 108, 146

Close Encounters of the Third Kind 107, 146, 290-92

Coburn, James 293, 296

Cohen, Jeff 7, 18, 21, 183, 185-6, 194-5, 198-9, 334

Cohen, Joan 7, 22-3, 28, 30, 32-3, 37-8, 44, 46, 169, 191, 193

Color Purple, The (book) 182, 291

Color Purple, The (film) 181, 215

Columbia 158, 169, 232, 245, 247-8, 252, 317; Columbia Sony *see* Sony

Columbus, Chris 84, 182

Combat! 53, 59-60, 244, 373

Commando 212, 221, 301

Connery, Sean 167-69

Connolly, Billy 336-7

Conrad, Robert 66

Conspiracy Theory 20, 279-80, 310-19, 386

Cooper, Alice 85, 199

Coppola, Francis Ford 97, 102, 172, 291, 314, 319, 333

Corliss, Richard 204, 221, 233

Cox, Wally 61

Cravat, Nick 61

Crawford, Joan 12

Crichton, Michael 247, 330, 332, 338

Cruise, Tom 225, 316

Curtin, Valerie 148, 151

Dachau 357

Dallas 78, 115

Daly, Bob 208-9, 240, 245, 256, 260, 270, 289, 297-8, 300-1, 319, 321, 323, 325-6, 348

Dante, Joe 61, 205, 247

Davey, Bruce 289, 311

Davi, Robert 183-4, 194, 198

Davis, Jr., Sammy 68-72, 129

DC Comics 96, 98, 114

de Bont, Jan 257, 332

Deer Hunter, The 150, 291

Defiant Ones, The 19, 222

Def, Mos 281, 345, 347

De Laurentiis Entertainment 246

De Palma, Brian 110, 168, 234

De Niro, Robert 150, 235

Di Bonaventura, Lorenzo 319, 323, 333

Diller, Barry 316-7

Dillon, Carmen 84

Disney 201, 245, 331-2

Dominguez, Berta 105-6

Donners Company, The 24, 332, 334

Donner/Shuler-Donner Productions 248, 285, 316, 332

Dorothy Chandler Pavilion 104, 145

Douglas, Michael 245, 247-8

Dragonheart 286-7

Earth Island Institute 287-8

Easy Rider 20, 150

Ebert, Roger 70, 220-1, 233, 239, 254, 259, 306, 318, 325, 341, 347

Edwards Air Force base 56-8

Eleventh Hour, The 59, 373

Empire of the Sun 182, 291

Entertainment Weekly 292, 335

E.T.: The Extraterrestrial 144, 148, 169, 182, 209, 245, 290, 333
Evans, Bob 148, 150
Evans, David Mickey 244-5, 247-9, 251
Exorcist, The 15, 78-9, 94, 104, 192
Factory, The 72, 354
Farr, Danny 7, 25, 30, 35, 40-2, 48, 192, 345, 357
Feldman, Corey 7, 182, 184-5, 189, 194-5, 198, 246, 298, 323, 334-5
Feldman, Phil 163-4
Feldon, Barbara 66-8
Felony Squad 377
Fetter, Tom 288-9
Filmways 50, 53, 58, 64, 97, 209
Flintstones, The 233, 300
Fonda, Jane 65, 104, 155
Ford, Harrison 197, 201, 227, 286, 317
48HRS 19, 169, 214, 222
Foster, Jodie 14, 274, 292-7, 300, 314
France 15, 73, 107, 118-9, 294, 332, 335-7, 339, 353
Freedman, Chauncey 45-6
Freedman, Claire 49, 352
Freedman, Gene 7, 29, 37-8, 41, 45-7, 49, 243, 345, 352, 357
Free Willy 25, 285-8, 307; Keiko 25, 287-8, 308
Friel, Anna 337-8
Fugitive, The 289, 327
Fugitive, The (television) 168, 376
Garner, Jim 274, 292-5, 299
Garrison, Michael 66
George Blake Enterprises 46-8, 124, 345
George, Susan 71, 129
Germany 337, 357
Get Smart (television) 66-8, 376
Ghostbusters 225, 228, 232, 245
Ghost Story 78, 377
Gibson, Channing 320, 322
Gibson, Mel 7, 14, 19-22, 24, 66, 173, 201, 210, 214-22, 234, 236-8, 256-60, 266, 269, 274, 276, 279, 282, 284, 289, 291-8, 300-1, 310-2, 314-6, 318-21, 324-5, 327, 334, 351-2, 354
Gibson, Robyn 214, 258
Gilbert, Bob 7, 49
Gilligan's Island 53, 63, 231, 374-5
Glazer, Mitch 226
Gleason, Jackie 18, 138, 158-63, 169
Glover, Danny 7, 19, 58, 214-6, 220, 222, 234, 237, 258-60, 269, 298, 320, 324-5

Glover, John 7, 227, 229-30
Godfather, The 74, 97, 291
Goldberg, Rube 125, 184, 205
Goldblatt, Stephen 7, 213, 215-9, 227-8, 234, 245, 257
Goldman, William 289, 291-2, 298, 312
Goldsmith, Jerry 89, 100, 104, 154, 180, 336, 340
Goodmark 150, 153
Goodwin, Bob 150, 153
Goonies, The 18-9, 21, 35, 184-7, 189, 191-9, 203-5, 209-10, 227, 230-1, 246, 263-4, 285, 298, 334, 337, 341, 351, 383
Gordon, Larry 212
Gordon, Shep 212, 278
Green, Chick 48, 125
Green, Kerri 7, 21, 183-5, 187, 198, 334
Greenlaw, Charlie 115, 119
Greenwich Village Theater 14, 44
Gremlins 61, 182, 184, 205
Grillo, Mike 152-3
Hackett, Buddy 230
Hackman, Gene 14, 97, 108, 135, 147-8,
Hagman, Larry 79, 114-5
Hall, Conrad 227-8
Hamilton, Guy 97, 107
Hanks, Tom 234, 253, 280
Hanna-Barbera 233
Harman, Bob 7, 116, 118
Harowitz, Harriet 22, 30-2, 35-7, 128, 249, 252, 356
Harowitz, Ida 31, 356
Harowitz, Joe 31-2
Harrison, George 244
Hauer, Rutger 18, 139, 173-5, 177-8, 180, 199, 201
Have Gun – Will Travel 372
Hawn, Goldie 108-9, 173
HBO 234, 237-8, 268, 286, 307
Helgeland, Brian 301, 306, 311, 313-4, 317, 351
Hill, Walter 234, 268, 286
Hinson, Hal 233, 254, 259, 306
Hoffman, Derek 7, 344-5, 347
Hoffman, Dustin 167
Holden, William 82, 207
Hong Kong 222, 324
Horn, Alan 326-7, 334, 342, 348
Horowitz, Mimi 37

Howard, Geoff 7, 171, 190, 208, 355
Howard, George 30-1, 356
Howard, Ron 84, 311
Humane Society of the United States 288, 308
Huy Quan, Key 7, 183, 192, 194, 198, 323, 334
Iceland 25, 288, 308
Icon Pictures 311, 327
Inside Moves (book) 95, 148
Inside Moves (film) 13, 18, 21, 96, 136,
    149-156, 159, 164, 209, 230, 244, 251, 253,
    255, 291-2, 305, 318, 345, 355, 382
Interns, The 78, 377
In the Heat of the Night 19, 222
Ironside 78, 378
Italy 84, 167, 172-4, 178-9, 191, 199, 245
It's About Time 63, 376
It's A Wonderful Life 149, 233
Jackman, Hugh 352
Jackson, Michael 197, 225
Jamieson, Brian 7, 203, 217, 220, 222
Jaws 21, 61, 94-5, 100, 144, 182, 228, 291
Jurassic Park (book) 247, 332
Jurassic Park (film) 247
Kahan, Steve 7, 14, 30, 32, 45, 73, 113, 150,
    156, 160, 230, 258, 298, 327, 335
Kamen, Michael 214, 244, 260, 305
Kamen, Stan 55
Kelmenson, Paul 245
Kemplen, Ralph 85
Kensit, Patsy 235-6
Kessler, Bruce 64
Khmara, Edward 157, 170, 200
Kidder, Margot 7, 21, 101, 110-1, 113, 118-9,
    144-5, 151, 157, 171, 255, 298, 348, 355
Kligerman, Thomas A. 331
Kojak 14, 78, 98, 236, 378-9
Kovács, László 7, 20, 150-3, 162-3, 248-52,
    254, 295
Kroll, Jack 155, 200, 204
Kubrick, Stanley 83, 146
Kushner-Locke 307
Ladd Company, The 157-8, 170-1, 311
Ladd, Jr., Alan 7, 69, 80-2, 89, 94-6, 145,
    157-8, 179, 202, 311, 335, 353, 355
Ladyhawke 18, 24, 34, 44, 59, 139-40, 157-8,
    167-81, 191, 199-202, 207, 214, 225, 314,
    318, 337, 383
Lange, Lisa 7, 25, 239, 288
Lauper, Cyndi 199, 203

Lawford, Peter 68-71
Lazzarino, Tony 56-7
Le Jouet 158, 169
Lester, Richard 112-3, 147-8, 156-7, 231, 342,
    348
Lethal Weapon 19-20, 44, 211-22, 227, 230-1,
    233-4, 236-9, 244-6, 266, 298, 301, 312,
    318-9, 351, 384; series 12, 20-1, 238, 251,
    286, 328, 351, 354
Lethal Weapon 2 234-40, 244, 269, 384
Lethal Weapon 3 25, 58, 256-60, 269-70, 286,
    300, 320, 325, 385
Lethal Weapon 4 256, 320-7, 387
Letter to Loretta 53, 55, 371-2
Levinson, Barry 148, 151, 184, 249
Levinson, David 78
Levitt, Gene 59
Lewis, Jerry 70, 155
Lew Tugend, Jennie 7, 182, 189, 205, 210-1,
    227-9, 232, 238, 245, 251, 254, 285, 287-8
Life 25, 213, 288
Li, Jet 321, 324
Lieutenant, The 63, 373
Linson, Art 226, 232, 243
Liska, Kathy 7, 25
London 68-71, 77, 80-3, 85, 88, 90, 93, 95,
    104-6, 108-10, 115, 119, 135, 144, 146, 154,
    159, 173, 213, 298, 348,
London, Jack 34, 194
Lord of the Rings 103, 148, 249
Los Angeles 12, 16, 23, 74, 77, 82, 88, 104, 145,
    151, 155, 159, 173, 209, 211, 214-5, 218-20,
    229, 236, 246, 249, 256, 287, 320-1, 337, 340
Los Angeles Times 200, 304, 318, 325, 347
Lost Boys, The 35, 210, 220, 246, 335, 389
Lucas, George 21, 58, 84, 120, 146, 180, 209,
    212, 250, 333
Lucas Tanner 63, 379
Lupus Research 25, 288
MacDonald, Peter 7, 85, 100-2, 108, 111, 119
MacPherson, Glen 345-6
Madalone, Dennis 153
Mad Max 173, 214
Madonna 168, 225
Man from U.N.C.L.E., The 14, 53, 62-3, 374-5
Mankiewicz, Tom 7, 13, 15-7, 93, 99-101,
    103-6, 108-9, 112-3, 115-6, 118, 133, 144,
    148, 158, 168-70, 172, 178, 180, 184, 207,
    209, 212, 221, 293, 342, 357-8

Mann's Chinese Theater 324, 326
Man Without a Face, The 289
Margret, Anne- 109
Maslin, Janet 155, 204, 221, 306, 325
Matrix, The 300, 326
Matuszak, John 195-7
Maverick (film) 20, 66, 274-6, 289-302, 314, 319, 345, 347, 386
Maverick (television) 289, 292
Mazzello, Joseph 43, 249-50, 271
McElwaine, Guy 7, 72, 159, 164, 207, 291
McKern, Leo 83, 169
McLean, David 56, 128
McQueen, Steve 14, 43-4, 52-6, 126
Mexico 213, 287
MGM 59-60
Molina, Alfred 169, 293, 297
Moore, Demi 191, 234
Moore, Julianne 25, 303
Morgan: A Suitable Case for Treatment 83, 316
Morrow, Vic 59-60
Morse, David 7, 13, 136, 150, 345
Moss, Jerry 7, 74, 278, 352-4
Mulligan, Robert 65, 80
Munger, Bob 77, 79
Murray, Bill 224-33, 267
NAACP 19, 215
NASA 56, 58
NBC 45, 50, 59, 66, 78
Neufeld, Mace 79-80, 87, 96
Newman, David 98-9, 144
Newman, Leslie 98-9, 144
Newman, Paul 45, 71-2, 292
Newsday 318
Newsweek 143, 155, 169, 200, 204
New York 11-4, 23, 31-2, 34, 42, 46-7, 49, 53, 58-9, 63, 65, 70-3, 101, 112-4, 123, 134, 155, 159, 184, 190, 208-9, 212, 225, 227-9, 311-4, 331, 337, 344-5, 347, 356; Bronx 30, 32; Clinton Corners 34-5, 37, 84, 244, 252, 287; Mount Vernon 22, 30, 32, 36-8, 41-2, 63, 244, 345, 357; Rolling Acres 34-5, 37, 84, 244, 252, 287
New York Times, The 70, 94, 155, 169, 200, 204, 221, 233, 253-4, 259, 299, 306, 320, 324, 340, 331, 324,
Nolan, Christopher 17, 354
Nolte, Nick 93, 214
Novak, Mr. 63, 373-5

Novato 249, 356
NRA 256, 306
Nurses, The 63, 373
O'Connor, Frances 337-8
O'Donoghue, Michael 226
Olympic Games 25, 287
Omen, The 12, 14-5, 19-20, 34-5, 61, 77-90, 94-6, 98, 100, 102, 104, 107, 117, 130-1, 144, 146, 169-70, 182, 186, 192, 202, 207, 210, 248, 253, 257, 286, 291, 301, 337, 340-1, 351, 353, 357, 381
Orlando 245, 257
Ovitz, Michael 147, 173, 225, 227, 232, 245-6, 286, 331-2, 338
Pacino, Al 168, 313
Packard Junior College 42-3, 252
Palmisano, Conrad 303
Pantoliano, Joe 183-4, 198, 238
Paramount 148-50, 226, 229, 232, 332, 334-5, 338, 340, 342
Peck, Gregory 14, 77, 82-3, 86-90
Peck, Veronique 82, 88
Peoples, David 157
Perisic, Zoran 118-9
Perry Mason 63, 374-5
Pesci, Joe 234-5, 237, 259-60, 320
PETA 25, 239, 288
Peters, Jon 245, 247, 251, 323, 333
Petrocelli 78, 379
Petrou, David 7, 17, 104-6, 111, 114, 116, 144
Pfeiffer, Michelle 14, 18, 139, 168-9, 177-8, 180, 199, 201
Picerni, Charlie 236
Pinewood Studios 111, 116, 118, 343
Polanski, Roman 83, 94, 119
Pollack, Sydney 168, 227, 232
Postman, The 319, 326
Powell, Andrew 180, 202
Preminger, Otto 11-3
Provincetown Players 44, 53
Pryor, Richard 18, 104, 137, 158-63, 169, 209
Puzo, Mario 97-8, 105, 114, 144, 148
Pyrford Court 83, 85
Radio Flyer 20, 43, 244-5, 247-56, 259, 271-3, 285-6, 291, 385
Raging Bull 156, 228, 235
Raiders of the Lost Ark 182, 202, 227, 290; *Indiana Jones* series 183, 202, 212, 239, 340

Rambo: First Blood Part II 211; *Rambo* series
   221, 301
Ramsey, Anne 183, 230
Rastar 158-9, 163
Redford, Robert 60, 93
Reeve, Christopher 15, 101, 103, 110-1, 114,
   118, 132-3, 143, 145, 209, 306-7, 333, 348,
   352
Remick, Lee 83, 86-7
Reventlow, Lance 64
Richard Donner Productions 181, 208, 234,
   238
Rich, John 63
Richardson, John 7, 78, 84, 86, 113-4, 157, 172,
   174
Rifleman, The 59, 372
Ritt, Martin 14, 45, 167, 353
Riva, J. Michael 125, 189, 195, 197, 203, 227,
   248
Roberts, Julia 14, 279, 311-2, 314-5
Robinson, Dar 246
Rocky 104, 149
Rolfe, Sam 62
Rosemary's Baby 79, 94
Rosen, Eddie 79, 232
Rosenberg, Mark 178
Roth, Richard A. 65
Roth, Steve 147, 225
Russell, Ken 85, 150
Russell, Kurt 168, 172-3, 225
Russo, Rene 257, 260, 320
Salkind, Alexander 96-9, 101, 103-9, 111-6,
   119-20, 143-4, 146-8, 156, 171, 212, 231,
   342, 349
Salkind, Ilya 7, 93, 96-7, 99, 101-2, 104-5,
   107-8, 111-2, 115-6, 119, 143-4, 146-8, 156,
   231, 342, 349
Salt and Pepper 68-71, 129, 150, 159, 380
Sam Benedict 372-3
Sanders, Tom 292, 299, 302
San Diego 289
San Francisco 215, 293, 331
Sarah T. – Portrait of a Teenage Alcoholic 78, 115,
   192, 379
Sarge 78, 377
Saturday Night Live 225-6, 228
Savage, John 136, 150
Scarwid, Diana 7, 13, 17, 136, 151, 156
Schindler's List 290-1

Schumacher, Joel 35, 210, 246
Schwartz, Julius 98
Schwartz, Sherwood 63
Schwartzberg, Fred 23, 30, 32, 34, 36-8, 43, 65,
   128, 357
Schwarzenegger, Arnold 212-3, 221, 234, 319
Scorsese, Martin 110, 156, 235, 296, 318
Scrooged 20, 225-33, 243, 267, 384
Seltzer, David 77, 79, 81, 94
Semel, Terry 190, 196, 203, 208-9, 240, 245,
   256, 260, 280, 289, 292-3, 297-8, 300-1, 311,
   319-21, 323, 325-6, 348
Senior Year 63, 378
Serling, Rod 60, 341
Shatner, William 60-1
Shepperton Studios 69, 84, 87, 89, 111, 343
Shuler Donner, Lauren 7, 24, 25, 32, 157-8,
   168-73, 177-9, 181, 191-2, 198, 201, 206-8,
   210, 212, 231, 240, 244-5, 248-51, 253-55,
   257-8, 264-5, 272-3, 276, 278, 285, 287-9,
   293, 298, 305-6, 308, 313, 316-7, 331-2, 335,
   338, 340, 352, 354-5
Shuster, Joe 16-7, 34
Siegel, Jerry 16-7, 34
Signal Productions 48, 50, 125
Silver, Joel 20, 206, 211-4, 218-9, 233-4, 238,
   257-8, 260, 285-6, 300-1, 307, 311-2, 315,
   319, 321, 327-8, 351
Silver Pictures 238, 279
Sinatra, Frank 57, 152, 159, 181, 203, 327
Singer, Bryan 17, 342
16 Blocks 20, 281, 343-7, 388
Sixth Sense, The (television) 78, 377
Smith, Robert Paul 92, 355
Sobieski, Carol 158, 163
Sony 245, 247
South Africa 191, 219, 231, 234-5, 239
Speed 257, 332
Spengler, Pierre 96, 108-9, 111, 115, 133,
   146-7, 342
Spiderman 17, 351
Spielberg, Steven 12, 18-9, 21, 58, 60-1, 84,
   94-5, 110, 146, 148, 152, 180-5, 189-90,
   198-9, 203-5, 209, 212, 215, 225, 247, 290-1,
   327, 333-4, 337-8
Stabler, Kenny 196
Stallone, Sylvester 14, 93, 211, 221, 277, 300-5
Stalmaster, Lynn 101
Stark, Ray 158-9, 161, 163-4, 169, 171, 212

Starlog 190, 229

Star Wars 21, 79, 84, 94, 100-1, 103, 107, 120, 143, 146, 209, 250, 257, 333

St. Elmo's Fire 191, 210

Stephens, Harvey 15, 76, 83, 86, 89, 131, 192

Stir Crazy 155, 160

Stonebridge Entertainment 245, 247

Stone, Oliver 308, 313

Storaro, Vittorio 172, 176-7

Streets of San Francisco, The 78, 378

Such Good Friends 11

Summer of '42 65, 80

Superman 12, 13, 15-21, 34, 44, 93, 96-120, 132-6, 143-4, 146-8, 153, 155-6, 164, 170, 172, 179, 182, 186, 202, 209, 219-20, 225, 230-1, 244, 247-8, 251-2, 286, 291, 298, 305-6, 318, 333, 337-8, 340-3, 348, 351, 354-5, 357

Superman Returns 342-3, 349

Superman II 102, 111, 115, 117, 146-8, 156-7, 342-3

Superman II: The Richard Donner Cut 347-8

Tales from the Crypt 234, 238-9, 268, 286, 301, 307, 327-8, 379-80

Tanz, Mark 150, 153

Taxi Driver 104, 228, 318

Taylor, Gil 83-4

Teamsters 57

Thau, Michael 7, 195, 219, 343, 347

Thomas, Michael 157-8

Three Musketeers, The 96, 98

Time 73, 94, 100, 143, 190, 200, 204, 221, 233, 299

Timeline (book) 330, 332, 338, 341

Timeline (film) 20, 210, 332-42, 344, 347, 387

To Kill a Mockingbird 80, 82

Toronto 107, 345

Travels of Jaimie McPheeters, The 63, 168, 374

Trippolette, Charlie 35-6

Toy, The 18, 96, 137-8, 158-64, 169-70, 202, 382

Twain, Mark 34, 188, 194, 204, 242

12 O'Clock High 375-6

Twentieth Century-Fox 80, 82, 86, 89, 94-5, 102, 131, 157, 163, 169, 171, 243, 245, 247, 286, 316-7, 320, 327

Twilight Zone, The 14, 53, 60-1, 63, 182, 238, 341, 373-4

Twinky 71, 129, 381

2001: A Space Odyssey 83, 146

Tyler Moore, Mary 55-6

Ullman, Liv 7, 13, 21, 25, 73-4, 107, 113, 118, 134, 144-5, 190, 202, 354

United Artists 57, 69-70, 128, 316

United Kingdom 70-1, 77, 81, 83-4, 97, 100, 106, 108, 115, 145, 147, 169, 172, 258, 337

Universal 78, 181-2, 247, 286, 290

Unsworth, Geoffrey 18, 83, 100, 114, 119, 143, 146

Urioste, Frank J. 282, 314

Van Wyck, Jim 7, 250, 255, 285, 292, 301-2, 313-4, 324, 336, 338-9, 341

Variety 13, 44, 143, 147, 169, 200, 204, 221, 293, 307, 315-6, 318, 323-4, 332, 347

Vaughn, Robert 62

Veber, Francis 158, 316

Wachowski, Andy 300-1

Wachowski, Larry 300-1

Walker, Paul 337-8

Walton, Todd 95, 148, 150-1

Wanted: Dead or Alive 14, 53-6, 126, 312, 371-2

Warner Bros. 35, 57, 65, 79-80, 96-7, 113, 115-6, 119-20, 147-8, 156-7, 171, 178-9, 181-2, 189-90, 199-201, 203, 208-12, 216-7, 220, 222, 225, 234, 237-40, 245, 247, 256, 260, 266, 269-70, 279-80, 288-9, 291, 293, 298, 300-1, 305, 311, 317, 319-23, 325-7, 332-4, 342-3, 347-9, 351; Warner Home Video 288, 343

Warner, David 7, 83-4, 86, 316

Warren, Lesley Ann 101, 110

Washington Post, The 70, 94, 155, 200, 202, 204, 221, 233, 239, 254, 259, 306, 318, 341

Watergate scandal 94, 120

Weir, Peter 214-5

Wells, H.G. 34, 194

Wenk, Richard 343-4, 346

Wild Wild West, The (television) 14, 63, 65-6, 68, 256, 375-7

William Morris 55, 225

William Wilson Elementary School 29, 357

Williams, John 100, 143, 154, 156, 342

Willis, Bruce 14, 214, 281, 344-7

Wood, Elijah 43, 249-50, 271-2

World War II 36, 42, 47, 59, 290

Wright, Amy 7, 151, 154

X-15 56-8, 60, 71, 128, 150, 203, 252, 380

X-Files, The 60, 150

X-Men 17, 103, 334, 342, 351

X-2: X-Men United 338, 342

Year of Living Dangerously, The 214, 298

Zemeckis, Robert 231, 268, 286

Zsigmond, Vilmos 7, 152, 248, 291, 293-6, 299, 302, 304

LaVergne, TN USA
27 November 2010
206464LV00009B/23/P